A MORMON BIBLIOGRAPHY

1830–1930

TEN YEAR SUPPLEMENT

A MORMON BIBLIOGRAPHY
1830–1930
TEN YEAR SUPPLEMENT

Compiled by

CHAD J. FLAKE

LARRY W. DRAPER

UNIVERSITY OF UTAH PRESS

SALT LAKE CITY

1989

Library of Congress Cataloging-in-Publication Data

Flake, Chad J.
    A Mormon bibliography, 1830–1930. Ten year supplement / compiled
by Chad J. Flake, Larry W. Draper.
      p.   cm.
    ISBN 0-87480-338-1
     1. Mormon Church— Bibliography.   2. United States—Church history—
Bibliography.   I. Draper, Larry W.   II. Title.
Z7845.M8F55   Suppl. BX8635.2
016.2893—dc20
                                      89-36679
                                         CIP

Contents

Preface

Dale Morgan set the stage for compiling a bibliography on Mormonism and his contribution to this project is well chronicled in the Introduction in *A Mormon Bibliography, 1830-1930.* Even though Morgan did not live to see the finished product, he understood that the process of building bibliography is a never ending one. Discovering rarities in institutional collections, in dealer catalogs, and from many other sources, is the "sort of thing that can go on forever." (*Flake* p. xxiii.)

Because there are the inevitable rare items discovered after the bibliography is published, a periodic supplement to the original volume is a necessity. This addendum represents ten years' worth of collecting additional items that fit the criteria for inclusion established for *A Mormon Bibliography.*

Some omissions that occurred in the original bibliography were the result of a variety of natural limitations found in the repositories from which the entries were compiled. One specific limitation was caused by differences in how source libraries handled the cataloging of their holdings. A case in point are two of the finest western American libraries in the world, the Bancroft and the Huntington.

At the Bancroft Library at the University of California, Berkeley, the books cataloged with the subject heading "Overland journeys to the Pacific" were quite accessible and were consequently examined with a high rate of efficiency. If the narrator had taken the Hudsputh cutoff or had gone through Fort Hall, then the likelihood of encountering the Mormons was small. The southern route through Fort Bridger, and thence probably through Salt Lake City, usually would have produced comment on the Mormons. This is how items containing material on the Mormons were identified and included in the bibliography.

But the Henry E. Huntington Library in San Marino -- said to have the best collection of "Overland journeys" in existence -- offered few relevant subject listings in its catalog. Consequently, one had to know the name of the author to check which route was taken and whether they encountered and made reference to the Mormons. Thus numerous books, particularly overland narratives, at the Huntington or elsewhere, failed to appear in the bibliography because searching the available subject headings proved to be inadequate. In the past ten years, scores of these narratives have been listed in dealer's or auction house catalogs, or made their way into the contributing libraries by other means and are now included in this supplement.

After the publication of the original bibliography, Donald T. Schmidt of the Historical Department of the Church of Jesus Christ of Latter-day Saints and I decided to inventory both the Historical Department of the Church of Jesus Christ of Latter-day Saints and Brigham Young University Lee Library to determine what might have been added to those collections since the research for the bibliography had been done and to incorporate into a working list those items that had been added up to that point (1984). After Schmidt's retirement in 1984, Larry W. Draper and I added new material to the list as it was received by each library over time. Also, there were collections at other institutions which had been recataloged or recently perused for their Mormon holdings, and the appropriate imprints from these libraries were added to this working list. These entries were again checked against the holdings of the church and BYU libraries, with the result being over eighteen hundred new entries added to the original bibliography.

The numbering of entries of the present volume is somewhat like that of the most recent edition of Wagner-Camp's, *The Plains & the Rockies,* edited by Robert H. Becker, 1982. That is, the numbering system from the original bibliography is retained while adding a, b, c, etc., to the appropriate new entries in this supplement. The reason for this is simple. We intend sometime in the future to combine this supplement with the original bibliography, and numbering the new entries in this manner will ease that integration.

It should be also noted that the entries from the Addenda section of the original bibliography have been included in this supplement. For example: Buell, Augustus. *The Cannoneer,* appears in the original bibliography as A6, while in the supplement this entry is given the number 1001a to properly place it alphabetically.

In 1988, when the time was deemed right to publish the supplement, copies of a preliminary list were sent to the University of Utah and Princeton University inasmuch as they are the libraries that are also currently vigorously collecting Mormon imprints. It was hoped that they would compare this preliminary list against their holdings, including new acquisitions of the past ten years. But, at present, neither library has responded. In the past year we have also checked the National Union Catalog for imprint information for items that are available in neither of the church nor the BYU collections. At the same time we noted other repositories in the holdings notes.

These then are the items added to *A Mormon Bibliography, 1830-1930* to make it more complete. The rules of inclusion are the same as those for the original bibliography. Only those imprints which contain information pertaining to Mormonism are included. Imprints devoted to Utah or Utah Territory which exclude comments on Mormonism are not included.

One notable set of exclusions from this volume are the imprints of bills introduced into Congress that relate to Mormonism. Imprints of abstracts or briefs that resulted from any Mormon court cases are included, but the bills introduced into Congress that relate to Mormonism are not. Those imprints are enumerated in *Mormons and Mormonism in U.S. Government Documents: A Bibliography* compiled by Susan L. Fales and I, published earlier this year.

Key to Library Symbols

United States Libraries

AAP	Auburn University
ArU	University of Arkansas
AzU	University of Arizona
C	California State Library
CLSU	University of Southern California, Los Angeles
CLU	University of California, Los Angeles
CoD	Denver Public Library
CoDu	University of Denver
CoU	University of Colorado
C-S	California State Library, Sutro Branch
CSmH	Henry F. Huntington Library
CSt	Stanford University
CtY	Yale University
CU	University of California, Berkeley
CU-B	Bancroft Library, University of California, Berkeley
CU-Riv	University of California, Riverside.
DAU	American University Library
DCU	Catholic University of America Library
DHU	Howard University Library
DI-GS	Geological Survey Library
DLC	Library of Congress
DN	U.S. Department of the Navy Library
DNAL	U.S. National Agricultural Library
DNLM	U.S. National Library of Medicine
DS	U.S. Department of State Library
DSI	Smithsonian Institute Library
FU	University of Florida, Gainsville
GU	University of Georgia, Athens
Hi	University of Hawaii
HLB	Brigham Young University, Hawaii
IaHi	State Historical Society of Iowa, Iowa City
IaLG	Graceland College
IaU	University of Iowa, Iowa City
ICHi	Chicago Historical Society
ICJ	John Crerar Library, Chicago
ICN	Newberry Library
ICRL	Center for Research Libraries, Chicago
ICU	University of Chicago
IdAr	Idaho State Archives
IdB	Boise Public Library
IdHi	Idaho State Historical Society
IdRR	Ricks College
IdTf	Twin Falls Public Library

OCi	Public Library of Cincinnati & Hamilton County
OCl	Cleveland Public Library
OCL	Lloyd Library and Museum
OClW	Case Western Reserve University
OCLWHi	Western Reserve Historical Society
OCU	University of Cincinnati
OFH	Rutherford B. Hayes Library
OHi	Ohio Historical Society
OkE	Public Library of Enid & Garfield County
OKentU	Kent State University
OkN	Pioneer Multi-County Library, Norman
OkU	Oklahoma University
OO	Oberlin College
OOxM	Miami University
Or	Oregon State Library
OrCS	Oregon State University Library, Carvallis
OrHi	Oregon Historical Society
OrP	Library Association of Portland
OrStbM	Mount Angel College
OrU	University of Oregon, Eugene
OT	Toledo-Lucas County Public Library
OU	Ohio State University
PBm	Bryn Mawr College
PCC	Crozer Theological Seminary, Chester
PHC	Haverford College
PHi	Historical Society of Pennsylvania
PP	Free Library of Philadelphia
PPA	Athenaeum of Philadelphia
PPC	College of Physicians of Philadelphia
PPi	University of Pennsylvania
PPL	Library Company of Philadelphia
PPLT	Lutheran Theological Seminary, Krauth
PPULC	Union Library Catalogue of Pennsylvania, Philadelphia
PSC	Swarthmore College, Swarthmore
PU	University of Pennsylvania
PV	Villanova College, Villanova
RPB	Brown University
TNJ	Joint University Libraries, Nashville
TNJ-R	Vanderbilt School of Religion, Nashville
TU	University of Tennessee, Knoxville
TxFTC	Texas Christian University
TxU	University of Texas
UAr	Utah State Archives
UHi	Utah Historical Society
ULA	Utah State University
UPB	Brigham Young University
USl	Salt Lake Public Library
USlC	Church of Jesus Christ of Latter-day Saints
UU	University of Utah
ViLxW	Washington & Lee University, Lexington

ViU	University of Virginia
Wa	Washington State Library, Olympia
WaS	Seattle Public Library
WaT	Tacoma Public Library
WaU	University of Washington, Seattle
WaWW	Whitman College, Walla Walla
WBB	Beloit College
WHi	Wisconsin Historical Society
WN	Neenah Public Library
WU	University of Wisconsin
WyU	University of Wyoming, Laramie

Foreign Country Libraries

Canadian Libraries

CaBVa	Vancouver Public Library
CaBVaU	University of British Columbia, Vancouver
CaBViP	British Columbia, Provincial Library, Victoria
CaBViPA	British Columbia, Provincial Archives, Victoria

Welsh Libraries

WalB	University College of North Wales
WalCC	County of South Glamorgan Library
WalCS	University College Library, Salisbury Collection
WalN	National Library of Wales
WalS	University College of Swansea
WalSW	West Glamorgan County Library

A

10a. *Der Abfall vom ursprunglichen evangelium und dessen wiederherstellung.* Chicago, Ill., Northern States Mission, 1907.

15 [2]p. 19½cm. (Traktat Nr. 1)

Title in English: The following from the original gospel and its restoration.

USIC, UPB

13a. *Action of the Utah Methodist Episcopal Church Mission Conference, Ogden, Utah, July 9th, 1881.* Ogden, Utah, Utah Methodist Episcopal Church Mission Conference, 1881.

Broadside. 25 x 15cm.

Anti-Mormon activities of the Methodist Episcopal Church.

USIC

23a. **Adams, Robert Chamblet.** *History of the United States in rhyme.* Boston, D. Lothrop and Co. [c1884]

72p. 17½cm.

Mormons mentioned, p. 60.

DLC, MH, NN, O, OT, USIC

25a. *Admission of Utah as a state in the union: memorial of citizens of the Territory of Utah asking for the admission of Utah as a state.* [n.p., 1882]

13p. 22cm.

Signed by Joseph F. Smith. Includes copy of proposed constitution.

UPB, USIC

27a. *Afterglow. Holiday edition of choice selections from the poets.* Lamoni, Iowa, 1892.

257p. illus. 20cm.

Published to be sold as Christmas gifts. Most of the poetry is by non RLDS poets. Poems by Vida Smith, David Smith, and Ina D. Coolbrith are included.

MoInRC

35a. **Ainsworth, William Francis, ed.** *All round the world: An illustrated record of voyages, travels, and adventures in all parts of the globe.* First series. London and Glasgow, William Collins, Sons, & Co., 1868.

xii, 820p. illus. 30½cm.

Mormons mentioned, p. 669-71.

USIC

35b. **Aitken, James.** *From the Clyde to California with jottings by the way.* Reprinted from the Greenock Herald. Illustrated. Greenock, William Johnston. Helensburgh, James Lamont. Glasgow, William Porteous and Co., 1882.

2p.l., iip. [1]l., 152p. fold. plate, 2 phot. 18cm.

Visit to Salt Lake City, with much on the Mormons, p. 50-63. Authorship established in *Howes A91* and *Cowan p. 6.*

CtY, DLC, NcU, UPB

35c. _____. *A run through the states: Supplementary to From the Clyde to California.* [Greenock] Printed at the Greenock Herald Office [1894?]

74p. 18cm.

In green printed wrapper.

A visit to the United States with his daughter. "Salt Lake City," p. 32-7.

UPB

40a. *Alberta, Canada, a complete and comprehensive description of the agricultural, stockraising and mineral resources of southern Alberta, Canada; also statistics in regard to its climate compiled from the latest reports.* [Salt Lake City, Taylor Bros., n.d.]

23 [8]p. tables. 22cm.

Mormons mentioned, p. 17.

USIC

40b. **Alberta Temple.** [n.p.] The Church of Jesus Christ of Latter-day Saints, 1923.

[4]p. 18cm.

Variant editions.

USIC

46a. Alexander, Edward Porter. *Military memoirs of a confederate; a critical narrative. With sketch-maps by the author.* New York, Charles Scribner's Sons, 1907.

viii, 634p. 2 ports. maps (1 fold) 23cm.

Brief description of his stint in Utah with the Utah Expedition.

DLC, MiU, MWA, NN, NjP, NN, ViU,

49a. *All Together Again.* [n.p., 1905]

Broadside. 11 x 12cm.

Lines sung at the Old Folks gathering at Nephi, Utah, October 15, 1905.

USlC

50a. Allen, Miss A. J. *Ten years in Oregon. Travels . . . of Dr. E. White and lady, west of the Rocky Mountains. With incidents of two sea voyages via Sandwich Islands around Cape Horn, also containing a brief history of the missions and settlement of the country . . . description of the soil, production and climate.* Ithaca, N.Y., Andrus, Gauntlett, & Co., 1850.

1p.l., [v]-xvi, [17]-430p. 20½cm.

Reference to shooting of Governor Boggs in 1842. A Mormon [Porter Rockwell] suspected and arrested, eventually freed, p. 144.

CLU, CtY, CU-B, DLC, MH, NN

50b. _____. *Thrilling adventures, travels and explorations of Dr. Elijah White among the Rocky Mountains and in the far west.* Compiled by Miss A. J. Allen. New York, J. W. Yale, 1859.

430p. front. 20½cm.

Supplement, p. 328-430. Contains reports on Oregon and Col. Fremont's adventures in crossing the California mountains, and his stay in Utah.

CaBViP, CU-B, ICN, WaWW

53a. Allred, Rhea. *Milk of the gospel.* [n.p., n.d.]

43p. 19½cm.

Doctrinal discussion.

USlC

58a. **America.** *Great crises in our history told by its makers. A library of original sources.* Chicago, Americanization Department. Veterans of Foreign Wars of the United States [c1925]

14v. illus., ports. 21½cm.

"The Mormon exodus to Utah" by B. H. Roberts in vol. 7.

DLC, CoDu, UHi, UU, WiU

64a. **American Journal of Industry.** *Salt Lake City, Utah. The industrial center of the intermountain region of western America. Her phenomenal progress, incomparable industries and remarkable resources. A glance at her history....* New York, American Journal of industry [1900]

114p. illus., ports, plates (part col.) 20 x 28cm.

Brief history of Mormonism in Utah, as well as some of its institutions such as ZCMI.

UPB

65a. **American Party. Utah.** *Ett Amerikanskt budskap. En strid som icke ar emot religion, utan emot missbruk af kyrkligt inflytande.* (Utgifvare: K. H. P. Nordberg, kandidat uppstalld af det Amerikanskt Partiet for medlem af Statslegislaturen) [Salt Lake City? n.d.]

4p. 23cm.

Mormon references.

Title in English: American Party.

USIC

69a. *Amnesty will not restore the right to vote, nor to hold office, nor to live with more than one wife, after the amnesty is granted.* [n.p., 1892]

Broadsheet. 23 x 14 cm.

Concerning the amnesty after the Woodruff Manifesto.

USIC

79a. **Anderson, Edward Henry.** *The Apostles of Jesus Christ. A brief account of their lives and acts; and of the rise and expansion of the Christian church up to A.D. 68. Written for the Deseret Sunday School Union.* Salt Lake City, Deseret Book Company, 1923.

xii, 284p. plates, maps. 19cm.

UPB

87a. _____. *A brief history of the Church of Jesus Christ of Latter-day Saints from the birth of the Prophet Joseph Smith to the present time.* Ten-cent ed. [Independence, Mo.] Zion's Printing and Publishing Co. [1916?]

143p. 18cm.

USIC

102a. Anderson, George Edward. *A key to the floral record of the Savior, the Prophet Joseph, the Patriarch Hyrum, First Presidency, Apostles and Temples of the Church of Jesus Christ of Latter-day Saints.* Temple Bazar, Manti. [Salt Lake City] Deseret News Co., 1887.

14p. 15cm.

USIC

108a. Anderson, James Henry. *The Church of Jesus Christ of Latter-day Saints. Its religion, history, condition, and destiny. An address delivered before the ethical society, at south place institute, London.* Liverpool, Millennial Star Office, [1895?]

64p. 13½cm.

USIC

114a. _____. *A personal letter.* [n.p.] 1920.

[4]p. 28cm.

"To my Utah friends."

USIC

131a. Anderson, Nephi. *Added upon; a story.* 9th ed. Salt Lake City, Deseret News Press, c1912.

4p.l. [7]-228p. 19cm.

DLC, OrU, RPB, USIC, UU

135a. _____. (Same in Dutch). *Verheerlijkt een verhaal.* Rotterdam, M-Mannen Club [n.d.]

201p. 22cm.

USIC

141a. _____. *The dimmed vision [a genealogical story].* 2nd ed. [Salt Lake City, Deseret Book, Seagull Press, n.d.]

19p. 15cm.

USIC

141b. _____. (same) 3rd ed. [Salt Lake City, Deseret Book, c1925]

16p. 15cm.

USlC

160a. **Anderson, Scott.** _Mormonism. By an ex-Mormon Elder. Showing the true teachings of Mormonism and how converts are made. Mormon idolatry. Mormon slavery. Blood atonement as preached by Brigham Young. The character of the Endowment House mysteries. Marriage and marriage laws, etc., etc. Also copy of a letter written to John Taylor, (the Mormon president,) giving his reasons why he withdrew from the Mormon Church._ Liverpool, Scott Anderson, T. Dobb & Co., 1885.

29 [3]p. 20½cm.

USlC

160b. **Anderson, William.** _Which is the Church? Jesus Christ established but one visible Church._ [Lamoni, Iowa, Herald Publishing House, 1883]

8p. 18cm. (No. 32).

Identified as A., W. in _Flake 1_.

CU-B, MoInRC

175a. _Anleitung um burger des Reiches Gottes zu werden._ [Bern, Buchdruckerei Steiger & Cie, 1896]

[4]p. 25½cm.

Title in English: Guidance on how to become a citizen of God's kingdom.

USlC

175b. _Anniversary of the birthday and baptismal day of the elect Lady of the Church of Jesus Christ of Latter-day Saints, Emmeline Blanche Woodward Wells._ [Salt Lake City, 1917]

[3]p. 8½cm.

Cover title.

UHi

175c. _Annual reunion of the Vermont Party, 1905-07._ [Salt Lake City, Deseret News, 1907?]

[8]p. illus. 19½cm.

USlC

175d. *Annual Scandinavian conference & reunion, August 28th and 29th, 1926, Ogden tabernacle.* [Ogden, Utah, 1926]

32p. 20cm.

USIC

175e. _____. *August 13 and 14, 1927, Utah Stake Tabernacle.* [Provo, Utah? 1927]

[14]p. illus. 19½cm.

Song words in Danish.

USIC

175f. *Ansichten hervorragender Personen Bezuglich des Charakters der Heiligen der letzten Tage.* [Berlin, Hugh J. Cannon, ca. 1890]

[4]p. 24cm.

Title in English: Opinion of prominent people with reference to the character of the Latter-day Saints.

USIC

175g. _____. (same) Berlin, Hugh J. Cannon, Leipzig, C. G. Rohder [1913]

[4]p. 24cm.

USIC

175h. **Anthony, Lenore.** *Pageant, Independence centennial celebration, October 2 to 7, 1927. Written and produced by Lenore Anthony.* [Independence, Mo., 1927]

20 [1]p. 23cm.

Mormons mentioned, p. 6, 11.

USIC

180a. **Anti-Polygamy Society.** *Polygamous assembly.* Salt Lake City, 1880.

Broadside. 21½ x 14½cm.

Signed: Mrs. S. A. Cooke, President, Mrs. M. Chislett, Secretary.

Dated: Salt Lake City, Utah, January 12, 1880.

USIC

187a. **Apperley, William Henry.** *A souvenir.* Logan, Utah, Earl & England Publishing Co., 1910.

[46]p. port. 22cm.

Poems concerning Mormon subjects.

UPB, USIC

191a. *Appletons' hand-book of American travel. Western tour. Embracing eighteen through routes to the West and far West, tours of the Great Lakes and rivers. . . .* New York, D. Appleton and Co., 1871.

x, 315p. illus., fold. maps. 19cm.

Utah and Mormons, p. 106-13, 254-60.

USIC

192a. **Appletons' illustrated hand-book of American travel:** *A full and reliable guide by railway, steamboat, and stage, to the cities, towns, waterfalls, battle-fields, mountains, rivers, lakes, hunting and fishing grounds, watering places, summer resorts, and all scenes and objects of importance and interest in the United States and the British providence. . . .* New York, D. Appleton & Co., 1857.

42p. 24 illus., maps (part fold) 20cm.

Mormons noted briefly in the section on Utah as well as Nauvoo in the section on Illinois.

UPB

192b. *Appreciative references to Elder A. Milton Musser's lecture on his missionary tour around the world without purse or scrip.* [n.p., n.d.]

Broadside. 28 x 22cm.

Brief testimonials, from Church leaders and others, concerning the value of Elder Musser's lecture.

USIC

201a. **Armstrong, K. L.** *The little giant encyclopedia and treasury of ready reference. 1,000,001 figures and facts.* Chicago, H. J. Smith & Co., 1890.

449p. illus., tables. 16cm.

Mormons mentioned, p. 12, 151, 214.

USIC

207a. *Articles of faith of the Church of Jesus Christ of Latter-day Saints,* by *Joseph Smith, partially completed by literal extracts from standard Latter-day Saints' works.* [Salt Lake City, Kinsman Publishing House, ca. 1900]

12p. 13½cm.

Caption title.

USIC

209a. **Ashley, F. B.** *Mormoniaeth: Neu draethawd ar y sect a elwir "Seintiau y Dyddiau Diweddaf," gan y parch. F. D. Ashley. Cyfieithedig i'r gymraeg gan y parch.* G. C. F. Harries . . . Merthyr-Tydfil, M. W. White, 1853.

34p. 17cm.

Title in English: Mormonism: Or a treatise on the sect called the "Latter-day Saints."

WalCS

221a. **Aubertin, John James.** *A fight with distances; the states, the Hawaiian Islands, Canada, British Columbia, Cuba, the Bahamas.* London, Kegan Paul, Trench & Co., 1888.

viii, 352p. illus., maps. 19½cm.

Mormons mentioned, p. 211-13.

CtY, DLC, DN, OClW, USIC, WaU

228a. *Augusta's story;* compiled by the Martha Board Chapter; Daughters of the American Revolution. [Augusta, Ill., Augusta Eable? 1921?]

219p. [48] leaves of plates., ports. 20cm.

"Reminiscenses of the Mormons," p. 45-55.

USIC

235a. *L'Autorite divine. Ordonnances nulles quand elles sont administrees sans autorite divine.* Zurich, Thos. E. McKay, 1909.

12p. 18½cm.

Title in English: Divine Authority.

USIC

B

243a. **Baedeker, Karl, ed.** *The United States with an excursion into Mexico. Handbook for travellers. With 19 maps and 24 plates.* 2nd. ed. rev. Leipsic, Karl Baedeker, 1899.

c, 579p. illus., col. maps (part fold). 16cm.

Brief history of Mormonism in its section on Salt Lake City, p. 478-81.

3rd ed. rev., 1904, DLC, MH, NN, MiU, OrU, USlC

4th ed. rev. DLC, OCU, PU, UHi, UU

DLC, ICJ, UHi, UPB, WyU

250a. **Baird, Robert.** *Religion in America; or, an account of the origin, progress, relation to the state, and present condition of the evangelical churches in the United States. With notices of the unevangelical denominations.* New York, Harper & Brothers, 1844.

xii, 343p. 24cm.

"The Mormons, or Latter Day Saints," p. 285-6.

CtY, CU, MH, NN, ViU, UPB

258a. **Baker, Sarah Schoonmaker (Tuthill).** *The Children on the plains. A story of travel and adventure from the Missouri to the Rocky Mountains.* London, T. Nelson and Sons; Edinburgh; and New York, 1864.

121p. illus. 16cm.

Descriptions of Fort Kearny, Fort Laramie and Salt Lake City.

UPB

258b. _____. (same) London, T. Nelson and Sons, 1867.

3p.l. [7]-121p. plates. 15½cm.

"Salt Lake City," p. [107]-112. Mrs. Nutten refuses to set foot in the "Mormon Babylon."

CtY, UPB

258c. **Baldwin, Nathan.** *An open letter from Nathan Baldwin, Jr. to the authorities of the Church in general and Heber J. Grant in particular. . . .* [Salt Lake City, ca. 1925]

Broadside. 20½cm.

A diatribe against the general authorities of the church.

USlC

259a. **Baldwin, Nathaniel.** *Law of tithing; the law of consecration; a discussion with scriptural references.* [Salt Lake City? 1921?]

52p. 15cm.

Variant printing.

USlC

272a. **Ballard, Melvin Joseph.** *Three degrees of glory.* [Ogden, Utah, Neuteboom Printing Co., 1922?]

32p. 15½cm.

At head of title: Published under the direction of Mount Ogden Stake Genealogical Committee.

USlC

294a. *Baptism for the dead: The font resembling somewhat the "molten sea" of Solomon's Temple. The first published photographs of the interior of the great Mormon Temple at Salt Lake City, Utah.* London, 1911.

IVp. illus. 35cm.

In Supplement to the Illustrated London news, Dec. 16, 1911, p. 1-4.

Also has title: The Interior of the Great Temple of the Mormons at Salt Lake City: the first published photographs.

USlC

295a. *Baptism, how and by whom administered.* [Liverpool, Millennial Star Office, ca. 1900]

[2]p. 21½cm.

USlC

295b. _____. (same) [Chicago, ca. 1911]

[2]p. 16½cm.

USlC

296a. _____. (same) [n.p., Missions of the Church of Jesus Christ of Latter-day Saints in the United States, n.d.]

[2]p. 16½cm.

USlC

297a. **Baptist Congress, 4th, Calvary Baptist Church, New York City, 1885.** *Fourth annual session of the Baptist Congress for the discussion of current quesions held at Calvary Baptist Church, New York City, November 10, 11, and 12, 1885.* New York, Century Co., 1886.

112p. 24cm.

Discussion of Mormon question, p. 15-22.

USIC

298a. **Barber, John Warner.** *All the western states and territories, from the Alleghanies to the Pacific, and from the lakes to the gulf, engravings. By John W. Barber and Henry Howe.* Cincinnati, O. Howe's Subscription Book Concern, 1868.

733p. illus. 23cm.

"Utah Territory," p. 535-44.

NjP, OCU, USIC

299a. _____. *Incidents in American history.* New York, Geo. F. Cooledge & Brothers, c1847.

404p. illus., plates, ports. 19cm.

Section 130. Account of the Mormons, p. 283-6.

USIC

302a. **Barker, James Louis.** *Was ist aus der Mission Jesu Christi geworden?* Zurich, Schweiz, Thomas E. McKay [1910?]

16p. 17cm. (Heft No. 1)

Title in English: What is become of the mission of Jesus Christ?

USIC

303a. **Barlow, James M.** *James M. Barlow, appellant, vs. Alexander Ramsey, A. S. Paddock, G. L. Godfrey, A. B. Carleton, J. R. Pettigrew, E. D. Hoge and Harmel Pratt. Appeal from the Supreme Court of the Territory of Utah.* Washington, Judd & Detweiler [1884?]

2p.l. 12p. 22cm.

At head of title: Transcript of record. Supreme Court of the United States. October term, 1884. No. 1031.

Cover title.

Case concerning registration to vote.

DLC

303b. **Barman, Ole.** *Mormonaren spelstykke i ei vending.* Oslo, Norigs Ungdomslag, MCMXVIII.

24p. 20cm.

Title in English: Mormons in a world of change.

Original in private hands.

USIC xerox

307a. **Barnes, Julia Katherine.** *Annals of a quiet country town; other sketches from life, by Julia Katherine Barnes; illustrated by E. Warde Blaisdell.* New York, London [etc.] Abbey Press [1902]

2p.l., 424p. illus., plates, port. 20½cm.

"A Mormon episode," p. 339-75.

DLC, USIC

326a. **Bartlett, S. M.** *Whig extra. Thursday, 12 o'clock, Sept. 3d. Letter from the editor.* Quincy, Ill., 1846.

Broadside. 45 x 20cm.

Extra of the Quincy Whig talking of the affairs in Nauvoo.

USIC

328a. **Baskin, Robert Newton.** *George H. Cope, appellant, vs. Thomas H. Cope and Janet Cope, respondents. Brief for respondents.* Washington, Judd & Detweiler [1890]

19p. 22cm.

At head of title: In the Supreme Court of the United States. October term, 1890. No. 1327.

Inheritance case for a plural wife.

DLC

329a. **Baskin, Robert Newton.** *Papers in the case of Baskin vs. Cannon, as delegate from Utah Territory. April 10, 1876. Papers for contestant.* Washington, 1876.

21 [1]p. 23cm. (U.S. 44th Cong. 1st Sess. House. Misc. Doc. No. 166)

"Papers for contestee," p. 17-21.

The right of George Q. Cannon to hold a seat in the Congress.

DLC, UPB, USIC

331a. **Bassett, Ernest Knight.** *Jubilee songs as sung by one thousand children at the semi-centennial celebration, July 1st, 1897, in honor of the pioneers of Utah.* [Salt Lake City? 1897]

[3]p. music. 32cm.

USlC

331b. **Bassett, William E.** *William E. Bassett, plaintiff in error, vs. the United States. In error to the Supreme Court of the Territory of Utah. Filed September 23, 1887.* [Washington? 1890?]

67p. 22cm.

At head of title: Transcript of record. Supreme Court of the United States. October term, 1890.

A polygamy case in which the defendant is divorcing his first wife.

DLC

335a. *Battle of Mormon.* *100 guineas, a meeting will be held in the New Temperance Hall . . . February 10 & 11, 1862.* Birmingham, Eagle Steam Press, 1862.

Broadside. illus., port. 39 x 35cm.

J.S. Wright's challenge for a Mormon debate.

USlC

342a. **Beadle, Charles.** *A trip to the United States in 1887. Printed for private circulation.* [London, J. S. Virtue and Co., 1887]

3p.l., 210p. fold. map. 19cm.

Brief stop over in Salt Lake City. Describes the ugly temple which he thinks is a device to get money out of the poor.

DLC, ICU, MoU, UHi, UPB

355a. **Beadle, John Hanson.** *Polygamy: or, the mysteries and crimes of Mormonism.* Philadelphia, Crawford & Co. [1882?]

[4]p. 21cm.

Advertisement from Crawford & Co., for books printed probably by the National Publishing Company.

UPB

356a. _____. (same) [Beaver Springs, Pa., American Publishing Company, 1904?]

Broadside. 49 x 31cm.

An advertisement for the sale of the 1904 edition of the author's book under the same title.

USlC

356b. _____. *Polygamy, or, the mysteries and crimes of Mormonism being a full and authentic history of this strange sect from its origin to the present time with a thrilling account of the inner life and teachings of the Mormons and an expose of the secret rites and ceremonies of the deluded followers of Brigham Young. Assisted by Hon. O. J. Hollister . . . with an introduction by Hon. Murat Halstead.* Philadelphia, Walter E. Dewey [c1904]

[126]p. 20 plates 23½cm.

Publishers dummy. Sheets in the back for orders.

UPB

356c. _____. (same) Chicago, Ill., A. B. Kuhlman Company [c1904]

[126]p. 20 plates 23½cm.

Publishers dummy. Sheets in the back for orders.

UPB

356d. _____. (same) Beaver Springs, Pa., American Publishing Co. [1904?]

vii, 599p. illus., plates. 23½cm.

Variant printing.

USlC

356e. _____. (same) *Illustrated with a great number of striking scenes of life among the Mormons.* [Philadelphia, World Bible House, c1904]

xvi, 604p. illus., plates, ports. 24cm.

UPB, USlC

360a. Beale, Joseph H. *Picturesque sketches of American progress. Comprising official descriptions of great American cities. Illustrated sketches of American scenery, and celebrated resorts. With historical sketches . . . of our country, under the various administrations.* New York, Empire Cooperative Associaiton, c1889.

445p. illus., ports, map, facsim. 24cm.

Salt Lake City, p. 155-6. Compares the Mormon emigration with that of the Israelites.

DLC, ICN, NIC, PHi

366a. **Bechtinger, Jos.** *Ein Jahr auf den Sandwich-Inseln. (Hawaiische Inseln.) Land, Leute, Sitten und Gebrauche, Import, Export, mit Berucksichtigung der klimatischen Verhaltnisse, vorkommenden Krankheilten, etc.* Vien, Im Selbstverlage des Verfassors, 1869.

4p.l., 202 [2]p. illus., ports., plates, fold. map. 23cm.

Title in English: A year on the Sandwich Islands.

Mormonism in Hawaii, p. 126-7.

AU, CU, MiU, MnU, NIC, UPB

378a. *Het begin van het evangelie van Jezus Christus.* *De verordeningen, waaraan allen, die leden van de Kerk van Christus worden, moeten gehoorzamen.* Fijfde druk, 57ste Duizendtal. Rotterdam, Gedrukt op last van Willard T. Cannon, 1905.

15p. 18½cm. (Tractaat No. 2)

Title in English: The beginning of the Gospel of Jesus Christ.

USIC

380a. *Bekesseg legyen e hazban!* [Zurich, Schweiz, Thomas E. McKay, ca. 1910]

[4]p. 22cm.

Title in English: Peace be in this house.

USIC

385a. **Bell, Alfreda Eva.** *Boadicea; the Mormon wife. Lifescenes in Utah. Beautifully illustrated.* Baltimore, Philadelphia, New York, and Buffalo, Arthur R. Orton [c1855]

2p.l., 11-[102]p. 23cm.

Second state. Page 98 of advertisement not printed on back of final leaf of text. It is blank. Page 98-99 of advertisement printed on a single sheet, followed by 2 pages of new advertisements by M.A. Milleitte.

UPB

394a. **Belnap, Gilbert.** *Impressions of the Prophet Joseph Smith.* [n.p., ca. 1880]

Broadside. 35 x 21½cm.

USIC

404a. **Bennett, Marshall & Bradley.** *In the matter of the estate of Orson Pratt, deceased. Abstract of record. Appeal from the District Court of the Third Judicial District.* [Salt Lake City] Star Printing Company [1891]

1p.l., 9p. 22cm.

At head of title: In the Supreme Court, of Utah Territory.

Cover title.

Probate case of a polygamist family.

DLC

404b. _____. (same) *Appellant's brief. Bennett, Marshall & Bradley, attorneys for appellants. S. Varian, attorney for respondents.* [Salt Lake City, 1891?]

12p. 22cm.

At head of title: In the Supreme Court of Utah Territory.

UAr

417a. **Bennion, Adam Samuel.** *What it means to be a Mormon. Written for The Deseret Sunday School Union. Revised by the author for the Junior Seminaries.* Salt Lake City, Deseret Book Company, 1929.

vi, [7]-168p. 18½cm.

UPB

439b. *Beproeft alle dingen; behoudt het goede.* [Rotterdam? Netherlands-Belgian Mission?] 1903.

4p. 21½cm.

Title in English: Prove all things, hold fast to that which is good.

USIC

439c. _____. (same) [Rotterdam? Netherlands-Belgian Mission?] 1904.

4p. 21½cm.

USIC

439d. _____. (same) 160ste Duizendtal. [Rotterdam? Netherlands-Belgian Mission?] 1905.

4p. 22cm.

USIC

439e. _____. (same) [Rotterdam? Netherlands-Belgian Mission? ca. 1906]

4p. 21½cm.

USIC

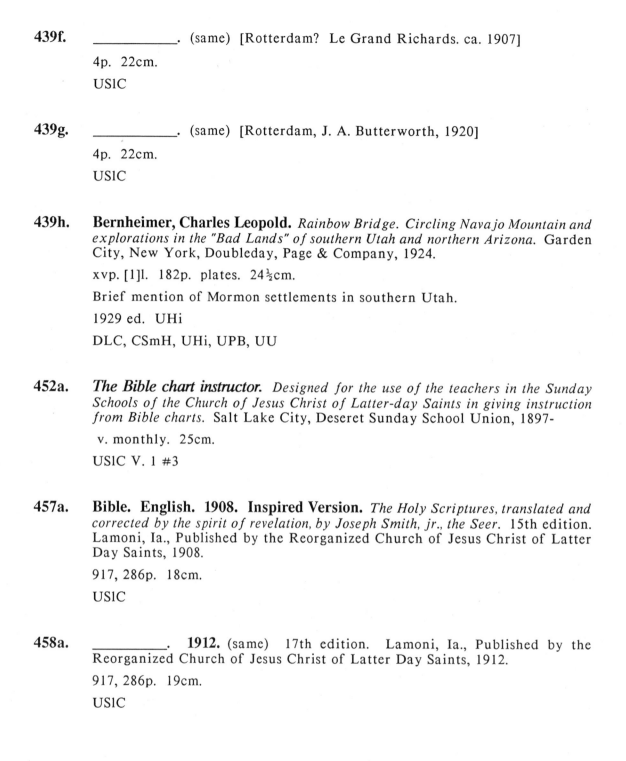

439f. _____. (same) [Rotterdam? Le Grand Richards. ca. 1907]

4p. 22cm.

USIC

439g. _____. (same) [Rotterdam, J. A. Butterworth, 1920]

4p. 22cm.

USIC

439h. Bernheimer, Charles Leopold. *Rainbow Bridge. Circling Navajo Mountain and explorations in the "Bad Lands" of southern Utah and northern Arizona.* Garden City, New York, Doubleday, Page & Company, 1924.

xvp. [1]l. 182p. plates. 24½cm.

Brief mention of Mormon settlements in southern Utah.

1929 ed. UHi

DLC, CSmH, UHi, UPB, UU

452a. *The Bible chart instructor. Designed for the use of the teachers in the Sunday Schools of the Church of Jesus Christ of Latter-day Saints in giving instruction from Bible charts.* Salt Lake City, Deseret Sunday School Union, 1897-

v. monthly. 25cm.

USIC V. 1 #3

457a. Bible. English. 1908. Inspired Version. *The Holy Scriptures, translated and corrected by the spirit of revelation, by Joseph Smith, jr., the Seer.* 15th edition. Lamoni, Ia., Published by the Reorganized Church of Jesus Christ of Latter Day Saints, 1908.

917, 286p. 18cm.

USIC

458a. _____. **1912.** (same) 17th edition. Lamoni, Ia., Published by the Reorganized Church of Jesus Christ of Latter Day Saints, 1912.

917, 286p. 19cm.

USIC

479a. **Bible. Selections. 1897.** *Bijbelsche Aanhalingen. Eene samenstelling van schriftuurplaatsen in subjectieve volgorde met talrijke citaten uit de werken van voorname schrijvers. In het bijzonder geschikt voor zendelingen en personen welke de heilige schriften studeeren.* Rotterdam, Uitgegeven door de Nederlandsche en Belgische. Zending van de Kerk van Jezus Christus van de Heiligen der laatste Dagen, 1897.

[1]p.l. [2]p. [5]-208[3]p. 16½cm.

Uit het Engelsch door Fred Pieper.

Title in English: Bible References. A compilation of scripture texts, arranged in subjective order . . . .

USIC

489a. **Bible. Selections. English. 1901.** *Ready references. A compilation of scripture texts, arranged in subjective order, with numerous annotations from eminent writers, Designed especially for the use of missionaries and scripture students.* Chattanooga, Tennessee, Southern States Mission, 1901.

2p.l. [5]-168p. 16½cm.

NjP, UPB

490a. _____. **1917.** (same) [Salt Lake City] Church of Jesus Christ of Latter-day Saints, 1917.

118p. 15½cm.

UPB

495a. _____. **German.** *Biblische Hinweisungen. Eine Zusammen-stellung von Schriftellen in thematischer Reihenfolge mit zahlreichen auffuhrungen von geschichtlichen Quellen. Besonders geeignet fur den Gebrauch der missionare und fur Solche, welche die heiligen Schriften studieren.* [Basel] Herausgegeben von Fred Tadje President der Schweizerischen und Deutschen Misison der Kirche Jesu Christi der Heiligen der Letzten Tage, 1924.

4p.l., 147p. 16½cm.

In green printed wrapper.

Title in English: Bible instructions.

UPB, USIC

501a. _____. **Swedish. 1853.** *Bibliska anvisningar.* Malmo, R. Capsson, 1853.

[2]p. 22cm.

Title in English: Bible references.

USIC

Biddle, George W. See *George Reynolds, Plaintiff in error, vs. the United States, Defendant in error.*

518a. *Bill of fare for Zion's camp.* October 10, 1865. [Great Salt Lake City, 1865]

Broadside. 18 x 8cm.

Menu for the dinner. Includes tea and coffee.

USlC

518b. **Billings, John Shaw.** *A report on barracks and hospitals, with descriptions of military posts.* Washington, Govt. Print. Off., 1870.

XXXIII, 494p. illus. 31cm.

In the article on Camp Douglas, p. 363-66, Mormonism is divided into four groups: Brighamites, Morrisites, Josephites, and Godbeites; other information on Mormonism. Catechism on the first principles of the Gospel.

UPB

522a. *Biographical and historical record of Ringgold and Decatur Counties, Iowa. A condensed history of the state of Iowa; portraits and biographies of the governors . . . engravings of prominent citizens in Ringgold and Decatur counties.* Chicago, Lewis Publishing Co., 1887.

796p. ports. 28cm.

Mormons and Reorganized Church, p. 132-3, 712, 746, 775-6, 783-91. Joseph Smith III, p. 512-4; Zenas H. Gurley, p. 539-44; Ebenezer J. Robinson, p. 544-5.

CoD, DLC, MnHi, OCl, UPB, USlC, WHi

522b. **Biographical and historical record of Wayne and Appanoose Counties, Iowa,** *containing portraits of all the Presidents of the United States from Washington to Cleveland, with accompanying biographies of each a condensed history of the state of Iowa; portraits and biographies of the governors of the territory and state; engravings of prominent citizens in Wayne and Appanoose Counties, with personal histories of many of the leading families, and a concise history of Wayne and Appanoose Counties, and their cities and villages.* Chicago, Inter-state Publishing Company, 1886.

5p.l., 9-746p. illus., ports. 28cm.

Mormon trail, p. 666. Second Mormon emigration, p. 671-3.

DLC, NN, UPB

Bird, Isabella Lucy. See Bishop, Isabella Lucy (Bird).

529a. *Birthday of the Lion House and of Susa Young Gates.* [Salt Lake City, 1926]

[2]p. illus., ports. 21cm.

Portraits of Brigham Young, Susa Young Gates and family and Lucy Bigelow Young.

UPB

533b. **Bishop, Francis Gladden.** *A proclamation from the Lord to his people, scattered throughout all the earth.* [Kirtland, Ohio, 1851]

Broadside. 61 x 23cm.

Included is a description of the golden plates and a revelation from the "Book of Life."

Dated: April 6, 1851.

USIC

536a. **Bishop, Isabella Lucy (Bird).** *Voyage d'une femme aux Montagnes Rocheuses.* Paris, E. Plon, Nourrit et Cie., 1888.

284 p. 18cm.

Title in English: Trip of a woman to the Rocky Mountains.

Translated from the English edition entitled: *A Lady's life in the Rocky Mountains.* She passed through Utah and remarks on the poor appearance of Mormon polygamous women.

USIC

538a. **Bixby-Smith, Sarah.** *Adobe days; being the truthful narrative of the events in the life of a California girl on a sheep ranch and in El Pueblo de Nuestra Sennoa de Los Angeles while it was yet a small, and humble town; together with an account of how three young men from Maine in eighteen hundred and fifty-three drove sheep and cattle across the plains, mountains and deserets from Illinois to the Pacific coast; and the strange prophecy of Admiral Thatcher about San Pedro harbor.* Rev. ed. Cedar Rapids, Iowa, Torch Press, 1926.

217p. plates, port. 19cm.

Mormons mentioned in the trip across the continent driving sheep.

UPB, USIC

539a. **Bjarnason, Lofter.** *Hith almenna truarfrafall.* [Reykjavik, Iceland? Prentsmithjan Gutenberg, 1905]

8p. 19½cm.

All but the final 5 pages is an Icelandic edition of Ben E. Rich "A friendly discussion."

Title in English: General apostasy from the faith.

USIC

540a. **Bjarnason, Thorarinn.** *Bibliu tilvisanir.* [Reykjavik, Iceland? 1894]

8p. 21cm.

Title in English: Bible references.

USIC

546a. **Blackburn, John W.** *The United States of America, plaintiff vs. the late corporation of the Church of Jesus Christ of Latter-day Saints, and others, defendants. June term, 1892. Opinion.* Salt Lake City, Star Print, 1892.

43p. 23cm.

Certified copy. Signed: John W. Blackburn and James A. Miner. At head of title: In the Supreme Court, Territory of Utah . . . .

USIC

548a. **Blackmore, Nellie Mussell.** *Principles of the junior church. An outline of lectures by Nellie Mussell Blackmore.* Independence, Mo., [Reorganized Church of Jesus Christ of Latter Day Saints] Centennial Conference Institute, 1930.

37p. 27½cm.

UPB

554a. **Blair, William Wallace.** *The inspired translation of the Holy Scriptures.* Lamoni, Iowa, The Reorganized Church of Jesus Christ of Latter Day Saints [ca. 1888]

[4]p. 19cm.

At head of title: No. 38.

USIC

562a. **Blanchard, Jonathan.** *Revised Odd-Fellowship illustrated; the complete revised ritual of the subordinate lodge and encampment, and the Redekah degrees, profusely illustrated by a past grand patriarch. With an historical sketch of the order, and an introduction and critical analysis of the character of each degree by Pres't J. Blanchard.* Cleveland, Ohio, A. Z. Wright & Co. [ca. 1902]

272p. illus. 17cm.

Published in many editions.

References to Mormon endowment, p. 14-15, 115.

USIC

563a. *De Blijde boodschap.* [Rotterdam? n.d.]

4p. 23½cm.

Title in English: The glad message.

USlC

572a. **Bliss, Charles H.** *Is baptism essential to salvation?* [Independence, Zion's Printing and Publishing Co., 1909]

[4]p. 15½cm.

UPB

573a. _____. (same) [Chicago, Church of Jesus Christ of Latter-day Saints, 1912]

[4]p. 16cm.

At head of title: No. 4.

Printed in Chicago by Allied Printing.

UPB, USlC

573b. _____. (same) [Independence, Mo., Missions of the Church of Jesus Chirst of Latter-day Saints, 1918?]

[4]p. 16½cm.

USlC

573c. _____. (same) [Independence, Zion's Printing and Publishing Company, 1925?]

[4]p. 16½cm.

Variant printings.

UPB

573d. _____. (same) [Liverpool, Millennial Star Office, n.d.]

[4]p. 22cm.

Includes Articles of Faith and catalogue of publications.

USlC

575a. _____. (Same in Armenian) *Mkrdouthuune eakan e phyyuthean.* [Murray, Utah, 1923]

6p. 7cm.

Title in English: Is baptism essential to salvation?

USlC

575b. _____. (same in Danish) *Er daab en betingelse for frelse?* [København, Joseph L. Petersen, 1926]

[2]p. 23cm.

Title in English: Is baptism essential to salvation?

USIC

575c. _____. (same) [København, Holger M. Larsen, 1930]

[2]p. 23½cm.

USIC

576a. _____. (same in Spanish) *Es el bautismo esencial a la salvacion? Traducido del Ingles por el Elder Rey L. Pratt, y El bautismo a quien y como debe ser administrado por Helaman Pratt.* Mexico, D. F., Publicado por la Mision Mexicana de la Iglesia de Jesu Cristo de Los Santos de los Ultimos Dias, 1912.

15 [1]p. 14 cm.

This pamphlet is composed of two items, the second entitled "El bautismo a quien y como debe ser administrado," is by Helaman Pratt and covers pages [6]-15.

Printed by Muller Hnos., Esq. Dr. Casimiro Liceaga y Dr. Carmona y Valle, Indianilla, Mexico [City]

USIC

576b. _____. (same) *Es el bautismo esencial a la salvacion? Traducido del Ingles por el Elder Rey L. Pratt y El bautismo a quien y como debe ser administrado por Elder Helaman Pratt.* El Paso Texas, Mision Mexicana de la Iglesia de Jesu Cristo de los Santos de los Ultimos Dias, 1925.

16p. 16½cm.

On verso of title: "Articulos de fe."

UPB

576c. _____. (same) 1928.

16p. 17½cm.

USIC

576d. _____. (same in Welch) *Mg'rdouthiun eagan eprgoutean.* [Murray, Utah, 1923]

6p. 16½cm.

UPB, USIC

577a. **Bloss, George M.D.** *Historic and literary miscellany.* Cincinnati, Robert Clarke & Co., Printers, 1875.

xi, 468p. port. 22cm.

"Who wrote the Book of Mormon?" (written in 1873), p. 440-2.

IaU, MWA, OC, OClFC, OClWhi, OCU, ODW, RPB, UPB, WaU

577b. **Blouet, Paul.** *John Bull & Co. The great colonial branches of the firm: Canada, Australia, New Zealand and South Africa.* New York, Charles L. Webster & Company, 1894.

319p. illus. 20cm.

Brief visit to Salt Lake City. Considers the Mormons harmless.

CtY, DLC, IEN, MB, TxU, UPB

577c. **Blunt, John Henry, ed.** *Dictionary of doctrinal and historical theology.* 2d ed. London, Oxford, and Cambridge, Rivingtons, 1872.

[8] 825 [1]p. 27cm.

Comments on Mormonism included.

DLC, ICN, NN, PU

578a. **Boddam-Whetham, John.** *Pearls of the Pacific.* London, Hurst and Blackett, 1876.

xiv, 362p. illus., plates. 22cm.

Brief mention of a Mormon settlement near Honolulu. Speculation concerning Mormon migration in case they are driven out of Salt Lake City.

UPB

581a. **Boles, W. H.** *Treason in Washington.* [Christopher, Ill.? 1908?]
2p.l., 171 [1]p. 20cm.

Title within border.

In gray printed wrapper.

Treason of the government in allowing Reed Smoot to retain his seat in the Senate.

UPB

581b. **Bolin, Johan.** *Beskrivning ofver Nord. Amerikas Forenta Stater.* Wexjo, A. F. Deurells Enka., 1853.

1p.l., 364p. 19½cm.

Title in English: Description of the United States of America.

A Swedish emigrant's guide to the United States. The California section contains information of the Mormons in Utah (Deseret.)

CtY, DLC, OC, NN

585a. **Bond, M. H.** *Spiritual gifts and spirit manifestations.* Providence, R.I., 1890.

103p. 19½cm.

Cover-title.

NjP

585b. _____. *Spritiual gifts and the Seer of Palmyra. Sequel to Spiritual Gifts and Spirit Manifestations.* Providence, R.I., 1891.

103, 58p. 19cm.

"Revised Edition" on cover.

NjP

594. **Bonwick, James.** *An octogenarian's reminiscences.* London, James Nichols, 1902.

xiv, 367 [4]p. 18½cm.

"Mormonland" p. 286-9. Impressions of Ogden and Salt Lake City in 1871-72. He was impressed with the Mormons.

DLC, UHi

632a. **Book of Mormon. English. 1900.** *The Book of Mormon. Translated by Joseph Smith, Jun.* Reprinted from the Third American Edition. Twenty-third edition. Lamoni, Iowa, Reorganized Church of Jesus Christ of Latter-day Saints. 1900.

xii, 545p. 16cm.

Reprint of the 1874 ed.

NjP

748a. *A book of startling revelations! . . . Mormonism unveiled! Being the only real expose of this creed ever given to the public.* [St. Louis, Sun Publishing Co., 1881?]

[4]p. illus. 28cm.

An advertisement for John D. Lee's *Mormonism Unveiled.*

UPB

752a. **Boquist, Laura (Brewster).** *Crossing the plains with ox teams in 1862.* [Los Angeles, c1930]

1p.l., 5-52p. 25cm.

A distrust of the Mormons while in Salt Lake City.

DLC

755a. *Boston Theatre.* *A rural comedy drama, the Mormon wife.* [Boston, Mass., 1901]

[20]p. illus. 19½cm.

Theater program for week of January 14, 1901.

USlC

759a. **Bourne, Henry Eldridge.** *A history of the United States. By Henry Elderidge Bourne and Elbert Jay Benton.* Boston, D.C. Heath & Co. [c1913]

viii, 534, lxip. illus. 20½cm.

Mormons mentioned, p. 360, 460, 488.

DLC, OCi, PP, PPL, USlC, WHi

763a. **Bowes, John.** *Mormonism exposed, in its swindling and licentious abominations, refuted in its principles, and in the claims of its head, the modern Mohammed, Joseph Smith, who is proved to have been a deceiver, and no prophet of God.* London, E. Ward, Manchester, Fletcher & Tubbs, Glasgow, G. Gallie, Edinburgh, A. Muirhead. [ca. 1850]

71 [1]p. 17½cm.

CtY, MiU, NN, OC1WHi, UPB, USlC

772a. **Boyd, James Penny.** *Red men on the war path, a thrilling story of sunset land and its tragedies. The peculiar intersting life, manners, customs, beliefs and ceremonials of the North American Indians, and a wholesome, interesting narration of the tragic events of their recent history, delightfully presented for the entertainment and instruction of youth, with a wealth of portraits and illustrations.* Philadelphia, and Chicago, J. H. Moore, & Co., [c1895]

395p. illus., 19 plates, 13 ports. 23cm.

"The affair of Mountain Meadows," p. 73-8.

UU, NN, OC1

790a. **Bradford, Ward.** *Biographical sketches of the life of Major Ward Bradford, as related by the author in his eighty-second year. Containing a graphic description of the manners and life of early times, vivid incidents in indian wars, and wilds of the mountains; life in the gold regions of Nevada; perils by land and sea. Together with reliable statements concerning the products and resources of many lands and many climes.* [Fresno, Ca.] Published for the author [1891]

92p. port. 17cm.

DLC, CSmH, MH, NN, NjP

801a. **Brandley, Theodore.** *Die grundung und lehren der Kirche Jesu Christi der Heiligen der letzten Tage. In kurze dargestellt vom Aeltesten Theodor Brandli.* Bern, Switzerland, J. U. Stucki, 1889.

24p. 23cm.

Title in English: The founding and teachings of the Church of Jesus Christ of Latter-day Saints.

USIC

803a. **Breakenridge, William M.** *Helldorado, bringing the law to the Mesquite.* Boston and New York, Houghton Mifflin Company, 1928.

[10]xix, 256 [5]p. illus. 23½cm.

Mormons mentioned, p. 55, 78-81, 219-20.

CU, DLC, MH, NM, TxU, UPB, USIC

813a. *Brief historical sketch of the life of Josiah Rhead and family.* [Ogden? 1926]

[2]p. 27½cm.

Josiah Rhead was convert to the Church in England in 1852. Family reunion in honor of Josiah Rhead's 95th birthday.

USIC

817a. **Briggs, Edmund C.** *Polygamy.* Great Salt Lake City [1864]

8p. 15cm.

Signed: Truth Conquers.

Dated: G.S.L. City, U.T., March 27, 1864.

USIC

826a. **Briggs, Jason W.** *Not Mormonism! As existing in Utah, but the doctrine of the true Church of Jesus Christ of Latter Day Saints.* [Salt Lake City? 1876]

Broadside. 22 x 31cm.

Announcement for a speech to be given in the Lutheran Church, March 5, 1876.

USIC

829a. *Brigham Young and the Mormons of the Salt Lake.* [n.p., 1871]

Broadside. 77 x 51cm.

This drama, based on the popular tale, "Jessie, the Mormon's Daughter," followed the presentation of "Woman, Her Rise or Fall in Life," at the Britannia Theatre, Hoston, England, November 1871. Occupies final one third of Broadside entitled "Britannia."

USIC

830. **Brigham Young College, Logan, Utah.** *Brigham Young College bulletin series.* Logan, Utah, 1884-1926.

v. 21-24cm.

Includes Alumni number, 1903, 1904, 1905, 1910, 1911, 1912, 1913, 1914, 1915, 1916, 1917, 1918. Commencement, 1926; The place of the junior college in our educational system, 1926; Views, 1907, 1909, 1911, 1914; Student directory 1910-1919, Alumni directory, 1910-1911. Catalogs listed separately.

USIC, UPB Alumni #1911

831. _____. *Catalog, 1884-1930.* [Logan, Utah, 1884-1926]

v. 21-24cm.

Called Prospectus in 1884-5, Circular 1885-1893. Catalogue, 1894-26
CU 1897, UPB 1884-5, 1885-6, 1888-9, 1889-90, 1890-91, 1891-2, 1892-3, 1893-4, 1894-5, 1895-6, 1896-7, 1897-8, 1898-9, 1899-1900, 1900-01, 1901-02, 1902-03, 1903-04, 1904-05, 1905-06, 1906-07, 1907-08, 1909-10, 1910-11, 1911-12, 1912-13, 1913-14, 1914-15, 1915-16, 1916-17, 1917-18, 1918-19, 1920-21, 1921-22, 1922-23, 1923-24, 1924-25, 1925-26. USIC 1885-1915.

838a. **Brigham Young University.** *Circular. To the heirs of the late President Brigham Young, greeting.* [Provo, Brigham Young Academy, 1884]

[2]l. 21cm.

Solicitation for funds after a fire destroys its building.

UHi, UPB

845a. *Brigham Young's birthday celebration.* Calder's Park. *A grand demonstration, celebrating the birthday of the great pioneer and leader, Brigham Young, in the Calder's Park, Thursday, June 1, 1899.* [Salt Lake City, 1899]

Broadside. 27 x 18cm.

An oration to be given by C. J. Freeman of Oxon, England and later a grand ball.

USIC

848a. **Brij, Elisabeth H. de.** *Ervaringen dan een Hollandsche vrouw in het land der Mormonen.* [n.p., n.d.]

15 [1]p. 21cm.

Title in English: Experiences of a Dutch woman in the land of the Mormons.

UPB

848b. **Brij, Wm. J. de.** *Leer en leven der Mormonen.* [n.p., n.d.]

16p. illus. 22cm.

Title in English: Teachings and life of the Mormons.

UPB

851a. **Brimhall, George Henry.** *Tithing.* [n.p., ca. 1909]

8p. 17½cm.

UPB

864a. **Broadbent, J. L., comp.** *Celestial marriage?* 3rd ed. [Salt Lake City? 1929]

30p. 20cm.

USIC

867a. **Broadhead, James Overton.** *The late corporation of the Church of Jesus Christ of Latter-day Saints et al., appellants, vs. the United States, appellees. Motion to advance cause. James O. Broadhead, Joseph E. McDonald, John M. Butler, Franklin S. Richards, for Appellants.* Washington, Gibson Bros., 1888.

11p. 22cm.

Case concerning the return of property that was confiscated when church was disenfranchised.

At head of title: Supreme Court of the United States. October term, 1888. No. 1423.

Cover title.

DLC

870a. _____. *The United States vs. The corporation of the Church of Jesus Christ of Latter-day Saints. Argument of Hon. James O. Broadhead delivered October 20, 1887.* [Salt Lake City? 1887?]

11p. 55cm.

At head of title: Supreme Court of Utah . . . .

An earlier version of above entry, *Flake/Draper Supplement 867a.*

USlC

877a. **Bromley, William Michael.** *Ko nga korerohari mo te haringa nui.* [Auckland, New Zealand, E. H. Fail, 1883?]

4p. 22cm.

Title in English: At the pleasant news concerning public rejoicing.

Translated by Pepene E. Ketone.

USlC

889a. **Bross, William.** *Address of the Hon. William Bross, Lieutenant-governor of Illinois on the resources of the far West, and the Pacific railway, before the Chamber of Commerce of the state of New York.* New York, John W. Amerman, 1866.

30p. 24cm.

The need for a railroad to the Pacific. Tells of the success the Mormons have had in agriculture in Utah.

CtY, DLC, ICN, NN, UPB

891a. **Brown, Adam Mercer.** *The gold region, and scenes by the way: Being the journal of a tour by the overland route and South Pass of the Rocky Mountains, across the Great Basin and through California.* Allegheny, Pa., Purviance & Co., 1851.

136p. 18cm.

In blue printed wrappers.

"Speaks in depth about the Mormons." *Mintz 55.*

UPB

901a. **Brown, John.** *The autobiography of John Brown the cordwainer; with his sayings and doings in town and country: Showing what part he took in the spread of church principles among the working classes.* Edited by a clerical friend. Third ed. Oxford, A. R. Mowbray, London, J. Masters & Sons, Simpkin, Marshall & Co., 1868.

iv, 219, 5p. illus., plates, music. 18cm.

Chapter XII. Mr. Brown continues the adventures of his friend Jaques, how he went off to the Great Salt Lake, what happened to him there, and what brought him back a wiser and a better man.

UPB

905a. **Brown, John Elward.** *In the cult kingdom; Mormonism, Eddysim and Russellism.* Siloam Springs, Arkansas, International Federation Publishing Co. [1918?]

117p. 19cm.

NjP, USIC

918a. **Browne, Charles Farrar.** *Artemus Ward among the Mormons.* London, Ward, Lock, and Tyler [1865?]

xxx, 192, 168 [32]p. illus. 17cm.

USIC

918b. _____. *Artemus Ward, "Among the Mormons" and "His book".* London, Ward, Lock [1882?]

xxx, 192, 168 [32]p. illus. 17cm.

USIC, ViLxW

923a. _____. *Artemus Ward, his book; with many comic illustrations.* New York, Carleton, 1866 (c1862)

vi, 224, 6p. illus. 19cm.

UPB, USIC

924a. _____. *Artemus Ward, his programme.* New York, S. Booth, [ca. 1865] [4]p. 24cm.

Program for entertainment of pictorial works on the Mormons.

USIC

924b. _____. *Artemus Ward, (his travels) among the Mormons.* London, Ward, Lock, and Tyler, [1865?]

xxx, 192, 168 [32]p. illus. 17cm.

Bound with: Artemus Ward, his book.

USIC

924c. _____. (same) London, Ward, Lock, [1882?]

xxx, 192, 168 [32]p. illus. 17cm.

Bound with: Artemus Ward, his book.

USIC

934. _____. *Artemus Ward's travels.* Girard, Ks., Haldeman-Julius, [187-]

96p. 13cm. (Ten cent pocket series, edited by E. Haldeman-Julius, no. 369).

Paperback ed. A Mormon romance. Reginald Gloverson, p. 56-92.

USIC

940a. _____. *The complete works of Charles F. Browne better known as "Artemus Ward". With a portrait by Geflowske, facsimile of handwriting, etc.* New ed. London, Chatto and Windus, 1893.

xi, 518 [32]p. facs., port. 20cm.

Includes: Artemus Ward (his travels) among the Mormons.

USIC

942a. _____. *Selected works of Artemus Ward; edited with an introduction by Albert Jay Nock.* New York, Albert Charles Boni, 1924.

295p. 20cm.

A visit to Brigham Young, p. 163-8; A Mormon romance -- Reginald Gloverson, p. 201-146.

USIC

945a. **Brownell, Henry Howard.** *The pioneer heroes of the new world. From the earliest period (982) to the present time.* New York, Dayton and Wentworth, 1855. [c1854]

736p. illus. 22½cm.

"The Mormon settlements," p. 617-25.

USIC

945b. _____. (same) New York, Dayton and Wentworth, 1855.

632p. col. plates, col. ports. 23cm.

"The Mormon settlements," p. 617-25.

Cty, NN, UPB

952a. **Buchanan, James.** *Mr. Buchanan's administration on the eve of the rebellion.* New York, D. Appleton and Company, 1866.

x, [9]-296p. 24cm.

Utah Expedition: p. 232-39.

UPB

961a. **Buchner, Max.** *Reise durch den Stillen Ozean.* Breslau, J. U. Kern's Verlag (Max Muller), 1878.

470p. 23½cm.

Title in English: Travels over the calm ocean.

Mormons mentioned, p. 436-47.

HU, CU, MH, USIC

961b. **Buck, Charles.** *A theological dictionary, containing definitions of all religious and ecclesiastical terms, an impartial account of the principal denominations which have subsisted in the religious world from the birth of Christ to the present day. By the late Rev. Charles Buck.* A new and greatly improved edition; by the Rev. E. Henderson. London, Printed for Thomas Tegg, 1841.

iv, 784, 8p. 22cm.

The edition probably used by Joseph Smith for his *Times and Seasons* article. "Mormonites," p. 537-38.

MWA, UPB

961c. **Buck, Franklin A.** *A yankee trader in the gold rush. The letters of Franklin A. Buck. Compiled by Katherine A. White, with illustrations.* Boston, Houghton Mifflin Company, 1930.

viii, 294p. illus., plates. 22cm.

Encounters Mormons in Pioche, Nevada.

DLC, MH, NjP, NN, OO, UPB

965a. **Budge, Alfred.** *Dudley D. Toncray, appellant, vs. Alfred Budge, defendant. Brief for respondent. Appeal from the District Court of the Fifth Judicial District of the State of Idaho, in and for the County of Bannock.* [Boise, Idaho? 1908]

40p. 25½cm.

At head of title: In the supreme court of the State of Idaho February Term, 1908.

USIC

968a. **Budge, William.** *The gospel message. Being a discourse, giving an explanation of some of the prominent doctrines of the Church of Jesus Christ of Latter-day Saints, delivered by Elder William Budge, at Chesterfield, August 10th, 1879.* (Reported by Joseph May, of Sheffield) [Liverpool, Latter-day Saints' Printing, Publishing, and Emigration Office, 1879]

12p. 22cm.

Variant of *Flake 968.*

USIC

978a. _____. *The only true gospel, or the primitive Christian faith.* [Liverpool, Printed and published by William Budge at the Latter-day Saints' Printing, Publishing and Emigration Office, 1879]

4p. 19½cm.

Dated Liverpool, Feb. 1, 1879.

Variant printings.

USIC

989a. _____. (same in Danish) *Det eneste sande Evangelium eller de forste Kristnes Tro.* [Kjøbenhavn, Martin Christophersen, 1913]

[4]p. 21½cm.

USIC

991a. _____. (same in German) *Das Einzig wahre evangelium.* Bern, J. J. Walser, 1883.

[4]p. 22cm.

USIC

992a. _____. (same in Swedish) *Det sanna evangelit eller de forsta kristnas tro.* [Stockholm, Gideon N. Hulterstrom, 1923]

4p. 22½cm.

USIC

992b. _____. (same) [Stockholm, Gideon N. Hulterstrom, 1930]

4p. 22½cm.

USIC

992c. _____. *Families in heaven.* [Paris, Idaho, Post Pub. Co., ca. 1900]

[6]p. 23½cm.

USIC

994a. _____. *Pre-existence of spirits. Discourse delivered by President William Budge, before the Elders' Quorum, December 19, 1895.* [Paris, Idaho? 1896?]

[4]p. 24cm.

Reported by Elder James H. Wallis.

USIC

997a. **Buel, James William.** *Heroes of the plains, or lives and wonderful adventures of Wild Bill, Buffalo Bill, Kit Carson, Capt. Payne, Capt. Jack, Texas Jack, California Joe, and other celebrated Indian fighters, scouts, hunters, and guides including a true and thrilling history of Gen. Custer's famous "last fight" on the little big horn, with Sitting Bull. Profusely illustrated.* St. Louis, Mo., Sun Publishing Co., 1882.

548p. illus. (part col.) 21cm.

Mormons mentioned in the biography of Buffalo Bill. Mormons use Indians to massacre wagon trains.

Other editions: New York, N. D. Thompson, 1882. ICN, OO; New York, Parks Bros., 1882.

NNC, UPB

1001a. **Buell, Augustus.** *"The cannoneer." Recollections of service in the Army of the Potomac. By "A detached volunteer" in the regular artillery.* Washington, National Tribune, 1890.

2p.l., 5-400p. illus. 21cm.

Supplementary chapter. Capt. Stewart's memoir of early service in the Battery. Includes his experiences with the Utah Expedition.

CSMH, MB, MH, UPB

1001b. *Buffalo Bill and the Danite kidnappers; or, the Green River massacre.* By the author of "Buffalo Bill." New York, Street & Smith, 1902.

29p. 27cm. (The Buffalo Bill Stories. February 1, 1902. No. 38)

One of Buffalo Bill's famous defeats of the Danites.

Colored printed cover.

UPB

1001c. *Buffalo-Bill; Le Complot des Mormons.* Seule edition originale autorisee par le Col. W. F. Cody, dit Buffalo Bill. [Paris, A. Eichler, edit. impr., n.d.]

32p. 27cm. (No. 89)

Title in English on cover: Buffalo Bill at war with the Danites, or The crafty Mormon's darkest plot.

UPB

1013a. **Burgess, Alice Chase.** *Fulfillment, a panorama of Christian cycle. Directed by Gladys Newton Six; given at the Centennial Conference of the Reorganized Church of Jesus Christ of Latter Day Saints, the auditorium, Independence, Missouri, April 18-19.* [Independence, 1930]

16p. 21cm.

Centennial program.

MoInRC

1019a. **Burnap, Willard A.** *What happened during one man's lifetime, 1840-1920; a review of some great, near great and little events.* Fergus Falls, Minn., W. L. Burnap, 1923.

461p. illus. 21cm.

Mormon Indian relations, p. 44; Mormon pioneers, p. 148-9.

UPB

1029a. **Burton, Sir Richard Francis.** *Viaje al pais de los Mormones.* Extractado y traducido por E. H. Y. F. Madrid, Imprenta de la Galeria Literaria, 1872.

2v. front. 16cm.

Title in English: Trip to the country of the Mormons.

At head of title: Galeria literaria. Murcia y Marti, editores.

In yellow printed wrappers.

Translation of his City of the Saints. V. 24 and 25 of Biblioteca Madrelena.

MH, UPB v. 1 only

1029b. _____. *Voyages du Capitaine Burton a la mecque aux grands lacs d'Afrique et chez les Mormons. Abreges par J. Belin-de Launay. D'apres le texte original et les traductions de Mme H. Loreau. Avec trois cartes.* Deuxieme edition. Paris, Librarie Hachette & Cie., 1873.

xvi, 336p. maps. 19½cm.

Title in English: Voyages of Captain Burton to the mecca, to the great lakes of Africa, and to the Mormons.

In green printed wrappers.

UPB

1047a. **Bushnell, Horace.** *A discourse for home missions, by Horace Bushnell, Pastor of the North Church, Hartford, Conn.* New York, Printed for the American Home Missionary Soceity, by William Osborn, 1847.

32p. 22cm.

At head of title: Barbarism the first danger.

Discusses the delusion of Mormonism, p. 25.

UPB

1049a. **Buss, Henry.** *Wanderings in the West, during the year 1870.* London, Printed for private circulation by Thomas Danks, 1871.

viii, 196p. 19cm.

Poetry. "Mormons," p. 153-68.

DLC, ICU, IEN, PPULC, PSC, UPB

1050a. **Butler, William.** *Proclamation from the Rocky Mountains. A voice of warning to the people of Canada!* [n.p., 1885]

Broadside. 23 x 15cm.

William Butler was set apart for a mission to Canada April 4, 1885 and returned in 1886.

USlC

C

1066a. **Caillot, Auguste Charles Eugene.** *Les Polynesiens orientaux au contact de la civilisation. Ouvrage illustre de 159 phototypier, reunies en 92 planches.* Paris, Ernest Leroux, 1909.

281p., 92 numb. plates 25cm.

Title in English: The Oriental Polynesians in contact with civilization.

Chapter 2 tells of Mormon influence at Tuamotu.

CtY, CU, DLC, ICJ, MiU

1081a. **Calderon, George.** *Tahiti, by Tihoti [pseud.]* New York, Harcourt, Brace and Co., 1922.

260p. front., plates. 23cm.

"Mormons," chapter XV, p. 54-7.

CoU, MB, OOxM, PPC, USIC, Vi

1085a. **California. Legislature.** *Resolution of the legislature of the State of California, in favor of the establishment of a territorial government in Carson Valley.* [Washington, William A. Harris, Printer?] 1858.

[1]p. 23cm. (U.S. 35th Cong. 1st Sess. Senate. Misc. Doc. No. 181)

Need to establish the territorial government, with the coming of the Utah Expedition.

UPB

1087a. **California. Legislature. Senate.** *Report of Mr. Flint, of the Select Committee, to whom was referred the resolutions of miner's convention at Shasta County. Submitted March 28, 1855.* [Sacramento] B. B. Redding, State Printer [1855]

13p. 21½cm. (Calif. Leg. Sen. Sess. 1855. Doc. No. 19)

USlC

1087b. **California. Legislature. Senate. Committee on Internal Improvements.** *Report of the Committee on Internal Improvements with reference to a road across the Sierra Nevada submitted April 10, 1855.* [Sacramento] B. B. Redding, state printer, 1855?

13p. 23cm.

Mentions the need to link up to the Mormon settlements.

CSmH, CU-B, MiU-C, TxFTC, UPB

1089a. **The Calimis.** Los Angeles, California Mission, 1922- .

v. 28cm.

A mission periodical.

USIC has v. 3- , 1922-

1090a. **Call, Lamoni.** *Anti-Mormon queries.* [Bountiful, Utah? ca. 1900]

[4]p. 13½cm.

USIC

1101a. **Callis, Charles Albert.** *Baptism of the Holy Ghost.* [n.p., n.d.]

14p. 15cm.

USIC

1126a. **Campbell, William R.** *Methods of Mormon missionaries.* [Salt Lake City, Gentile Bureau of Information, ca. 1910]

11 [1]p. 14½cm.

Variant.

USIC

1127a. _____. *The political aspects of Mormonism. Mr. Roberts not a Democrat. No member of this polygamous Priesthood can be a Democrat, or a Republican in any true sense of the term. No patriotic party can afford to compromise with the polygamists.* [Salt Lake City, 1900?]

[4]p. 28cm. (Circular No. 1)

USIC

1129a. _____. *Reasons why B. H. Roberts, of Utah, should be expelled from the House of Representatives of the Fifty-sixth Congress.* [Salt Lake City? 1900?]

[4]p. 28cm. (Circular No. 2)

USIC

1129b. _____. *Rev. Wm. R. Campbell, Box 1061, Salt Lake City, Utah, October 7, 1899. Mr. Editor.* [Salt Lake City, 1899]

2l. 28½cm.

At head of title: [To be published October 18th.]

Concerning the seating of B. H. Roberts.

USIC

1139a.   **Cannon, Angus Munn.** *Angus M. Cannon, plaintiff in error, vs. the United States. Brief for defendant in error.* [Washington? 1885?] 45p. 22cm.

At head of title: Supreme Court of the United States, October term, 1885. No. 1169.

Cover title.

The polygamy case of Cannon and his wives Clara, Sarah, and Amanda Cannon.

DLC

1139b.   _____. *Angus M. Cannon, plaintiff in error, vs. the United States. In error to the Supreme Court of the Territory of Utah.* [Washington? 1885?] 41p. 22cm.

At head of title: In the Supreme Court of the United States, October term, 1885. No. 1169.

Cover title.

Polygamy case of Cannon and his three wives.

DLC

1139c.   **Cannon, Anne Wells.** *Daughters of Zion. Song, written for the Relief Society conference, April, 1908.* [Salt Lake City? General Board of Relief Society? 1908?]

Broadside. 19 x 11cm.

USIC

1155a.   **Cannon, George Quayle.** *Die geschichte der Mormonen. Ihre bersolgungen und reisen.* Salt Lake City, J. H. Ward, 1892.

41 [3]p. 15½cm.

Title in English: The History of the Mormons.

USIC

1174a.   **Cannon, George Q., and Sons.** *Catalogue and price list of church publications, school and college text books, miscellaneous books, etc., etc., . . . Jan 1st.* Salt Lake City, George Q. Cannon & Sons Co., 1900.

52p. 15cm.

USIC

1176a. **Cannon, George Q., and Sons Company.** *Catalogue and price-list of church publications and other books, etc.* Salt Lake City, Geo. Q. Cannon & Sons Co., 1897.

36p. 14½cm.

USIC

1179a. **Cannon, Hugh J.** *Liebe Bruder, was soll ich thun, dass ich selig werde?* Eine kurze Erklarung der fur jeden Menschen zur Seligkeit notwendigen Grundsatze des Evangeliums Jesu Christi. (Apostelgeschichte 16, 30) Tracktat II. Hamburg, Herausgegeben von der Redaktion des "Stern," 1900.

16p. 18cm.

Title in English: Dear brother, what must I do to be saved?

Druck von Schroder & Jede.

In salmon printed wrappers.

USIC

1179b. _____. (same) Berlin, 1901.

16p. 19cm.

In pink printed wrappers.

USIC

1179c. _____. (same) Berlin, Herausgegeben von Hugh J. Cannon [1902?]

16p. 18cm.

Druck von G. T. Roder, Leipzig.

In green printed wrappers.

USIC

1180a. _____. (same) Chicago, Herausgegeben von Northern States Mission, 1907.

14p. 19cm.

In printed wrappers.

Druck von H. C. Etten & Co., Chicago.

UPB, USIC

1182a. _____. (same) Basel, 1922.

16p. 15cm.

Variant printing.

In salmon printed wrappers.

T. U. Wagner, Buchdruckerei, Freiburg.

USIC

1183a. _____. *Why is it? Pertinent questions regarding "Mormonism".* [Liverpool, Millennial Star Office? ca. 1900]

4p. 21cm.

UPB

1184a. **Cannon, Joseph Jenne.** *The struggle to attain righteousness; address delivered over Radio Station KSL Sunday evening, April 1, 1928.* [Salt Lake City, Deseret News, 1928]

Broadside. 59 x 24cm.

"Reprint from the Deseret News on Saturday, April 7th."

Conduct of life, immorality of war, etc.

USIC

1186b. **Card, Charles Ora.** *200 men with teams wanted who will become actual settlers in southern Alberta, Canada.* [n.p., 189-?]

Broadside. 30 x 21cm.

USIC

1187a. **Carey, Joseph.** *By the Golden Gate, or San Francisco, the queen city of the Pacific Coast, with scenes and incidents characteristic of its life.* Albany, New York, The Albany Diocesan Press, 1902.

29p. port. 21cm.

Cary visits Utah, p. 30-7.

RLV, UHi

1189. **Carleton, James Henry.** *Report on the subject of the massacre at the Mountain Meadows, in Utah Territory in September, 1857, of one hundred and twenty men, women and children who were from Arkansas. By Brevet Major James Henry Carleton, U. S. Army. And report of the Hon. William C. Mitchell, relative to the seventeen surviving children who were brought back by the authorities of the U. S. after their parents and others, with whom they were emigrating, had been murdered.* Little Rock, [J]ohnson & Yerkes, State Printers, 1860.

32p. 22cm.

At head of title: [Senate Doc.]

Probably the first edition of two printed at Little Rock in 1860. Addressed to the Governor of Arkansas.

Howes C 147.

ArU, KU, UPB

1190. _____. (same) Little Rock, Democrat Steam Press Print. 1860.

32p. 22½cm.

Probably the second of two editions printed at Little Rock in 1860.

W-C 354.

CtY, ICN, NjP, UPB, UU

1190b. _____. *Report on the subject of the massacre at the Mountain Meadows, in Utah Territory in September, 1857, of one hundred and twenty men, women and children who were from Arkansas. By Brevet Major James Henry Carleton U. S. Army. And report of the Hon. William C. Mitchell, relative to the seventeen surviving children who were brought back by the authorities of the United States after their parents and others, with whom they were emigrating, had been murdered.* Little Rock, True Democrat Steam Press Print, 1860. Reprint by Press Printing Company. 1889.

23p. 23½cm.

Printed wrappers.

CSmH

1192a. **Carlton, Ambrose Bolivar.** *Judge A. B. Carlton's views on the qualification of voters of Utah under the antipolygamy laws of Congress.* Correspondence. [Salt Lake City, 1887]

Broadside. 29 x 21cm.

USlC

1201a. **Carmichael, Albert.** *The Order of Enoch.* Independence, Missouri, Herald Publishing House [n.d.]

39p. 19cm.

Reorganized Church doctrinal pamphlet.

UPB

1210a. **Carrington, Albert.** *Prospectus of the 15th volume of the Deseret News weekly and the first volume of the Deseret News semi-weekly.* [Great Salt Lake City, Deseret News, 1865]

Broadside. 36 x 22cm.

Dated July 6th, 1865.

USIC

1210b. **Carrington, Janette.** *An apostrophe to Zion.* Published in Zion's Home Monthly, June 1, 1894. [Salt Lake City, 1894?]

Broadside. 21 x 14cm.

Mormon poetry.

USIC

1214a. **Carroll, Henry K.** *The religious forces of the United States enumerated, classified, and described on the basis of the government census of 1890. With an introduction on the condition and character of American Christianity.* New York, The Christian Literature Co., MDCCCXCIII.

lxvi, 478p. illus., plates. 21cm. (American church history series, vol. 1)

Chapter XXVI. The Latter-day Saints, 165-74.

DLC, ICN, NjP, OCl, UPB

1222a. *The Carthage Jail.* [n.p., n.d.]

[4]p. illus. 18cm.

USIC

1224a. *The case against delegate Cannon, of Utah.* [Salt Lake City, 1881?]

4p. 23cm.

At head of title: [From the Daily Evening News of November 1.]

Against the seating of George Q. Cannon.

USIC

1229a. **Cassity, L. J.** *Fruits of the gospel of Jesus Christ.* Compiled by L. J. Cassity. Auckland [NZ] Messenger Publishing [1913?]

16p. illus. 14cm.

USIC

1235a. **Caswall, Henry.** *Mormonism and its author; or, a statement of the doctrines of the "Latter-day Saints."* London, Printed for the Society for Promoting Christian Knowledge, 1854.

22p. 16½cm.

UPB

1236a. _____. (same) London, Printed for the Society for Promoting Christian Knowledge, 1857.

16p. 18cm.

In green printed wrapper.

UPB

1238a. *Catechism on the first principles of the gospel.* [Salt Lake City, Juvenile Instructor Office, ca. 1890]

Card. 16 x 12cm.

Title within a double lined border.

Twenty seven questions and answers. Ten general questions and ten [11-20] questions under the caption: Faith. Seven questions under the caption: Repentance.

UPB, USIC

1239b. **Catherwood, Mary Hartwell.** *Mackinac and lake stories.* New York and London, Harper & Brothers, 1899.

4p.l., 211 [1]p. 10 plates 19cm.

Two stories: "King of Beaver," and "Beaver Lights," are about the Strang group.

DLC, USIC

1239c. **Catlin, George B.** *The story of Detroit.* Detriot, Mich., The Detroit News, 1923.

xix 764p. illus. 20cm.

Chapter LXXXI, "Michigan's Mormon Colony," p. 449-53. Discusses the Strangites; includes illustrations.

USIC

1242. **Cavling, Henrik.** *Fra Amerika, af Henrik Cavling. Med 74 helsidebilleder paa særligt papir, flere hundreds afbildninger i teksten, samt et koloreret kort over Nordamerika.* København, Gyldendal, 1897.

2v. illus., pl., port., fold map, plan, facsim. 24cm.

Title in English: From America.

Description of Mormonism in the section on the west.

Cty, DLC, MB, MH, MnU, MsU, MoU

1250a. **Chambers, Julius.** *The Mississippi River and its wonderful valley. Twenty-seven hundred and seventy-five miles from source to sea.* New York, G. P. Putnam's Sons, 1910.

xvi, 308p. illus., plates. 25cm.

Includes a visit to Nauvoo and a conversation with Emma Smith.

CU, DLC, ICN, NjP, NN, UPB

1256a. *Chapter on prayer.* [Salt Lake City] Printed at the Juvenile Instructor Office [ca. 1900]

Broadsheet. 19 x 12cm.

On verso: The Ten Commandments.

Questions and answers on gospel questions. On various colored cards.

USIC

1257a. **Charteris, Francis.** *Letters & journal by the Hon. Francis Charteris, during a journey in America, across the Pacific, Japan, China, and home by Mongolia, in fourteen months; and in Italy.* [London, Harrison and Sons, 1868?]

1p.l., 155p. 25cm.

Two letters written while in Salt Lake City, with very little on the Mormons. Heard Brigham Young talk.

N, NBuG, UPB

1259a. **Chase, Edward R.** *Territory of Utah, County of Box Elder. Edward R. Chase, of said County, being duly sworn before me, says. . . .* [Salt Lake City? 1886]

3p. 23½cm.

Letter from E. R. Chase to Edwin F. Conely, dated Salt Lake City, Jan. 26, 1886, concerns the trial of Lorenzo Snow and the confirmation of O. W. Powers who is perceived as a friend of the Mormons, p. 2-3.

USIC

1260a. **Chase, William Ingraham.** *Some account of the rulers of the world. Prepared for use in the schools.* Chicago, W. I. Chase, School Herald Office, 1887.

96p. 17cm. (School Herald Extra for January, 1887)

George F. Edmunds and Mormons, p. 91-2.

DLC, USlC

1261a. **Chasles, Philarete.** *Moeurs et voyages ou recits du monde nouveau, par M. Philarete Chasles, Professeur au college de France.* Paris, Eugene Didier, editeur, MDCCCLV.

327p. [2]l. 18cm.

Title in English: Customs and voyages or stories of the new world.

In chapter one he encounters a Mormon and discusses their beliefs; visits Nauvoo while the Icarians were there. Dated 1849.

CtY, KyU, MiU, TxU, UPB

1261b. **Cheftele, Sophie.** *Les forces morales aux Etats-Unis (l'eglise, l'ecole, la femme).* Paris, Payot & Cie, 1920.

212p. 18cm.

Title in English: Moral forces in the United States.

Mormons, p. 53-9.

CtY, MH, NN, USlC

1264a. **Chicago. Citizens.** *Dear Sir: At a mass meeting held in this city on the 23rd ultimo, a committee of prominent citizens was appointed for the purpose of organizing a movement in this and other states against polygamous Mormonism.* [Chicago, 1882]

Broadside. 21½ x 14cm.

Form letter. With text signed: John A. Jameson [and others], Committee for Vermont.

WHi

1264b. _____. *Dear Sir: We are today face to face with polygamous Mormonism.* [Chicago, 1882]

Broadside. 26½ x 21cm.

Caption-title.

Form letter. With text signed: Thomas Hoyne [and others].

WHi

1264c. **Chicago Daily Journal.** *Crime and treason of the Mormon Church exposed. Reprinted from the Chicago Daily Journal.* [Chicago, 1912?]

30p. 18½cm.

"The only Eastern journal with the 'courage' to tell the truth about Mormonism."

DLC, NN, USlC

1264e. **Chicago. World's Columbian Exposition. 1893. Board of Lady Managers. Utah.** *World's Fair ecclesiastical history of Utah.* Compiled by representatives of the religious denominations. Salt Lake City, George Q. Cannon & Sons, Co., Printers, 1893.

vii, [9] 318p. illus. plates, ports. 22cm.

CSmH, ICN, NN, UHi, UPB, USl, USlC, UU

1264f. **Child, Hamilton.** *Gazetteer and business directory of Ontario County, N.Y., for 1867-8.* Syracuse, Printed at the Journal Office, 1867.

240p. 21cm.

Includes early history of Mormonism in New York.

DLC, UHi, UPB

1264g. _____. *Gazetteer and business directory of Wayne County, N.Y., for 1867-8.* Hang up this book for future reference. Syracuse, Journal Office, 1867.

264p. fold. map. 21½cm.

The insidious monster, Mormonism, p. 52-54.

DLC, UPB, USlC

The Children on the plains. See Baker, Sarah Schoonmaker (Tuthill).

1265a. *The "Children's Friend" as a missionary.* [Salt Lake City, n.d.]

Broadside. 22 x 14cm.

USlC

1267a. **Chisholm Brothers.** *Historical and descriptive sketches of Salt Lake City.* Portland, Maine, Chisholm Brothers, 1891.

1v. (Unpaged) illus. 16 x 24½cm.

Title on cover: Views of Salt Lake City. Mormon references throughout.

USlC

1275a. **Christensen, Thomas P.** *Dansk Amerikansk historie.* Cedar Falls, Iowa, Holst Printing Co. [c1927]

192 [3]p. 19½cm.

Title in English: Danish American History.

Mormons mentioned, p. 44-52.

DLC, ICN, KU, MnU, NN, USlC

1275b. *Christensen's grand historical exhibition, consisting of 22 beautiful paintings on more than 2,000 square feet of Canvas, and illustrating the principle events in connection with the rise and progress of the Church of Jesus Christ of Latter-day Saints.* [Salt Lake City, Merchant Co., ca. 1882]

Broadside. 39 x 17cm.

Advertisement for Carl C. Christensen's exhibition of painting on the history of the Church.

USIC

Christian Education and New West Gleanor. See *New West Gleanor.*

1276a. *A Christian messenger to all people.* Published by authority of The Church of Jesus Christ. Glenwood, Iowa, Journal Book and Job Print, 1877.

80p. 23cm.

Publication of the Church of Jesus Christ (Rigdonite).

USIC

1283a. *Christ's bride.* [n.p., n.d.]

[4]p. 14½cm.

Perhaps a RLDS church publication.

NjP

1283b. **Church, John H. C.** *Diary of a trip through Mexico and California, with visits at Cincinnati, New Orleans, Galveston, Houston, San Antonio, El Paso, Paso Del Norte, Chihuahua, Zacatecas, Aguas Clientes, Leon, Silao, Guanajuato, Queretaro, City of Mexico, Toluca, Puebla, Pyramid of Cholula, Tlascala, Orizaba, Los Angeles, Pasadena, San Francisco, Monterey, Santa Cruz, San Jose, Napa Soda Springs, Sacramento, Salt Lake City, Manitou Springs, Denver, Georgetown, Chicago and Niagra Falls.* Pittsfield, Mass., Marcus H. Rogers, printer, 1887.

72p. 17½cm.

Mormons and Utah, p. 59-62.

C, CU-B, OkN, UPB, USIC

1283c.   **The Church.** [Salt Lake City, Juvenile Instructor Print? ca. 1887]

Broadsheet. 16½ x 11cm.

Deseret Sunday School catechism.

CtY

1291a.   **Church of Christ (Temple lot).** *The sacred spot is definitely located. The stone markers planted in 1831 tell the story.* [Independence, 1929?]

[3]p. illus. 30½cm.

Locating the cornerstone of the temple site.

UPB

1298a.   **Church of Jesus Christ (Bickerton).** *Hymns and spiritual songs, original and selected, for the use of the Church of Jesus Christ of Latter Day Saints, revised and compiled by W. Bickerton, T. Bickerton, and J. Stranger, Elders of the Church, in West Elizabeth, Pa.* Pittsburgh, Printed by J. T. Shryock, Book and Job Printer, 1855.

378p. 11cm.

Edition with the 1855 title page, but revised as the 1864 edition.

UPB

1310a.   **Church of Jesus Christ of Latter-day Saints.** *An address. The Church of Jesus Christ of Latter-day Saints to the world.* Salt Lake City, 1907.

19p. 23cm.

In gray printed cover.

Signed: Joseph F. Smith, John R. Winder, Anothon H. Lund, in behalf of the Church of Jesus Christ of Latter-day Saints, March 26, 1907.

UPB, USIC

1321a.   _____. *Bp._____ We today forward to you blank forms for Statement of Poor Account.* [Salt Lake City, 1887]

Broadside. 21 x 14cm.

Signed: Wm. B. Preston.

Form to register the poor in each ward.

USIC

1324a. _____. *By-laws of the Church Association of* _____ *Stake of Zion.* [Salt Lake City, 1898]

4p. 15cm.

Cover title: By-laws.

"Notice is hereby given that a meeting of the members of the 'Church Association of the Salt Lake Stake of Zion' . . . 2nd day of July, A.D. 1898," tipped in.

USlC

1329. _____. *Catalogue of publications of the Church of Jesus Christ of Latter-day Saints for sale by the Deseret News Co.* Salt Lake City, 1887.

[8]p. 18cm.

In tan printed wrapper. Cover title.

UPB

1337c. _____. *Circular of instructions. Settlement of tithes for the year 1896.* Salt Lake City, 1896.

[4]p. 28cm.

Need for tithing settlement.

USlC

1337d. _____. *Circular of instructions. Settlement of tithes for the year 1897.* Salt Lake City, 1897.

[3]p. 28cm.

Need for tithing settlement.

USlC

1344a. _____. *Congregational hymns for general conference friday afternoon, April 6, 1923.* [Salt Lake City?] 1923.

[3]p. 18cm.

USlC

1349a. _____. *Course of study for the quorums of the Priesthood. Church of Jesus Christ of Latter-day Saints. Deacons.* [Salt Lake City] Prepared and issued under the direction of the General Authorities of the Church, 1925.

96p. 18cm.

In green printed wrapper.

UPB, USlC

1350a. _____. *Divine authority.* [Liverpool? ca. 1895]

4p. 21½cm.

Caption title.

Missionary tract.

USIC

1354a. _____. *Eine gottliche offenbarung und Belehrung uber den Ehestand. Aus dem Englishchen ubersetzt von Dan. Carn.* Hamburg, 1854.

8, 32p. 23½cm.

Title in English: A revelation from God and teachings on marriage.

Translation of the *Deseret News Extra*, September 14, 1852, and Orson Spencer's *Patriarchal order or plurality of wives.*

USIC (incomplete)

1366a. _____. *"He that readeth, let him understand." "The faith and doctrines of the Latter-day Saints, with scriptural proofs.* [London] To be had of T. C. Armstrong, Printed by W. Aubrey [1852?]

[4]p. 18cm.

UPB

1366b. _____. *History of America B.C. 200 - 420 A.D. Book of Mormon; an authentic account of the origin of the American Indian.* [Independence, Mo.? Missions of the Church of Jesus Christ of Latter-day Saints, 1912?]

[4]p. 16½cm.

USIC

1366c. _____. (same) [Chicago, Ill., 1912?]

[4]p. 16½cm. (No. 3)

USIC

1366d. _____. (same) [Independence, Mo.? Missions of the Church of Jesus Christ of Latter-day Saints, 1916?]

[4]p. 16½cm.

USIC

1369a.   . *Hymns for semi-annual conference Latter-day Saints, held January 8, 1905.* [Handsworth, William O. Creer, 1905?]

[2]p. music. 21cm.

USIC

1383a.   . *De Kerk van Jezus Christus van de Heiligen der Laatste Dagen aan de wereld.* [Rotterdam, Nederlandsch-Belfische Zending] 1907.

16p. 20½cm.

Title in English: Church of Jesus Christ of Latter-day Saints to the world.

USIC

1386a.   . *The Latter-day Saints church office building, Salt Lake City, Utah.* [Salt Lake City, Deseret Book Company [ca. 1920]

[8]p. illus. 11 x 16cm.

Colored illus. on front.

UPB, USIC

1387a.   . *L.D.S. hymns for the Scandinavian Conference in the Assembly Hall, Sunday, October 3rd, at 4 p.m.* [Salt Lake City? n.d.]

[4]p. music. 21½cm.

USIC

1391a.   . *Letters. Dear Brethren of the Seventies.* [Salt Lake City, 1884]

[3]p. 20cm.

Letter of inquiry from Horace S. Eldredge, in behalf of the First Council of Seventies, in regard to quorum membership, and a reply signed by John Taylor, in behalf of the First Presidency, Wilford Woodruff, in behalf of the Twelve Apostles.

USIC, UPB

1397a.   . *List of tithing prices, weights and measures.* Salt Lake City, 1883.

Broadside. 25 x 19cm.

Within ornamental border.

Dated Salt Lake City, August 6, 1883.

USIC

1399a. _____. *He mau haawina no ke kula ana i ka Oihana Kahuna a me na lala o na Hui Manawalea iloko o Ka Ekalesia o Iesu Kristo o na La Hope Nei.* [Honolulu? ca. 1920?]

61p. 23cm.

Title in English: Lessons for Priesthood and Relief Society.

HLB

1405a. _____. *Names of presidency and bishops of the organized stakes of Zion.* [Salt Lake City, 1893?]

Broadside. 54 x 32cm.

USlC

1406a. _____. (same) [Salt Lake City, Deseret News, 1894?]

Broadside. 56 x 32cm.

USlC

1411. _____. *Official delcaration. To whom it may concern.* [Salt Lake City, 1890]

Broadsheet. 19 x 10½cm.

Signed: Wildford Woodruff.

Includes sustaining motion by Lorenzo Snow.

The polygamy manifesto.

UPB, USlC

1419a. _____. *Popular songs of the Church of Jesus Christ of Latter-day Saints.* [Salt Lake City? Church of Jesus Christ of Latter-day Saints, 1904]

Broadside. 35½ x 23½cm.

USlC

1449a. _____. *The truth about the "Mormons."* [Independence, Mo., Zion's Printing and Publishing Company, 1925?]

[4]p. 15½cm.

Variant Printing

UPB

1450a. _____. *The Twelve Apostles . . . [4 lines of text] The Seven Presidents of the Seventy Elders. [2 lines] The First Seventy Elders. [21 lines] The Second Seventy Elders [23 lines].* [Kirtland? 1836?].

Broadside. 31 x 20cm.

Text enclosed within border.

Printed between the organization of the Twelve Apostles in 1835 and the apostasy of John Boynton in 1837.

List of Members of the various organizations.

UPB, USIC

1450b. _____. *Twentieth general annual conference of the Y. M. and Y. L. M. I. A. and the thirteenth annual conference of the Primary Associations of the Church of Jesus Christ of Latter-day Saints.* Salt Lake City, 1915.

[8]p. 17½cm.

Cover title. In brown printed wrapper.

UPB

1450c. _____. *The United States, appellant, vs. the late corporation of the Church of Jesus Christ of Latter-day Saints et al.* [Washington? 1893?]

22p. 22cm.

At head of title: In the Supreme Court of the United States. October term, 1893. No. 887

Cover title.

Property owned by the church was taken over by the government and used for Territorial schools.

DLC

1461a. **Church of Jesus Christ of Latter-day Saints. Bureau of Information. Salt Lake City.** *Information for tourists.* [Salt Lake City, Magazine Printing Co., ca. 1903]

8p. illus. 15cm.

USIC

1485a. _____. *Utah; its people, resources, attractions, and institutions.* Compiled from authentic information and the latest reports. Salt Lake City [1928?]

2p.l., [5]-90 [2]p. illus. (part col.) 18cm.

Cover title: Utah; the tourist's guide.

UPB

1495a. **Church of Jesus Christ of Latter-day Saints. Church Music Committee.** *Deseret anthems. Vol. 1. Six anthems selected from the publications of Novello & Company and published by the L.D.S. Church Music Committee.* "Second Edition." [Salt Lake City, Deseret Book Company, 1927?]

1p.l., 36p. music. 25½cm.

UPB

1498a. **Church of Jesus Christ of Latter-day Saints. Conferences. Iowa.** *The members of the Iowa Conference of the Church of Jesus Christ of Latter-day Saints will hold their semi-annual conference.* [Council Bluffs, Iowa, 1905]

Broadside. 30 x 23cm.

Announcement of meeting in Council Bluffs, Iowa, and that the principles and history of the Church would be explained by Elders from Utah.

Dated, April, 1905.

USIC

1502. **Church of Jesus Christ of Latter-day Saints. Council of the Twelve Apostles.** *An epistle of the Council of the Twelve Apostles of the Church of Jesus Christ of Latter-day Saints, read October 10, 1887, at the general semi-annual conference, held in Salt Lake City.* [Salt Lake City] Deseret News Co. [1887]

16p. 21cm.

Caption title. An epistle to the members of the Church of Jesus Christ of Latter-day Saints.

Cover title.

In tan printed wrapper.

After the death of John Taylor it was difficult getting the Quorum together to choose a new President.

UPB, USIC

1510a. _____. (same) *Priesthood conferences. 1928.* [Salt Lake City, Council of the Twelve, 1928]

[8]p. 17cm.

UPB

1512a. _____. *Suggestions for Melchizedek Quorum Committees. Committee on Church Service.* [Salt Lake City] 1929.

5p. 23cm.

UPB, USIC

1518a. **Church of Jesus Christ of Latter-day Saints. Department of Education.**
A handbook for the officers and teachers in the religion classes of the Church of Jesus Christ of Latter-day Saints. Salt Lake City, The Deseret Book Company, 1924.

118p. 18cm.

UPB

1524a. _____. *Outlines in religious education. Second year New Testament.* Salt Lake City, Deseret Book Co. [c1928]

237p. 19½cm. (Outlines in religious education)

Cover title: New Testament dispensation.

USIC

1532a. **Church of Jesus Christ of Latter-day Saints. Deseret Sunday School Union.** *Arrest of Ammon by the guards of King Limhi.* Salt Lake City, 1897.

[2]p. illus. 11cm.

Little Book of Mormon lesson pictures.

USIC

1539a. _____. *Class work for 1917.* [Salt Lake City, 1916?]

Broadside. 22 x 8½cm.

List of courses and books for 1917.

USIC

1539b. _____. *Collect 1930 dime fund in one day.* [Salt Lake City, 1930]

[3]p. 15½cm.

USIC

1551a. _____. *Deseret Sunday School Union leaflets. Lesson 1, June 2nd, 1889 -- Lesson 56, December 21, 1890.* [Salt Lake City, 1890?]

[116]p. 25cm.

USIC

1551b. _____. *(same)* [Lessons 1 to 56 inclusive. Salt Lake City? 1895?]

[116]p. 25cm.

Title page missing.

Includes hand written note dated 1895.

USIC

1552a. _____. (same) Lessons 1 to 212, inclusive. With index to leaflet notes and chapter of subjects, etc. Salt Lake City, Deseret Sunday School Union, 1902.

viii [428]p. 25cm.

USlC

1555a. _____. _Financing and distributing Sunday School lessons._ Salt Lake City, Deseret Sunday School Union Board [1928]

Broadside. 24cm.

USlC

1557a. _____. _Hints for Sunday School Superintendents._ [Salt Lake City, n.d.]

[4]p. 16cm.

Vest pocket ed.

USlC

1565a. _____. _The Lord's Supper from a revelation given to Joseph the Prophet in April, 1830._ [Salt Lake City? 1890?]

[2]p. 16½cm.

On verso: Blessing on the wine.

UHi

1566a. _____. _Minutes of annual conference meeting of the Sunday School Union._ Salt Lake City, Deseret Sunday School Union, 1894-95.

2v. 25cm.

USlC

1571a. _____. _Program, district Sunday School convention, Saturday and Sunday, June 3rd and 4th, 1905, at Logan, Utah. Cache, Hyrum, Benson, Malad and Oneida Stakes._ [Logan, Utah, J. W. Harry, Logan Republican, 1905]

[16]p. 22½cm.

USlC

1571c. _____. _Program for Sunday School annual stake conferences to be held during the year 1900._ [Salt Lake City, 1900]

4p. 14cm.

NjP

1571d.   _____. *Program, 1918 Apr. 7.* Salt Lake City, Utah, 1918.

Broadsheet. 23 x 12cm.

Program for annual conference held in the tabernacle. Includes a list of the speakers and special numbers.

USIC

1576a.   _____. *Regulations for the guidance of Sunday Schools, adopted by the Deseret Sunday School Union Board.* [Salt Lake City, Deseret Sunday School Union Board, 1900?]

3 [1]p. 25½cm.

USIC

1579a.   _____. *Reverence.* [Salt Lake City, 1926]

16p. 19cm.

In gray printed wrapper.

Contents: Master builder, by Elder Winslow Farr Smith, Respect for law and government, by Elder Byron D. Anderson, Reverence for the home, by Lynn S. Richards, Reverence for the priesthood, by Elder Orson D. Romney, Jr., Reverence for House of the Lord by Elder Herman Wells. Application, by Elder David O. McKay.

UPB

1579b.   _____. *Rules for the guidance of Sunday Schools in the Stakes of Zion.* [Salt Lake City] Deseret Sunday School Union, Juvenile Instructor Office [1895?]

2p. 17cm.

UHi

1580a.   _____. *Songs to be sung by the congregation at the semi-annual Sunday School conference, Tabernacle, Sunday evening, April 8, 1906. Under the direction of Elder Geo. D. Pyper.* [Salt Lake City, Clayton Music Company] 1906.

[4]p. music. 18cm.

UPB, USIC

1583a.   _____. *Stories from the Old Testament for the Primary Department of the Sunday School.* Salt Lake City, Deseret Book Co., 1921.

202p. 18½cm.

NjP

1585a. _____. *Sunday morning in the Kindergarten. Illustrated lessons for the kindergarten department of the Sunday School.* First year. Salt Lake City, Deseret Sunday School Union, 1917.

99 [7]p. illus. 19½cm.

USIC

1588a. _____. *Sunday School conferences, 1917.* [Salt Lake City, 1917]

Broadside. 21 x 15cm.

USIC

1595a. _____. *Sunday School officers and teachers handbook.* Salt Lake City, Deseret Sunday Union, Deseret Book Company [1929?]

84p. [6]l. 19cm.

"Notes and additions," [6] l. following text.

UPB

1599a. _____. *Sunday School outlines of the Parents' Department.* [Salt Lake City] Deseret Sunday School Union [1906]

32p. 19½cm. (Series A6)

Eight pages of advertisement before and eight pages after text. Date of printing established from advertisement.

Cover title. Printed gray wrapper.

UPB

1599b. _____. *Superintendents will please report on the following questions at the annual Sunday School conference of their stake in the year 1898.* [Salt Lake City, 1898]

Broadside. 27½cm.

USIC

1600a. _____. *Zondagsschool-bladeren.* [Les 1 - Les 32] [n.p., 1900?]

[64]p. 27½cm.

Lessons on the life of Christ.

Title in English: Deseret Sunday School leaflets.

USIC

1600b. _____. *Zondagsschool-schetsen. De artikelen des geloofs.* Rotterdam, Nederlandsch-Belgische Zending [1907?]

12p. 21cm.

Title in English: Sunday School outlines. The Articles of Faith.

Theological department, fourth year. Doctrine of the Church.

USIC

1600c. _____. (same) *Jezus, de Christus.* Rotterdam, Nederlandsch-Belgische Zending [1907?]

12p. 20½cm.

Title in English: Jesus the Christ.

Sunday School outlines: Theological Department, first year.

USIC

1600d. _____. (same) *Jongens en meisjes uit den bijbel. Het leven der apostelen.* Rotterdam, Nederlandsch-Belgische Zending [1907?]

8p. 20½cm.

Title in English: Young men and girls from the Bible. The life of the Apostles.

Sunday School outlines: Primary Department.

USIC

1600e. _____. (same) *Ouder en kind.* Rotterdam, Nederlandsch-Belgische Zending [1907?]

27p. 19½cm.

Title in English: Parent and child.

Sunday School outlines: Parents' Department.

USIC

1600f. _____. (same) *Ten dienste der Zondagsscholen in de Nederlandsch-Belgische Zending van de Heiligen der Laatste Dagen voor 1907. Departementen: Eerste Middelbare Afdeeling, Tweede Middelbare Afdeeling.* Rotterdam, Alex Nibley [1907]

15p. 16cm.

Title in English: Sunday School services in the Netherlands/Belgium Mission of Latter-day Saints for 1907.

Sunday School outlines: First and Second Intermediate Departments.

USIC

1605a. **Church of Jesus Christ of Latter-day Saints. Deseret Sunday School Union. Hymnal. English.** [Salt Lake City, 1877?]

24 numb. cards. music. 22 x 15cm.

Cards printed in 1877, according to the Historical Department, and bound in 1879.

UPB, USIC

1605b. _____. **1879?**

[Music cards. Salt Lake City, 1879]

12 cards. 24 nos. music. 14 x 22cm.

USIC

1622a. _____. *Deseret Sunday School song book. A collection of choice songs for the use of Sunday Schools, and suitable for Primary Associations, Religion Classes, Quorum meetings, social gatherings, etc.* Salt Lake City, Deseret Sunday School Union, 1908.

8p.l., 220p. music. 13 x 17cm.

"Eleventh edition."

UPB

1623a. _____. *Deseret Sunday School songs. For the use of Sunday Schools and suitable for Primary Associations, Religion Classes, Quorum meetings, social gatherings, and the home.* Salt Lake City, Deseret Book Company [c1909]

32p. music. 20½cm.

Cover title.

Songs from the 1909 Sunday School hymnal.

UPB, USIC

1623b. _____. **1909.** (same) Salt Lake City, Deseret Sunday School Union, c1909.

295 nos., [6]p. music. 19½cm.

Printed by "Press of Henry C. Etten & Co., edition printers and binders, Chicago."

UPB, USIC

1623c. _____. **1909.** (same) Salt Lake City, Deseret Sunday School Union [ca. 1909]

295 nos., [6]p. music. 19½cm.

Printed by "The Deseret News Press."

Issued in several printings.

UPB, USIC

1636a. _____. **Hymnal. German. 1929.** *Deseret Sonntagschulliederbuch fur die schweizerische und deutsche Mission de Kirche Jesu Christi der Heiligen der letzten Tage.* 3e. aufl. Basel, F. Tadje, 1929.

178p. 12cm.

Title in English: Deseret Sunday School song book for the Swiss and German Mission of The Church of Jesus Christ of Latter-day Saints.

UU

1640a. _____. **Salt Lake Stake.** *Salt Lake Stake Sunday Schools. Missionary districts and appointments, 1898.* [Salt Lake City, 1898]

[4]p. 21cm.

List of the visiting districts and names of the superintendents.

UPB

1640b. **Church of Jesus Christ of Latter-day Saints. First Council of the Seventy.** *Elder* _____ *Dear Brother:* [Salt Lake City, 188-]

Broadside. 21 x 14cm.

Concerns information about Elders who might wish to perform missionary labor abroad.

Signed by Jacob Gates.

USIC

1644a. _____. *Letters.* Salt Lake City, 1884.

3p. 20cm.

Letter to the First Presidency and Twelve Apostles from Horace S. Eldredge in behalf of the First Council of Seventies.

USIC

1644b. _____. *Presidents of _____ Quorum of Seventy: Dear brethren: It is the design of some of the members of the First Council of Seventy to visit your quorum* . . . . Salt Lake City, 1902.

7p. 15½cm.

Dated: October 1902.

Instruction: For Seventies to get Temple recommends and presidents to live in the locality of their quorums.

USlC

1644c. _____. *To the presidents of the . . . Quorum of Seventies.* Salt Lake City, 1891.

4p. 21cm.

Dated: March 1891.

General epistle concerning status of local quorums; older members should be made High Priests.

Signed: Jacob Gates, in behalf of the First Council of Seventies.

At head of title: Seventies' Council Rooms.

UPB, USlC

1644d. _____. *To the presidents of the . . . Quorum of Seventies.* Salt Lake City, 1892.

4p. 22cm.

Dated: September, 1892.

General Epistle concerning local quorums and in particular the selections of missionaries.

Signed: John M. Whitaker [and others]

At head of title: Seventies' Council Rooms . . .

UPB, USlC

1645a. _____. *The Seventy's calling, and local service in the Church. A communication from the First Council from the editorial pages of the Improvement Era from January, 1912.* Salt Lake City, Skelton Publishing Company, 1912.

[8]p. 21cm.

Cover title.

Instructions from the First Council of Seventy relating to the assignments of local Seventies in the wards and stakes.

UPB

1645b. _____. *To all presidents and members of the Seventies' quorums. Dear Brethren:* [Salt Lake City, 1886]

Broadside. 22 x 14cm.

At head of title: Note: Presidents of Stakes, Bishops and all presiding officers will please give this appeal all possible publicity in their meetings. An appeal to have proper records.

USIC

1645c. _____. *To the presidents and clerks of the Quorum of Seventies.* Salt Lake City, 1886.

Broadside. 23 x 13cm.

Need to get better information on local quorums.

USIC

1646a. _____. *To the presidents of the* _____ *Quorum of Seventies. Dear Brethren.* [Salt Lake City, 1883]

[4]p. 18½cm.

Instructions to local quorums as instructed by the First Presidency April 13th and 14th, 1883.

UPB

1646b. _____. *To the presidents of the* _____ *Quorum of Seventies. Dear Brethren.* Salt Lake City [188-]

[4]p. 18½cm.

The need to fill vacancies in local quorums as well as the Seven Presidents. Signed: Henry Herriman, H. S. Eldredge. Jacob Gates, Abraham H. Cannon, Seymour B. Young, C. D. Fjedlsted, John Morgan.

USIC

1648a. _____. *To the presidents of the* _____ *Quorum of Seventies. Dear Brethen:* [Salt Lake City, 1893?]

4p. 21cm.

Concerning the publication in 1893 of B. H. Robert's *Outlines of Ecclesiastical History.*

UPB

1649a. **Church of Jesus Christ of Latter-day Saints. First Presidency.** *An Address. The Church of Jesus Christ of Latter-day Saints to the world. "Let the facts be submitted to a candid world."* Salt Lake City, 1907.

16p. 21½cm.

"Headquarters Australian Mission -- 'Victory,' Pemell Street, Enmore, Sydney," on p. 16.

UPB

1652a. _____. *An address. To the officers and members of the Church of Jesus Christ of Latter-day Saints.* [Salt Lake City, 1893]

[2]p. 29cm.

Signed: Wilford Woodruff, George Q. Cannon, Joseph F. Smith.

Same material also published in a pamphlet entitled: Recent discussion in Mormon affairs.

In Brown printed wrapper, and variant wrappers.

UPB, USIC

1652b. _____. *Bishop* _____ *Dear Brother.* Salt Lake City, 1891.

Broadside. 27 x 21cm.

Letter to solicit funds for the completion of the Salt Lake Temple.

UPB

1655b. _____. *Circular of instructions; settlement of tithes for the year 1890[-1897]. To the presidents of stakes, bishops of wards and stake tithing clerks in Zion.* Salt Lake City, 1890 [-1897]

v. 22cm.

USIC 1890, 1891, 1893, 1894, 1896, 1897.

1658a. _____. *Dear Brethren:* [Salt Lake City, 1920]

Broadside. 28 x 22cm.

Dated August 23, 1920, and signed by Heber J. Grant, Anthon H. Lund, and Charles W. Penrose.

Concerns "Arizona Temple day."

USIC

1658c. _____. *Dear Brother:* [Great Salt Lake City, 1865] [4]p. 17cm.

Letter sent for colonization missions. "You will report to President Erastus Snow, St. George, who will direct you where to go." Letter dated Great Salt Lake City, Oct. 18, 1865, and signed by First Prsidency and Quorum of the Twelve.

USIC

1658e. _____. *Dear Brother: The Pioneer Electric Power Company, whose works are at Ogden, Utah . . . .* Salt Lake City, 1896.

[2]l. 22cm.

Dated: October 2nd, 1896. Church's involvement in non-church funtions. Second leaf blank.

USIC

1658f. _____. *Dear Sister. The dedication of the great Temple.* [Salt Lake City, 1893]

Broadside. 18 x 11½cm.

Dated: Salt Lake City, Utah Territory, March 29th, 1893.

Signed: Wilford Woodruff, George Q. Cannon, Joseph F. Smith.

UPB

1662. _____. *An epistle of the First Presidency, to the Church of Jesus Christ of Latter-day Saints, in general conference assembled. Read April 6, 1886, at the 56th general annual conference, held at Provo, Utah.* Salt Lake City, Deseret News Company, 1886.

19p. 22½cm.

Cover title.

Signed: John Taylor, George Q. Cannon, March, 1886.

Polygamy and other subjects.

CSmH, CU-B ICHi, ICN, NjP, NN, UPB, USIC

1662a. _____. (same) Salt Lake City, Deseret News Company, 1886.

19p. 22½cm.

Variant printed wrapper with type reset.

UPB

1668a. _____. *Greeting: Beloved Brethren.* [Liverpool, 1851]

[2]l. 38cm.

Signed: Brigham Young, Heber C. Kimball, Willard Richards, Great Salt Lake City, Deseret, September 27, 1850.

Reprinted from the *Millennial Star* v. 13, #4, p. 49-54.

Also published in the *Deseret News*, and the *Frontier Guardian.*

Title from *Deseret News*: "Fourth general epistle of the Presidency of the Church of Jesus Christ of Latter-day Saints, from the Great Salt Lake Valley in the state of Deseret, to the saints scattered throughout the earth."

Probably galley proofs.

USIC

1669a. _____. *Greetings from the First Presidency, President Heber J. Grant, Prest. Anthony W. Ivins, first counselor, Prest. Charles W. Nibley, second counselor.* [Salt Lake City] Church of Jesus Christ of Latter-day Saints [1929?]

[4]p. 17cm.

Christmas greeting.

USIC

1671a. _____. *International Association of Municipal Electricians, special organ recital, Tabernacle, Wednesday, August 17th, 1927.* [Salt Lake City, Courtesy of the First Presidency of the Church of Jesus Christ of Latter-day Saints, 1927]

[5]p. illus. 16½cm.

USIC

1674b. _____. *Official announcement . . . to the officers and members of the Church of Jesus Christ of Latter-day Saints.* Salt Lake City, 1894.

[4]p. 21½cm.

Dated August 18, 1894 and signed: Wilford Woodruff, Geo. Q. Cannon, Jos. F. Smith.

The closing of church university to support University of Utah.

USIC

1677a. _____. *Special organ recital in honor of H.R.H. Gustavus Adolphus, crown prince of Sweden and H.R.H. Louise, crown princess of Sweden, Tabernacle, Salt Lake City, July 9, 1926.* [Salt Lake City, 1926]

[8]p. illus. 18½cm.

USIC

1677b. _____. *Special organ recital in the tabernacle, Salt Lake City, Utah, given under the direction of the First Presidency . . . in honor of the officers and enlisted men of the United States Army located at Fort Douglas.* [Salt Lake City, 1917]

[4]p. 15½cm.

USIC

1680b. _____. *To conductor Evan Stephens, and the members of the Tabernacle Choir.* Salt Lake City, 1895.

Broadside. 19 x 14cm.

Dated Feb. 14, 1895. Signed by Wilford Woodruff, George Q. Cannon, Joseph F. Smith.

Memoranda expressing First Presidency's feelings that members of the Tabernacle Choir are acting as missionaries for the chruch.

USIC

1681a. _____. *To presidents of stakes and bishops of wards: Dear Brethren. Your attention is called to the documents issued for the office of the "Irrigation Commission for Utah."* Salt Lake City, 1895.

Broadside. 28 x 22cm.

Irrigation matter addressed to Stake Presidents or Bishop. Dated April 26, 1895, and signed by the members of the First Presidency.

USIC

1682a. _____. *To the bishops and members of the Church of Jesus Christ of Latter-day Saints, residing in the various settlements throughout these mountains: Beloved brethren and sisters . . .* [Salt Lake City, 1876]

[2]l. 28cm.

Dated: October 25, 1876.

Concerning the temples under construction.

UPB, USIC

1685a. _____. *To the presidency and bishopric of _____ Stake. Dear Brethren:* Salt Lake City, 1891.

3p. 21½cm.

Dated: June 1st, 1891.

Regarding church finance and fast offerings.

USIC

1685b. _____. *To the presidents, bishop's agents and bishops of the several stakes and wards of Zion.* Salt Lake City, 1887.

4p. 21½cm.

Dated: December 13, 1887.

Instructions for annual settlement of tithes and offerings.

USIC

1685c. _____. *To the presidents of stakes and bishops of wards.* [Salt Lake City] 1891.

Broadside. 20½ x 13½cm.

At head of title: Office of the First Presidency, November 10th, 1891.

Second letter concerning temple recommends.

USIC

1685d. _____. *To the presidents of stakes and bishops of wards.* [Salt Lake City, 1894]

[2]l. 28½cm.

At head of title: Office of the First Presidency of the Church of Jesus Christ of Latter-day Saints, Salt Lake City, Utah, November 22, 1894. Letter concerning contributions for Brigham Young memorial fund.

USIC

1685e. _____. *To the presidents of stakes and bishops of wards.* [Salt Lake City, ca. 1895]

Broadsheet. 19 x 13½cm.

Letter concerning interruptions to Sunday School meetings.

USIC

1687c. _____. *To the presidents of stakes and their counselors.* Salt Lake City, 1889.

2 [1]p. 21 x 24cm.

At head of title: President's Office, Church of Jesus Christ of Latter-day Saints, Salt Lake City, Utah, Dec. 2, 1889.

Letter recommending Dec. 23 as a day of fasting and prayer due to legal persecutions.

Reprint with recommendation of Salt Lake Stake presidency.

USIC

1691a. _____. *To the presidents of stakes, bishops and parents in Zion.* [Salt Lake City, c1922]

[3]p. 17½cm.

Reprint of the 1916 publication (*Flake 1691*) regarding family life with an added paragraph stating the current First Presidency's endorsement of it.

UPB

1691b. _____. *To the presidents of stakes, bishops of wards and stake tithing clerks in Zion.* Salt Lake City, 1888.

4p. 24½cm.

Dated: December 10, 1888.

Instructions for annual settlement of tithes and offerings.

USIC

1709a. **Church of Jesus Christ of Latter-day Saints. Genealogical Society of Utah.** *The Genealogical Society of Utah.* [Salt Lake City, 1921?]

2p. 23cm.

UHi

1762a. **Church of Jesus Christ of Latter-day Saints. Hymnal. 1841.** *A collection of sacred hymns, for the Church of Jesus Christ of Latter-day Saints, in Europe. Selected by Brigham Young, Parley P. Pratt, and John Taylor.* Second edition. Manchester, Printed and sold by P. P. Pratt, 47, Oxford Street, and by the agents throughout England, 1841.

2p.l., 5-336p. 10½cm.

NcD

1766. _____. **1849.** *A collection of sacred hymns, for the Church of Jesus Christ of Latter-day Saints, in Europe. Selected by Brigham Young, Parley P. Pratt, and John Taylor.* Eighth Edition. Liverpool, Published and sold by Orson Pratt, 15, Wilton Street, Soho Street; and sold by the agents throughout England, 1849.

352p. 10½cm.

UPB, USIC (inc.)

1767a. _____. **1852?** *Latter Day Saints' hymns.* [Sidney, Australia? 1852?]

16p. 21cm.

51 nos.

Caption title.

Imprint information from a comparison of other Australian Mission imprints.

UPB

1798a. _____. **1908.** *The songs of Zion. A collection of choice songs especially selected and arranged for the home and for all meetings, Sunday Schools and gatherings of elders and saints in the mission field.* Chicago, Published by the Missions of the Church of Jesus Christ of Latter-day Saints, c1908.

246 nos. music. 14cm.

UPB

1815a. _____. **1924.** *A selection from the songs of Zion.* Published by the Missions of the Church of Jesus Christ of Latter-day Saints. Independence, Press of Zion's Printing and Publishing Company [1924]

[32]p. music. 15cm.

In green printed wrapper with mission addresses on front and printed verses on back.

UPB

1822a. _____. **1925?** *Hymns used by the Latter-day Saints.* [n.p. 192-]

16p. 11cm.

Eighteen common hymns.

Variant printings.

USIC

1845a. _____. **Hymnal. Japanese. 1905.** *Matsu Jitsu Seito sanbika.* [Tokyo] Matsu Jitsu Seito Iesu Kirisuto Kyokai [1905]

101p. 9 x 13cm.

Title in English: Songbook for the Church of Jesus Christ of Latter-day Saints.

Compiled by Horace S. Ensign and Frederick A. Caine.

USIC

1848b. _____. Hymnal. Maori. 1910. *Nga himene hunga taper.* Salt Lake City, 1910.

15p. 14½cm.

Title in English: Songs of Zion.

A number of hymns presented in anticipation of a regular hymnal.

UPB

1849a. _____. Hymnal. Norwegian. 1903. *Aandelige sange til brug i mission og Sondagsskole.* Forlagt af Peter Andersen. Porsgrund [Norway] Brodrene Dyrings Bogtrykkeri, 1903.

32p. 15½cm.

Title in English: Selected songs for use on missions and Sunday School.

USIC

1866. _____. Hymnal. Swedish. 1910. *Zions sanger en samling af utvalda sanger for de Sista dagars heliges Moten, sondagsskolor, missionarsforeningar och hemmet. Utgifven och forlagd af Iesu Kristi Kyrka af sista dagars helige. Salt Lake City, Utah.* Forlagsrattighet, af Joseph Smith, 1910.

1p.l., 209 nos. [3]p. music. 20cm.

Title in English: Zions songs a collection of selected songs for the Latter-day Saint meeting.

Printed in Chicago by Henry C. Etten.

Close score compiled by Hugo D. E. Peterson.

NN, UHi, UPB, USIC, UU

1870a. _____. Hymnal. Turkish. 1899. *Roihani ilahiler.* [Istanbul?] 1899.

73p. 13cm. mimeograph.

Title in English: Spiritual hymns.

Turkish hymnal with Armenian characters.

USIC

1870b. _____. Hymnal. Welsh. 1846. *Hymnau, wedi eu cyfansoddi a'u casglu, yn fwyaf neillduol, at wasanaeth Saint Y Dyddiau Diweddaf.* Rhydybont, printed by John Jones, 1846.

viii, [56]p. 10½cm.

Title in English: Hymns, composed and collected most particularly for Latter-day Saints service.

Dennis 7

UPB Incomplete. Title page and pages after p. 16 missing.

1873a. **Church of Jesus Christ of Latter-day Saints. Industrial Bureau.** *Dear Brother....* [Salt Lake City, Committee of the Bureau, 1897]

Broadside. 27 x 16cm.

Signed by the committee members. Unemployment of immigrant church members.

USlC

1883a. **Church of Jesus Christ of Latter-day Saints. Missions.** *Invitation....* [Liverpool, 1851]

3 [1]p. 19cm.

Dated from list of works on page [1].

UPB

1884a. _____. **Missions. Australian.** *Lovers of truth are most respectfully invited to attend a course of lectures.* [Melbourne, B. M. Lucas, 1876]

Broadside. 22 x 14cm.

Lectures by J. Welling and E. T. Hoagland on gospel themes.

USlC

1884b. _____. **Missions. British.** *Catalogue of works published by the Church of Jesus Christ of Latter-day Saints, and for sale at the Millennial Star Office, 42, Islington, Liverpool.* Liverpool [n.d.]

Broadside. 21 x 13½cm.

A line of text has been cut from copy.

UPB

1884c. _____. (same) [Liverpool, ca. 1879]

Broadside. 21 x 13½cm.

UPB

1887a. _____. Character of the Latter-day Saints. [London, 1912?]

4p. 23cm.

Introductory material the same as *Flake 1887*. Quotations of opinions differ.

UPB, USlC

1888a. _____. *Convention of the elders of the British Mission, 1913; "Deseret," London, September 9th & 10th.* [London, 1913]

[7]p. illus. 21½cm.

USlC

1891a. _____. *Invitation! A great and marvelous work has come forth to which we invite your serious attention.* [Islington? ca. 1905]

Broadside. 20 x 12cm.

Invitation to attend meetings.

USIC

1891b. _____. *Invitation. All persons are respectfully invited to attend the Latter-day Saints' meetings, to investigate their faith and doctrines, and to examine their publications.* [Liverpool, Printed by J. Sadler, 1852?]

4p. 18½cm.

Signed: C. H. Wheelock . . . [and] A. F. McDonald.

UPB

1891c. _____. (same) *To examine their publications, and to investigate their faith and doctrines.* [Liverpool? 1852?]

[3]p. 15½cm.

UPB

1900a. _____. *Three district meetings of the Church of Jesus Christ of Latter-day Saints, will be held in the Foresters' Hall, . . . on Sunday, March 25, 1900.* [Hull, 1900]

Broadsheet. 23 x 14cm.

Articles of Faith printed on the verso.

USIC

1904a. _____. **Missions. British. Bradford Conference.** *Conference. The Church of Jesus Christ of Latter-day Saints will hold their Conference in the Philadelphia Chapel, North Wing, Bradford, on Sunday, February 23rd, 1845 . . . When there will be present on the occasion, two Americans, one of whom belongs to the Quorum of the Twelve Apostles.* Bradford, J. Parkinson, Printer, 1845.

Broadside. 33 x 34cm.

The two Americans were Wilford Woodruff and Elijah Sheets. A summary was published in the Millennial Star, March, 1845.

USIC

1911a. _____. **Missions. British. Cheltenham Branch.** *A conference of the Cheltenham Branch of the Church of Jesus Christ of Latter-day Saints . . . Sunday, Aug. 13th, 1911 . . . at which President John F. Snedaker of the Bristol Conference . . . will address the meetings.* [n.p., 1911]

Broadside. 22 x 14½cm.

USIC

1929a. _____. **Missions. British. Hull District.** *Souvenir program, Hull District. Centennial Jubilee Conference. Church of Jesus Christ of Latter-day Saints.* The Metropole, Hull. Sunday, March 30th, 1930. Hull, Printed by Larter & Bottamlay [1930]

[4]p. 26cm.

UPB, UU

1930a. _____. **Missions. British. Liverpool Conference.** *Testimonial presented to Elder Henry Clegg, president of the Rose Place Branch of the Church of Jesus Christ of Latter-day Saints, of the Liverpool Conference.* Liverpool, 1855.

Broadside. 33 x 21cm.

Signed: Daniel Caveen, traveling elder; John Matthews, elder; Henry Hughes, elder; Samuel Carlisle, secretary.

Within ornamental border.

Dated: Liverpool, March 5, 1855.

USIC

1940b. _____. **Missions. British. London Conference.** *Half yearly report of the London Conference of the Church of Jesus Christ of Latter-day Saints, held on Saturday & Sunday, 2nd & 3rd July, 1853.* [London? 1853]

2 [2]p. 21½cm.

Caption-title.

UPB

1942a. _____. **Missions. British. London District.** *"Deseret". Programme of closing meeting, Sunday, June 19, 1927.* London [1927]

[4]p. 21½cm.

USIC

1942b. _____. **Missions. British. Manchester Conference.** *Church of Jesus Christ of Latter-day Saints. The Manchester semi-annual conference.* Oldham, Engl., Chronicle Printing Works, 1897.

Broadside. 57 x 51cm.

Announcing conference to be held Feb. 21, 1897 at Unity Hall.

USIC

1942c. _____. **Missions. British. Newcastle Conference.** *Conference meetings.* 1895 Nov. 17, Stockton-on-Tees [Newcastle?] Printed by Randolph Stephenson [1895]

Broadside. 52 x 39cm.

Announcing the meetings of the Newcastle Conference.

USIC

1945a. _____. **Missions. British. Norwich Conference.** *Roll of honour. Church of Jesus Christ of Latter-day Saints. The Saints of the Norwich Conference have pleasure in placing on record the below mentioned brethren who served their country during the great war, 1914-1919.* [Norwich? 1919]

Broadside. 38 x 31cm.

With ornamental border with pictures of the Kirtland, Nauvoo, Salt Lake, and Manti temples at side and bottom.

USIC

1945b. _____. **Missions. British. Nottingham Conference.** *Conference minutes of the Church of Jesus Christ of Latter-day Saints, held at St. Ann's Chapel, Nottingham, October 2 and 3, 1852.* [Nottingham, 1852]

1p.l., 4-13 [2]p. 21cm.

UPB (defective copy).

1945c. _____. *[Report of the Nottingham Conference of the Church of Jesus Christ of Latter-day Saints held at St. Ann's Chapel, October 2nd and 3rd, 1852.]* [Nottingham, 1852]

13 [2]p. tables. 20½cm.

UPB copy lacks title page, USIC

1947a. _____. *[Report of the Nottinghamshire Conference of the Church of Jesus Christ of Latter-day Saints.]* [Nottingham, 1849?]

6p. 21cm.

UPB copy lacks title page.

1948a.   _____. *Second quarterly report of the Church of Jesus Christ of Latter-day Saints, held in St. Ann's Street Chapel, Nottingham, on the Twenty-ninth day of June, 1852. Henry Savage, President. John Wigley, Secretary. John Pymm, Assistant.* [Nottingham?] 1852.

8p. 21cm.

UPB

1952a.   _____. **Missions. British. Sheffield Conference.** *Report of the Sheffield Conference of the Church of Jesus Chirst of Latter-day Saints, held in the Hall of Science, Rickingham-St. Sheffield, on the eighth of June, 1851 . . . J. V. Long, reporter.* [Sheffield, Stephen New, printer, 1851]

8p. 21cm.

Variant printing with new colophon pasted at bottom of page 8 to eliminate discourse of G. P. Dykes.

USIC

1953a.   _____. **Missions. British. Southampton Conference.** *Half-yearly reports of the Southampton Conferences of the Church of Jesus Christ of Latter-day Saints, held in Southampton, Saturday, December 8, 1850 . . . Sunday, May 25, 1851 . . . and in Portsmouth, Saturday and Sunday, December 13 and 14, 1851.* Portsmouth, W. Eddington [1851]

16p. 21½cm.

Cover title.

Title within lined border.

T. B. H. Stenhouse was president of the conference in 1850, W. C. Dunbar in 1851.

UHi, UPB

1956a.   _____. **Missions.   British.   Welsh District.** *The Welsh District Conference.* [n.p., 1927]

Broadside. 23 x 14cm.

Held in Memorial Hall, Varteg, Sunday, April 24, 1927. Speakers include James E. Talmage, president of the European Mission and Mrs. May Booth Talmage, president of the European Mission Relief Societies. Verso includes "Truth gems, extracts from 'Mormon' teachings."

USIC

1956b.   _____. **Missions. Central States.** *The "Mutual" cook book.* Kansas City, Jackson County, Mo., Young Ladies' Mutual Improvement Association of the Kansas City Branch of the Church of Jesus Christ of Latter-day Saints, 1920.

128p. 24cm.

UPB, USIC

1968a. _____. **Missions. Eastern States.** *A statement from Josiah Quincy, mayor of Boston, 1845-1849, concerning an interview had in 1844 with Joseph Smith, the Mormon prophet. Some of the sayings and predictions made by the prophet Joseph Smith. A letter to Mr. Wentworth from the Prophet in answer to a request from him for a statement of belief, to be published in the Chicago Democrat.* New York City, Eastern States Mission [ca. 1915]

32p. 18½cm.

A large paper edition of *Flake 1968.*

UPB

1968b. _____. **Missions. Eastern States. Brooklyn Branch.** *Program dedicatory services, Brooklyn chapel . . . February sixteenth, nineteen nineteen.* [Brooklyn, New York, 1919]

[8]p. illus. 27½cm.

USlC

1970a. _____. **Missions. European.** *Exposition des premiers principes de la doctrine de l'Eglise de Jesus-Christ des Saints des-derniers-jours.* Rotterdam, Publiee par Eillard T. Cannon, 1904.

16p. 17cm.

Cover-title.

Title in English: Explanation of the first principles of the doctrine of the Church of Jesus Christ of Latter-day Saints.

UPB, USlC

1973a. _____. *Price list: Publishing Department of the European Mission of the Church of Jesus Christ of Latter-day Saints.* Liverpool, England [1920]

13p. 18cm.

USlC

1977a. _____. *The word of wisdom. A demonstrated way to health, long life and happiness.* [Dresden, Druck, Krueger & Horn, n.d.]

[4]p. 21cm.

UPB

1978a. _____. **Missions. French.** *An epistle to the Church of Jesus Christ of Latter-day Saints in France, and the Channel Islands, from the Presidency of the French Mission.* [St. Helier's, Jersey, 1854]

10p. 20½cm.

Signed: Andrew L. Lamoreaux, James H. Hart, Louis A. Bertrand, William Taylor. Saint Helier's, Jersey, January 2nd, 1854.

Formerly *Flake 4734.* This item is the English edition of *Flake 1979.*

Cty, UPB, USIC

1986a. _____. **Missions. German.** *Wahrend der Konferenz der Kirche Jesu Christi der letzten Tage.* [n.p., 1901]

Broadside. 28 x 22cm.

A handbill advertising meeting for a conference March 10, 1901.

Signed: Fr. Hufner.

Title in English: During the conference of the Church of Jesus Christ of Latter-days.

USIC

1988a. _____. **Missions. German-Austrian.** *Unsre Sonntagsschule.* [Dresden, Deutsch-Osterreichische Mission und Basel, Schweizerisch-Deutsche Mission, ca. 1930]

[4]p. illus. 19½cm.

Title in English: Our Sunday School.

USIC

1995a. _____. **Missions. Netherlands.** *Enkele getuigenissen aangaande de Kerk van Jezus Christus van de Heiligen der laatste Dagen, den Profeet Joseph Smith, en het "Mormon" volk.* [Rotterdam, 1904]

Broadsheet. 22 x 18cm.

Title in English: A few testimonies concerning the Church of Jesus Christ of Latter-day Saints, the Prophet of Joseph Smith, and the "Mormon" people.

UPB, USIC

2001a. _____. *Onze buurman, de heer S.* [Rotterdam, Uitgave van T. C. Hair, n.d.]

5 pts. 21½cm.

Pt. 5 under title: De Heer S. en de zendeligen van de Heiligen der Laatste Dagen. [Mr. S. and the Missionaries of the Latter-day Saints]

Title in English: Our Neighbor, Mr. S.

UPB 1, 2, 5; USIC

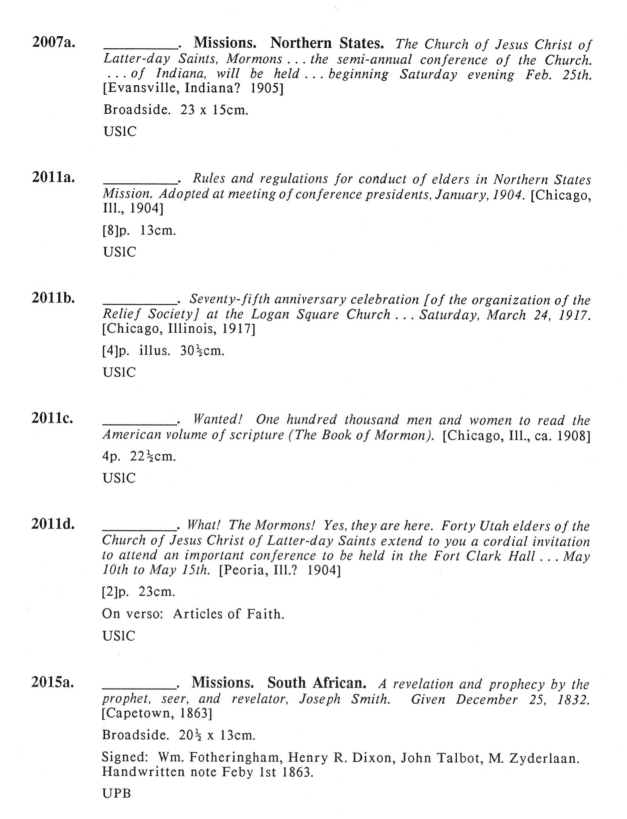

2007a.   _____. **Missions. Northern States.** *The Church of Jesus Christ of Latter-day Saints, Mormons . . . the semi-annual conference of the Church. . . . of Indiana, will be held . . . beginning Saturday evening Feb. 25th.* [Evansville, Indiana? 1905]

Broadside. 23 x 15cm.

USlC

2011a.   _____. *Rules and regulations for conduct of elders in Northern States Mission. Adopted at meeting of conference presidents, January, 1904.* [Chicago, Ill., 1904]

[8]p. 13cm.

USlC

2011b.   _____. *Seventy-fifth anniversary celebration [of the organization of the Relief Society] at the Logan Square Church . . . Saturday, March 24, 1917.* [Chicago, Illinois, 1917]

[4]p. illus. 30½cm.

USlC

2011c.   _____. *Wanted! One hundred thousand men and women to read the American volume of scripture (The Book of Mormon).* [Chicago, Ill., ca. 1908]

4p. 22½cm.

USlC

2011d.   _____. *What! The Mormons! Yes, they are here. Forty Utah elders of the Church of Jesus Christ of Latter-day Saints extend to you a cordial invitation to attend an important conference to be held in the Fort Clark Hall . . . May 10th to May 15th.* [Peoria, Ill.? 1904]

[2]p. 23cm.

On verso: Articles of Faith.

USlC

2015a.   _____. **Missions. South African.** *A revelation and prophecy by the prophet, seer, and revelator, Joseph Smith. Given December 25, 1832.* [Capetown, 1863]

Broadside. 20½ x 13cm.

Signed: Wm. Fotheringham, Henry R. Dixon, John Talbot, M. Zyderlaan. Handwritten note Feby 1st 1863.

UPB

2018a. _____. **Missions. Swiss.** _Die ewige wahrheit; der gegenwartige Bustand der religiosen Welt und Die Wiederbringung des wahren Evangeliums._ Bern, Herausgegeben vom Missionsbureau, Buchdruckerei T. Sturzenegger, 1900.

16p. 18½cm.

Title in English: The eternal truth; the modern position of the religious world.

UPB

2018b. _____. **Missions. Swiss-German.** _Anleitungen zur organization und tatigkeit der gemeinschaftlichen fortbildungsvereine fur junge manner und damen._ Basel, Kirche Jesu Christi der Heiligen der Letzten Tage, 1924.

44p. 21½cm.

Title in English: Guide to the organization and activities of the common continuing education for young men and women.

USIC

2021a. _____. _Erlosung fur die Toten. Praerestenz und herkunft des Menschen. Taufe fur die toten. Herausgegeben von der Redaktion des "Stern"_ . . . Bern, Buchdruckerei Steiger & Cie., 1897.

15 [1]p. 18½cm.

Title in English: Salvation for the dead.

UPB, USIC

2022a. _____. (same) Zurich, Switzerland, Hugh J. Cannon, 1904.

16p. 18cm. (Tractat. No. 4)

UPB

2042a. _____. **Missions. Tahitian.** _Te Raau a Iosepha ra. Te moe vea ei Na Mua i te Buka a Mormona. Papeete, Tahiti._ Neneihia i te piha neneiraa a te Ekalesia a Iesu Mesia i te Feia Mo'a i te Mau Mahana Hopea Nei, 1906.

1p.l., 12p. 19cm.

Title in English: The Stick of Joseph.

Book of Mormon evidences.

UPB

2042b. _____. (same) Papeete Tahiti, Ekalesia a Iesu Mesia i te Feia Mo'a i te Mau Mahana Hopea Nei, 1906.

1p.l., 12p. 18cm.

UPB

2042c. **Church of Jesus Christ of Latter-day Saints. Music Committee.** *Organists manual; a course of instruction in playing the reed organ.* Published for the use of the organists of the Church of Jesus Christ of Latter-day Saints by the Church Music Committee. Salt Lake City, 1923.

30p. music. 23cm.

USIC

2053a. **Church of Jesus Christ of Latter-day Saints. Mutual Improvement Association.** *M.I.A. banquet, tendered by general officers of Mutual Improvement.* July 17th, 1897. Salt Lake City, 1897.

[4]p. 16½cm.

Printed in gold.

Printed wrapper.

UPB

2074a. _____. *Prospectus of eleven lectures and recitals on sociology, literature, science and music, by the most eminent American artists and literateurs.* [Salt Lake City] Deseret News [1904]

20p. illus. 17cm.

Cover-title: M.I.A. Lecture Bureau, Salt Lake City.

At head of title: Lecture course of 1904-1905.

USIC

2080b. _____. *Salt Lake's fall carnival and terpsichorea melange as presented by F. M. Agostini and P. L. Lynwood under auspices of Mutual Improvement Associations, Salt Lake City, Utah.* [Salt Lake City, 1908]

26p. illus. 24 x 31½cm.

USIC

2086a. _____. The word of wisdom. [Salt Lake City, 1928?]

[6]p. folded. 11½cm.

USIC

2086c. **Church of Jesus Christ of Latter-day Saints. Old Folks Committee.** *11th annual old folk's excursion, 1886.* [Salt Lake City? 1886]

Broadside. 19 x 14cm.

Excursion of all Salt Lake citizens over seventy years old on a trip to American Fork.

USIC

2087a. _____. *Fraternal greeting issued by Old Folks' Central Committee of Salt Lake City, Utah.* [Salt Lake City, 1908?]

[4]p. 16cm.

Honor given to the aged in the local wards. Text within line border.

USIC

2087b. _____. *Free outing for old folks.* [Salt Lake City, 1904]

Broadside. 23 x 18cm.

USIC

2087c. _____. *Good news for the aged.* [Salt Lake City, 1912]

Broadside. 28 x 22cm.

Invitation to join with the Davis Stake for a social at Lagoon on June 26, 1902.

USIC

2087d. _____. *Old Folks Day a big jubilee.* [Salt Lake City, 1906]

Broadside. 22 x 15cm.

In two columns.

Invitation for the aged to attend the 1906 jubilee.

USIC

2087e. _____. *Old Folks will go to Brigham City.* [Salt Lake City, 1905]

Broadside. 19 x 9cm.

USIC

2087f. _____. *Outing of the Old folks.* [Salt Lake City, 1900]

Broadside. 20 x 15cm.

USIC

2087g. _____. *Outing of the Old folks. Grand excursion to Lagoon -- a free ride to all over seventy years of age. Salt Lake & Ogden Railroad and Salt Lake City street railways will treat the aged to a free ride.* [Salt Lake City, 1900]

Broadside. 20½ x 15cm.

Signed: Wm. B. Preston and others.

USIC

2087h.   _____. *"Peace on earth, good will to man."* [Salt Lake City, 1890?]

Broadside. 23 x 15cm.

Excursion of Weber County Old Folks to the Exposition building in Salt Lake City.

USIC

2087i.   _____. *Presidential reception tendered to the old folks of Utah irrespective of creed, race or color, on the occasion of President William Howard Taft's visit.* [Salt Lake City] 1911.

[6]p. illus. 20cm.

USIC

2096a.   _____. **Church of Jesus Christ of Latter-day Saints. Presiding Bishopric.** *Bishop _____ Dear Brother: The tithing and offerings due the church.* Salt Lake City, 1868.

Broadside. 19 x 12cm.

Dated Nov. 1, 1868, and signed by Edward Hunter, L. W. Hardy, and J. C. Little.

USIC

2098a.   _____. *Circular. To Bishop _____* [Salt Lake City, 1868]

Broadsheet. 25 x 21cm.

On verso: A postscript by President Brigham Young.

Concerning the Union Pacific Railroad and its impact on Utah.

USIC

2099a.   _____. *Dear Brother: _____* [Salt Lake City, 1889]

Broadside. 28 x 22cm.

Dated Salt Lake City, July 20, 1889.

Need for tithing payment due to lacks of money from investments.

USIC

2103a.   _____. *Instructions and suggested program, Aaronic Priesthood Centenary Celebration, 1929.* [Salt Lake City, 1929]

12l. 27cm.

USIC

2114a. _____. *Thoughts on tithing.* Salt Lake City [n.d.]

7p. 14½cm.

USIC

2117a. **Church of Jesus Christ of Latter-day Saints. Primary Association.** *Bulletin for Primary Associations of the Church of Jesus Christ of Latter-day Saints in Missions of the Church.* [Salt Lake City? 1927?]

16p. 15½cm.

USIC

2117b. _____. *Children's jubilee of the Primary Association of the Church of Jesus Christ of Latter-day Saints, Tabernacle, Sunday, June 10th, 1928.* [Salt Lake City, Seagull Press, 1928]

[4]p. 26½cm.

USIC

2119a. _____. *Instructions to officers of the Primary Association, 1914.* [Salt Lake City, General Board of Primary Association, 1914]

16p. 23cm.

Instructions to officers regarding organization of ward and stake primaries.

USIC

2121a. _____. *The Primary song book.* Salt Lake City, The General Board of Primary Associations, 1905.

93 nos. music. 19½cm.

USIC

2126a. _____. *Seagull girls.* [Salt Lake City, 1925?]

10l. 28cm.

Cover title: Segolia.

Publication for eleven year old girls of the Primary Association. In illustrated printed paper wrapper.

UHi

2136a. **Church of Jesus Christ of Latter-day Saints. Relief Society.** *Plan and program for the study of child culture and the Book of Mormon. Arranged for the Relief Societies of the Utah Stake of Zion.* [Provo?] 1902.

2p.l., 22p. 18½cm.

In red printed wrapper.

UPB

2137. _____. (same) [Provo, New Century Printing Co.] 1903.

2p.l., 22p. 18½cm.

UPB

2155a. **Church of Jesus Christ of Latter-day Saints. Social Advisory Committee.** *The cigarette evil.* [Salt Lake City, 1919?]

[4]p. 23cm. (Bulletin No. 1)

Discusses the increase in use of tobacco and how to fight it.

UPB, USIC

2161a. **Church of Jesus Christ of Latter-day Saints. Stakes. Benson.** *Benson Stake ward teachers' message.* [Logan?] 1924.

v. 20cm.

UPB Feb. 1925

2165a. _____. **Stakes. Box Elder.** *Course of study for the Y.M.M.I. Association of Box Elder Stake of Zion, copied from contributors of 1893-94.* [Brigham City, 1894]

45p. 24cm.

UHi

2165b. _____. *Sunday School plan for the first intermediate department, Box Elder Stake.* [Box Elder, Utah, Box Elder News Print, 1902]

16p. 20cm.

Cover title: Plan of study for the first intermediate department of Box Elder Stake Sunday Schools for 1902.

USIC

2165c. _____. **Stakes. Cache.** *M.I.A. outlines for summer work, 1908. Young Men's and Young Ladies' Mutual Improvement Associations, Cache Stake.* Logan, Utah, J. P. Smith [1908]

12p. 17cm.

USIC

2167a. _____. **Stakes. Davis.** *Sunday School manual. Published at the suggestion of the six missionaries from Davis Stake. William Beazer, Thomas Thornley, Frederick Walton, T. J. Howard, Mahonri Brown, W. X. Pack. Contains the methods of teaching and the principal diagrams given the missionaries. Is designed to assist the teacher in systematizing his work.* Bountiful, Utah, Lamoni Call [n.d.]

30p. 16½cm.

USIC

2169a. _____. **Stakes. Fremont.** *To the superintendents and Sunday School workers of the Fremont Stake of Zion. Dear brethren and sisters.* [Rexburg, 1900]

Broadside. 36 x 14cm.

A reception planned so that President Lorenzo Snow could shake hands with all the children.

USIC

2176a. _____. **Stakes. Granite.** *Invitation to attend the dedication of the Granite Stake Tabernacle . . . Sunday, December 27, 1903.* [Salt Lake City, 1903]

[8]p. illus. 17cm.

USIC

2177a. _____. *Program for ward teaching and home evening. February - April - July. Spiritual standard for Granite Stake.* [Salt Lake City, 1924.]

[8]p. 22cm.

Family home evening.

UPB, USIC

2185a. _____. **Stakes. Jordan.** *Jordan Stake of the Church of Jesus Christ of Latter-day Saints. Recommendations.* [Salt Lake City, 1906]

[5]p. 18cm.

USIC

2192a.   _____. **Stakes. Liberty.** *"Of all that Thou shall give me I will surely give the tenth unto thee." Liberty Stake Presidency.* [Salt Lake City?] 1928.

[4]p. 15½cm.

Signed: Bryant S. Hinckley, President, Fred M. Michelsen, First Counselor, Wilson McCarthy, Second Counselor.

Need to pay tithing.

UPB

2192b.   _____. *Second elders' conference of the Liberty Stake of Zion to be held March 11, 17 and 18, 1907.* [Salt Lake City, 1907]

[3]p. 17½cm.

USlC

2196a.   _____. **Stakes. Lost River.** *Theology. D. & C., Sec. 88: 77.* Salt Lake, Magazine Printing Co., 1929.

Broadside. 16 x 9cm. (Ward teacher's leaflet).

UPB

2202a.   _____. **Stakes. North Weber.** *Ward teachers manual. North Weber Stake. "Gospel Doctrines."* Ogden, Utah, Prepared by the Committee of the High Council under the direction of the Stake Presidency, North Weber Stake of Zion, 1930.

20p. 19½cm.

In orange printed wrapper.

UPB

2202b.   _____. **Stakes. Ogden.** *Ogden Stake Relief Society work in outline for the year nineteen hundred thirteen. Issued under the direction of the Relief Society Board of Ogden Stake and sanctioned by the Relief Society General Board of the Church.* 5th ed. [Ogden, Utah] 1913.

22p. 17cm.

USlC

2208a.   _____. **Stakes. Pioneer.** *Pioneer Stake Mutual Improvement activity guide, 1918-19.* [Salt Lake City, 1918]

24p. 15cm.

USlC

2210b. _____. **Stakes. Rigby.** *Regarding law enforcement.* [n.p., 1914]

Broadside. 20 x 14cm.

Social problems affecting Idaho Mormons.

USlC

2210c. _____. **Stakes. St. George.** *Programme of exercises of the joint conference of M. I. Associations and Sabbath Schools, of St. George Stake, to be held on Sunday and Monday, July 14th and 15th, 1889, at Pine Valley, Utah Territory.* [St. George, Utah, 1889]

[4]p. 21½cm.

USlC

2214a. _____. **Stakes. St. Joseph.** *Ward teachers' subjects.* Thatcher, Ariz. [ca. 1925]

14p. 18½cm.

USlC

2216a. _____. **Stakes. Salt Lake.** *Bishop's message for April, 1928.* [Salt Lake City, 1928]

Broadside. 19 x 14cm.

UPB

2224a. _____. **Stakes. Salt Lake. Young Men's Mutual Improvement Association.** *Annual oratorical contest.* [Salt Lake City, ca. 1901]

Broadside. 22 x 13cm.

Boyd Park, Salt Lake City jeweler, donated a silver loving cup in mid-May 1901. This broadside gives rules to determine who shall hold the Boyd Park Orators' Cup. This could be a later contest, as one of the deadlines specified is "not later than April 27."

USlC

2229a. _____. **Stakes. Summit.** *Lessons for mothers work, Summit Stake Relief Society.* [Coalville? Utah, ca. 1904]

[6]l. 17½cm.

Lectures 7 - 12 only.

USlC

2232a. _____. **Stakes. Uintah.** *Uintah Stake Relief Society outlines for the year nineteen hundred and thirteen. Endorsed by stake presidency.* [Vernal, Utah, 1913]

35p. 21cm.

USIC

2233a. _____. **Stakes. Utah.** *By-laws of the Church Association of the Utah Stake of Zion.* [Provo, 1894]

4p. 18cm.

Forming of a corporation.

USIC

2233b. _____. *Official program, pioneer day celebration, under the direction of the Utah Stake Sunday Schools.* Provo, Utah, 1912.

19p. 23cm.

UHi

2233c. _____. *Plan and program for the study of child culture and the Book of Mormon. Arranged for the Relief Societies of the Utah Stake of Zion.* [Provo, New Century Printing Co.] 1902.

22p. 18½cm.

UPB, USIC

2233d. _____. *(same)* 2nd ed. [Provo, Utah] 1903.

22p. 18½cm.

USIC

2233e. _____. *Resolutions of respect to the memory of Miss Evelyn Billings, who departed this life September 13, 1892.* [Provo?] 1892.

Broadside. 20 x 11cm.

Miss Billings was secretary of the Young Ladies' Mutual Improvement Association of Utah Stake. Signed: Donna Nechan, Mattie Harding, Teenie Johnson.

Within ornamental border.

USIC

2235a. _____. *Ward teaching, explanation and revelation.* [Provo, ca. 1925]

[6]p. 16cm.

UPB

2238a. _____. **Stakes. Weber.** *Priesthood convention of Weber Stake. Weber Normal College, 9:55, Ogden Tabernacle, 1:55, Sunday March the twenty-first, nineteen hundred and twenty.* [Ogden, Scoville Press, 1920]

[6]p. 20½cm.

Priesthood convention program.

USlC

2239a. _____. *Rules for the guidance of members of the Weber Stake Sunday School Board and the government of Sunday Schools throughout the stake revised and adopted May 20th, 1908.* [Ogden? Utah, 1908]

22p. 18cm.

USlC

2240a. _____. *Ward Teachers Department. Weber Stake High Council. Lesson.* [Ogden? 1909?-1917?]

v. 21½cm.

UPB Lesson 94. June, 1917.

2240b. _____. **Stakes. Weber. High Council.** *Circular. To the members of the Hooper Irrigation Company: Brethren* _____. *Ogden, 1874.*

Broadside. 17 x 15cm.

Encourages members of the company to pay their irrigation tax, etc.

USlC (incomplete).

2241a. **Church of Jesus Christ of Latter-day Saints. Tabernacle Choir.** *Mormon Tabernacle Choir, 175 voices . . . Metropolitan Temple, Wednesday, April 15, 1896.* [n.p., 1896]

[4]p. illus. 24cm.

USlC

2249a. **Church of Jesus Christ of Latter-day Saints. Wards. Ensign.** *Dedicatory services, Ensign Ward Chapel, Sunday, April 1, 1923.* [Salt Lake City, 1923]

[8]p. illus. 22cm.

NjP, USlC

2250a. _____. **Wards. Fifteenth.** *Roll of honor of the Fifteenth Ward Sunday School.* [Salt Lake City] J.N. Perry & Co. [ca. 1888]

Broadside. 31 x 46cm.

Marks given for attendance, good conduct, etc.

USlC

2250b. _____. **Wards. Forest Dale.** *Annual ward conference of the Forest Dale Ward . . . January 7th to 14th, 1923.* [Salt Lake City, 1923]

8p. illus. 24cm.

USlC

2250d. _____. **Wards. Gooding.** *Ordinations and ceremonies. [Compiled by the elders of Gooding Ward, Gooding, Idaho for the benefit of the building fund.]* [Gooding, Idaho, ca. 1925]

[16]p. 6½ x 10cm.

USlC

2254a. _____. **Wards. Liberty Second.** *Program; the Elder's missionary benefit, given under the auspices of the Fourth Quorum of Elders; Second Ward, November 16, 1921.* [Salt Lake City, 1921]

[12]p. illus. 23cm.

USlC

2258a. _____. **Wards. Provo 1st.** *The law of tithing, as set forth in the old scriptures and in modern revelation -- comments thereon by President Brigham Young, President John Taylor, President George A. Smith, Apostle F. D. Richards, and the Presiding Bishopric of the Church.* [Provo, Utah, Silver the Printer, 1898?]

4p. 24½cm.

USlC

2258b. _____. **Wards. Richards.** *Christmas testimonial to our missionaries in the field . . . December 5th, 1924.* [Salt Lake City, Arrow Press, 1924]

[8]p. illus. 24½cm.

USlC

2260a. _____. **Wards. Seventeenth.** *Program of dedicatory and opening services. Seventeenth Ward Chapel.* [Salt Lake City] Deseret News [n.d.]

4p. 17½cm.

NjP

2261a. _____. **Wards. Twentieth.** *Outline of three years' course of study for Twentieth Ward Sunday School.* [Salt Lake City, n.d.]

[3]p. 24cm.

USIC

2262a. _____. **Wards. Twenty-second.** *Dedication, 22nd Ward Chapel and Amusement Hall . . . Sunday evening, September 7th, 1919.* [Salt Lake City] 1919.

[4]p. illus. 21½cm.

USIC

2264a. _____. **Wards. Wells.** *Souvenir program. Formal opening of Wells Ward Chapel . . . October seventeenth, nineteen hundred twenty-six.* [Salt Lake City, 1926]

[4]p. illus. 23cm.

USIC

2279. **Church of Jesus Christ of Latter-day Saints. Young Men's Mutual Improvement Association.** *Manual, 1897-8. The life of Jesus.* Salt Lake City, Published by the General Board, 1898.

73p. 23cm.

USIC

2303a. _____. *Offenbarungen der Neuzeit. Geschichte und Botschaft der "Lehre und Bundnisse". Aus dem englischen "Manual for the Young Men's Mutual Improvement Associations" ubersetzt.* Basel, Herausgegeben von der Schweizerisch-Deutschen Mission der Kirche Jesu Christi der Heiligen der litzten Tage, 1920.

144p. 18cm.

Title in English: Modern revelation, the history and message of the Doctrine and Covenants.

UPB, USIC

2303b. _____. (same) Basel, Herausgegeben von Fred Tadje, 1925.

140p. 20cm.

UPB

2318a. _____. *To stake and ward officers of the Y.M.M.I.A.* [Salt Lake City? 1906]

8p. 21cm.

A review of topics treated at the 11th annual M.I.A. conference, held June, 1906.

USlC

2318b. _____. *To the stake officers, Y.M.M.I.A. Dear Brethren* _____. [Salt Lake City, 1891]

Broadside. 22 x 16cm.

Concerning the approaching April conference.

USlC

2319a. _____. *Über charakterbildung und lebensführung.* Basel, Schweizerischen und Deutschen Mission, 1924.

102p. 20½cm.

Title in English: Manual for junior classes 1917-18.

Translated by H. Dressen from the English.

USlC

2335a. **Church of Jesus Christ of Latter-day Saints. Young Women's Mutual Improvement Association.** *Courses of study; Adult Women's Department of the Young Ladies Mutual Improvement Association; the ethics of the Doctrine and Covenants, four music programs, Indian lore, 1930-31.* Salt Lake City, Young Ladies Mutual Improvement Association, 1930.

93p. illus. 23cm.

USlC

2338a. _____. *Guide to the first year's course of study in the Young Ladies Mutual Improvement Association; prepared by the General Board of the Young Ladies' Mutual Improvement Association and issued as sanctioned by the First Presidency of the Church.* Salt Lake City, George Q. Cannon & Sons Co. [ca. 1895]

41p. 22cm.

USlC

2350a. _____. *Handbuch fur die bienenkorbaadchen des fortbildungsvereins fur junge damen.* [Basel?] Schweizerisch-Deutschen und Deutsch-Ost Oesterreichischen Mission, 1928.

182p. illus. 24½cm.

Title in English: Handbook for the beehive girls of the YWMIA.

USlC

2365a. **Church of Jesus Christ of Latter Day Saints. (Strang).** *Facts for thinkers. In defense of James J. Strang as the legally appointed and ordained successor of Joseph the Martyr.* Pueblo, Colo., H. D. Anderson [ca. 1915]

[4]p. 20cm.

The "One Mighty and Strong" published in 1915 by Wingfield Watson is not included.

UPB

2365b. _____. (same) [Pueblo, Colo., ca. 1927]

4p. 21½cm.

USlC

2367a. **Church of Jesus Christ of Latter Day Saints. (Wight).** *A collection of sacred hymns for the use of all the Saints. Selected by a committee in a branch of the Church of Jesus Christ of Latter Day Saints.* Austin, Printed at the New Era Office, 1847.

1p.l., [3]-94p. [1]l. 13½cm.

IaLG

2370a. **Church of the Firstborn (Morrisites).** *Stray lights on different principles. Poetry and prose for the comfort of friends.* San Francisco [James Dove?] 1885.

[50]p. 23½cm.

Portions in Danish and in English.

USlC

2374a. **Circular. To the citizens of Utah.** [Great Salt Lake City, 1864]

Broadside. 21½ x 19½cm.

Hand written note at end: G. S. L. City, July 5, 1864.

Because of the fact that the nation was going on the gold standard, the undersigned agree to save a years supply of grain.

UPB, USlC

2374b. _____. Great Salt Lake City, July 16th, 1864.

Broadsheet. 36 x 23cm.

To call a meeting due to the "Gold Act" passed in the United States and its impact on the wheat market. On the verso is a copy of the "Gold Act."

UPB, USIC

2404a. **Clawson, Ellen C.** *Ellen C. Clawson and Hiram B. Clawson, appellants, vs. Alexander Ramsey, A. S. Paddock, G. L. Godfrey, A. B. Carleton, J. R. Pettigrew, E. D. Hoge and James T. Little. Appeal from the Supreme Court of the Territory of Utah.* Washington, Judd & Detweiler [1884?]

2p.l., 12p. 22cm.

At head of title: Transcript of record. Supreme Court of the United States. October term, 1884. No. 1030.

Cover title.

Case concerning registration to vote.

DLC

2404b. **Clawson, Hiram Bradley.** *Bishop _____ Dear Sir:* [Great Salt Lake City, 1855]

Broadside. 17 x 20cm.

Advises those members holding land warrants to keep them.

USIC

2411a. **Clawson, Rudger.** *Rudger Clawson, appellant, vs. the United States. Appeal from the Supreme Court of the Territory of Utah.* Filed December 3, 1884. [Washington, Judd & Detweiler, Printers, 1885]

7p. 22cm.

At head of title: Transcript of record. Supreme Court of the United States. October term, 1884. No. 1235.

Challenges the way the jurors were selected for his polygamy trial.

Fales/Flake 690.

DLC

2411b. _____. *Rudger Clawson, plaintiff in error, vs. the United States. In error to the Supreme Court of the Territory of Utah.* Filed February 5, 1885. [Washington, Judd & Detweiler, Printers, 1885]

23 [1]p. 22cm.

Transcript of record. Supreme Court of the United States. October term, 1884. No. 1263.

The defense contends that the possible jurors were asked improper questions.

DLC

2423a. **Clayton, John Middleton.** *Speech of John M. Clayton, of Delaware, on the bill to organize territorial governments in Nebraska and Kansas; discussing the Missouri compromise and the doctrine of non-intervention. Delivered in the Senate of the United States, March 1 and 2, 1854.* Washington, Printed at the Congressional Globe Office, 1854.

22p. 23cm.

Reasons for not making Utah a separate territory due to the fact that the Mormons would make it a theocracy. Part of the compromise of 1850.

MH, RPB, UPB

2430a. **Clegg, William.** *Utah. The prize poem.* [Salt Lake City? ca. 1896]

Broadside. 15 x 21cm.

Divine destiny of Utah.

USlC

2434a. **Clerc, Alexis.** *Voyage au pays du petrole.* Paris, A. Degorce-Cadot, Editeur. 9, Rue de Verneuil [1882?]

2p.l., [5]-323 [1]p. 18½cm.

At head of title: Bibliotheèque de vulgarisation. A travers le Monde. I.

Title in English: Voyage to the land of petroleum.

Chapter VI. Chez les Mormons.

UPB

2445a. **Cody, William Frederick.** *Buffalo Bill's own story of his life and deeds. His autobiography brought up to date including a full account of his death and burial. By ... William Lightfoot Visscher.* [n.p.] John R. Stanton, c1917.

xiii, 352p. illus., ports. 21cm.

Memorial edition.

Mormons p. 50-53.

DLC, Or, OU, TxU, UPB

2449a. **Coke, Henry John.** *Tracks of a rolling stone. By the Honorable Henry J. Coke.* 2d ed. London, Smith Elder & Co. 1905.

3p.l., 359p. port. 21½cm.

Brief encounter with a Mormon while going west in 1850.

CtY, MB, MH, NN, PU, UPB

2450a. **Colborn, Edward Fenton.** *Utah revealed.* [Salt Lake City, 1896]

47p. illus. 23cm.

Cover title.

"Mormonism," p. 45 and other references.

USlC

2455a. **Colfax, Schuyler.** *The Mormon defiance to the nation. Suggestions as to how it should be met.* [Salt Lake City? 1882?]

Broadside. 41 x 21½cm.

At end of article: South Bend, Ind.

From the *Advance*, Chicago, Dec, 22, 1881.

USlC

2457a. **The College Record.** *Devoted to the Interests of Education.* Logan, Utah, 1893-

v. 21cm.

Published by Brigham Young College.

USlC v.1 #12

2460a. **Colorado-Utah Advertising and Curio Co.** *We carry a full line of curios and souvenirs . . . all questions answered and information furnished concerning the "Mormon" Church.* Manitou, Colo. [1905?]

[2]p. 11½cm.

Includes: Chronological information concerning the Church . . . and Articles of Faith.

USlC

2461a. *Columbus and Columbia; a pictorial history of the man and the nation embracing a review of our country's progress, a complete history of America, a new life of Columbus and an illustrated description of the Great Columbian exposition.* Four books in one volume. New York, N.D. Thompson Publ. Co. [c1892]

832p. illus. 27cm.

"Rise of the Mormons," p. 599-600.

NN, USlC

2465b.   **Comettant, Jean Pierre Oscar.** *Tre ar i Forenta Staterna. Iakttagelser och skildringar af Oscar Commetant [sic].* Stockholm, C. H. Fahlsteds forlag, 1860.

[1]p.l. 342p. 20cm.

Title in English: Three years in the United States.

In light brown printed wrappers.

Mormons mentioned, p. 170-73.

CU, MdBP, MiU, HjP, PPL, USlC

2466a.   *[Compilation of statements on plural marriage and priesthood].* [Salt Lake City? Gems Publishing Co.? n.d.]

84p. 27½cm.

USlC

2471a.   *Concordance and reference guide to the Book of Doctrine and Covenants.* Published by the Reorganized Church of Jesus Christ of Latter Day Saints. Plano, Ill., Printed at the True Latter Day Saints, Herald Steam Book and Job Office, 1870.

23p. 15½cm.

Copy in private hands.

UPB xerox copy.

2473b.   *A conference of the Church of Jesus Christ of Latter-day Saints, will be held at Saddlers Wells theatre.* Landport, Taynton Steam Printer, 1877.

Broadside. 19 x 13cm.

Apostle Albert Carrington would be the main speaker.

USlC

2481a.   **Conway, Moncure Daniel.** *My pilgrimage to the wise men of the East.* Boston and New York, Houghton, Mifflin and Company, The Riverside Press, Cambridge, 1906.

viiip. [1]l., 416p. 23cm.

Chapter 2 includes "Journey to Salt Lake City; John W. Young; Mormonism and human nature; Elder Penrose as a preacher; Mormon wives and Mormon husbands; The fate of repudiated wives."

UPB

2489a. **Cook, Joel.** *America, picturesque and descriptive.* New York, P. F. Collier & Son [c1900]

3v. illus. 20½cm.

Utah and Mormons, Vol. 3, p. 48, 270, 216, 393-94, 473-76.

CoU, DLC, MH, USlC, WaU

2504a. **Coop, Timothy.** *A trip around the world. A series of letters by Timothy Coop and Henry Exley.* Cincinnati, H. S. Hall & Co. 1882.

x, 11-221p. illus., ports. 19cm.

Authors pass through Salt Lake City in 1880, p. 13-21.

DLC, OCL, UPB, WHi

2505a. **Cooper, Charles.** *Signs of the day. No. 9.* [Salt Lake City, 1883]

[3]p. 17½cm.

Dated: Salt Lake City, Feb. 2nd, 1883.

Mormon poetry.

USlC

2514a. **Cope, Thomas H.** *C. O. Whittemore, appellant, vs. Thomas H. Cope, Mary Ann Jack and B. S. Young, respondents and George H. Cope, appellant. Brief of respondent Thomas H. Cope.* Salt Lake, Star Print [1895]

23p. 22cm.

At head of title: Supreme Court of Utah Territory, January term, 1895.

Inheritance case with polygamist wives and children.

DLC

2520a. **Cornish, John J.** *Rogers - Cornish debate. Christian Church vs. Reorganized Church of Jesus Christ of Latter Day Saints. Held at Sanford, Michigan, December 14-22, 1891. Arranged by J. Cole Moxon. Scott-Cornish debate held at Burnham, Michigan, January 20-22, 1892. Arranged by J. J. Cornish.* Independence, Missouri, Zion's Ensign Print., 1892.

36p. 19cm.

First debate with M. D. Rogers; second with E. B. Scott.

Formerly *Flake 7407.*

MoInRC

2530a. **Cory, Winifred Graham.** *Judas of Salt Lake.* London, Eveleigh Nash Company Limited, 1916.

2p.l., 309p. [1]l. 19cm.

Leaf of book advertisement after text.

UPB

2536a. **Cotteau, Edmond.** *Promenades dans les deux Ameriques 1876-1877 avec deux cartes itineraires de l'Amerique du nord et de l'Amerique du sud.* Paris, G. Charpentier et Cie, Editeurs ... 1886.

1p.l., 320p. 2 fold. maps. 18cm.

Title in English: Excursions in the two Americas 1876-1877 with two itinerary maps of North America and South America.

Chapter 6. "Utah; Salt Lake City; Les Mormons."

CLSU, UPB

2542a. **Coughlin, Jere., comp.** *Jefferson County centennial, 1905; Speeches, addresses and stories of the towns.* Watertown, Hungerford-Holbrook Co. [1905]

440p. 23cm.

Brief vitrolic history of Mormonism.

NcAS, UPB, WHi

2542b. **Courier Printing Company.** *Manual of the churches of Seneca County with sketches of their pastors. 1895-96.* Seneca Falls, N.Y. Compiled and published by the Courier Printing Company, 1896.

240p. illus. 25cm.

Mormons mentioned in the introduction and on page 232.

CLU, MiD, NN, NRU, PCC, USlC

2552a. **Cowen, Edward David.** *Newspaper career of E. D. Cowen, with biographic sketches by Charles A. Murray, Slason Thompson, R. E. M. Strickland, C. E. Arney, Hugh Hune, Frank M. Dallam, Jr.* [Seattle, Western Printing Company, c1930]

4p.l., 151p. [4]l. port. 21cm.

"John D. Lee among the Indians," p. 49-56.

UPB

2564a. **Cox, James.** *Our own country; representing our native land and its splendid natural scenery, rivers, lakes, waterfalls, geysers, glaciers, mountains, canons, and entrancing landscapes, reproduced in a series of five hundred superb original photographs* . . . . St. Louis, Mo., The National Co. [c1894]

vi, 319p. illus. 33cm.

Mormons and Salt Lake, p. 162-73.

InU, MH, NN, OC, USlC

2575a. **Crary, A. M.** *The A. M. Crary memoirs and memoranda written by himself.* Herington, Kansas, Herington Times Printers [c1915]

4p.l., 164 [2]p. plates, ports. 19cm.

"Elder Childs and Brother Johnny," p. 40-42. Mormon proselyting in St. Lawrence County.

DLC, OCl, PHi, UPB, WHi

2581a. **Creigg, Alfred.** *History of Washington County from its first settlement to the present time, first under Virginia as Yokogania, Ohio, or Augusta County until 1781, and subsequently under Pennsylvania; with sketches of all the townships, boroughs, and villages, etc.; and to which is added, a full account of the celebrated Mason and Dixon's line, the whickey insurrection, Indian warefare, traditional and local historical events.* 2d ed., rev. and cor. by Alfred Creigh. Harrisburg, Pa., B. Singerly, printer, 1871.

375, 132p. 23½cm.

Chapter 5. "Mormonism," p. 89-93.

First published in 1870.

DLC, OCl, MWA, OOxM, OClW, MdBP, MnHi, PHi

2587a. **Crocheron, Augusta B. Joyce.** *To my friends.* [Salt Lake City? 1888]

Broadside. 46 x 16cm.

Signed. South Bountiful, Davis Co., Utah, August 25, 1888. Requesting subscriptions for Dan Weggeland painting from a pencil sketch by Crocheron. The subscription is for a photograph. Title: Joseph rebuking the guard at Richmond Jail.

USlC

2596a. **Crofutt, George Andrews.** *Crofutt's trans-continental tourist's guide, containing a full and authentic description of over five hundred cities, towns, villages, stations, government forts and camps, mountains, lakes, rivers, sulphur, soda and hot springs, scenery, watering places, summer resorts.* New York, Geo. A. Crofutt, 1873.

224, 4p. illus. (part fold.) 17½cm.

Utah, p. 93-106, with history of the Mormon church and its immigration to Utah.

UPB

2597a. **Crooks, James.** *The autobiography of James Crooks.* Terre Haute, Indiana, Moore & Langen Printing Company, 1900.

228p. Port. 18cm.

A brief report of a visit to Salt Lake City in 1879 with reference to the Mormon settlement.

InU, UPB

2608a. **Culmer, Henry L. A.** *Tourists' guide book to Salt Lake City.* Salt Lake City, J. C. Graham & Co., 1879.

26p. 18½cm.

DLC, USlC

2608b. _____, ed. *Utah directory and gazetteer for 1879-1880, containing the name and occupation of every resident in the towns and cities of Salt Lake, Utah, Weber, and Davis counties and a very complete list of the merchants, manufacturers, professional men and officials together with full gazetteer information.* Compiled and edited by H. L. A. Culmer. Salt Lake City, J. C. Graham & Co., [1879]

xiii, 13-389p. 23½cm.

UPB

2614a. **Curtis, George Ticknor.** *Ex parte: In the matter of Lorenzo Snow, petitioner, appellant. Appeal from the Third Judicial District Court, Salt Lake County, Territory of Utah.* [Washington? 1886?]

2p. 22cm.

At head of title: Supreme Court of the United States. October term, 1886. No. 1282.

Lorenzo Snow was in confinement in the Utah Penitentiary for bigamy.

Cover-title.

DLC

2618a.   _____. *A plea for religious liberty and the rights of conscience. An argument delivered in the Supreme Court of the United States April 28, 1886, in three cases of Lorenzo Snow, Plaintiff in error, v. the United States, on writs of error to the Supreme Court of Utah Territory.* Washington, D. C., Printed for the author by Gibson Brothers, Printers and Bookbinders, 1886.

55p. 21½cm.

Extracts from an argument delivered in the Supreme Court of the United States, April 28, 1886, in three cases of Lorenzo Snow, Plaintiff in error, v. The United States, on writs of error to the Supreme Court of Utah Territory. By Franklin S. Richards. p. 43-55.

In Green printed wrapper.

DLC, MH, NcD, UPB, ViU

2629a.   **Curtis, William E.** *A summer scamper along the old Santa Fe Trail and through the gorges of Colorado to Zion.* Chicago, Inter-Ocean Publishing Company, 1883.

2p.l., [7]-113p. 17cm.

Chapter VII. The city of the Saints, p. 97-113.

NN, USIC

2630a.   **Custer, George Armstrong.** *Wild life on the plains and horrors of Indian warfare, by General G. A. Custer, U. S. A. With a graphic account of his last fight on the Little Big Horn, as told by his foe Sitting Bull, also sketches and anecdotes of the most renowned guides, scouts and plainsmen of the west. General Crook and the Apaches.* St. Louis, Sun Publishing Co., 1883.

526p. ill., plates 23cm.

Account of the Mountain Meadows massacre by John Tobin, p. 498-528.

CLSU, DLC, KU, ODW

2632.   **Cutler, Frank.** *Haapiiraa I-[XX] Papaihia e Farani Tuterera.* Papeete, Tahiti, Te Ekalesia a Isu Mesia i to Feia Mo a i te Mau Mahana Hopea Nei [ca. 1908]

20v. 22cm.

Title in English: Lessons 1-20.

USIC has 1-17, 20.

2632a. _____. *Te hoe aratai no te mau taata i roto i te Ekalesia a Iesu Mesia i te feia mo'a i te mau mahano hopea nei. Papaihia e Iosepha Heta, i Tahiti. I te Matahiti 1901, eifaaapia e faarahihia e Viliamu Setemila i te Matahiti 1990.* Neneihia e Eraneta a Rositera. Papeete, Tahiti, Neia i te piha neneiraa a te Ekalesia a Iesu Mesia i te Feia Mo'a i te Mau Mahana Hopea Nei, 1917.

28p. 17½cm.

Title in English: One who leads about the men inside the Church of Jesus Christ of Latter-day Saints.

In gray printed wrapper.

UPB, USlC

2634a. _____. *Te monoraa mau i te toroa peretiteniraa no te Etaretia a Iesu Mesia no te Feia Mo'a no te Mau Mahana Hopea Nei. Ei pahonoraa i te parau a Farani raua Butera na nia i "Te mamoraa i te toroa peterireniraa no te etaretia." I papaihia e Tehare H. Leka.* Papeete, Tahiti, I neneihia i te piha neneiraa no te Etaretia a Iesu Mesia no te Mau Mahana Hopea Nei, 1909.

24p. 23cm.

Title in English: The succession of the office of presidency in The Church of Jesus Christ of Latter-day Saints.

UPB

2635a. **Cutler, John Christopher.** *England to Holland, Belgium and France. Salt Laker and his brother Bert journey across tossing North Sea to Rotterdam and the Hague; visit Antwerp, Brussels and Paris.* [Salt Lake City, ca. 1920]

[4]p. 21cm.

Also published with title: "Hull to Holland," see *Flake/Draper 2635c.* Mentions missionary experiences.

USIC

2635b. _____. *Financial review no. 561. John C. Cutler, Jr., investment banker.* Salt Lake City, 1915.

[4]p. 21cm.

Includes extensive quote from Elbert Hubbard on Utah Pioneers.

USIC

2635c. _____. *Hull to Holland. A Utah boy describes scenes and events on the trip. The quaint old land of dykes. A preliminary note of Manchester, England, and finishing touches about little Belgium and France.* [Salt Lake City, ca. 1920]

[4]p. 21cm.

Also published with title: "England to Holland, Belgium and France," see *Flake/Draper 2635a.* Mentions missionary experiences.

USIC

2635d. _____. *Lincoln's earliest home; Utah boy's visit to Abraham Lincoln's birthplace, on the Old Kentucky Farm. Carry off relics -- a lesson from the martyred president's life for American boys.* [Salt Lake City, ca. 1920]

[3]p. 21cm.

Visit occurred during author's mission.

CtY, USlC

2637a. *Cyclopaedia of religious denominations:* Containing authentic accounts of the different creeds and systems prevailing throughout the world. Written by members of the respective bodies. London, Published by John Joseph Griffin & Company . . . 1853.

2p.l., [vii]-xii, xxviii, 359 [1]p. 19½cm.

"The Mormons, or Latter-day Saints. By Joseph Smith, Nauvoo, Illinois," p. 289-300. Each article is separately paginated.

CtY, MH, OCl, USlC, WHi

D

2640a. *Daab, hvorledes og af hvem udfores den.* [Kjøbenhavn, Udgivet og forlagt af Joseph L. Petersen, Trykt i "Aka," 1926]

[2]p. 23cm.

Title in English: Baptism, how and by whom administered.

USlC

2641a. **Dabney, Owen P.** *True story of the lost shackle; or seven years with the Indians.* [n.p., c1897]

98p. illus. 19cm.

The strange companion (p. 66-67) tells of his conversion to Mormonism. Wife stealing by Brigham Young, p. 66-69.

UPB

2641b. _____. (same) [Salem, Or., Capital Printing Co., c1897]

3p.l., 98p. illus. 20cm.

CtY, CoU, DLC, NjP, OU, UPB, WaU

2648a. **Dalby, Oliver C.** *Faith.* [Salt Lake City, 1920]

[4]p. 18cm.

Ensign Stake of Zion Ward Teachers' leaflet. June, 1920.

USlC

2657a. **Dana, F. L.** *The great West; a vast empire. A comprehensive history of the trans-Mississippi states and territories. Containing detailed statistics and other information in support of the movement for deep harbors on the Texas-Gulf coast.* Denver, Colo., Excelsior Printing Co., 1889.

262, xxxvp. illus. 23cm.

"Utah -- 1847 to 1889," p. 223-33.

CoU, DLC, KyU, MB, NN, USlC

2657b. **The Daniel Hanmer Wells Association.** *Annual reunion of the Wells family.* Salt Lake City, 1900-[1930]

    v. 20-27 cm.

    Also has title changes such as 1901: The Wells Annual.
Includes information concerning the Wells family.

    UPB 1900, 1901, 1908, 1910, 1912, 1913. 1928.

2659a. **Daniels, William M.** *Correct account of the murder of Generals Joseph and Hyrum Smith at Carthage on the 27th day of June 1844. By Wm. M. Daniels, an eye witness.* Nauvoo, Ill. Published by John Taylor for the proprietor, 1845. [Independence? Daniel Macgregor, ca. 1917]

    26p. 20½cm.

    CtY, UPB

2671b. **Daughters of the American Revolution. Martha Board Chapter.** *Augusta's story.* Compiled by the Martha Board Chapter, Daughters of the American Revolution. Augusta, Ill., Augusta Eagle? [ca. 1921]

    219p. illus., ports., plates. 20cm.

    "Reminiscenses of the Mormons," p.45-55.

    USIC

2672a. **Daughters of Utah Pioneers.** *Constitution and by-laws. Daughters of Utah Pioneers.* Organized, April 11, 1903. Amended, April 2, 1924. [Salt Lake City, 1924?]

    11p. 15cm.

    In green printed wrapper.

    Printed before 1927 when it was also amended.

    UPB

2674a. _____. **Weber County, Company.** *Programme of the Daughters of Utah Pioneers, Weber County Company, 1928-1929.* [Ogden, 1928]

    3p. 19½cm.

    UHi

2681a. **Davies, John.** *Y doniau gwyrthiol fel eu darlunir yn yr ysgrythyrau sanctaidd, gyda sylwadau ar bynciau eraill cysylltiedig a gwyrthiau.* Gan John Davies . . . Brynmawr, argraffwyd gan John Davies, Hoel y Brenin, MDCCCLII.

60p. 13cm.

Title in English: The miraculous gifts as they are depicted in the Holy Scriptures.

Mormon miracles discussed.

WalCS

2682b. **Davies, W. R.** *Y Seintiau Diweddaf. Sylwedd pregeth a draddodwyd ar y gwyrthiau.* Er mwyn goleuo y cyffredin, a dangos twyll y creaduriaid a alwant eu hunain yn Seintiau y Dyddiau Diweddaf, Merthyr Tydfil, argraffwyd gan David Jones, Heol-fawr, 1846.

20p. 16cm.

Title in English: The Latter Saints.[sic]

WalN

2697a. **Davis, John.** *Y casgl; neu grynhoad o draethodau, caniadau, a llythyron, perthynol i Saint y Dyddiau Diweddaf.* Merthyr Tydfil, argraffwyd ac ar werth gan J. Davis, Georgetown, 1853.

ivp. 17cm.

Second edition.

Title in English: The compilement; or a collection of treatises, songs, and letters, pertaining to the Latter-day Saints.

Title page for miscellaneous pamphlets.

The copies at USIC and WalN vary in content which is also reflected in variant tables of contents.

Dennis 71

USIC, WalN

2702a. _____. *Llyfrau Saint y Dyddiau Diweddaf, ar werth gan J. Davis, argraffydd, Georgetown, Merthyr, a chan y Saint trwy Gymru.* Merthyr Tydfil, argraffwyd, ac ar werth gan J. Davis, Georgetown, 1851.

Broadsheet. 17½cm.

Title in English: Book of the Latter-day Saints, for sale by J. Davis.

On the verso is an advertisement concerning the printing of a Welsh Book of Mormon.

Dennis 58

MH, USIC

2702b. _____. *Pregeth gwrth-Formonaidd. At y Parch T. Williams, Ebenezer, ger Caerfyrddin.* Rhydybont, John Jones, [1848].

4p. 17½cm.

Title in English: Anti-Mormon sermon.

Dennis 21

NjP

2727a. **Davison, Matilda Spaulding.** *Folly and falsehood of the golden Book of Mormon.* Hexham, Edward, Edward Pruddah [1840?]

4p. 16cm.

Wife of Solomon Spaulding.

Reprinted from Lunenburgh Colonial Churchman, Jan. 25, 1839.

Date in original is erroneous because her statement was first published in the Boston Recorder April 5, 1839.

NN

2734a. *A day school in Utah.* by M.C.A. [New York, Woman's Home Missionary Society, Methodist Episcopal Church, n.d.]

[4]p. 15½cm.

Need for non-Mormon education.

USIC

2734b. **Daynes, Joseph John.** *Brigham Young's funeral march.* Salt Lake City, Daynes & Son, 1877.

5p. port., music. 34cm.

Portrait of Brigham Young mounted on cover. Words and music.

UPB

2734c. _____. *The Latter-day Saint anthems book. Composed exclusively by Prof. Joseph J. Daynes.* Salt Lake City, Daynes-Beebe Music Co. [1916]

62p. music. 26cm.

USIC

2734d. **Deam, William H.** *Fruit in the season thereof.* [n.p., n.d.]

8p. 19cm.

Concerning the word of wisdom. Deam worked at the Herald House as a printer.

MoInRC

2734e. _____. *Songs of praise, new songs to old tunes.* Independence, Missouri, 1923.

8p. 28cm.

MoInRC

2738a. **Dean, Joseph Henry.** *He leo kahea. E. J. H. Dina.* [Honolulu, Hawaii? ca. 1888]

[3]p. 20½cm.

Title in English: The calling voice.

USlC

2744a. **De Brij, Elisabeth H.** *Ervaringen van een Hollandsche vrouw in het land der Mormonen.* [n.p., ca. 1909]

15 [1]p. 21cm.

In orange printed wrappers.

Title in English: Experiences of a Dutch woman in the land of the Mormons.

A Dutch convert's feelings about Mormonism and Utah.

USlC

2761a. **Demetrius, Jr., [pseud.]** *An epistle of Demetrius, Junior, the silversmith.* Birmingham, England; J. Taylor [1842?]

Broadside. 37 x 25cm.

USlC

2761b. **Demetrius, Junior.** *An epistle of Demetrius, Junior, the silver-smith, to the workmen of the occupation, and all others whom it may concern: greeting: showing the best way to preserve our craft, and to put down the Latter Day Saints.* Peterboro [New Hampshire?] Printed for Elder E. P. Maginn [1842?]

Broadside. 35 x 22cm.

Text within ornamental border.

Reprinted from the Manchester edition. In this edition "Manchester" has been changed to "America" in the first paragraph, and the Church from "about 10" to "about 12" suggesting an 1842 American. Eli P. Maginn, for whom the broadside was printed labored in the vicinity of Peterboro from the fall of 1841 until the spring of 1843.

Right margin cropped with some loss of border.

UPB

2762a. **Democratic Party. Utah.** *Proceedings of the Democratic State convention held at Ogden, Utah, August 18, 1916, including . . . The speech of Hon. B. H. Roberts in nomination of Hon. Simon Bamberger for the office of Governor. . . .* Salt Lake City, Democratic State Committee, 1916.

32p. 23cm.

Mormons, p. 21.

USlC

2762b. _____. *The Utah contest. Indisputable facts which ought to settle the question.* [Salt Lake City? 1892?]

[2]p. 23cm.

Mormons mentioned.

USlC

2777a. **Derry, Charles.** *The voice of the good shepherd.* [Lamoni, Iowa, ca. 1881]

4p. 21cm. ([Tract] No. 3)

MoInRC

2779a. **DeRupert, A. E. D.** *Californians and Mormons.* New York, John W. Lovell [ca. 1881]

Broadside. 23½ x 15cm.

At head of title: (New editon)

Advertisement for a new edition which was apparently not published.

UPB, USlC

2779b. *The descendants of father John Tanner, of Bolton, Warren Co., State of New York.* [n.p., 1884]

Broadside. 22 x 14cm.

The Tanner family announce a family reunion at Payson, Utah, on Christmas Day, 1884, marking the fiftieth anniversary of his leaving his Bolton home to cast his lot with the church then gathering at Kirtland.

UPB, USlC

2779c. *Description of the Joseph Smith Monument.* [Salt Lake City? 1905?]

Broadside. 31 x 31cm.

Describes the monument built in Sharon, Vermont to honor Joseph Smith.

USlC

2780b. *The Deseret alphabet.* [Salt Lake City, ca. 1869]

Broadside. 20 x 14cm.

List of Deseret alphabet characters with English equivalents.

USlC

2780c. **Deseret Book Company.** *Catalog and price list. L. D. S. Church publications, bibles and miscellaneous books.* [Salt Lake City, 1927]

63p. 25½cm.

List of Mormon books in print.

UPB

2780d. _____. *Reading course books adopted by the Mutual Improvement Asociation for 1930-1931.* [Salt Lake City, Deseret Book Co., 1930]

[2]p. 20cm.

UHi

2780e. _____. *The Seven Presidents of the Mormon Church.* Salt Lake City [Deseret Book Company, 1919?]

[2]p. illus. 17½ x 27½cm.

UHi

2787a. **Deseret (State). Constitution.** *Constitution of the State of Deseret and memorial to Congress. Adopted in Convention, March 18, 1872.* Salt Lake City, 1872.

28p. 23½cm.

UPB, USlC

2787b. _____. *Letter of the delegate of the Territory of Utah in Congress, enclosing the memorial of the delegates of the convention which assembled in Great Salt Lake City, and adopted a constitution with a view to the admission of Utah into the Union as a State, together with a copy of that constitution.* [Washington, William A. Harris, Printer, 1858]

10p. 22cm. (U. S. 35th Cong. 1st sess. Mis. Doc. No. 240)

UPB

2799a. **Deseret Museum.** *The Deseret Museum, the pioneer museum of the intermountain West.* [Salt Lake City, 1910?]

[4]p. illus. 23cm.

UHi

2804a.   **Deseret News. Extra. 1852.** *List of Mormon emigrants of 1852.* [Salt Lake City, Deseret News, 1852]

Broadside. 49 x 28cm.

USIC

2804b.   _____. **Extra. 1854, June 19.** *List of persons shipped at Liverpool, England, from January, 1854, to March 21st, 1854 by Samuel W. Richards.* [Salt Lake City, Deseret News, 1854]

Broadside. 57 x 31cm.

USIC

2811a.   **Deseret News Office.** *Catalogue of publications of the Church of Jesus Christ of Latter-day Saints.* For sale at the Deseret News Office. Salt Lake City, 1883.

[6]p. 17cm.

USIC

2811b.   **Deseret News Publishing Co.** *For all kinds of Mormon publications address the Deseret News Publishing Co.* Salt Lake City [ca. 1895]

[2]p. 17½cm.

On verso: Advertisements for *Deseret Evening News, Deseret Semi-weekly News,* and *Deseret Weekly.*

USIC

2811c.   *Deseret News white book, automobile maps and logs.* Salt Lake City, Deseret News, 1922.

48p. illus., maps. 21½cm.

"The old Mormon trail to . . . Los Angeles."

UHi

2823a.   **Devens, Charles.** *John Miles vs. United States. No. 592. Error to Supreme Court of Utah. Government brief.* [Washington? 1880]

13p. 22cm.

At head of title: In the Supreme Court of the United States. October term, 1880.

A case in which a juror was asked if he believed in polygamy.

DLC

2827a. **Dey & Street.** *In the matter of the estate of George Handley, deceased. On petition of Sarah Chapman et al. for a rehearing. Brief for respondents. Dey & Street, W. H. Bramel, attorneys for respondent.* [Salt Lake City] Star Printing Company [1897]

12p. 22cm.

At head of title: In the Supreme Court of the State of Utah.

Cover title.

A polygamy inheritance case.

UAr

2829a. **Dick, William Brisbane.** *Dick's Ethiopian scenes, variety sketches, and stump speeches, containing end men's jokes.* New York, Fitzgerald Publishing Corporation [c1873]

178p. [7]l. 17cm.

In printed wrapper.

"Artemus Ward's panorama" and "Among the Mormons," p. 167-69.

Another edition: 1879. UPB

UPB

2832b. **Dickout, Hiram.** *Marriage suit. Latter Day Saints find justice in the High Court of Canada.* June, 1905. [n.p., n.d.]

15p. 18cm.

Third edition.

MoInRC

2833a. **Dickson, William Howard.** *Extracts from "Solid facts from a loyal man".* [n.p., ca. 1895]

Broadside. 27 x 9cm.

Extract from a speech charging the Mormons of being disloyal to the government and trying to overthrow the American home.

USlC

2834a.   _____. *In the matter of the estate of Oscar A. Amy, deceased; Jennie Amy, appellant, vs. Royal D. Amy et al., appellants, vs. Adelia Young et al., respondents. Abstract. Appeal from Third District Court. W. H. Dickson and S. P. Armstrong, attorneys for Jennie Amy, appellant. LeGrant Young, attorney for Adelia Young, et al., respondents. Pence & Allen, attorneys for Royal D. Amy, et al., appellants.* [Salt Lake City] Tribune Job Printing Co., 1895.

40p. 22cm.

At head of title: In the Supreme Court of Utah Territory. No. 602.

Cover title.

In the testimony of Elliot Butterworth, his membership in the Mormon church is questioned.

UAr

2841a.   **Dinsmore, Isabella Kimball.** *Trips and travel. Letters to the Unitarian Alliance.* Belfast, Maine, 1929.

5p.l., 180p. port. 18½cm.

"Salt Lake City," p. [89]-111.

A description of her tour of the Salt Lake Temple Square.

UPB

2841b.   *Directory of Ogden City, and North Utah record. Containing a complete exhibit of the principal business firms of Ogden; the name, occupation and residence of every resident in the city; and a statement embodying the history, present facilities and future prospects of the great railway centre of the Pacific Coast. Together with a reliable showing of the population, resources, etc., of the other towns in Weber County, and the principal Settlements along the line of the Utah Northern Railroad in this Territory. Published by S. A. Kenner and Thos. Wallace.* Ogden, Utah, Printed at the Ogden "Junction" Office, March 15, 1878.

xii, 134 [1]p. 19cm.

A great deal of information concerning the Mormon settlements in Weber, Box Elder, and Cache counties.

CtY, UPB

2845a.   **Dixie College, St. George, Utah.** *A home school for all.* [St. George, 1881]

[2]l. 21½cm.

The establishment of the St. George Academy.

USIC

2846a. **Dixon, William Hepworth.** *Les Etats-Unis d'Amerique. Impressions de voyage. Abreges par H. Vattemare.* Paris, Librairie Hachette et Cie, 1879.

190 [2]p. illus., port., maps. 22½cm.

Title in English: United States of America. Impressions of a trip.

Chapter 4. Utah, Les Mormons, Le Territoire Indien.

C, UPB

2851a. *Do you wish the world to go Mormon?* [Binghampton, N. Y., Plymouth Congregational Church, 1927]

Broadside. port. 29 x 21½cm.

First of a series of four meetings at Plymouth Congregational Church, March 7, 1927, in which B. H. Roberts spoke and answered questions. Protestant ministers also invited to show their side of the issue.

USIC

2851b. **Dobson, Eli T.** *Biographical sketch of the life of Elder Thomas Dobson, with a short record of family descent. By his son, E. T. Dobson.* Denison, Iowa, Printed at the Bulletin Office, 1878.

8p. 22cm.

An early LDS member, he joined the RLDS church and made many trips to Utah for the RLDS Church.

MoInRC

2853a. **Dr. Williams & Co., College of Anatomy.** *Descriptive catalogue of Dr. Williams & Co. College of Anatomy, 298 State Street, Chicago, Ill. Mammoth gallery of science, art, and curiosities. Mysteries of man and woman. Chamber of horrors.* [Chicago, 1878?]

44p. 22cm.

"The Chamber of Horrors. Life size figures in wax representing Brigham Young, surrounded by his harem of twenty wives. John D. Lee, the leader of the Mountain Meadow murders, as he appeared on the day of his execution. The celebrated Danite chiefs," p. [38-43]

Published after the deaths of Brigham Young and John D. Lee in 1877 and of Porter Rockwell in 1878.

UPB

2881a. **Doctrine and Covenants. English. 1900?** *The Doctrine and Covenants, of the Church of Jesus Christ of Latter-day Saints, containing the revelations given to Joseph Smith, Jr., the Prophet, for the building up of the kingdom of God in the last days. Divided into verses, with references, by Orson Pratt, Sen.* Salt Lake City, Utah, The Deseret News, Printers and Publishers [1900?]

2p.l., 503p. 17½cm.

Printed between 1898 and 1907.

UPB

2888a. _____. **1904.** (same) Salt Lake City, The Deseret News [1904]

503p. 18cm.

Published as a separate, as well as a double combination.

USlC

2895a. _____. **1909.** (same) Salt Lake City, The Deseret Sunday School Union, 1909.

503p. 13cm.

Vest pocket edition.

Published also in a double combination.

USlC

2900a. _____. **1915.** (same) Salt Lake City, The Deseret Sunday School Union, 1915.

503p. 13cm.

Vest pocket edition.

Published also in a double combination.

USlC

2914b. **Doctrine and Covenants. Section 76. English.** *A striking and remarkable vision, disclosing the real and final state of man, after the period of his existence in this world, by Joseph Smith Jun., and Sidney Rigdon.* Preston, Whittle's, Printers, 25, Fishergate [1838?]

Broadside. 45 x 36cm.

Printed before the death of Joseph Smith, Sr. An Elder's certificate with a similar border, dated 1838, printed in Preston suggests the date and place of printing of this broadside.

UPB

2916a. _____. **Section 87. English.** *A prophecy and revelation concerning the present war and future destiny of America and all other nations; by the Prophet, Seer, and Revelator, Joseph Smith; given Dec. 25th, 1832, extracted from the "Pearl of Great Price".* [Droylsden? John Schofield? ca. 1864]

Broadside. 18½ x 13cm.

At head of title: My brother, read, and then judge.

"Any works of the church or any further information, can be obtained by applying to Mr. John Schofield, Daisy Bank, Droylsden."

Civil War prophecy.

USlC

2916b. _____. (same) **1864.** *A revelation and prophecy. By the Prophet, Seer, and Revelator, Joseph Smith. Given December 25, 1832.* [n.p., 1864]

Broadside. 15 x 10cm.

Published in the *Saints' Herald* November, 1860.

MoInRC, UPB

2916c. _____. (same) *"A revelation and prophecy by the Prophet, Seer, and Revelator, Joseph Smith. Given December 25th, 1832 [sic]* [n.p., n.d.]

Broadside. 28 x 21cm.

In three columns. The Joseph Smith revelation appears in column one. Columns two and three contain, "A vision of Joseph Hoag. Who was an eminent min,ister[sic] of the Society of Friends, of New York."

USlC

2929. **Doctrine and Covenants. Dutch. 1929.** *Het Boek der Leer en Verbonden van de Kerk van Jezus Christus van de Heiligen der Laatste Dagen, Vevattende de openbaringen ann den profeet Joseph Smith, Jr., voor de oplouwing vanhet koninkrijk Gods in de Laatste Dagen. Uit het Engelisch vertaald door H. De Brij Fz. met medewerking van Sylvester Q. Cannon. Eerste Nederlandsche Uitgave.* Rotterdam, Uitgegeven door Sylvester Q. Cannon, 1908.

2p.l., 547 [3]p. 17cm.

Title in English: The Book of the Doctrine of Covenants of the Church of Jesus Christ of Latter-day Saints.

When Frank I. Kooyman was made Mission President in 1929, he found pages 177-192 lacking from existing copies, so reprinted them with a new translation.

UPB, USlC

2933a. _____. **German. 1920.** *Das Buch der Lehre und Bundnisse der Kirche Jesu Christi der Heiligen der letzten Tage, welches die Offenbarungen enthalt dem Propheten Joseph Smith, jun. gegeben, nbest einem Anhang von Offenbarungen der Prasidentschaft der Kirche Jesu Christi, exteilt. Aus dem Englischen ubersetzt von Heinrich Ehring...Vierte Auflage.* Basil, Herausgegeben von der Schweigerisch-Deutschen Mission, 1920.

[1-5] 6-32, 490p. 17½cm.

Includes an appendix with sections 133-138.

Title in English: Book of the Doctrine and Covenants of the Church of Jesus Christ of Latter-day Saints.

USlC

2933b. _____. (same) *Vierta Auflage.* Basel, Herausgegeben voh der Schweizerisch-Deutschen Misison, 1920.

2p.l., [5]-32, 499p. 17cm.

"Index," 32p.

USlC

2943a. **Doctrine and Covenants (Reorganized Church) English. 1872.** *The Book of Doctrine and Covenants of the Church of Jesus Christ of Latter-Day Saints. Carefully selected from the revelations of God, and given in the order of their dates.* Cincinnati [Plano, Ill.] Printed by the Publishing Committee of the Reorganized Church of Jesus Christ of Latter-Day Saints, [ca. 1872]

vi, 335p. 17cm.

First edition, second issue. October 1, 1870 edition of True Latter Day Saints' Herald mentions a new edition of the 1864 printing "printed on sized and calendered paper."

Bound in contemporary brown sheep. Gilt stamped label on spine.

MoInRC

2944a. _____. **1882.** Plano, Ill. [ca. 1882]

342p. 16cm.

Includes section 118.

MoInRC

2945a. _____. **1887.** Lamoni, Iowa, Printed by the Board of Publication of the Reorganized Church of Jesus Christ of Latter Day Saints, 1880 [ca. 1887]

vi, 346p. 17cm.

Contains Section 119 given in 1887. Same plates and copyright of the 1864 edition.

MoInRC, UPB, USlC

2945b. _____. **1891.** Lamoni, Iowa, Printed by the Board of Publicaiton of the Reorganized Church of Jesus Christ of Latter Day Saints, 1880 [ca. 1891]

352p. 15½cm.

Includes section 121.

MoInRC, UPB

2945c. _____. **1894.** Lamoni, Iowa, Printed by the Board of Publication of the Reorganized Church of Jesus Christ of Latter Day Saints, 1880 [ca. 1894]

359p. 16½cm.

Includes section 122, given in 1894.

USlC

2960a. _____. **1914.** Lamoni, Iowa, Printed by the Board of Publication of the Reorganized Church of Jesus Christ of Latter Day Saints. 1913 [ca. 1914].

298, 60p. 18cm.

Contains Section 131. Reissue of the 1911 edition.

USlC

2962a. _____. **1919.** Lamoni, Iowa, Printed by the Board of Publication of the Reorganized Church of Jesus Christ of Latter Day Saints, 1919.

299, 60p. 19cm.

Contains Section 133.

USlC

2968a. _____. **Section 126. English. 1902.** [Lamoni, Iowa, Reorganized Church of Jesus Christ of Latter Day Saints, 1902]

391-394p. 17cm.

At head of title: Supplement to Saint's Herald, May 21, 1902.

Dated: Lamoni, Iowa, April 18, 1902.

To be added to the Doctrine and Covenants of 1901.

UPB

2969a. *The doctrine of the first resurrection, a light which cannot any longer be hid in darkness.* Independence, Mo., 1878.

8p. 20cm.

MoInRC

2971a. **Dodge, Augustus Caesar.** *Nebraska and Kansas. Speech of Mr. Dodge, of Iowa, in the Senate of the United States, Feb. 25, 1854, the Senate having under consideration the bill to organize the Territories of Nebraska and Kansas.* [Washington, Printed at the Congressional Globe Office, 1854?]

15p. 23cm

Speaks of the institution of polygamy and states that no law of the Utah Legislature which condoned it would pass.

DLC, NN, UPB, ViU

2972a. **Dodge, Ida Flood.** *Arizona under our flag.* Tucson, Arizona Daily Star, 1928.

198p. 23cm.

In tan printed cover.

Mormons in Arizona.

DLC, UPB

2973a. **Domin, Karel.** *Dvacet tisic mil po sousi a po mori. Kniha draha.* Praha, Makladatelstvi J. Otto, Spolecnost S. R. O., 1929.

736p. illus., plates, fold. map. 24½cm.

Title in English: 10,000 miles by land and by sea.

Chapter XXIV. V meste Mormonu.

UPB

2976a. **Donan, Patrick.** *The heart of the continent: An historical and descriptive treatise for business men, home seekers and tourists, of the advantages, resources and scenery of the great West.* Published by the Passenger Department, Chicago Burlington & Quincy Railroad. Chicago [Buffalo, N. Y., Clay & Richmond] 1882.

63 [1]p. illus., map. 17cm.

Speaks of the non-polygamist Mormons at Plano, and Mormon migration through Council Bluffs.

CtY, DLC, NNC, UPB, WHi

2976b. _____. *Utah; being a concise description of the vast resources of a wonderful region.* 10th ed. [Denver] Passenger department of the Denver and the Rio Grande and Western, 1902.

80p. illus. 23½cm.

Other editions 1903. UHi, 1905. UHi, DLC

Includes material on Mormonism.

UPB

2983a. **Dougall, Lily.** *The Mormon prophet.* London, Grant Richards, 1899.

444p. 19½cm.

"Printed by R. & R. Clark, Limited, Edinburgh," p. 444.

UPB

2983b. **Douglas, Stephen Arnold.** *Kansas, Utah, and the Dred Scott decision. Remarks of Hon. Stephen A. Douglass [sic], delivered in the State House at Springfield, Illinois, on 12th of June, 1857.* [Springfield?, 1857]

8p. 24½cm.

Includes information on polygamy.

IaU, IU, MiU, UPB

2999a. **Drake, Emma Frances (Angel).** *Het vermoorden van ongeboren kinderen.* [Rotterdam?] Uitgereikt door De Kerk van Jezus Christus van de Heiligen der laatste Dagen (Mormonen) [n.d.]

7 [1]p. 20cm.

Title in English: The murdering of unborn children.

A doctrinal tract.

USIC

3001a. **Drannan, William F.** *Thirty-one years on the plains and the mountains. Or, the last voice from the plains. An authentic record of a life time of hunting, trapping, scouting and Indian fighting in the Far West. By Capt. William Drannan who went onto the plains when fifteen years old. Copiously illustrated by H. S. DeLay. And many reproductions from photographs.* Chicago, Rhodes & McClure Publishing Company, 1899.

[2]p.l. [7]-8p. [1]l. 9-586 [9]p. 19½cm.

Nine pages of advertisements follow page 586.

"Mormons," p. 362-71, 395-98.

UPB, USIC

3013a. **Drumm, Mark.** *Drumm's manual of Utah, and souvenir of the first state legislature, 1896.* [Salt Lake City, 1896]

95 [1]p. 19½cm.

Brief history of the settlement of Utah.

At head of title "The beehive state."

UHi, UPB

3023a. **Dufferin and Ava, Hariot Georgina (Hamilton) Hamilton-Temple-Blackwood Marchioness of,** *My Canadian journal 1872-8. Extracts from my letters home written while Lord Dufferin was Governor-General . . . With illustrations from sketches by Lord Dufferin. Portraits and map.* London, John Murray, 1891.

[18] [1] 422 [6]p. illus., port., plates, fold. col. map. 21cm.

Visit to Salt Lake City in 1876.

UPB

3023b. _____. (same) New York, D. Appleton and Company, 1891.

xvi, 456p. illus., maps, ports. 19cm.

USlC

3027a. **Dugard, Marie.** *La Societé Américaine: Moers et caractere -- la famille -- role de la femme -- écoles et universites.* 2d ed. Paris, Libraire Hachette, 1896.

1p.l., 320p. 18½cm.

Title in English: The American Society: Mores and character -- the family -- role of the women -- schools an universities.

Includes a section on Mormonism, in the chapter entitled: La prairie et le bassin du Lac Sale.

DLC, MiU, MoU, NN, UPB

3027b. **Duguet, Raymond.** *La Polygamie aux Etats-Unis: Les Mormons.* Paris, Eds. du "Nouveau Mercure", 1921.

2p.l., [5]-98p. 19½cm.

Title in English: Polygamy in the United States: The Mormons.

In brown printed wrapper dated 1922.

UPB, USlC

3028a. **Dumbell, Kate Ethel Mary.** *Seeing the West; suggestions for the west-bound traveller.* Garden City, New York, Doubleday, Page & Company, 1930.

xiv, 206p. 1l. illus. (map) 18cm.

"Salt Lake City and the Zion National Park," p. 17-26.

A brief discussion of the Mormons.

DLC, MiU, OO, UPB, WaT, ViU

3033a.   **Dundas, J. H.** *A Zetetic sermon.* Auburn, Nebraska [ca. 1920]

36p. 15cm.

Mormons, p. 14-15, 31.

USIC

3040a.   **Dunn, Ballard S.** *The twin monsters: And how national legislation may help to solve the Mormon problem, and restore to society, somewhat of the sacramental character of the rite of holy matrimony.* By Rev. Ballard S. Dunn. New York, James Pott & Co. [ca. 1885]

31p. 23½cm.

Cover title.

Gray printed wrappers with title within border. Advertisements on inner wrappers. Printed after Sept. 1884 and before 1886.

CtY, NN, UHi, USIC, WHi

3040b.   _____. (same) 2d. ed. New York, James Pott & Co., publishers [1885?]

31p. 23½cm.

Cover title.

At head of title: Price, 25 cents.

Gray printed wrappers with title within border. Advertisement on inner wrappers. Printed after Sept. 1884 and before 1886.

CtY, DLC, ICN, MH, ULA, UPB, WHi.

3040c.   _____. (same) New York, James Pott & Co., Publishers [c1886]

31p. 23½cm.

Cover title.

At head of title: Third edition. Price, 25 cents.

In gray printed wrapper with title with border.

CtY, DLC, OCiWHi, UHi, UPB, WHi

3047a.   **Dunne, Finley Peter.** *Mr. Dooley's philosophy. Illustrated by William Nicholson, E. W. Kemble, F. Opper.* New York, R. H. Russell, 1900.

2p.l., 7-263p. 18½cm.

"Polygamy," p. 109-114.

USIC

3083a. *Dynoethiad Mormoniaeth; yn cynwys hanes Joseph Smith, saith gradd y deml, gwreigiaeth ysbrydol, yn nghyda'r seremoniau a arferir ar Dderbyniad i'r Urdd hono. O enau tystion profedig. Wedi eu casglu gan y lefiad.* Abertawy, Argraffwyd gan Joseph Rosser, Heol fawr, 1853.

44p. 16½cm.

Title in English: Exposure of Mormonism; including the story of Joseph Smith.

WalCS

E

3099a. **Eastman, Samuel.** *Ten years of my mission. Called of God, not of man. Legal heir to the priesthood and keys of the kingdom.* [Salt Lake City, 1914]

193p. 20cm.

Preface signed: Salt Lake City, August 1st, 1914.

UPB

3104a. **Eaton, Horace.** *A memorial of the celebration at Palmyra, N. Y. of the centennial fourth of July, 1876, including the oration by Theodore Bacon, and a sketch of the early history of Palmyra.* Rochester N. Y., E. R. Andrews, book and job printer, 1876.

34p. 22½cm.

In blue printed wrapper.

Joseph Smith, p. 33-34.

DLC, NIC, UPB

3107a. **Eckfeldt, Jacob Reese.** *Supplement to the manual of coins and bullion. By Jacob R. Eckfeldt, and William E. Du Bois.* Philadelphia [Assay Office of the Mint] 1849.

[1]p.l. 240p., [1]l. plates. 27½cm.

One plate shows "California and Mormon coins," in embossed gilt on dark blue paper, tipped in at time of publication between page 60 and 61. Another plate, "The Mormon Coins," only 17cm. in size, is tipped in at time of publication following page 240.

This *Supplement* . . . is a companion volume to "A manual of gold and silver coins of all nations," published by the same authors in Philadelphia in 1842.

In private possession.

3118a. **Edwards, William Seymour.** *In to the Yukon.* Cincinnati, Robert Clark Company, 1904.

312 [4]p. illus. 19½cm.

On his return he visit Salt Lake City and discusses Mormonism.

Another edition. 1905. UHi, UPB

DLC, MB, PPL, UHi, UPB, WaS

3123a. *Eighty-ninth anniversary of the birth of Joseph F. Smith, University Ward Hall, November 12th, 1927.* [Salt Lake City, 1927]

[4]p. port. 17½cm.

UHi

3127a. **Eldredge, Charles Augustus.** *Robert N. Baskin, contestant, v. George Q. Cannon, contestee. Brief and argument of Chas. A. Eldredge.* [Washington? Gibson Brothers, Printers, 1876]

31p. 23cm.

At head of title: House of Representatives. Forty-fourth Congress, Committee on Elections.

DLC, USlC

3128a. **Eldredge, Horace S.** *The United States of America, plaintiff, vs. Horace S. Eldredge and Francis Armstrong, defendants, No. 6,600. Transcript of record. Appeal from the Third District Court. F. S. Richards, LeGrand Young, Sheeks & Rawlins, Attorneys for Appellants. Dickson & Varian, Attorneys for Respondent.* [Salt Lake City?] Parker, Printer [1887]

28p. 24cm.

At head of title: In the Supreme Court of Utah Territory, January term, 1887.

USlC

3128b. **Eldredge, Jane (Jennings).** *Descendants of John Walker of Gringley-on-the-Hill, Nottingham, England.* [Salt Lake City? ca. 1920]

12p. ports. 23cm.

Includes Mormon descendants.

USlC

3133a. **Eliza [Pseud.]** *Truth made manifest. A dialogue on the first principles of the oracles of God.* By Eliza. [n.p., n.d.]

12p. 22cm.

MoInRC

3133b. _____. (same) Plano, Ill. [before 1881]

12p. 22cm.

Includes poem "An angel chair" by Perla Wild and "Helps" on the last page.

MoInRC

3137a. **Elliott, A. B.** *Travelers' handbook across the continent; Pacific Railroad and California sketches.* Troy, New York, Thornton, Nims & Co., 1870.

x, 85 [1]p. 14cm.

Brief stop in Salt Lake City, with description of Mormonism.

DLC, DHU, ICU, OrStbM, UHi

3150a. **Ellis, Charles.** *Press comments on Mr. Charles Ellis' lectures.* Salt Lake City [1891?]

[4]p. 22cm.

Insert letter "To whom it may concern" recommending the lectures and signed by Wilford Woodruff, Geo. Q. Cannon and Jos. F. Smith. Dated January 9th, 1891.

USIC

3155a. **Ellis, John B.** *Free love and its votaries; or, American socialism unmasked, being an historical and descriptive account of the rise and progress of the various free love associations in the United States, and of the effects of their vicious teachings upon American society.* New York, United States Publishing Company [c1870]

502p. illus. 24cm.

Notes that Mormonism does not go as far as the Oneida community.

NBuC, OKE, UPB, USIC

3163a. **Emmons, Samuel Bulfinch.** *Philosophy of popular superstitions and the effects of credulity and imagination upon the moral, social, and intellectual condition of the human race.* Boston, L. P. Crown & Co., 1853.

288p. 20cm.

Chapter XIII. "Mormon superstition." A very critical view of Mormonism.

DLC, ICN, ICRL, MB, NjP, UPB

3166a. **Engelhardt, Zephyrin.** *San Diego Mission.* By Fr. Zephyrin Engelhardt, O. F. M. San Francisco, James H. Barry Company, 1920.

xiv, 358, 8p. illus., maps. 23½cm. (The Missions and Missionaries of California, new series, local history).

A brief account of the Mormon Batallion's stay in San Diego in a mission.

CU, DLC, DHU, ICU, OrStbM, UHi, UPB

3171a. **Ensign Circulating Library.** Independence, Missouri, Ensign Publishing House [1893?]

    v. quarterly. 16cm.

Vest pocket edition. Not individually volumed, and appears under individual titles.

USIC

3178a. *Er de Sidste-Dages Hellige Kristne?* [København, Udgivet og forlagt af Joseph L. Petersen, Trykt i "Aka," 1926]

4p. 22cm.

Title in English: Are the Latter-day Saints Christians?

USIC

3179a. **Erdan, Alexandre.** *La France mystique. Tableau des excentricites religieuses de ce temps.* 2e edition avec portraits. Revue par l'auteur, et augmentee d'une nouvelle preface. Par Charles Potvin. Amsterdam, R. C. Meijer, 1858.

2v. ports. 19cm.

Title in English: Mysterious France.

In gray printed wrappers.

Chapitre IV, Les Mormons. Taken from Lorenzo Snow's *Voix de Joseph.*

IaU, MiU, OClW, UPB

3180a. **Ericksen, Ephraim Edward.** *The psychological and ethical aspects of Mormon group life. A dissertation submitted to the faculty of the graduate school of arts and literature in candidacy for the degree of Doctor of philosophy . . .* Chicago, University of Chicago Press [1922]

100 [1]p. 23cm.

In tan printed wrapper.

Dissertation information on the title page.

UPB

3183a. **Estournelles de Constant, Paul Henri Benjamin, Baron d'.** *Les Etats-Unis d'Amerique.* Paris, Librairie Armand Colin, 1913.

ix, 536p. fold. col. map. 18½cm.

Title in English: The United States of America.

"Les Mormons," p. 83-87; Chapter 4, pt. 5 on dry farming and the Mormons. Is positively impressed with both.

CoU, CtY, DLC, DSI, NcD, UPB, USIC

3210a. **Evans, David.** *Saint y dyddiau diweddaf a doniau gwyrthiol. sef pregeth a draddodwyd, dydd Sul y 27ain Awst. 1848, yn Eglwys Sant Dewi, Caerfyrddin, gan y parch.* David Evans ... Caerfyrddin, Argraffwyd gan William Spurrell, Heol-y-brenin, MDCCCXLVIII.

20p. 18cm.

Title in English: The Latter-day Saints and miraculous gifts.

WalCS, WalN

3210b. **Evans, Frederick William.** *Autobiography of a Shaker, and revelation of the apocalypse. With an appendix.* Mt. Lebanon, N. Y., E. W. Evans, 1869.

162p. 21cm.

Mormon practice of polygamy one fulfillment of the Apocalypse.

CtY, DLC, ICJ, MB, N, UPB

3233a. **Evans, Richard C.** *Bishopric of Canada, Reorganized Church of Jesus Christ of Latter Day Saints; to the saints of Canada Mission.* [Toronto?, 1909?]

4p. illus. 26cm.

MoInRC

3241a. _____. *Faulty creeds. Prominent ministers confirm the angel's message.* By Elder R. C. Evans. Independence, Missouri, Ensign Publishing House [n.d.]

70p. 22cm.

MoInRC

3251a. _____. *Joseph Smith, was he a prophet of God? Sermon by Elder R. C. Evans.* [Independence, Mo., Ensign Published House, 1902]

64p. port. 16cm. (*The Gospel Banner.* V. 9. No. 2. Extra A. April 1902)

In pink printed wrapper.

Portrait of Evans on the title page.

UPB

3270a. **Evans, T. B.** *From Geneva to Mexico. A record of a tour through the western part of the United States and the greater part of old Mexico, with illustrations.* Geneva, Ill., From the press of the Geneva Republican, 1893.

3p.l., 87p. port., plates. 24cm.

Includes a chapter on his visit to Salt Lake City.

TxU, UPB

3278a. *Everybody should read the Book of Mormon.* [Liverpool?, 1889?]

Broadside. 15 x 27cm.

Brief description of the Book of Mormon. Handwritten note: England, March, 1889.

USlC

3278b. *Die ewige wahrheit. Erklarung uber die lehren der Kirche Jesu Christi der Heiligen der letzten Tage. Vom abfall und wiederbringung des wahren evangeliums.* Hamburg und Bern, Herausgegeben von der redaktion des "Stern," 1898.

16p. 18cm.

Title in English: The eternal truth.

Missionary tract.

USlC

3280a. **Ewing, Leon R.** *A rejected manuscript. The other side.* [n.p., ca. 1902] 16p.

17cm.

In grey printed wrapper.

A defense of Mormonism by a non-member.

UPB

3283a. *Exposure of clerical slander.* Battle Creek, Mich., Steam Press of the Seventh-day Adventist Publishing Association, 1864.

15p. 22½cm.

Seventh-day Adventists not responsible for Mormonism.

MiBsA

3284a. *The extermination of the Latter Day Saints from the state of Missouri in the fall of 1838.* New York, S. Brannan, Prophet Office [ca. 1845]

Broadside. 35½ x 49cm.

Lithograph by H. R. Robinson, 142 Nassau St., N.Y.

USlC

3284b. **Eyma, Louis Xavier.** *Excentricites Americaines par Xavier Eyma.* Edition autorisee pour la Beligique et l'etranger, interdite pour la France. Leipzig, Alph. Durr, Libaire-editeur, [1860]

193 (i.e. 197)p. [1]l. 14cm. (Collection Hetzel)

Title in English: American eccentricities.

Brigham Young, p. 43-46.

DLC, LU, MB, NN, TxU, UPB

3284c. _____. *Les trente-quatre etoiles de l'union Americaine. Histoire des etats et des territoires.* Paris, Michel Levy freres, Libraires-editeurs, Bruxelles et Leipzig, A. Lacrois, Verboeckhoven et Cie., 1862.

2v. 22cm.

Title in English: The thirty-four stars of the American Union.

Mormons discussed in v. 2, p. 211-14.

CtY, DLC, NjP, NN, RPB, UPB, USlC

F

3289a.   *A fac-simile from the Book of Abraham, No. 2.* [Nauvoo, Ill., Times and Seasons, 1842]

Broadside. illus. 31 x 24cm.

Reprinted from *Times and Seasons*, Vol. 3, No. 10.

USIC

3291a.   *Facts for thinkers. In defense of James J. Strang as the legally appointed and ordained successor of Joseph the Martyr.* Pueblo, Colo. [1915?]

[4]p. 20½cm.

List of pamphlets available from H. C. Anderson in Pueblo.

UPB

3301a.   **Farewell entertainment and dance in honor of Elder Louis Iverson.** [Salt Lake City] 1897.

Broadside. 23 x 15cm.

Elder Iverson was going to the Indian Territory.

USIC

3319a.   *Fellow country women.* [n.p., ca. 1885]

Broadside. 20½ x 13½cm.

Printed after the Edmunds Act of 1882 but before the Edmunds-Tucker of 1887.

UPB

3319b.   **Felt, Charles B.** *Organizations of the Church of Jesus Christ of Latter-day Saints.* [Salt Lake City, 1921]

[4]p. 18cm.

USIC

3323a.   **Fenzi, Sebastiano.** *Gita intorno alla terra dal gennaio al Settembre dell' anno 1876.* Firenze, Coi tipi dei successori le monnier, 1877.

259 [1]p. 22½cm.

Title in English: Trip to the land of January to September of the year 1876.

In grey printed wrappers.

Discussion of Mormonism, p. 215-16.

UPB

3325a.   **Fergusson, J. C.** *The Alta California Pacific Coast and Trans-continental Railroad guide. Contains more information about the states and territories of the Pacific Coast, and those traversed by the great trans-continental railroad than any other book extant.* San Francisco, Fred. MacCrellish & Co. [1871]

8 [4] xii, 293 [3]p. illus., plates, maps (1 fold). 18cm.

Salt Lake City, p. 217-21, with mention of the "New Zion movement."

DLC, CSmH, UPB

3331a.   **Ferris, Jacob.** *The states and territories of the great West; including Ohio, Indiana, Illinois, Missouri, Michigan, Wisconsin, Iowa, Minesota, [sic] Kansas, and Nebraska.* New York and Auburn, Miller, Orton, and Mulligan, Buffalo, E. F. Beadle, 1856.

xii, [13]-352p. [6]l. illus., plates fold map. 20cm.

In the back are advertisements for books including "History of the Mormons" and calls it the most singular delusion of modern times.

CU, DLC, IdU, MB, MiU, NN, UPB

3332a.   **Fetting, Otto.** *Eighteenth Message.* [Port Huron, Mich. Mrs. Otto Fetting, 1930?]

[4]p. 22cm.

At head of title: John the Baptist has come, as Christ said he would. Matt. 17:11.

Printed in double columns and can be folded to [4]p.

UPB

3332b.   _____. *Eighteenth Message. A warning to all people of the second coming of Christ. John the Baptist (Ressurrected) has come.* [Independence, Board of Publication of the Church of Christ, 1930]

[4]p. 19cm.

Dated: January 6, 1930.

UPB

3333a. _____. *John the Baptist (Resurrected) has come. Twenty-second message.* [Independence, Mo., 1930?]

[4]p. 19½cm.

Caption title.

Message dated July 29, 1929.

UPB

3338d. _____. *Supplement revelations on the building of the Temple and instruction to the Church of Christ.* [Port Huron, Michigan, 1930?]

Broadside. 22 x 21cm.

Dated: February 28th, 1930.

UPB, USIC

3338e. _____. (same) *The time is at hand. The Lord has spoken and revealed his purpose by the mouth of His servant "John."* [Port Huron, Michigan, 1929?] [4]p. 22cm.

Includes visitations thirteenth through sixteenth, dated September 20, 1929 to October 27, 1929.

UPB, USIC

3338f. _____. *Supplement revelations on the building of the Temple and instructions to the Church. Seventeenth visitation [and] eighteenth visitation.* [Independence, Mo.? 1930?]

Broadsheet. 22 x 21cm.

USIC

3338g. _____. *Twelfth visitation of the messenger to Elder Otto Fetting, Port Huron, Mich. Supplement to revelation on building the temple.* [Port Huron, Mich. Mrs. Otto Fetting, 1929?]

[6]p. 21½cm.

UPB, USIC

3338h. _____. *Twenty-second Message. July, 1930.* [Port Huron, Mich., Mrs. Otto Fetting, 1930?]

Broadsheet. 22 x 21cm.

At head of title: John the Baptist has come, as Christ said he would. Matt. 17:11.

Printed in double columns and can be folded to [4]p.

Variant printing without date July, 1930 after title.

UPB

3338i. _____. *Twenty-third Message.* [Port Huron, Mich., Mrs. Otto Fetting, 1930?]

Broadsheet. 22 x 21cm.

At head of title: John the Baptist has come, as Christ said he would. Matt. 17:11.

Printed in double columns and can be folded to [4]p.

Dated Oct. 31, 1930.

UPB

3338j. _____. *A warning to all people of the second coming of Christ. One of the series of revelations on the building of the temple and instruction to the Church of Christ.* [Independence, Missouri, Printed by the Board of Publication of the Church of Christ, 1930?]

[4]p. 21½cm.

Dated November 30, 1930.

Twenty-fourth message.

UPB, USlC

3339a. _____. (same) *Revelations on the building of the temple and instruction to the Church of Christ.* [Port Huron, Michigan, Mrs. Otto Fetting, 1930?]

25p. 22½cm.

Includes messages 1 through 22.

USlC

3348a. **Field, Jasper Newton.** *Isms, fads & fakes. A series of Sunday night discourses.* Indianapolis, Hollenbeck Press [c1904]

3p.l. [9]-227p. 19½cm.

"Mormonism, or, the so-called Latter-day Saints," p. [9]-21.

DLC, OClWHi, UPB

3359a. *[First Presidency, Council of the Twelve, and Patriarch to the Church]* [n.p., 1906?]

Broadside. illus., ports. 51 x 21cm.

Photographs of the First Presidency, the Apostles, and the Patriarch-- brethren sustained by church membership as Prophets, Seers, and Revelators. Broadside apparently issued some time between April 1906, when Elders George F. Richards, Orson F. Whitney, and David O. McKay were sustained, and June 1907, when Elder George Teasdale passed away.

USlC

3368a.   **Fisk, James L.** *Expedition of Captain Fisk to the Rocky Mountains. Letter from the Secretary of War, in answer to a resolution of the House of February 26, transmitting report of Captain Fisk of his late expedition to the Rocky Mountains and Idaho.* [Washington, Govt. Print. Off., 1864]

39p. 22cm. (U.S. 39th Cong., 1st Sess. House. Ex. Doc. No. 45)

Meets the Morrisites at Soda Springs then went on to Salt Lake City. Includes a formula to break up Mormonism.

UPB

3368b.   **Fitch, Franklin Y.** *The the [sic] life, travels and adventures of an American wanderer: A truthful narrative of events in the life of Alonzo P. DeMilt. Containing his early adventures among the Indians of Florida; His life in the gold mines of California and Australia; his explorations of the Andes and the Amazon and its tributaries, etc., etc., interspersed with sketches and narratives. Illustrating life, manners, customs and scenery in Mexico, Central America, Peru, Brazil, Australia, the South Sea Islands, and the United States. With numerous engravings.* New York, John W. Lovell Company [c1883]

viii, [9]-228, 43 [5]p. illus., port., plates. 19½cm.

Spent a winter in "Mormon gulch." After leaving he watched Sam Brannan risk $18,000 on the roulette table.

CtY, DLC, ICU, KyU, UPB, ViU

3372a.   **Fitzhugh, George.** *Cannibals all; or, slavers without masters.* Richmond, Va., A. Morris, 1857.

xxiii, [25]-379p. 18½cm.

Scattered references to Mormonism and Brigham Young.

AU, DLC, MHi, MiU, MU, PPL, PU, TU

3373a.   **Flagg, James Montgomery.** *Boulevards all the way-maybe. Being an artist's truthful impression of the U.S.A. from New York to California and return, by motor.* New York, George H. Doran Company [1925]

4p.l., 11-225p. 19½cm.

Brief visit to Salt Lake City. Comments that the Mormons have one thing on their mind -- sex.

DLC, MB, NN, OCl, PPL, UHi

3373b. **Flamank, Robert.** *On the departure from earth of Beatrice Lillian Driggs, on March 14, 1874, at Pleasant Grove, Utah Co.* [Stafford? 1874]

Broadside. 30 x 17cm.

Text within ornamental border.

Dated: 35 Peel Terrance, Stafford, April 27, 1874.

Funeral poem.

USlC

3377a. **Fletcher, Lawrence.** *Into the unknown; a romance of South Africa.* London, Paris & Melbourne, Cassell & Company, Limited, 1892.

viii, [9]-215p. 21cm.

A strange story in which Mormonism is transported to Africa as a local cult.

IEN, MH, NcU, TxU, USlC

3380a. *The flower of the Mormon city.* [Newton, Australia, Burrows, 1912]

Broadside. 29 x 15cm.

At head of title: The great masterpiece.

Advertisement for a film which came from Denmark in 1912 entitled "Mormonbyens Blomst." In English speaking areas it was sometimes titled "The Flower of the Mormon town."

Charles H. Hyde, president of the Australian Mission (1911-1913) sent this broadside to Pres. Joseph F. Smith in a letter dated July 25, 1912.

USlC

Flowers, R. W. *See From Ocean to Ocean.*

3382a. **Fogg, William Perry.** *"Round the world." Letters from Japan, China, India, and Egypt.* Cleveland, Ohio, 1872.

6p.l. [7]-237p. 24cm.

Reprinted from the *Cleveland Leader.*

Includes a stop over in Utah, with a description on Mormonism and a prediction that it would fold after the death of Brigham Young.

DLC, MWA, NN, OClW, OrU, OC, UPB

3383a. **Fohlin, Ernest Victor.** *Salt Lake City and Utah by pen and pictures.* Vol. 1, Part 1. [Salt Lake City, c1913]

[20]l. illus., plates. 26 x 35cm.

"A tribute to the pioneers of Utah" by C. C. Goodwin, p. 5. Other Mormon references.

UPB, USIC

3397a. **Ford, Thomas.** *Presentation of a flag to Governor Ford and his troops by the ladies of Hancock County.* [n.p., 1846]

Broadside. 35 x 18cm.

Address by Mary J. Borbridge, Nov. 9, 1846, as the ladies of Hancock County presented a flag to Governor Ford and his men.   Also includes Governor Ford's response.

USIC

3402a. **Forman, S. E.** *A history of the United States for schools.* New York, Century Co. [c1910]

xiii, 419, lxxi p. illus., maps. 21cm.

Mentions Mormons, p. 274, 283, 379-80.

DLC, OU, PP, PV, USIC

3403a. **Forrest, Earle Robert.** *History of Washington County, Pennsylvania.* Chicago, S. J. Clarke Publishing Company, 1926.

3v. illus. (incl. facsims) plates, ports. 27½cm.

"The Book of Mormon," v. 1, Chapter 75, p. 636-644.

DLC, PHi, WHi

3405a. *Fort Sutter papers. A transcript of the Fort Sutter papers together with the historical commentaries accompanying them brought together in one volume for purposes of reference.* [New York? De Vinne Press? 1921]

22p.l., 29v. in 1. 35cm.

Manuscript 26 tells of the arrival of the ship Brooklyn, the fear of thousands of Mormons arriving from the East, and a note on Sam Brannan.

UPB

3412a. **Fountain, Paul.** *The great deserts and forests of North America.* London, New York and Bombay, Longmans, Green, and Co., 1901.

ix, 295p. 23cm.

Mormons, p. 204-7.

DLC, OO, UHi, USIC, Wa

3415a. **Fox, Henry J.** *Fox and Hoyt's quadrennial register of the Methodist Episcopal Church, and universal church gazetteer.* Hartford, Case, Tiffany & Co., Wm. Jas. Hamersley, 1852.

iv, [5]-311[1]p. 19cm.

"Mormons, or Latter Day Saints," p. 271.

ICU, IU, UPB

3419a. *Framstaende mans vittnesbord om de sista dagars heliga.* Stockholm, Nordstjarnan [1913]

4p. 23cm.

Title in English: Prominent men's testimonies about the Latter-day Saints.

USlC

3420a. **Francis, Harriet Elisabeth.** *By land and sea; incidents of travel, with chats about history and legends.* Troy, N. Y., Nims and Knight, 1891.

ix, 198p. port., plates 25cm.

A two hour stop over in Salt Lake City; attends a meeting in the Tabernacle and describes the meeting.

DLC, PPL, UPB

3420c. **Frankua, Gilbert.** *Among the Mormons.* [London? 1926?]

Broadside. 77 x 51cm.

Advertising an article in the "Sunday Pictorial."

USlC

3434a. **Frazier, Walter Jerome.** *Salt Lake City busy man's pocket directory, 1922.* [Salt Lake City, c1922]

151p. 14cm.

Mormon chapels, p. 21-24.

USlC

3434b. *A Free lecture on character education will be given by Dr. John T. Miller [Tuesday, Aug. 7 - Friday, Aug. 12].* [Sunderland] Sunderland Post [1906?]

Broadside. 22 x 14cm.

Lectures held in Mormon chapels in Sunderland and West Hartlepool.

USlC

3436a. **Freece, Hans Peter.** *Hans P. Freece, popular lectures.* Des Moines, Iowa, Midland Chautauqua Circuit [1909?]

[4]p. port. 27½cm.

Freece was an excommunicated Mormon.

USIC

3443a. _____. *The Mormon Elder and how to meet him.* [New York, 1908?]

6p. 16cm.

UHi

3444a. _____. *The Mormon peril.* [New York City, Printed under the direction of the International Reform Bureau, Washington, D. C., n.d.]

Broadsheet. 22½ x 15cm.

Freece apparently printed a series of anti-Mormon tracts under this heading.

MoInRC

3445a. _____. *Uncle Sam says the Mormons still practice polygamy.* [New York] 1913.

Broadside. 21½ x 10cm.

UHi

3447a. **Freemasons. Salt Lake City Grand Lodge.** *Catalogue of books and rules and regulations of the Masonic Library in Salt Lake City, Utah.* Salt Lake City, Tribune Printing and Publishing Co., 1880.

122 [1]p. 22cm.

Mormon books, p. 74, 112-115, 117-120.

USIC

3450a. **Fremont, John Charles.** *Central railroad route to the Pacific. Letter of J. C. Fremont to the editors of the National Intelligencer, communicating some general results of a recent winter expedition across the Rocky Mountains, for the survey of a route for a railroad to the Pacific.* [Washington, 1854]

7p. 22½cm.

Describes his winter journey of 1853-54, with an account of the Mormon settlements of Parowan and Cedar City.

CSmH, MOU, UPB

3459a. **French, Augustus C.** *To the citizens of Hancock.* [Springfield, 1846]

Broadside. 16 x 16cm.

Governor French of Illinois, Dec. 12, 1846, announced that he was withdrawing the troops from Hancock County because they were no longer needed to keep order. He asked the citizens to prevent any further acts of violence.

USlC

3461a. **French, Joseph Lewis, ed.** *The pioneer west. Narratives of the westward march of empire. Selected and edited by Joseph Lewis French. With a foreward by Hamlin Garland. Illustrations in color by Remington Schuyler.* Boston, Little, Brown, and Company, 1923.

xivp., [1]l., 386p. col. plates. 21cm.

Includes an extract of "The city of the Saints," by Richard Burton, p. 174-201.

Another edition: 1924. MiU, MtHi, OO, OrSaW, PP, UPB, WaU

CU, DLC, MB, NN, UHi, USlC, WHi

3469a. **Frisbie, Barnes.** *The history of Middletown, Vermont, in three discourses, delivered before the citizens of that town, February 7 and 21 and March 30, 1867.* Poultney, Vt., Published by request of the citizens of Middletown, 1867.

130p. 22½cm.

Brief mention of Oliver Cowdery and his relationship to Mormonism.

DLC, ICN, MB, Phi

3472a. **Froiseth, Jennie Anderson, ed.** *The women of Mormonism: or, The story of polygamy as told by the victims themselves. With an introduction by Miss Frances E. Willard, and supplementary papers by Rev. Leonard Bacon, Hon. P.T. Van Zile, and others.* New York, Wm. H. Shepard, 1882.

xviii, 19-416p. illus., plates, ports. 20cm.

UPB

3476a. *From ocean to ocean, being a diary of a three months' expedition from Liverpool to California and back.* [London] Printed for private circulation, 1871.

2p.l., 108p. [1]l. 23cm.

"Salt Lake," p. 37-39.

Attributed to R. W. Flowers.

UPB

3489a. **Fullom, Stephen Watson.** *The great highway. A story of the world's struggles.* London, Longman, Brown, Green, and Longmans, 1854.

viii, 302 [1]p. illus. 20½cm.

In chapter called "The unknown tongue," Fullom discusses the deluted Joseph Smith and in later chapters comments on Joseph Smith's death.

CtY, NcU, USIC

3492a. *Funeral services for Mrs. Phileus Tempest.* [Rexburg? 1928]

Broadside. 26 x 13cm.

Died in Rexburg, Idaho, January 9, 1928.

USIC

3492b. *Funeral services for Mrs. Rebecca N. Nibley held in the Assembly Hall, Salt Lake City, Utah, July 5, 1928.* Salt Lake City, 1928.

28p. port. 22cm.

Added title page: In memorium, Rebecca Neibaur Nibley.

Cover title: Rebecca Neibaur Nibley.

USIC

3494a. *Funeral services, Patriarch John Smith.* [Salt Lake City, 1911]

[4]p. illus., port. 18 x 14cm.

Funeral, Salt Lake Tabernacle, Nov. 12, 1911.

USIC

G

3498a. **Gabriac, Alexis.** *Course humoristique autour du Monde, Indes Chine, Japon. Illustree de huit gravures sur bois.* Paris, Michel Levy Freres, editeurs, 1872.

4p.l., 308p. music. plates. 24½cm.

Title in English: Humorous route around the world, Indochina, Japan.

In blue printed wrappers.

Passed out Salt Lake City in 1869. Includes notes concerning Mormonism.

CtY, DLC, NjP, UPB

3498b. **Gabriel, Ralph Henry.** *Toilers of land and sea.* New Haven, Yale University Press, 1926.

340p. illus. 26½cm. (Pageant of America, 3)

Liberty bell edition. Mormons mentioned, p. 234.

DLC, IdB, MB, MH, OrP, USIC

3498c. **Gaillardet, Frederic.** *Ancien redacteur en chef du Courrier des 'Etats-Unis.* Paris, E. Dentu, editeur, 1883.

2p.l., 371 p. [2]l. 18½cm.

Title in English: Former editor and chief of the courier of the United States.

Chapter XI. Les Mormonisme et ses Fondateurs.

UPB

3508b. **Garner, Mary J.** *The happiest Christ. By Mary J. Garner and Callie B. Stevvins.* Lamoni, Iowa, 1893.

55p. 16cm. (Birth Offering Series, No. 2)

Sponsored by the Daughters of Zion teaching children the spirit of giving.

MoInRC

3509a. **Garretty, J. R.** *Garretty's guide, a vest pocket business directory, memorandum and reference book, and tourists guide to Salt Lake City, Utah.* [Salt Lake City] 1890.

129p. 15cm.

"The Church of Jesus Christ of Latter-day Saints," p. 26.

UHi, UPB

3522a.   **Gates, Susa (Young).** *Polygamy! World wide after the war?* San Francisco, Pacific Bureau Service, 1917.

Broadside. illus., port. 53 x 36cm.

"Probably, but only on high moral ground," said a notable Mormon.

UPB

3525a.   _____. *Utah women in politics.* [Salt Lake City, 1914]

16p. 23cm.

UHi, UPB

3526a.   _____. *Why I believe the gospel of Jesus Christ.* [Salt Lake City, Deseret News Press, 1930?]

29p. illus, port. 29cm.

UPB

3528a.   _____. *Women of the "Mormon" Church. By Susa Young Gates and Leah D. Widtsoe.* [Independence, Press of Zion's Printing and Publishing Company, 1926.]

34p. illus., ports. 22½cm.

UPB

3535a.   **Gay, F. D. B.** *The white book road guide . . . published from the standpoint of the man in the car.* Provo, Utah, 1920.

48p. illus., map. 28cm.

"Old Mormon trail," p. 3. Brief history of the route from Salt Lake City to Southern Utah with some historical information.

UHi

3543a.   **Geoghegan, J. B.** *Brigham Young, written and composed by J. B. Geoghegan.* London, 1870.

8p. 28cm.

USIC

3560a. **Gibson, Walter Murray.** *The Shepherd Saint of Lanai. Rich "primary" revelations, gathered from various sources and produced in historical for the first time in the "Saturday Press," Dec. 24, 1881 to Jan. 21, 1882.* Honolulu, Thos. G. Thrum, Publisher, 1882.

45p. 22cm.

Extracts of writings by Gibson; letters from Gibson; statements of contributions and miscellaneous material about Gibson.

USIC

3560b. _____. (same) Honolulu, Thos. G. Thrum, Publisher, 1882.

46p. 22cm.

"Truth versus falsehood, p. 46, added to the original edition."

UPB (inc.)

3560c. _____. (same) Honolulu, Thos. G. Thrum, Publisher, 1882.

47p. 22cm.

Appendix added to 46 page edition. Gibson and the Mormons, p. 47.

CtY, CU-B, DLC, MH, NN, UHi

3571a. **Giles, Barnet Moses.** *Zion's trumpet.* Salt Lake City, 1878.

14p. 24cm.

A controversial work on Israel and Brigham Young.

USIC

3580a. **Gillen, C. W.** *Minnen fran mina resor genom Norra Amerikas forenta staten och Canada.* Orebro [1897]

272p. illus. 18cm.

Title in English: Memories from my trip through the United States of America and Canada.

Account of a trip made in the [1870's] to Utah, with material on Salt Lake City and Brigham Young.

MnHi

3584a. **Gilman, Arthur.** *A history of the American people.* Boston, D. Lothrop and Co. [c1883]

xxiii, 668p. illus. 18½cm.

Mormons, p. 447-50.

DLC, MnHi, MWA, PHC, USIC

3588a. *Glad Tidings. Supplement to The Glad Tidings.* [Clifford, Ontario, Canada, Reorganized Church of Jesus Christ of Latter Day Saints, 1892]

Broadside. 28 x 28cm.

Includes a letter addressed "Dear Tidings" by A. E. Mortimer. Concerns information on the Canadian Mission of the RLDS Church.

USIC

3588b. **Gladding, Effie Price.** *Across the continent by the Lincoln Highway. Illustrated by photographs.* New York, Bretano's, 1915.

ix, [11]-262p. illus., plates, fold. map. 21cm.

Luncheon at a Mormon ranch in Nevada. Mormon ranch at Kanada, Salt Lake City, p. 150-157.

CU-Riv, DLC, MB, NN, OCI, Phi

3589a. *Ett gladt bundskap; inbjudning till Guds rike.* Stockholm, K. B. Bostroms Boktr., 1908.

12p. 17½cm.

Title in English: The glad message.

USIC

3589b. _____. (same) Sjatte svenska upplagan. Stockholm, P. Sundwall, 1909.

12p. 19cm.

In blue printed wrapper.

USIC

3589c. _____. (same) *Attonde svenska upplagan.* Stockholm, Utgiven och forlagd av Theo. Tobiason, 1919.

12p. 18cm.

In gray printed wrapper. Articles of Faith on the back cover.

On page 12: Kindbergs Tryckeriaktiebolag, Jonkoping. 1920.

UPB, USIC

3599a. **Glisan, Rodney.** *Journal of army life.* San Francisco, A. L. Bancroft and Company, 1874.

xi, 511p. illus., plates, fold. chart. 23cm.

Chapter XXVIII has information on the Utah expedition.

UPB

3608a. **Goemaere, Pierre.** *Across America with the king of the Belgians. Authorized translation from the French by Beatrice Sorchan.* New York, E. P. Dutton & Co. [c1921]

3p.l., 149p. 19cm.

Stopped in Salt Lake City for two hours. Summary of Mormons beliefs.

DAU, DLC, MB, OCl, PPL, UPB

3609a. **Goldberger, Ludwig Max.** *Das Land der unbegrenzten Moglichkeiten. Boebachtungen uber das Wirtschaftsleben der Vereinigten Staaten von Amerika.* Berlin, F. Fontane, Chicago, Brehtano's, 1903.

299p. 23½cm.

Title in English: The land of the unrestricted possibilities.

Mormons, p. 151-55.

DLC, ICJ, MH, NN, PU, USlC

3610a. *Goldkoerner von wahrheit und auszueg aus den reden und briefen hervorragender manner Utahs (aus der bergangenheit und gegenwart).* [Salt Lake City? Frank J. Cannon? 1895?]

12p. ports. 18½cm.

Title in English: Nuggets of truth . . .

USlC

3611a. *Gone to rest.* [Springville? 1899?]

Broadside. 27 x 16cm.

Tribute to Sarah Lovell Mendenhall, wife of William Mendenhall.

USlC

3611b. **Gontard, Jean.** *Au pays des gratte-ciel (Etats-Unis) 20 planches hors texte.* Paris, Librairie Pierre Roger, c1925.

3p.l., [7]-272p. illus. 20cm.

At head of title "Les pays modernes".

Bound in red and blue printed wrappers.

Title in English: Land of the Sky Scrapers (United States)

"Au Pays mormon," p. [245]-258.

CtY, DLC, NG, NN, NNC, OCU, UPB

3617a. **Goodrich, Samuel Griswold.** *The world as it is, and it has been; or a comprehensive geography and history ancient and modern.* New York, J. H. Colton and Company, 1855.

272, 4 [3]p. illus., col. maps 27cm.

"Territory of Utah," p. 130-31. Gives brief history of Mormonism.

UPB

3618a. **Goodwin, Charles Carroll.** *As I remember them.* Salt Lake City, Published by a special committee of the Salt Lake Commercial Club, 1913.

360p. 23cm.

Biography of William S. Godbe p. [336]-37.

CoU, DLC, IdB, IdU, MB, UPB, USlC

3618b. _____. *At a meeting held at Independence Hall, Salt Lake City, August 22, 1872, it was resolved . . .* [Salt Lake City, 1872]

Broadside. 17 x 11cm.

Creation of Utah's Liberating League to oppose the tyranny of church leaders.

USlC

3622a. **Goodwin, Samuel Henry.** *Freemasonry in Utah. A chapter from the early history of Mt. Moriah Lodge No. 2. Nov. 11th, 1865 - Nov. 25th. 1867.* [Salt Lake City? 1924]

16p. 22cm. (Educational bulletin. No. 2)

The exclusion of Mormons from the Utah Lodge.

Caption title.

UPB

3624a. _____. *Freemasonry in Utah. The first lodge - 1859-1861.* [Salt Lake City? 1924]

12p. 22cm. (Educational bulletin. No. 1)

Caption title.

The first lodge began as a result of the Utah Expedition and the creation of Camp Floyd.

UPB

3638a. *The Gospel Banner.* Independence, Missouri, Ensign Publishing House, 1894-1900.

14v. quarterly. 16cm.

Series of tracts which carried sermons of well known RLDS ministers. The sermons originally appeared in *Zion's Ensign.*

MoInRC

3649a. **Gottfredson, Peter, comp.** *Supplement to History of Indian depredations.* [Salt Lake City? Skeleton Publishing Co.? ca. 1920]

16[1]p. ports. 20½cm.

USlC

3655a. **Graceland College.** *Annual catalogue of Graceland College.* Lamoni, Iowa, 1895-

v. 21cm.

IaLG, MoInRC

3656a. **Graham, Harry.** *More misrepresentative men. Pictures by Malcolm Strauss.* New York, Fox, Duffield & Company, MCMV.

112p. illus., plates. 17½cm.

"Joseph F. Smith," p. 90-5; satire with a caricature portrait which bears no resemblance.

DLC, MiU, NIC, PU, UPB

3662a. **Grand Army of the Republic.** *Forty-third national encampment.* G.A.R. Salt Lake City, August, 1909.

[22]p. illus. 21½cm.

Historic Mormon sites described.

UPB

3662b. _____. *Forty-third annual G. A. R. national encampment. Salt Lake City, Aug. 9th-14th, 1909. Souvenir book of views. Compiled by Thomas & Lynch.* Salt Lake City, Amos News Company, publishers, 1909.

[52]p. illus. 23cm.

Includes portraits of the First Presidency of Mormon Church, scenes in and around the Temple grounds, and other Mormon buildings.

UHi

3662c. _____. *Salt Lake City, Utah, for the National Encampment of the Grand Army of the Republic in 1900.* [Salt Lake City? 1900]

8p. 23cm.

Mormon references.

USlC

3662d. _____. *Farragut Post.* The G. A. R. and Utah. [n.p.,n.d.]

Broadside. 24 x 14cm.

Resolutions adopted at the last meeting concerning Utah becoming a state and the good work Angie F. Newman is doing to prevent it.

USlC

3662e. *Grand concert.* The inhabitants of Nauvoo and its vicinity, are respectfully informed that a grand concert of vocal and instrumental music, will be held at the Concert Hall, in this city, on Monday, Tuesday, and Wednesday, April 7, 8, & 9, 1845. [Nauvoo, 1845]

Broadside. 60 x 21cm.

Members of the W. Pitt band listed.

USlC

3662f. *Grand Scandinavian jubilee concert in the great Tabernacle,* Salt Lake City, June 14, 1900. [Salt Lake City, 1900]

[4]p. 20cm.

USlC

3665a. **Grant, Heber Jeddy.** *Appalling evils of the liquor traffic shown in statistics from various lands. Address delivered in Tabernacle, Salt Lake City, Sunday, July 30, 1916.* (Reported by F. W. Otterstrom) [Salt Lake City? 1916?]

[8]p. 23½cm.

Mormon references.

USlC

3673a. _____. *My dear brother.* Salt Lake City, 1917.

[4]p. 20cm.

Includes "Oh say what is truth?" on page [2]. A pamphlet on the subject of the Word of Wisdom.

Cover letter to go with copy of Henry Ford's "Little White Slaver." Includes three pages of poems. Dated: December, 1917.

USlC

3676a. _____. *Speaking of the Era, President Grant says:* [Salt Lake City, ca. 1925]

[2]l. 36cm.

Era refers to the *Improvement Era.*

USlC

3680a. _____. *When great sorrows are our portion.* [Salt Lake City, 1912?]

[4]p. 23cm.

Letter to Mr. and Mrs. O. L. Winters of Ogden on the occasion of the death of their young daughter.

Dated: March 21, 1912.

UPB, USlC

3693a. **Graves, A. P.** *Twenty-five letters to a young lady.* 6th ed. Chicago and New York, Fairbanks, Palmer & Co., 1884.

135p. 17½cm.

Mormons mentioned, p. 59.

ICJ, ICRL, NRAB, USlC

3698b. *The great Mormon remedy!* [n.p. 1889?]

Broadsheet. 17 x 10½cm.

On verso: Twin Lakes, Colo. H. T. Koerner, c1889.

A recipe for various Mormon cures.

USlC

3698e. *The Great Salt Lake country.* Denver, The Williamson-Haffner Engraving Company, 1906.

[4]p. [24] leaves of col. plates. 25 x 30cm.

Brief mention of the Mormons.

UHi, UPB

3726a. **Griffiths, Gomer T.** *The doctrine of Christ.* Llanelly, Mecury [n.d.]

4p. 23cm.

MoInRC

3727a. _____. *Griffith's parliamentary chart and key to parliamentary practice.* Sydney, Australia, 1914.

28p. 18cm.

MoInRC

3728a. _____. **comp.** *The instructor; a synopsis of the faith and doctrine of the Reorganized Church of Jesus Christ of Latter Day Saints, together with historical and general evidences from the works of eminent theological writers past and present . . . to which is added memorable events and items of interest connected with the history of the church.* [Lamoni, Iowa, Reorganized Church of Jesus Christ of Latter Day Saints, ca. 1900]

iv, 231p. 19cm.

UPB

3728b. _____. (same) 9th ed. Lamoni, Iowa, Reorganized Church of Jesus Christ of Latter Day Saints, 1904.

iv, 231p. 19cm.

USlC, UPB

3733b. **Grisson, Wilhelm.** *Beitrage zur Charakteristik der Vereinigten Staaten von Nord-Amerika.* Hamberg, Perthes-Besser & Mauke, 1844.

xiip., [1]l., 480p. 21½cm.

Title in English: Contribution to the characteristics of the United States of North America.

Mormonism, p. 370-78.

DLC, MiU, OCl, UPB

3733c. **Griswold, J. comp.** *James' railroad and route book for the western and southern states.* Cincinnati, U. P. James, 1856.

1p.l., xi, [10]-93p. map. 15cm.

Includes the Mormon route from Kanesville, to the city of the Great Salt Lake, Utah.

KyU

3733d. **Groussac, Paul.** *Del Plata al Niagara.* Buenos Aires, Jesus Mendez, 1925.

xxiv, 495 [1]p. 22½cm.

Chapter XI. "Salt Lake City," p. 256-98. Chapter XII. El Mormonismo, p. 282-98.

Title in English: From Plata to Niagara.

DCU, DLC, MoU, PU, UPB

3733e. **Grout, William Wallace.** *Case of Brigham H. Roberts, of Utah. Speech of Hon. William W. Grout, of Vermont, in the House of Representatives, Thursday, January 25, 1900.* Washington, 1900.

13p. 24cm.

Speech concerning Robert's exclusion from Congress.

UPB

3734a. *Die Grundprinzipien des Evangeliums Jesu Christi wie sie von ihm selbst singesetzt wurden.* *Glaube, Buke, Taufe, Spendung des hl. Geistes. Autoritat und Offenbarung.* *Herausgegeben von der Redaktion des "Stern."* Hamburg, Buchdruckerie Schroder & Jeve, 1898.

16p. 18cm. (Traktat Nr. 2)

Title in English: The fundamental principles of the Gospel of Jesus Christ.

USlC

3734b. _____. (same) Bern, Buchdruckerei Steiger & Cie., 1899.

16 [2]p. 18cm.

USlC

3755a. **Gunnison, John Williams.** *The Mormons, or, Latter-day Saints. In the valley of the Great Salt Lake: A history of their rise and progress, peculiar doctrines, present condition, and prospects, derived from personal observation, during a residence among them.* New York, George Munro's [1904?]

xvii, 168, 81p. 18½cm.

In blue printed wrapper.

USlC

3757a. **Gunsolley, J. A.** *Our boys and the public schools.* Lamoni, Iowa, 1893.

12p. 16cm. (Daughters of Zion leaflets, No. 5)

Included as a supplement with a *Saints' Herald* subscription.

MoInRC

H

3768a. **Haddock, John A.** *The growth of a century: As illustrated in the history of Jefferson County, New York, from 1793 to 1894. Comp. from state, county and town records, with many original articles upon interesting subjects.* Philadelphia, Sherman, 1894.

842 (i.e. 920)p. illus., plates, ports., facsims. 23cm.

Mormonism in the town of Adams, p. 386-87, and in Theresa, p. 700-704.

CLU, CtY, ICN, NjP, NN

3770a. **Hadwen, Walter Robert.** *First impressions of America.* London, Hutchinson & Co. [1921]

320p. illus., ports. 22cm.

Chapter 11, "The Mormons." Chapter 12, "Salt Lake City."

DLC, ICU, NN, OrU, UPB, USIC

3778a. **Hahn, F. J.** *Et par ord om Mormonerne. Andet oplag.* Kjøbenhavn, F. E. Bording, 1852.

16p. 22cm.

Title in English: A few words about the Mormons.

USIC

Haigh, Sarahanne. See *Handcart song.*

3793a. **Hall, Edward Hepple.** *The picturesque tourist. A handy guide round the world for the use of all travellers between Europe, America, Australia, India, China, and Japan.* London, Elzevir Press, 1877.

viii, 196, xxviiip. illus., fold maps. 19cm.

Describes towns along the Union Pacific Railroad, with a side trip to Salt Lake City.

CtY, MH, PP, PPl, UPB

3807a. **Hamilton, Thomas.** *Men and manners in America. By the author of Cyril Thornton, etc.* Philadelphia, Carey, Lea & Blanchard, 1833.

vi, 410 [6]p. 23½cm.

Six pages of advertising material at end of the volume.

"History of Mormonism." Passed several parties of Mormons going to join the settlement at Kirtland.

CtY, DLC, MB, NN, PPL, UPB, ViU

3807b. **Hamilton, William Thomas.** *My sixty years on the plains. Trapping, trading, and Indian fighting.* By W. T. Hamilton, edited by E. T. Sieber, with eight full page illustrations by Charles M. Russell. New York, Forest and Stream Publishing Co., 1905.

244p. 21½cm.

Contains various brief references to the Mormons.

CaBVaU, GU, TxU, UPB, UU, WaWW

3809a. **Hanchett, Lafayette.** *Two prayers.* [Salt Lake City, 1923?]

Broadside. 24½cm x 17cm.

From the *Improvement Era,* Vol. 26, no. 11, Sept. 1923, p. 1050.

USlC

3828a. *Hancock Eagle. Hancock Eagle -- Extra.* Nauvoo, Hancock County, October 24, 1846.

Broadside. 46 x 30cm.

Information concerning the status of the regulars for the winter. Includes financial matters. Signed: Almon W. Babbitt, Joseph L. Heywood, John S. Fullmer.

USlC

3829a. *Handcart song. Written from dictation of Sarahanne Miller, nee Haigh, who crossed in Martin and Tyler's company in the year 1856.* [n.p., n.d.]

Broadside. 21 x 18cm.

Davidson attributed authorship to William Hobbs. Hafen attributed authorship to John D. T. McAllister.

USlC

3837a. **Hanks, Nymphus Coridon.** *Up from the hills.* Independence, Missouri, Press of Zion's Printing and Publishing Co. [1921]

57p. 16cm.

UHi

3841a.   **Hanson, Paul M.** *Baptism of the spirit.* Independence, Herald Publishing House [1900?]

1p.l., 67-81p. 19cm.

At head of title: The Angel Message Series. Chapter 5.

Cover title.

UPB, USIC

3849b.   _____. *The true church.* [Sydney, Australia] Reorganized Church of Jesus Christ of Latter Day Saints [ca. 1918]

24p. 20½cm.

Printed by the Standard Publishing House.

NjP

3863a.   **Harris, Albert Wadsworth.** *The cruise of a schooner.* Chicago, Charles Daniel Frey, c1911.

xiv, 265p. illus., photos, map, plates. 20½cm.

Chapter VI, "The Dixie country of Utah," with some mention of the Mormons, including photographs of "Mormon" homes.

C, CtY, DLC, IEN, KyU, UPB, USIC

3869a.   **Harrison, Elias L. T.** *An address to the visitors to conference with extracts from a variety of articles.* [Salt Lake City, ca. 1870]

8p. 31cm.

USIC

3869b.   **Harrison, Elias Lacy Thomas.** *Defense of Mr. Bright and rationalism. A lecture delivered by Mr. E. L. Harrison, at the Walker Opera House, Tuesday evening, Feb. 20, 1883. Being a reply to the strictures of Rev. R. G. McNiece, and other clergymen of Salt Lake City, in reference to Mr. Chas. Bright's position relative to civilation and Christianity.* [Salt Lake City, 1883?]

16p. 21cm.

Mormons and polygamy mentioned.

UPB, USIC

3871a. **Hart, Henry Martyn.** *Recollections and reflections.* [Denver, Smith-Brook Printing Company, 1917].

205p. illus., plates, ports. 21cm.

Brief stop in Salt Lake City and his unsuccessful attempt to see Brigham Young, p. 95.

DLC, OrU, UPB, WHi

3873a. **Hart, William Surrey.** *My life, east and west.* Boston and New York, Houghton Mifflin Company, 1929.

1p.l. [x], 362 [1]p. illus. ports. 22cm.

Suggests the Mormons were in favor of United States participation in World War I.

CU-B, DLC, MH, NN, OCl, UPB, USlC

3891a. **Haven, Jesse.** *An epistle of Elder J. Haven, President of the Cape of Good Hope Mission; to the saints in the Cape of Good Hope, greeting: Beloved brethren:* [Cape Town, W. Foelscher, 1855]

3p. 19cm.

Farewell letter of Elder Haven.

UPB

3891b. _____. *On the first principles of the gospel.* [Cape Town, Van de Sandt de Villiers & Tier, Printers, 1853]

14p. 16½cm.

Formerly *Flake A40*.

UPB, USlC

3892a. _____. *A warning to all.* [Capetown, South Africa, 1853]

Broadsheet. 21 x 12½cm.

Signed: Jesse Haven, William Walker, Leonard I. Smith.

UPB, USlC

3930a. *"He that readeth, let him understand."* [London, Printed by W. Aubrey [1852]

[4]p. 19cm.

Missionary tract.

Formerly *Flake 201*.

USlC

3930b. _____. (same) [London, to be had of Edmund C. Brant. Printed by B. Briscoe [1852?]

[4]p. 19cm.

Variant printing.

CSmH

3935a. *Hear, o ye people! Three lectures will be delivered* . . . [Brimingham, Printed for Elder James Holly, 1896]

Broadside. 40 x 28cm.

Space provided to write in the time and place of each lecture. Handwritten note at the bottom "Printed for Elder James Holly in Birmingham, in 1896 (250 copies)."

USIC

3935b. *Hear the testimony -- then judge ye.* **Mormonism!** *Gen. Bennett, author of the "Mormon Expose," will lecture at the court room.* [n.p., 1843]

Broadside. 40 x 29cm.

Anti-Mormon lecture for gentlemen only.

USIC

3946a. **Hellwald, Friedrich Anton Heller von.** *Die Erde und ihre Volker. Ein geographisches hausbuch von Friedrich von Hellwald. Funfte Auflage Neu bearbeitet von Ernst Waechter.* Stuttgart, Berlin, Leipzig, Union Deutsche Verlagsgesellschaft [1906?]

2v. illus., col. map. 24cm.

Title in English: The earth and its people.

His trip through Utah, v. 2, p. 126-32.

DLC, UPB

3948a. *Help! Twelve men met in solemn conclave in Salt Lake City.* [Salt Lake City, Salt Lake Tribune] 1905.

Broadside. 28 x 15cm.

How the gentiles of Salt Lake City help assist the Committee on Privileges and Elections in its hearings on Reed Smoot.

UPB

3953a. **Henderson, Alice Palmer.** *The ninety-first; the first at Camp Lewis.* Tacoma, Washington, John C. Barr [c1918]

5p.l., 510p. illus., ports. 24cm.

Description of Mormon members on p. 145, 446-49.

DLC, MB, OrCS, UPB, WaT

3956a. **Henrichsen, Erick Christian.** *Afskrift. Til Bergens politimester!* [Bergen, Norway, 1904]

[4]p. 22cm.

Title in English: Transcript. Letter to Bergen's chief of police.

Letter dated Bergen, Norway, July 6, 1904, written by Bergen Conference President explaining church beliefs. Articles of Faith, p. [4].

USIC

3956b. _____. *Det første store drama (syndefaldet). Bergen, den 7 Februar 1905.* [Bergen, 1905]

[6]p. 22cm.

Title in English: The first grand drama (the fall of man).

USIC

3956c. _____. *Missionaer-sang. Bergen, den juli 1905.* [Bergen, John Griegs Bogtrykkeri, 1905]

[3]p. 23½cm.

Title in English: Missionary hymn.

USIC

3956d. _____. *Tre digte. Bergen, den 8 mai 1905.* [Bergen, Griegs Bogtrykkeri, 1905]

[7]p. 22½cm.

Title in English: Three poems.

USIC

3957a. *Henry S. Tanner, president of the California "Mormon" Mission from Salt Lake City.* [San Diego, Hildreth Printing House, 1895]

Broadside. 22 x 15cm.

Title of his addresses, "The organization of the Kingdom of God" and "The cause of the pecularities of Mormonism."

USIC

3961a.   **Herald House.** *Herald Publishing House and Bookbindery, catalogue and price list of publications and books.* Lamoni, Iowa [1895]

27p. 15cm.

A descriptive catalogue was available as early as 1894. Ensign Publishing House also published a catalogue.

USlC

3961b.   _____. (same) Lamoni, Iowa [1900]

27p. 15cm.

MoInRC

3975a.   **Heydenfeldt, Solomon, Jr.** *Danger to your wives and daughters -- theosophy and demonology -- the mysteries of satanism -- unison of the conscious force.* Washington, Geo. R. Fray, Printer, Globe Office. [189-]

Broadside. 43 x 34cm.

Brief mention of Mormon fanaticism.

DLC, DNLM, USlC

3976a.   **Heywood, A. R.** *Joseph P. Ledwidge, as County Clerk and clerk of the Probate Court of Weber County, Utah, plaintiff and respondent, vs. George H. Matson, as County Registration Officer of Weber County, Utah, and F. L. Chapin, O. P. Herriman, George L. Corey, Jr., A. I. Stone, and H. M. Durbrow, as Deputy Registrars. Defendants and Appellants. A. R. Heywood, and John E. Bagley, attorneys for defendants and appellants.* Ogden, Acme Printing Co. [1893]

10p. illus. 22cm.

Election of probate judges under the Edmunds act and the Utah Commission.

Fales/Flake 1127.

UAr

3991a.   **Hicks, Geo. A.** *Celestial mrriage [sic] A drama. In five acts. A domestic tragedy, designed for the stage.* [Clinton, Utah?, 1886]

Broadside. 19½ x 14cm.

Publicity for his play.

UPB

3994a.   **Higgins, Charles A.** *To California and back. Illustrations by J. T. McCutcheon.* Chicago, Passenger Department, Santa Fe Route, 1893.

151p. illus., map. 21cm.

Visits Salt Lake City; gives a digest of Mormon beliefs.

CU, DLC, MoU, OO, UPB

3998a. **Hill, Laurence L.** *La Reina; Los Angeles in three centuries.* *A volume commemorating the fortieth anniversary of the founding of the Security Trust & Savings Bank of Los Angeles, February 11, 1889.* [Los Angeles] Security-First National Bank, c1929.

208p. 23cm.

"The Mormons and the first Fourth of July," p. 41.

DLC, MB, NjP, USIC, ViU, WaU

4010a. **Hinckley, Alonzo Arza.** *The Church and its divine mission.* [Salt Lake City, Deseret News, 1928]

Broadside. 57 x 21cm.

Reprint from the *Deseret News* of August 11, 1928.

Radio address given on KSL radio, Salt Lake City, August 5, 1928.

USIC

4010b. **Hinckley, Bryant Stringham.** *Some distinctive features of Mormonism . . .* [Chicago, Bryant S. Hinckley, n.d.]

Broadsheet. 10 x 7cm.

On verso: "A series of cards presenting facts of vital importance to all people." Issued when the author was president of the Northern States Mission.

USIC

4013a. **Hinds, Peter M.** *Lamoni illustrated.* Lamoni, Iowa, 1892.

29p. illus. 16cm.

Includes a history of Lamoni, and a description of the town.

MoInRC

4020a. **Hirschberg, Julius.** *Meine dritte Amerika-fahrt.* Berlin, Urban & Schwarzenberg [1905?]

54p. 25½cm.

Title in English: My third American trip.

Sondersbdruck aus der "Medizinischen Klinik" 1905, Nr. 42, 43, 45, u. 46.

Mormons mentioned, p. 37.

USIC

4020b. _____. *Von New York nach San Francisco. Tagebuchblatter. Von J. Hirschberg M. D.* Leipzig, Verlag von Veit & Comp., 1888.

viii, 276p. 21½cm.

Title in English: From New York to San Francisco.

Made the trip in 1887. Describes Utah and the history of Mormonism, p. 215-45. UPB copy has remnants of a black wrapper.

CtY, DLC, ICN, NcD, NjP, NN, UPB

4020c. *Historical biography of the United States, classified. Containing all the historical, noted events, and interesting incidents connected with the settlement of the United States since its first discovery, up to the present time. Classified and arranged under appropriate headings.* New York and Philadelphia, Keystone Publishing Company, c1885.

403p. 23½cm.

Advertisements interspersed throughout. "Mormonism," etc., p. 81.

UPB

4022a. **The History Company.** *History of Utah.* [San Francisco? 1889?]

[4]p. 22cm.

Advertisement for H. H. Bancroft's *History of Utah* with James Dwyer as the local agent.

USlC

4023. *The history of Adams County, Illinois. Containing a history of the county -- its cities, towns, etc. A biographical directory of its citizens, war record of its volunteers in the late rebellion; general and local statistics. Portraits of early settlers and prominent men. History of the northwest, history of Illinois, map of Adams County, constitution fo the United States, miscellaneous matters, etc. Illustrated.* Chicago, Murray, Williamson & Phelps, 1879.

xii, [7]-822p. illus., ports, fold. col. map. 24cm.

The "Mormon war," p. 104-118.

DLC, ICN, MB, NN, OCl, OClWhi, UPB

4031a. *History of Howard and Chariton counties, Missouri, written and compiled from the most official, authentic and private sources, including a history of its townships, towns and villages. Together with a condensed history of Missouri; a reliable and detailed history of Howard and Chariton Counties -- its pioneer record, resources, biographical sketches of Great value; incidents and reminiscences. Illustrated.* St. Louis, National Historical Company, 1883.

ix, 1224p. illus., ports. 28½cm.

"Mormon difficulties," p. 54-57.

C-S, ICN, TxU, UPB

4031b. _____. (same) St. Louis, National Historical Company, 1883.

xi, 1224p. illus., ports. 26½cm.

"Mormon difficulties," p. 54-57.

Publisher's dummy.

In gray printed wrapper with advertisements and recommendations printed on both inside covers, on verso of back cover, and on final page.

UPB

4053a. **Hittell, Theodore Henry.** *The adventures of James Capen Adams, Mountaineer and Grizzly Bear hunter, of California. Illustrated.* Boston, Crosby, Nichols, Lee and Company, 1860.

vi [1] [9] 378p. illus., plates, port. 19½cm.

Chapter XI, visits the Rocky Mountians, spends the Fourth of July in Salt Lake City; material on the Mormons.

CSmH, CtY, DLC, MiU, UPB, UU

Hobbs, William. See *Handcart song.*

4056c. **Hoge, E. D.** *Sarah A. Chapman, et al., appellants, vs. Elizabeth Handley, respondent. Respondent's brief. E. D. Hage, Arthur Brown, attorneys for respondent.* [Washington? 1893?]

14p. 22cm.

Record case no. 14,191. Supreme Court of the United States.

Sarah A. Chapman was the polygmous wife of George Handley.

DLC

4056d. **Hoge & Burmester.** *In the matter of the estate of George Handley, deceased. Sarah A. Chapman, et al., appellants, vs. Elizabeth handley, et al., respondents. Brief of respondents.* Hoge & Burmester, Arthur Brown, attorneys for respondents. [Salt Lake City? 1890?]

8p. 22cm.

At head of title: In the Supreme Court of the Territory of Utah.

Cover title.

A polygamy inheritance trial.

UAr

4056e. **Holbrook, Alfred.** *Reminiscences of the happy life of a teacher.* Cincinnati, Elm Street Printing Company, 1885.

2p.l., v-vi, [7]-362p. 19½cm.

Mormons in Ohio during his residence there in 1837, p. 222-26.

DLC, FU, ICN, OC, OClWHi, UHi, UPB, USlC

4056g. **Hole, James.** *Letter from Mr. James Hole, to Mr. Samuel Bradfield, on the false and wicked teaching of the Latter-day imposture, by Joseph Smith, the false prophet.* [n.p.] 1886.

Broadside. 20 x 12cm.

Dated 27th, 1886.

USlC

4059a. **Holley, James.** *Hear, O ye people.* [Birmingham, 1896]

Broadside. 40 x 28cm.

Announcement of lectures on three subjects dealing with the Church. Provides a place to write in the time and place of the lectures.

USlC

4076a. *The home library of knowledge "Multum in parvo."* *More than sixteen thousand subjects, with cross references, over two thousand illustrations. Maps charts and gazetteer.* Editor-in-chief Paul I. Neergaard. Kansas City, Mutual Publishing Company, 1924.

2v. illus (part col.), maps. 28cm.

V. 2, "Mormons."

Includes information under Brigham Young and Joseph Smith.

UPB

4088a. **Hord's Cambrian Theatre, Merthyr.** *Mormon's daughter! or, The mysteries of Salt Lake.* Neath [Wales] Wm. Harry Rees, 1869.

Broadside. 74 x 25cm.

Advertisement for an anti-Mormon play. Dated Dec. 8, 1869.

USlC

4099a. **Houston, Samuel.** *Speeches of Sam Houston, of Texas, on the subject of an increase of the army, and the Indian policy of the government, delivered in the Senate of the United States, January 29 and 31, 1855.* Washington, Printed at the Congressional Globe Office, 1855.

20p. 22½cm.

Brief mention of the Mormon cow incident near Fort Laramie.

CtY, DLC, TxU, UPB

4110. **Howe, Henry.** *Historical collections of the great West: Containing narratives of the most important and interesting events in western history -- remarkable individual adventures -- sketches of frontier life -- descriptions of natural curiosities: To which is appended historical and descriptive sketches of Oregon, New Mexico, Texas, Minnesota, Utah and California. Illustrated with numerous engravings.* Cincinnati, Henry Howe, 1851.

2v. in 1. illus., plates (part col.), map. 24cm.

"Utah," p. 417-34. Includes early history of Mormonism as well as its development.

Paged continuously.

Other editions: 1852, 1853, 1855, 1857, 1858, 1872.

DLC, MB, NjP, OCl, OClWHi, OFH, UPB

4112a. **Howells, William.** *L'Evangile.* Merthyr Tydfil, printed by John Davis, Georgetown [1849]

2p. 17cm.

Title in English: The gospel.

Dennis 29.

USlC

4128a. **Hughes, Thomas.** *Darlithiau ar dwyll Mormoniaeth. Darlith I. Ar dwyll dechreuad Mormoniaeth: a draddodwyd yn Neuadd Tref Rhuthyn, Medi 3ydd, 1852.* Rhuthyn, I. Clarke [1852?]

16p. 15cm.

Title in English: Lectures on the deceit of Mormonism. Lecture I.

WalCS

4128b. _____. (same) *Darlith II. Ar Farn y Saint am Dduw, Angylion, ac Enaid Dyn. A draddodwyd yn Neuadd Tref Rhuthin, Chwefror 25ain, 1853.* Rhuthyn, I. Clarke, [1853?]

16p. 16cm.

Title in English: Lectures on the deceit of Mormonism. Lecture II.

Mormonism's opinion of God, etc.

WalCS

4131a. **Hulot, Etienne Gabriel Joseph.** *De l'Atlantique au Pacifique a travers le Canada et le nord des Etats-Unis.* Paris, E. Plon, Nourrit et C., 1888.

3p.l., 339p. 2 fold. maps. 19cm.

Title in English: From the Atlantic to the Pacific across Canada and the northern United States.

Mormons mentioned, p. 332-33.

DLC, USlC

4135a. **Hunt, Charles J.** *A brief history and financial summary of the Gallands Grove, Iowa, District from 1859 to 1912.* Dow City, Iowa, Enterprise Print, 1912.

Unpaged. illus. 19cm. (Circular No. 8)

MoInRC

4141a. **Hunt, Elvid.** *History of Fort Leavenworth, 1827-1927. With a preface by Brigadier General Edward L. King.* Fort Leavenworth, Kansas, The General Service Bookstore, 1926.

6p.l., 286p. illus., plates (1 fold.), maps (1 fold.) 24cm.

Mormons mentioned p. 78, 82, 115-16.

CU, DLC, MH, NjP, TxU, UPB, WaU

4148a. **Huntsman, Sara.** *Book of the words. A historical pageant of the Utah Agricultural College. Written and directed by Miss Sara Huntsman. Presented on the College campus, June 5, 1915.* [Logan, 1915]

48p. 22cm.

Begins with the sowing of the grain by Orson Pratt and Brigham Young.

UHi, UPB

4150a. **Hurtado, Evaristo.** *A new and wonderful revelation to mankind. By Rev. Evaristo Hurtado.* Boston, 1907.

104p. 17½cm.

Cover title: Good for everybody; it reveals the truth.

Mormons mentioned, p. 57, 60, 73, 100-101.

MH, USIC

4169a. **Hyde, Orson.** *A sketch of the travels and ministry of Elder Orson Hyde, Missionary of the Church of Jesus Christ of Latter-day Saints, to Germany, Constantinople and Jerusalem, containing a description of Mount Zion, the Pool of Siloam and other ancient places, and some account of the manners and customs of east, as illustrative of scripture texts, with a sketch of several interviews and conversations with Jews, missionaries, etc., with a variety of information on the present state of that and other countries, with regard to coming events and the restoration of Israel. Compiled from his late letters and documents, the last of which bears date at Bavaria, on the Danube, Jan. 18, 1842.* Salt Lake City, Printed at the Deseret News Office, 1869.

24p. 21cm.

MH, NjP, UPB, USIC

4177a. *Hymns to be sung at the dedication of the Masonic Temple; April 5, 1844.* [Nauvoo, 1844]

Broadside. 23 x 17cm.

Hymns: The hod carrier's song. The entered 'prentices' song. Glee. For the anniversary of St. John.

USIC

4177b. *Hyrum Ricks & Company, Rexburg, Idaho, Real Estate Loans and Insurance.* [Rexburg, Idaho, ca. 1910]

[20]p. illus. 22½ x 19cm.

Photo of Rexburg 3rd Ward meeting house, p. [18]

USIC

I

4179a. **Idaho. Governor, 1880-1883 (Neil).** *Biennial message of John B. Neil, Governor of Idaho, to the Eleventh Session of the Legislature of Idaho Territory.* Boise City, Idaho, Printed at the Statesman Office. 1880.

19p. 21cm.

Cover title; title within lined border.

"Polygamy," p. 16-18.

IdHi, UPB

4179b. **Idaho. Governor, 1880-1883 (Neil).** *Second biennial message of John B. Neil, Governor, to the twelfth session of the Legislative Assembly of Idaho Territory.* Boise City, Printed by Milton Kelly, 1882.

24p. 21cm.

Cover title.

In gray printed wrapper; title within a border.

"Polygamy," p. 20-23.

IdU, UPB, USIC

4180a. **Idaho. Governor, 1884-1885 (Bunn).** *Biennial message of William M. Bunn, Governor of Idaho to the thirteenth session of the Legislative Assembly of Idaho Territory.* Boise City, Milton Kelly, Printer, 1884.

22p. 20cm.

Cover title.

In blue printed wrapper.

"Polygamous and treasonous Mormonism," p. 21-22.

IdU, UPB

4180b. **Idaho. Governor, 1885-1889 (Stevenson).** *Biennial message of Edward A. Stevenson, Governor of Idaho, to the fourteenth session of the Legislature of Idaho Territory.* Boise City, 1886.

21p. 22cm.

Cover title.

In printed wrapper.

"The Mormon question," p. 20-21.

IdU, USIC

4180c. _____. *Biennial message of Edward A. Stevenson, Governor of Idaho to the fifteenth session of the Legislature of Idaho Territory, 1888-1889.* Boise City, Statesman Print. [1888]

32p. 22cm.

Cover title.

In printed wrapper.

"The Mormon question," p. 17.

IdU

4180d. _____. *Report of the governor of Idaho to the Secretary of the Interior. 1886.* Washington, Govt. Print. Off., 1886.

22p. 24cm.

"The Mormon question," p. 18.

UPB

4180e. _____. *Report of the governor of Idaho to the Secretary of the Interior. 1887.* Washington, Govt. Print. Off., 1887.

53p. 24cm.

Includes material on the Mormons and the test oath, under "Mormon counties," p. 32-33.

UPB

4180f. _____. *Report of the Governor of Idaho to the Secretary of the Interior. 1888.* Washington, Govt. Print. Off., 1888.

68p. 23cm.

Mormons, p. 13-14, 22-23.

UPB

4181a. **Idaho. Governor. 1889 (Shoup).** *Governor's message to the first legislature of the State of Idaho.* [Boise City, Idaho, 1890]

24p. 22cm.

Mormons mentioned, p. 3.

UPB

4181b. **Idaho Home Missions Council.** *Report of the Every-Community survey of southern Idaho conducted under the auspices of The Idaho Home Missions Council and The National Home Missions Council, June 10-19, 1923. Report edited and published by the president and secretary of the Council by order of the Executive Committee.* [Boise, Idaho? 1923]

26p. tables, map. 23cm.

Mormon statistics.

USlC

4183a. **Ide, Simeon.** *A biographical sketch of the life of William B. Ide: With a minute and interesting account of one of the largest emigrating companies. (3000 miles over land), from the East to the Pacific Coast. And what is claimed as the most authentic and reliable account of "the virtual conquest of California, in June, 1846, by the Bear Flag Party," as given by its leader, The late Hon. William Brown Ide.* [Claremont, N. H., 1880]

2p.l., [3]-25, 239 [1]p. 17cm.

During the wait at the garrison, Ide is accused of being a Mormon with intentions of turning the land over to them. p. 161-64.

CtY, CU-B, DLC, MB, NjP, UPB, USlC

4199a. **Illinois. Governor, 1842-1846 (Ford).** *Proclamation by the Governor ... Executive Department, Springfield, Illinois, September 20, 1845.* [Springfield, 1845]

Broadside. 45½ x 32cm.

One of the proclamations on the state of supposed Mormon insurrection in Adams and Hancock counties.

IHi

4210a. *Important from the Great Salt Lake. Progress of the Mormon settlement, From the New York "Weekly Herald," of Oct. 13, 1849.* Woolwich, Printed by John Grant, Woolwich, for Thomas Bradshaw, Elder, Carlton Vale [ca. 1850]

Broadside. 48 x 37½cm.

Printed after Oct. 1849, probably in 1850 or 1851.

UPB

4210b. *Important to all.* [Landport?] Printed by Toynton, Steam Printer [n.p.]

Broadside. 19 x 12cm.

Announcement of preaching by Elders of the Church of Jesus Christ of Latter-day Saints from Salt Lake City, Utah, U.S., North America. Includes space to write in the time and place of meeting.

USlC

4210c. *Important. To whom this may concern.* [Independence? 1927?]

Broadside. 21 x 11cm.

A challenge for Fred M. Smith of the Reorganized Church of Jesus Christ of Latter Day Saints to debate the Strang claim of being the true successor to Joseph Smith.

UPB

4213a. *In consequence of the sickness of President Brigham Young.* [Salt Lake City, ca. 1887]

Broadside. 36 x 29cm.

Listing of meetings held and not held by the general authorities from 1877 to 1887.

UPB, USIC

4217a. *In memoriam. George A. Blakeslee. September 20, 1890.* [n.p., n.d.]

Unpaged. 21cm.

Blakeslee was the Presiding Bishop of the RLDS church at the time of his death.

MoInRC

4219a. *In memoriam; President Anthon H. Lund.* [Salt Lake City, 1924]

[4]p. illus. 21cm.

"Program to be rendered at the unveiling of President Anthon H. Lund's monument, Sunday, August 17, 1924."

USIC

4232a. *Indbydelse til Guds Rige. Kollun til Guthsrikis.* [Kanpamannahofn, Utgifith og upplagt af N. C. Flygare, Prentath hja F. E. Bording, 1876]

8p. 21cm.

Title in English: Invitation to the kingdom of God.

UPB

4237a. *Independence, Missouri, an illustrated description; its schools, churches, residences, improvements, etc.: including a complete descriptive history of the Latter Day Saints Church in Independence and many of its members.* [n.p., ca. 1902]

85p. illus. 28cm.

MoInRC

4248a.   **Ingersoll, Robert Green.** *Mistakes of Moses.* [Chicago, Baldwin's Book Store, 187-?]

14p. 22cm.

Mormons, p. 10.

DLC, ICN, IHi, USIC

4255a.   **Installation, Nauvoo Lodge.** Nauvoo, Printed at the office of the *Times and Seasons* [1842]

Broadside. 40 x 28cm.

Mormons and Masonry in Nauvoo.

USIC

4258a.   **Interdenominational Council of Women.** *Plan of campaign for the anti-polygamy constitutional amendment.* New York [1900]

[4]p. 16cm.

NNUT

4259a.   _____. *Results of the anti-polygamy crusade.* New York [1900?]

[4]p. 16cm.

NNUT

4272a.   *Iowa contested election case. Evidence taken in the Iowa contested election case, and referred to the Committee on Elections.* Washington, Wm. M. Belt, 1850.

122p. 23cm. (U. S. 31st Cong. 1st Sess. House Misc. Doc. No. 48).

Includes Mormon activity during the election events.

UPB

4275a.   **Ironside, Henry Allen.** *The Mormon's mistake; or, what is the gospel?* New York, Loizeaux Brothers, Publishers [n.d.]

[16]p. 16½cm.

"Printed at the Bible Proof Press . . ."

Book price list on the verso of the final leaf.

UPB

4295a. **Ivins, Virginia (Wilcox).** *Pen pictures of early Western days. Illustrations by Wm. S. Ivins.* [Keokuk, Iowa] c1905.

160p. 22½cm.

She was a niece of Isaac Galland who accompanied her party overland via Salt Lake City in 1853.

DLC, ICN, KU, NjP, UPB, UU

J

4304a. **Jackson, Thomas.** *The Book of Mormon weighed in the balances of the scriptures, and found wanting. A lecture delivered at Coalville, December 25, 1844.* Leicester, Printed for the author, by T. Cook, 1845.

28p. 22cm.

UPB

4315a. **James, Jason W.** *Memorial events in the life of Captain Jason W. James.* [Roswell, N.M., 1911]

150p. port. 19cm.

Hauled freight to Camp Floyd in 1858; recounts the Mountain Meadows massacre.

CtY, TxU, UPB

4316a. **James, Uriah Pierson.** *James' River guide containing descriptions of all the cities, towns, and principal objects of interest, on the navigable waters of the Mississippi Valley flowing west from the Alleghany Mountains, east from the Rocky Mountains, and south from near the northern lakes, including the rivers of Alabama and Texas, flowing into the Gulf of Mexico: also, an account of the sources of the rivers; with full tables of distances, and many interesting historical sketches of the country, statistics of population products, commerce, manufactures, mineral resources scenery, &c. &c. Illustrated with forty-four maps, and a number of engravings.* Cincinnati, Published by U. P. James, 1863.

128p. illus., maps. 23cm.

"Nauvoo," p. 17-18.

In green printed wrapper.

UPB

4318a. **James O. Wright & Co.** *Just published, the Mormon Bible . . .* [New York City, 1858]

Broadside. 26 x 20cm.

Advertisement of a reprint of the third edition of the Book of Mormon. Publishers state that it was re-issued because the Mormon leaders were suppressing that edition. Holograph note on broadside indicates that this copy was sent by J. M. Bernhisel to President Brigham Young. Broadside is torn and lower left corner is missing.

USIC

4325a. **Jaques, John.** *Catechism for children, exhibiting the prominent doctrines of the Church of Jesus Christ of Latter-day Saints.* Liverpool, Printed and Published by Horace S. Eldridge [1870]

iv, [5]-81p. 17cm.

"Seventeenth thousand."

UPB

4354a. **Jaques, Mary J.** *Texas ranch life: With three months through Mexico in a "Prairie schooner."* London, H. Cox, 1894.

ix, [1]l., 353p. illus., plates. 25cm.

Stop in Salt Lake City, with a brief description of the temple, etc.

CU-B, DLC, ICJ, NjP, UPB

4360a. **Jarman, William.** *Mormonism and exhibition of Mormon life.* [Boston, 1881?]

Broadside. 74 x 19cm.

An illustrated lecture with many sub-titles such as "American polygamy," and "The washing and anointing in the Endowment House." Broadside indicates place of lecture as Town Hall -- Westford, Friday eve., July 22. Verso includes testimonies dated 1880 and 1881.

USIC

4362a. _____. *The Mountain Meadow massacre, and the confession and execution of the Mormon Bishop John D. Lee. 120 men, women, and children murdered by the Utah "Latter-day Saints."* [Leicester, England, n.d.]

8p. 19½cm.

At head of title: Anti-Mormon works, by W. Jarman, ex-Mormon priest, from Salt Lake City.

UPB

4363a. _____. *U.S.A. Uncle Sam's abscess, or Hell upon earth for U.S. Uncle Sam. By W. Jarman, esq., K.G.L., T.C.K., Knight of the Grand Legion of North America, who suffered twelve years in the Mormon Hell on earth, as one of the "Virgins without guile," and a priest after the order of Melchizedek: Where polygamy, incest, under the Lord."* Exeter, England. Printed at H. Leduc's Steam Printing Works, 1884.

34p. 20cm.

UPB

4376a. **Jefferies, William.** *The gospel pioneer. By Wm. Jefferies, an Elder of the Church of Jesus Christ of Latter-day Saints.* [Salt Lake City, Juvenile Instructor Office, 1890?]

23 [1]p. 18½cm.

UPB

4382a. **Jensen, Nephi.** *Jimin no tokucho.* [Tokyo] Matsu Jitsu Seito Iesu Kirisuto Kyokai [1920]

7p. 15½cm.

Title in English: Characteristics of the citizens of God.

USIC

John the Baptist has come, as Christ said he would. See Fetting, Otto. Twenty-second message and Twenty-third message.

4432a. **Johnson, Clifton.** *What to see in America . . . with five hundred illustrations.* New York, The Macmillan Company, 1919.

xv [1] 541 [4] p. illus., plates, maps. 19½cm.

[4] pages of advertisements.

Chapter 43. Utah, with references to the Mormons.

DLC, MH, NN, UHi

4442. **Johnson, Joseph.** *The great Mormon fraud; or, the Church of Latter-day Saints proved to have had a falsehood for its origin; A record of crime for its history; And for its doctrines: curelty, absurdity, and infamy. The detestable and immoral system of polygamy exposed, and the horrible Mormon doctrine of "blood atonement" explained.* Manchester, Butterworth & Nodal, Printers, 1885.

31 [1]p. 18½cm.

DLC, NN, UPB, USIC

4457a. **Jones, Dan.** *Ai duw a ddanfonodd Joseph Smith?* [Abertawy, argraffwyd a chyhoeddwyd gan D. Jones, 1855]

16p. 18cm.

Title in English: Was it God who sent Joseph Smith?

Formerly *Flake A41. Dennis 89.*

MH, USIC, WalN, WalS

4457b. _____. *Ai dwyfol oedd cenadwri Joseph Smith?* [Abertawy, argraffwyd a chyhoeddwyd gan D. Jones, 1855]

16p. 18cm.

Title in English: Was Joseph Smith's mission divine?

Identical, with the exception of the title only, to *Flake/Draper Supplement 4457a.*

Dennis 89.

MH, USlC, WalN

4457c. _____. *Amddiffyniad y Saint; sef, gwrth-brofion o gam-gyhuddiadau maleis-ddrwg dyn o'r enw Rees Davies, o New Orleans, yn erbyn y Saint.* Swansea, D. Jones [1854?]

12p. 17½cm.

Title in English: Defense of the Saints. Refutation of claims made by Rees Davis against the Mormons sailing from Wales to New Orleans.

Formerly *Flake 9879. Dennis 80.*

CSmH, UPB, USl, USlC, UU

4463a. _____. *Atebydd y gwrthddadleuon a ddygir yn fwyaf cyffredinol drwy y wyad yn erbyn Saint y Dyddiau Diweddaf, a'r athrawiaeth a broffesant; mewn ffurf o ymddyddan, er symud y rhwystrau oddiar ffordd y Cymry ymofyngar, heb "anmhwyllo ynghylch cwestiynau, ac ymryson ynghylch geiriau, o'r rhai y mae cenfigen, ymryson, cableddau, a drwg dybiau yn dyfod; ac na ddaliont ar chwedlau ac achau anorphen, y rhai sydd yn peri cwestiynau, yn hytrach nag adeiladaeth dduwiol, yr hon sydd trwy ffydd: gwnaed [pawb] felly." Gan. Capt. D. Jones.* Merthyr-Tydfil, Cyhoeddwyd ac ar werth gan yr awdwr [1847]

24p. 19cm.

Cover title.

Title in English: A conversational rebuttal to the anti-Mormon arguments prevalent throughout the country.

Formerly *Flake A42. Dennis 3.*

CSmH, UPB, USlC, WalCS, WalN

4463b. _____. *Beth ydyw yr efengyl?* Rhydybont, John Jones [1846?]

8p. 17cm.

Title in English: What is the Gospel?

Dennis 10.

UPB

4467a. _____. *Dadl rhwng Bedyddiwr ac anffyddiwr.* Merthyr Tydfil, D. Jones [1854]

16p. 17½cm.

Title in English: A debate between a Baptist and an atheist.

Translation of an article published by Orson Hyde in the *Millennial Star,* v. 12, p. 4-9. The Bible teachings ignored by the Baptists are central to Mormonism.

Dennis 76.

USIC

4467b. _____. *Dammeg y pren a ddwg naw math o ffrwythau!* [Abertawy, argraffwyd a chyhoeddwyd gan D. Jones, ca. 1855]

4p. 18cm.

Title in English: The parable of the tree that brought forth nine different kinds of fruits.

Formerly *Flake A43. Dennis 93.*

UPB, USIC, WalN, WalS

4467c. _____. *Darlun o'r byd crefyddol.* [Abertawy, cyhoeddwyd ac argraffwyd gan D. Jones, ca. 1855]

4p. 18cm.

Title in English: A picture of the religious world.

Formerly *Flake A44. Dennis 94.*

MH, USIC, WalN, WalS

4477a. _____. *Llyfr Mormon, ei darddiad.* [Abertawy, argraffwyd a chyhoeddwyd gan D. Jones, ca. 1855]

12p. 18cm.

At head of title: [Traethawd Iaf. [sic]

Title in English: The Book of Mormon, its Origin. [First treatise]

Formerly *Flake A45. Dennis 95.*

MH, UPB, USIC, WalN

4477b. _____. *Llyfr Mormon, ei darddiad. Gweinidogaeth angylaidd bresennol yn rhesymol ac ysgrythyrol.* [Abertawy, Cyhoeddwyd ac argraffwyd gan D. Jones, ca. 1855]

12p. 18cm.

At head of title: [Traethawd 2il. [sic]

Title in English: The Book of Mormon, its Origin. [Second treatise]

Formerly *Flake A46. Dennis 96.*

MH, USlC, WalN

4478a. _____. *"Peidiwch a'u gwrando."* [Aertawy, argraffwyd a chyhoeddwyd gan D. Jones, 1854]

8p. 18cm.

Title in English: Do not listen to them.

Formerly *Flake 6224. Dennis 82.*

CSmH, UPB, USl, USlC, UU, WalCC, WalN

4478b. _____. *Profion o eirwiredd Llyfr Mormon.* [Rhydybont, John Jones, 1847?]

12p. 17½cm.

Title in English: Proofs of the truthfulness of the Book of Mormon.

Dennis 15.

WalN

4483a. **Jones, Daniel.** *Y drych cywir, lle y gellir canfod yn eglur twyll y Mormoniaid, neu "Seintiau y Dyddiau Diweddaf" mewn dull o holiodau ac atebion, rhwng Daniel a'i gyfaill.* Gan Daniel Jones . . . Caerfyrddin, argraffwyd gan J. T. Jones, Heol Las., 1847.

12p. 18½cm.

Title in English: The true mirror.

Deceit of the Mormons.

"Haman" hanging from his own gallows! *Flake 4474*, is a response to this item.

WalN

4483b. _____. (same) Llanymddyfri, argraffwyd gan E. Morris, Heol-y-Brenin, MDCCCXLVIII.

12p. 18cm.

Title in English: The true mirror.

In private possession.

4484a. **Jones, Daniel Webster.** *To those interested in the Mexican Mission.* Salt Lake City, 1886.

Broadside. 27 x 21cm.

Concerning sale of land in Chiluahua for settling.

USIC

4484b. **Jones, Dewi Elfed.** *Annerchiad ar ymadawiad W. S. Phillips a J. Davis, ynghyd a lliaws o'r Saint, i dir Seion.* Gan Dewi Elfed Jones, Llanelli. Llanelli, John Thomas [1854?]

4p. 23cm.

Title in English: Greeting on the departure of W. S. Phillips and J. Davis, together with a host of the Saints, to the land of Zion.

Dewi Elfed Jones is a pseudonym for David Bevan Jones.

A song.

Dennis 74.

MH

4485a. **Jones, Henry M.** *His final admonition.* [Salt Lake City? 1918?]

Broadside. port. 38 x 33cm.

Dated: Somewhere in France, July 14, 1918.

Letter concerning his religious feeling and about the war.

USIC

4485b. **Jones, Hugh.** *Dirgelion Saint Y Dyddiau Diweddaf, yn cael eu dinoethi.* Caernarfon, argraffwyd gan Thomas Jones Evans, 1852.

24p. 15cm.

Title in English: Mysteries of the Latter-day Saints exposed.

Claims to have been a teacher with the Mormons for two years.

WalCS

4493a. **Jones, Noah R.** *Cwyn yr ymfudwr, a'i ddau anerchiad.* Merthyr Tydfil, Printed by John Davis, Georgetown [1849?]

4p. 18cm.

Title in English: Lament of the emigrant, and his two greetings.

Dennis 33.

CSmH

4496a. **Jones, Robert Webster.** *Light interviews with shades.* Philadelphia, Dorrance [c1922]

151p. 20cm.

"The author . . . has endeavored to give the logical views of famous historical characters on strictly modern questions." Chapter VI, "Brigham Young endorses woman suffrage," p. 50-55.

DLC, UPB

4498a. **Jones, Thomas.** *Traethodau ar ail-ddyfodiad Crist, yr adgyfodiad, a'r mil blynyddau.* Llanelli, Cyhoeddwyd ac ar Werth gan Thomas Jones, 1853.

12p. 17½cm.

Title in English: Treatises on the second coming of Christ, the resurrection, and the thousand years.

Dennis 72.

WalN

4498b. _____. *Traethodau ar y doniau gwyrthiol, a'r mil blynyddoedd, etc.* Llanelli, Cyhoeddwyd ac ar werth gan Thomas Jones, 1853.

12p. 17½cm.

Title in English: Treatises on the spiritual gift, and the thousand years, etc.

Formerly *Flake A47. Dennis 73.*

WalN

4498c. **Jones, Thomas Rees.** *The Seventy. Dedicated to the Seventy.* [n.p., 189-?]

Broadside. 26 x 13cm.

Poetry.

USlC

4498d. **Jones, William.** *Egwyddorion Saint y Dyddiau Diweddaf yn cael eu pwyso yn nglorianau rhesymau ac ysgrythyrau, gan William Jones, Bethesda . . . .* Bethesda, argraffwyd tros yr awdwr, gan R. Jones, 1851.

24p. 16cm.

Title in English: Principles of the Latter-day Saints weighed in the scales of logic and scriptures.

UPB

4502a. *Joseph Smith, the martyr, in his own defense.* Rozelle [Australia] Published by the Australian Tract Club of the Re-organized Church of Jesus Christ of Latter Day Saints [1908?]

[24]p. port. 21cm.

In pink printed wrappers.

Author's initials: F. E.

Reprint of three articles from the *Salt Lake Tribune,* Sunday, July 26, 1908.

Joseph's opposition to polygamy.

UPB

4502b. _____. (same) Published by the Australian Tract Club of the Re-organized Church of Jesus Christ of Latter Day Saints. Rozelle [Australia] Printed at the Standard Publishing House. 1908.

[12]l. port. 21½cm.

In tan printed wrapper.

Signed: Joseph Smith, Per F. E.

UPB

4503a. **Josiah Rhead Family.** *Brief historical sketch of the life of Josiah Rhead and family.* Ogden, Utah, 1926.

[4]p. 28cm.

USIC

4510. *Jubilee songs.* [Nauvoo, 1843]

Broadside. 32 x 34cm.

Text within border.

Two poems. The first concerning one of Joseph Smith's trials, in Illinois, written Jan. 7, 1843 was not signed. It was written by Wilson Law and Willard Richards. The second signed by Miss E. R. Snow, and was included in v. 1 of her published poems.

USIC

4510a. **Judd, J. W.** *United States, vs. The late corporation of the Church of Jesus Christ of Latter-day Saints, and others. Brief of J. W. Judd, for the petitioners, the Trustees of Brigham Young Academy, at Provo, Utah County.* [Salt Lake City? 1892]

9p. 22½cm.

At head of title: In the Supreme Court, Utah Territory. June term, 1892.

UHi, USIC

4511a.   *Junction extra! August 29, 1877. 10 p.m. Death. Which loves a shining mark, has seized a mighty man. Prest. Brigham Young called home.* [Ogden, 1877]

Broadside. 37 x 15cm.

Probably the second extra printed at the *Ogden Junction* upon the death of Brigham Young.

USIC

4511b.   *Junction extra. Death of Prest. B. Young.* [Ogden, 1877]

Broadside. 17 x 14cm.

Announcement of the death of Brigham Young and the notice that full particulars would be published later.

USIC

4514a.   *Juvenile Instructor. Is your heart in the work? Do you believe the gospel is true? Are you magnifying your calling as officer, teacher or parent?* [Salt Lake City, Juvenile Instructor Office, 1915?]

[4]p. 15½cm.

USIC

4514b.   _____. *Prospectus for volume XXVIII of the Juvenile Instructor.* [Salt Lake City, Geo. Q. Cannon & Sons Co., 1892?]

[4]p. 28cm.

Outlines of what would be included such as "A Mormon at the World's Fair." Also price lists for the *Instructor* and various books.

UPB

4514c.   Juvenile Instructor Office. *Books for sale at Juvenile Instructor Office, Salt Lake City, and its branch house, Cannon & Sons, Ogden, Utah.* Salt Lake City, Juvenile Instructor Office [1884]

[4]p. 12½cm.

The books advertised on p. [1]-[2] were published in 1884.

UPB

4515.   _____. *Catalogue of books and stationary for sale at the Juvenile Instructor Office, Salt Lake City, Utah, also for sale by A. H. Cannon, dealer in books, stationary and toys, Ogden, Utah . . . April, 1887.* [Salt Lake City?] 1887.

16p. 15cm.

USIC

4515a.   _____. *Catalogue of books and stationery for sale at the Juvenile Instructor Office. Catalogue and price list.* Salt Lake City, George Q. Cannon & Sons Company. 1895.

32p. 13cm.

USIC

4516a.   _____. *A fatal blow to infidelity!* [Salt Lake City, 189-?]

[4]p. 13cm.

Price list of LDS books and miscellaneous publications.

USIC

K

4536a. **Keeler, Joseph Brigham, comp.** *Genealogical record of the Keeler family.* Provo, Utah, Enquirer Steam Print, 1891.

14p. 20½cm.

MH, NjP, USlC, UU

4543a. *The Keep apichinin.* Salt Lake City, August 25, 1867-July 4, 1871.

3v. 21½ to 40cm.

"A semi-occasional paper devoted to cents, scents, sense and nonsense." Mormon references throughout. Opposed the Godbeite movement in 1870. Discontinued with the July 4, 1871 issue, V. 3, #1.

Advertised in *The Deseret News,* March 9, 1870 p. 6.

UPB V.1: #7, 9-11; V.2: #2-3, 9-14, 17, 19-23; V.3: #1; USlC comp.

4562a. **Kelley, William H.** *Presidency and priesthood. The apostasy, reformation, and restoration.* Lamoni, Iowa, Herald Publishing House and Bookbindery, 1904 [c1890]

xx, 486 [10]p. port., facsims. 20½cm.

UPB

4576a. **Kelsch, Louis A.** *Eine praktische hinweisung auf Bibelstellen fur die Lehren des Evangeliums.* [n.p., n.d.]

24p. 15cm.

Title in English: A practical reference of Bible references for the teaching of the gospel.

UPB

4586a. **Kennedy, James Henry.** *An interesting address on "The three witnesses of the Book of Mormon."* [Utica? 1890]

[4]p. 34cm.

At head of title: From *Utica Herald,* January 28th, 1890. Historical meeting of the Oneida Historical Society.

UPB

4587a. **Kenner, Scipio Africanus.** *Album of state and other public officers of Utah.* Salt Lake City, The Great Campaign, 1901.

38 [2]p. ports. 23½cm.

Biographies of Utah public officers including many Mormons.

Issued by "The Great Campaign" as a souvenir of the 4th Legislature.

USIC

4595a. **Kesler, Alonzo Pratt.** *Apostacy and restoration.* [Brooklyn, N.Y., ca. 1898]

4p. 21½cm.

Signed: A.P.K.

USIC

4595b. _____. *Distinguishing characteristics of Mormonism.* [Brooklyn, 1898?]

4p. 21cm.

Missionary tract.

UPB, USIC

4613a. **Kimball, Heber Chase.** *Address to my children.* [Salt Lake City? n.d.]

Broadside. ports. 28½ x 36cm.

Within ornamental border.

USIC

4622a. **Kimball, Soloman Farnham.** *Temple report for June 14, 1900, giving the amount of ordinance work performed by the Kimball family and their friends since June 14, 1897. Also the amount of cash contributed by them and how expended.* [Salt Lake City] 1900.

Broadside. 27½ x 21cm.

UHi

4633a. **Kingsley, George Henry.** *Notes on sport and travel. With a memoir by his daughter Mary H. Kingsley.* London, Macmillan and Co., Limited, 1900.

4p.l., 544p. port. 21cm.

The party was snowed in in Salt Lake City with nothing to do, since actresses were no longer supplied by the prophet.

CtY, MH, MiU, NN, PP, UPB

4633b. **Kingsley, Rose Georgina.** *South be west; or, winter in the Rocky Mountains and spring in Mexico. Edited with a preface by the Rev. Charles Kingsley.* London, W. Isbister & Co., 1874.

xvii, 411p. illus., plates, folded map. 22cm.

A visit to Salt Lake City with inaccurate material on the Mormons.

CtY, CU, DLC, NN, PPL, UPB

4643a. *The Kinsman. The "stone" in the "hat."* Salt Lake City, Kinsman Literature [ca. 1900]

27p. 13cm.

Cover title.

The editor of *Kinsman* was William R. Campbell.

UPB

4643b. _____. (same) *Whitmer vs. Josephites and the source of some revelations. From The Kinsman.* Salt Lake City, Kinsman Publishing Co. [ca. 1899]

35p. 13½cm.

Final section signed: A. T. Schroeder.

USIC

4656b. **Kirtland Safety Society Bank.** *Minutes of a meeting of the stockholders of the Kirtland Safety Society Bank; held on the 2nd day of November, A. D. 1836.* [Kirtland, 1836]

Broadside. 31½ x 17½cm.

At head of title: Kirtland, Ohio, December, 1836.

A variant printing without the *Messenger Extra* designation.

USIC

4657a. _____. *Minutes of a meeting of the members of the "Kirtland Safety Society," held on the 2d day of January, 1837.* [Kirtland, 1837]

Broadside. 32 x 17½cm.

At head of title: *Messenger Extra.* Kirtland, Ohio, March, 1837.

Meeting to incorporate the Bank.

USIC

4659a. **Kneeder, H. S.** *Through storyhood to the sunset seas. What four people saw on a journey through the Southwest to the Pacific Coast.* Chicago, Knight, Leonard & Co., 1895.

205p. illus. 24cm.

First printed in 1893.

Brief visit to Salt Lake City with information about its founding.

CtY, DLC, MB, MWA, NIC, TxU

4659b. **Kneeland, Samuel.** *The wonders of the Yosemite Valley, and of California. With original photographs by John P. Soule.* Boston, Alexander Moore, 1871.

xi, 13-71p. photo. 27cm.

In gilt tooled red cloth.

"Salt Lake and the Central Pacific Railroad," p. 19-25. Describes Salt Lake City and his insight on Mormonism.

Another edition: Boston, Alexander Moore, 1872. CU-B, DLC, MH, NjP, OCl, UPB.

CU-B, MH, UPB

4659c. **Knight, Elleanor (Warner).** *A narrative of the Christian experience, life and adventures, trials and labours of Elleanor Knight, written by herself. To which is added a few remarks and verses.* Providence, 1839.

1p.l., [iii]-iv, [5]-126p. 14cm.

Encounters Mormon missionaries in Vermont in 1857 and was not impressed by them.

ICN, NNU-W, RPB, UPB

4667a. **Knortz, Karl.** *Amerikanische Skizzen.* Halle, Hermann Gesenius, 1876.

311p. 18cm.

Title in English: American sketches.

"Geschichte des Mormonenthums," p. 171-205.

ICN, IU, NN, OCU, RPB, UPB, USIC

4668a. **Knower, Daniel.** *The adventures of a forty-niner. An historic description of California, with events and ideas of San Francisco and its people in those early days.* Albany, Weed-Parsons Printing Co., 1894.

[3]p.l. [5]-200p. ports. illus. 19cm.

Mormons, Sam Brannan, and Mormon Island mentioned, p. 9, 65, 114, 194-95.

Decker II: 735.

UPB, USIC

4669a. **Knox, Philander Chase.** *In opposition to the resolution reported from the Committee on Privileges and Elections "that Reed Smoot is not entitled to a seat as a Senator of the United States from the State of Utah." Speech of Hon. Philander C. Knox, of Pennsylvania, in the Senate of the United States, _____, February __, 1907.* [n.p., 1907?]

30p. 23cm.

At head of title: Confidential! Not to be released until the delivery of the speech has been begun. Accepted on this condition.

DLC, UPB

4671a. **Knox, Thomas Lowell, ed.** *Scenes from every land. Over five hundred photographic views. Designed to take the place of an extended tour of the world. With an introduction by Gen. Lew Wallace.* Springfield, O., Mast, Crowell & Kirkpatrick, 1892.

xvi, [17]-400p. of illus., (ports.) 28 x 34½cm.

View of the Salt Lake Temple with a graveyard in the foreground, p. 253. Includes description.

DLC, MB, UHi

4675a. *Ko te inoi.* [Auckland? 189-?]

Broadside. 18 x 12cm.

Title in English: The prayer.

A Catechism on prayer in Maori.

USlC

4675b. *Ko te whakahokinga mai o te rongo pai.* Auckland [189-?]

Broadsheet. 18 x 12cm.

Title in English: The restoration of the good news (gospel).

A catechism on the restoration of the gospel in Maori.

USlC

4675c. *Ko te Whanautanga o thu karati.* [Auckland? 189-?]

Broadside. 18 x 12cm.

Title in English: The birth of Jesus Christ.

A catechism on the birth of Christ in Maori.

USlC

4683a. **Kooyman, Frank Iemke.** *Levensvragen.* [Rotterdam? Nederlandsche Zending? 1905]

4p. 22cm.

Signed: I. K.

Title in English: Life's questions.

USIC

4683b. _____. (same) [Rotterdam, Uitgave van LeGrand Richards, ca.1907]

4p. 21½cm.

USIC

4690a. **Kuykendall, Ralph S.** *A history of Hawaii, prepared under the direction of the Historical Commission of the Territory of Hawaii. With introductory chapters by Herbert E. Gregory.* New York, Macmillan Company, 1926.

x, 375p. illus., ports., col. map. 21cm.

"The Mormons" p. 215-16. "Walter Murray Gibson," p. 268-71.

DLC, LU, PP, UPB

L

4692a. **L., C.** *Fralsningens vag.* [Kristiania, Nikolai Olsens boktryckeri, 1898]

36p. 20½cm.

Title in English: Plan of salvation.

Mormon beliefs on pre-existence, p. 28.

USIC

4711a. *Lambach.* *The sililoquy [sic] of Brigham.* [n.p. 188-?]

Broadside. 22 x 15cm.

A poem ridiculing Brigham Young and polygamy. Signed merely Lambach.

USIC

4711b. **Lambert de Sainte-Croix, Alexander.** *De Paris a San Francisco. Notes de voyage.* Paris, Calmann Levy, editeur, 1885.

2p.l., [i]-iii, 319 [1] p. illus., fold. map. 19cm.

Title in English: From Paris to San Francisco.

In grey printed paper cover.

Mormons mentioned, p. 137-39.

USIC

4735a. **Lander, Frederick West.** *Practicability of railroads through the South Pass. Letter from the Secretary of the Interior, transmitting a report from F. W. Lander, esq., relative to the practicability of a railroad through the South Pass.* [Washington, James B. Steedman, 1858]

20p. 23cm. (U. S. 35th Congress. 1st Sess. House. Ex. Doc. No. 70).

Need to cultivate the Mormons despite the furor against them.

UPB

4737a. **Landon, Melville De Lancey.** *Wise, witty, eloquent kings of the platform and pulpit. Biographies, reminiscences and lectures. Profusely illustrated.* Chicago. F. C. Smidley & Co., 1891.

ix, 19-570p. Illus. 24cm.

Artemus Ward's Panorama, on Mormonism, p. 33-74.

CoU, DLC, MtU, NcD, OCl, OFH, UPB

4741a. **Langley, Henry G.** *The Pacific Coast business directory for 1871-73: Containing the name and post office address of each merchant, manufacturer and professional residing in the states of California, Oregon, and Nevada; the territories of Washington, Idaho, Montana, Utah, Arizona, and Alaska; and the colony of British Columbia* . . . San Francisco, Henry G. Langley, 1871.

cxii, 792, 87p. illus. 24cm.

Brief information on the Mormons in the Utah sections under "Area and resources," p. 150 and "Salt Lake City," p. 423.

DLC, UPB

4742a. **Lanier, Roy H.** *Mistakes of "Latter Day Saints;" a review of the books, doctrines and practices of "Church of Jesus Christ of Latter Day Saints: Utah Branch.* [Fort W, Tx, 1930]

60 [4]p. 15cm.

Printed on back: Church of Christ, Fourth and State Streets, E. R. Harper, Minister, Little Rock, Ark.

NN, UPB, UU

4755a. **Larson, Daisy Deen (Barger).** *Courtship, marriage and the home, by Daisy B. Larson.* Salt Lake City, Utah, Deseret News Press [1927]

91p. 15½cm.

DLC, USIC

4758a. **Larus, John Rouse.** *Women of America.* Philadelphia, The Rittenhouse Press, 1908.

xii, 389p. 20cm. (Woman in all ages and in all countries [series])

References to Mormons, p. 304-6.

NcC, UPB, USIC

4761a. **Latimer, A. C.** *Mormon horrors exposed or why I left the Mormon Church, an expose of the most secret temple rites, strange scenes and treasonable oath.* [Springfield, Mo., American Appeal Pub. Co., ca. 1915]

16p. 16cm.

USIC

4764a. *Latter day pilgrim.* [n.p., 185-?]

Broadside. 31 x 19cm.

A two part poem concerning the Saints gathering to the West and building the temple and the New Jerusalem.

USIC

4765a.   *Latter-day Saint Literature.* [Salt Lake City, Juvenile Instructor, 1882?]

Broadside. 30 x 20cm.

Price list for LDS books.

USlC

4765b.   *Latter-day Saint seminaries and American education.* [Salt Lake City, 1928?]

Broadside. illus., port. 56 x 46cm.

Development of the seminary system.

USlC

4765c.   *Latter-day Saints.* [n.p., 1847]

Broadside. 21 x 26cm.

"The Edinburgh Branch of this society now meet, for public worship, in Mr. M'Pherson's large hall." Dated, May 1847.

USlC

4766a.   *The Latter Day Saints' belief.* Hull, Oliver's Printing Est. [1852?]

Broadside. 21 x 14cm.

Title within ornamental border.

Space provided to write time and location of meeting. A free rendition of the Articles of Faith.

USlC

4768a.   *Latter-day Saints: the dupes of a foolish and wicked imposture.* New York, Tract Society [ca. 1849]

2pts. (16, 16p) 18cm.

Republication of the London edition. At head of title: No. 396, No. 397.

USlC

4774a.   *Latter-day Saints' faith.* [n.p., 1850?]

Broadside. 19 x 26cm.

Includes the Articles of Faith, passages of scripture referring to the work of the Lord in the last days, and meeting times and addresses.

USlC

4787a.   *The Latter-day Saints (Mormons).* *What people of distinction say about them.*
[Chicago, Ill., Northern States Mission, 1904?]

4p. 22½cm.

UPB, USlC

4812a.   **Lawrence, William.** *Life of Amos A. Lawrence, with extracts from his diary and correspondence.* Boston and New York, Houghton, Mifflin and Company, 1888.

x, 289p. illus., ports., plates 20cm.

Need to fill Utah with Christians to suppress Mormonism, p. 270-71.

DLC, ICN, NIC, PP, ViN

4822a.   *The Leavitts of America;* *a compilation of five branches and gleanings from New England to California and Canada.* Woods Cross, Utah, Published by Mrs. Jane Jennings Eldredge for the Leavitt Family Association, 1924.

254p. 23½cm.

Includes Utah Leavitts.

UHi, UPB

4837a.   *Lecture! Rattling roaring rhymes.* *Mormon Utah and her institutions. Life among the Rocky Mountain saints. The land of many wives and much silver.*
[n.p.] 1873.

Broadside 69 x 16cm.

Five parts: 1. Brigham and his harem. 2. Say, have you ever been to Zion? 3. The Great Basin 4. The Weber and its echo. 5. Brigham's sermons.

NjP

4837b.   **Ledyard, Edgar M.** *Gidex (registered) for Utah.* [Salt Lake City, Legal Printing Co.] 1928.

10p. fold. map. 28cm.

Includes the early history of Utah and the Mormons.

CU-B, MB, UHi, UPB

4848a. **Lee, John Doyle.** *La vie, la confession et l'execution de l'eveque John D. Lee, le monstre Mormon. Ses dix-sept epouses -- details terribles depuisas mort -- implication de Brigham Young -- le massacre de Mountain Meadows -- aussi la fuite de sa fille de Salt Lake City. Les Danites la pursuivent, parcequ'elle ne veut pass epouser Orson Pratt. Elle expose les affaires de la "maison du lion."* Philadelphia, Publie par l'ancienne maison de publication de Franklin, c1877.

78p. [1]l. illus. 23½cm.

In purple printed wrappers.

Title in English: The life, the confessions and the execution of Bishop John D. Lee.

UPB

4865a. **Lee, Mrs. S. M.** *Glimpses of Mexico and Californa.* Boston, Geo. H. Ellis, Printer, 1887.

124p. 18½cm.

Wrote from Salt Lake City, April 25, 1886. View of the Temple, Brigham Young's grave, and includes remarks about Mormonism.

DLC, UPB, UU

4870a. *Lehi City Rustler Supplement.* [Lehi, Utah, 1897]

Broadsheet. 29½cm.

Mormon references.

USIC

4871a. **Leigh, James Wentworth.** *Other days. With a preface by Owen Wister.* New York, The Macmillan Company, 1921.

255p. illus., ports., plates 23cm.

"In the seventies." Visit to Salt Lake City; visited Brigham Young; other comments of Mormonism.

ICU, GU, MB, NN, UPB

4871b. **Leishman, James Allen.** *The event of the 19th century.* [Logan, Utah? 1900?]

Broadside. 28 x 22cm.

Stamped on bottom: James A. Leishman. Handwritten date: 31 Dec. 1900, Logan, Utah. Poem on restoration of the gospel.

USIC

4874a. **Leonard, Ambrose V.** *Born in the living law, third from Adam and Christ.* [n.p., n.d.]

Broadside. 27 x 36cm.

Announcing his lecture concerning the millennium. Provides space to write in the time and place of lecture. Tickets one dollar.

USIC

4881a. **Lewis, Carl.** *Abraham, yourself and Jacob; a changeable God.* [Lamoni, Ia, n.d.]

[4]p. 30cm.

Doctrinal tract for the Reorganized Church.

USIC

4891a. **Lewis, Evan.** *Hanes chwech o benboethiaid crefyddol sef, Joseph Smith, Mahomet, Richard Brothers, Jemimah Wilson, Ann Lee, a Joanna Southcotte. Gan Evan Lewis.* Merthyr Tydfil, argraffwyd gan Rees Lewis, Heol-fawr, 1849.

23p. 17½cm.

Title in English: History of six religious hotheads.

WalS, WalN

4896a. **Lewis, William A.** *The Church of Jesus Christ. Where is it -- How shall I know it? There are many churches of men, only the one Church of Christ.* [Lamoni, Iowa?] Reorganized Church of Jesus Christ of Latter-day Saints [1912?]

18p. 19cm.

USIC

4897a. _____. (same) [Independence, Mo.] Reorganized Church of Jesus Christ of Latter Day Saints [n.d.]

30p. 18cm.

UPB

4911a. *The Liahona. Prospectus of the Liahona.* Independence, Mo., 1907.

Broadside. 28 x 21½cm.

Signed: Independence, Mo., 1907.

Printed to serve all the missions in the United States.

UPB, USIC

4923a. *Life history of brother Lars R. Jensen.* [n.p., ca. 1900]

Broadside. 22 x 17cm.

Biography.

USlC

4925a. *The life sketch of Lydia Mamreoff von Finkelstein (Madame Mountford).* *With original photographic views taken by the author in the Holy Land.* New York, 1908.

48 [1]p. illus. 20½cm.

Mormons mentioned, p. 33.

DLC, NN, USlC

4937a. **Lindsay, Agnes Yullo.** *Farewell Hymn. Dedicated to President William Gibson, on his being called to leave the Edinburgh Conference of the Church of Jesus Christ of Latter-day Saints.* [Dundee? 1849?]

Broadside. 21 x 23cm.

Text within ornamental border. Printed in gold.

Poem in eight 4-line stanzas, dated at end: Dundee, Oct. 31, 1849.

UPB

4956a. *A little talk, between John Robinson and his master about Mormonism, shewing its origin, absurity, and impiety.* [Bedford: Printed and sold by W. White: Also by Hamilton, Adams, & Co., London, 1840?]

8p. 16½cm.

An anti-Mormon polemic.

UPB

4958a. **Littlefield, Lyman O.** *Celestial marriage, evidence that the revelation on celestial marriage was revealed through Joseph Smith. Positive proof that Joseph Smith had plural wives.* [n.p., ca. 1886]

4p. 27cm.

Smith (Joseph III) -- Littlefield correspondence, testimony of Mercy Thompson, David Fullmer, etc.

MoInRC

4963a. **Livesey, Richard.** *An exposure of Mormonism, being a statement of facts relating to the self-styled "Latter Day Saints," and the origin of the Book of Mormons, by Richard Livesey, of Winchendon, Massachusetts, America, Minister of the Methodist Episcopal Church.* Manchester, Wm. Shackleton and Son, Printers, 1840.

12p. 21½cm.

UPB

4969a. *Llyfr cronicl prophwydi Mormonaidd. Ychydig o hanes gweithredoedd twyllodrus, rhai o'r "Seintiau y Dyddiau Diweddaf." Ynghyd a melldithion ofnadwy Duw, ar gau brophwydi a'r rhyfygus* ... Llanymddyfri, Argrffwyd gan E. Morriss, Heol-y-brenin, MDCCCXLVIII.

12p. 19½cm.

Title in English: Chronicle of the Mormon prophets.

Brief account of deceitful acts of some Latter-day Saints.

WalN

4972a. **London, Jack.** *The Iron heel.* New York, The Macmillan Company, London, Macmillan & Co., Ltd. 1908.

2p.l., vii-xivp., [1]l. 354 [4]p. 19½cm.

A note for chapter 25, p. 353, concerns the Danites.

DLC, MH, NjP, TxU, UPB, UU, ViU

4975a. **Long, Elmer E.** *Facts about the Bible and what it teaches.* [Douglas, Arizona, n.d.]

[15]p. 22½cm.

USlC

4995a. *A Lover of truth. Remarks on the doctrines, practices, &c. of the Latter-day Saints: Setting forth the marvellous things connected with this new light from America.* Preston, Printed by J. Livesey [n.d.]

8p. 20cm.

Lancaster Record Office, UPB (xerox)

5001a. **Lowell, James Russell.** *The Biglow papers, edited, with an introduction, notes, glossary, and copious index, by Homer Wilbur.* Cambridge, Published by George Nichols, New York, George P. Putnam, 1848.

12, xxxii, 163p. 19cm.

At head of title: Meliboeus-Hipponax.

Brief discussion of Joseph Smith, p. 74-75.

DLC, MB, MH, MiU, OO, OU, UPB, ViU

5001b.   *Loyal celebration of Utah County, Provo, July 4, 1887 at Tanner's Grove.* Provo, American Print., 1887.

Broadside. 31 x 14cm.

At head of title: 1776. 1887.

Independence day program.

USlC

5005a.   **Luce, Amante.** *Errors and inconsistencies concerning the presidency of the dominant church in Utah.* [Lamoni, Iowa, Herald Publishing House, 1901?]

12p. 18cm.

Variant printing without "No. 207."

UPB, USlC

5006a.   _____. *The reorganization of the Church of Jesus Christ of Latter Day Saints. A brief treatise setting forth the law and revelations governing such exigencies as arose in the church after the death of Joseph Smith.* [Independence, Mo.] Reorganized Church of Jesus Christ of Latter Day Saints [n.d.]

11p. [2]l. 18cm.

Place of publication from leaf following text. The final leaf has a seal on the verso.

UPB

5008a.   _____. (same) [n.p., n.d.]

11p. [1] 19cm.

CU-B, NjP, UPB

5018a.   **Luff, Joseph.** *Funeral sermon of President Joseph Smith; sermon by Joseph Luff.* [n.p., 1918?]

26p. 19cm.

MoInRC

5035a.   _____. *The way called heresy. Sermon. By Joseph Luff, delivered at the general church reunion, Logan, Iowa, October 16, 1892.* Lamoni, Iowa, [189-]

89-96p. 27cm. *(Saints' Herald Supplement)*

Also reprinted as a tract.

MoInRC

5044a. **Lund, Anthon Hendrik.** *Temple records adjusted and genealogical information obtained.* [Salt Lake City, 191-?]

Broadside. 22 x 14cm.

Letter offering the services of the Genealogical Society of Utah to help individuals keep their temple records.

USIC

5045a. **Lutaud, Auguste Joseph.** *Les Etats-Unis en 1900.* Paris, Societe d'Editions Scientifiques, 1896.

xvi, [17]-300p. 18cm.

Title in English: The United States in 1900.

"Les Mormons," p. 222-36. The basis of Mormon theology is polygamy.

PPL, UPB

5046a. **Lyell, Sir Charles.** *A second visit to the United States of North America. by Sir Charles Lyell, F. R. S.* New York, Harper & Brothers, Publishers, London, John Murray, 1849.

2v. 19½cm.

Brief mention of the Mormons, v.1, p. 77, v.2, p. 51.

CtY, CU, DLC, MB, PPA, UPB, WaU

5048a. **Lyford, C. P.** *The Mormon problem. An appeal to the American people. With an appendix, containing four original stories of Mormon life, founded upon fact, and a graphic and thrilling account of the Mountain Meadows massacre. By Rev. C. P. Lyford.* New York, Hunt & Eston, Cincinnati, Cranston & Stowe [c1886]

323p. 19cm.

CSmH, CtY, CU, MH, TxU, UPB, UU

Lykkejaeger, Hans. See Smith, Andrew Madsen.

5050a. **Lyman, Amasa Mason.** *Circular.* [San Bernardino, Ca., 1855]

Broadside. 28 x 20cm.

Circular is signed by Amasa Lyman and Charles C. Rich, and is an invitation for people to settle in San Bernardino.

USIC

5063a.   **Lyman, Richard Roswell.** *Prohibition; not state control. An address in the Tabernacle, Salt Lake City, Oct. 3, 1930.* [Salt Lake City, 1930]

12p. 23cm.

UPB, USlC

5064a.   **Lynch, Frank E.** *The pathfinder of the great western empire, by Frank E. Lynch, Sr. Devoted to the purpose of assisting the public in finding useful government land for farms, timber grazing and minerals. Describes vacant land in California, Oregon, Washington, Arizona, Nevada, Utah, Idaho, Montana, and New Mexico.* Los Angeles, Gem Publishing Co. [c1920]

103p. illus., plates. 22½cm.

Brief section on Utah in which he places the Mormons in Utah in 1845 and the Mountain Meadows massacre in 1846.

DI-GS, DLC, OrU, UHi, UPB

5066a.   **Lyon, Caleb.** *No government bounty to polygamy. Speech of Hon. Caleb Lyon, of Lyonsdale, New York, in the House of Representatives, May 4, 1854.* [Washington, Printed at the Congressional Globe Office, 1854?]

2p. 21½cm.

OC

5066b.   **Lyon, John.** *Address to Franklin D. and Samuel W. Richards, brothers, on leaving their field of labour for the Camp of Israel, February 15th, 1848.* Kilmarnock [1848?]

Broadside. 22½ x 14½cm.

USlC

5066c.   _____. *Dairy [sic] of a voyage from Liverpool to New Orleans, on board the ship International, commanded by Capt. David Brown, with a crew 26 in number, and a company of 419 members of the Church of Jesus Christ of Latter-day Saints, under the presidency of Elders Arthur, Lyon, and Waddington.* [Liverpool? 1854]

7 [1]p. 19½cm.

A whitewashed edition of John Lyon's diary.

USlC

5068a.   _____. *To Cyrus H. Wheelock, pastor of the Manchester, Liverpool, and Preston Conferences. December 18th, 1852.* [Glasgow, J. Midgley, 1852]

Broadside. 27 x 22cm.

Within an ornamental border. Poem in honor of Wheelock.

USlC

M

5075a. *The M. Official publication of the Mutual Improvement Association.*

Maricopa Stake of Zion. Mesa, Ariz. 1924-

　v. 22cm.

UPB v. 1 #8

5076a. **Mabie, Hamilton Wright.** *Our own country, its history and achievements and the story of our great men and women.* [By] *Hamilton W. Mabie [and others].* Chicago, Ill., Philadelphia, Pa., Stockton, Cal., Monarch Book Co. [c1895]

560p. illus. 25cm.

Mormons, p. 223, 412-13.

At head of title: A new history for American homes.

USlC

5078a. **McAfee, Joseph Ernest.** *Light for Utah.* [New York, Board of Home Missions of the Presbyterian Church in the U.S.A., 1906]

[2]p. folded. 14cm. (No. 240)

Need for missionary work in Utah.

USlC

5078b. **McAfee, Lucy H.** *Tim.* 2d ed. New York City, Literature Department of the Woman's Board of Home Missions of the Presbyterian Church in the U.S.A. [1903]

31 [1]p. 14cm. (No. 244)

Anti-Mormon fiction.

USlC

5090a. **McAllister, Duncan McNeil.** *How to prevent sickness.* Salt Lake City [1885?]

4p. 21cm.

Caption title.

At head of title: Please do not destroy this.

Concerning the word of wisdom.

USlC

5099b. _____. *Temples of the Church of Jesus Christ of Latter-day Saints and the sacred purposes to which they are dedicated.* Independence, Mo., Zion's Printing and Publishing Co., 1930.

16p. 18½ cm.

USlC

McAllister, John D. T. See *Handcart song.*

5100b. **Macbride, Thomas Huston.** *In cabins and sod-houses.* Iowa City, The State Historical Society of Iowa, 1928.

xv, 368p. plate. 23cm.

Expulsion of the Mormons from Nauvoo and their trek through Iowa briefly treated in a conversational form.

DLC, IdU, MB, NN, TxU, UHi, UPB

5116a. **McClellan, John J.** *Prize ode to irrigation. Words by Mrs. G. McClurg. Music by J. J. McClellan.* Chicago, National Music Company [1907]

45p. 23cm.

Includes the Mormon pioneer use of irrigation.

UHi

5116b. _____. (same) *Written and composed for the 11th National Irrigation Congress, Ogden, Utah, September 15-18, 1903. Written by Mrs. Gilbert McClurg, of Colorado Springs. Composed by J. J. McClellan, of Salt Lake City.* [Salt Lake City, Press of The Deseret News, 1903]

24p. music. 26cm.

Cover title.

MiU, OO, UPB

5117a. **McClellan, Rolander Guy.** *The golden state: A history of the region west of the Rocky Mountains; embracing California, Oregon, Nevada, Utah, Arizona, Idaho, Washington Territory, British Columbia, and Alaska, from the earliest period to the present time with a history of Mormonism and the Mormons.* Philadelphia, Flint & Co., 1874 [c1872]

711p. illus. 23cm.

Utah and Mormons, p. 549-99.

CoU, CtY, DLC, IdU, MB, NN, OU, UPB, UU

McClurg, Mrs. Gilbert. See McClellan, John J. *Prize ode to irrigation.*

5127a. **McConkie, Oscar Walter.** *Tradition and the Book of Mormon. Address delivered over Radio Station KSL Sunday evening, March 25, 1928.* [Salt Lake City, Deseret News, 1928]

Broadside. 47 x 24cm.

Reprinted from *The Deseret News* of Saturday, March 31, 1928.

USlC

5142a. **McDonald, Joseph E.** *The United States vs. The Corporation of the Church of Jesus Christ of Latter-day Saints. Argument of Senator Joseph E. McDonald, delivered October 21, 1887.* [Salt Lake City, 1887?]

At head of title: Supreme Court of Utah.

Broadside. 55 x 42cm.

USlC

5150a. **McDowell, Floyd M.** *What can we do at our Religio? A manual of social and recreational activities for the Religio.* Lamoni, Ia., Reorganized Church of Jesus Christ of Latter Day Saints, 1921.

48p. 19cm.

MoInRC

5152a. **McDowell, Joseph F.** *Disciplism; or the claims of Alexander Campbell to a restored, primitive Christianity examined.* [n.p., n.d.]

12p. 22cm.

MoInRC

5152b. _____. *The present truth.* [n.p., n.d.]

4p. 22cm.

MoInRC

5170a. **McGuire, Benjamin R.** *The facts in the case.* [n.p., n.d.]

4p. 16cm.

MoInRC

5170b. _____. (same) [n.p., n.d.]

8p. 16cm.

Signed by Benjamin R. McGuire and Arthur E. McKim.

MoInRC

5195a. **McKay, David Oman.** *Birth control.* [Salt Lake City? ca. 1916]

Broadside. 28 x 22cm.

Originally published in the Relief Society Magazine, V.3, July, 1916, p. 366-67.

USlC

5195b. _____. *Ki nga Hunga Tapu o te Mihana o Niu Tirini e Noho huihui ana ki te Hui Tau ki Porirua.* [n.p., 1922]

[4]p. 22½cm.

Title in English: Latter-day Saints of New Zealand who have assembled for the annual conference at Porirua.

Dated on p.[4]: Salt Lake City, Utah, November 8th, 1922.

USlC

5199a. _____. *To the priesthood quorums generally.* [Salt Lake City, 1911]

[4]p. 22½cm.

Report of a sub-committee to the General Priesthood Outlines Committee, signed by the chairman, David O. McKay, and dated April 7th, 1911. Report concerns missionary work and methods of making outlines more effective.

USlC

5213. **McKinley, Henry J.** *Brigham Young; or, the prophet's last love. A play in three acts.* San Francisco, Excelsior Press, Bacon & Company, Printers, 1870.

30p. 18cm.

Cover title.

NN, USlC

5220a. **McLeod, Norman W., ed.** *A souvenir of Mesa City and environments. The resources and attractions of Arizona's paradise graphically described. Edited by Norman W. McLeod, John Beach Chattin.* [Mesa, Arizona? 1894]

35 [1]p. 21cm.

Includes the "Mormons of Mesa."

USlC

5231a. **McMillen, A. W.** *An American Red Cross study to the needs of disabled World War veterans in Salt Lake County, Utah with particular reference to Salt Lake County Red Cross Chapter's contribution in this field . . . conducted August 18, 1925 to September 18, 1925.* [Salt Lake City? 1925]

75p. 22½cm.

Relief Society, p. 34-39.

USlC

5231b. **McMohon, J. P.** *The ne [sic] plus ultra invention of the nineteenth century! The patent human digester; and consumer of wind.* Council Bluffs, Western Trumpeter, 1854.

Broadside. 36 x 23cm.

Satire on Mormonism.

USlC

5238a. *The (Madras) "Christian Instructor" versus Mormonism.* [Madras: Printed by Henry Texter, at the Hindu Press . . . and published by John McCarthy, 1856]

12p. 22cm.

CSmH

5242a. *Magic, pretended miracles, and remarkable natural phenomena. Remarkable delusions; or, illustrations of popular errors.* London, The Religious Tract Society [1855]

192p. [1]l. illus. 16cm.

"The Mormonites," p. 171-88. Mormons mentioned as the final delusion.

DLC, InU, MH, MrU, PU, UPB

5246b. **Maine. Legislature.** *Assassination of John K. Robinson. Resolution of the Legislature of Maine, relating to the assassination of John King Robinson, at Salt Lake City.* [Washington, Govt. Print. Off., 1867.]

2p. 23cm. (U. S. 40th Cong. 2d Sess. Misc. Doc. No. 4)

Assassination blamed on a band of Mormons acting under the direction of leading authorities.

UPB, USlC

5264a. **Manning, William Henry.** *The Danite chief; or, the Mormon's plot. By Capt. Mark Wilton [pseud.]* New York, Nickel Library, 1887.

30p. 17cm.

UPB

5282a. **Marshall, J. H.** *Saints of a latter-day: A rhyme for the principality of Wales.* [Hereford, Printed at the Times office, 1851?]

12p. 15½cm.

Dated: Llandovery, May 8th, 1851.

Municipal Library, Swansea, South Wales. UPB (Xerox).

5282b. **Marshall, John A.** *Edwin B. Ayers and Edward A. Kessler, appellants, vs. Mary Ann Jack, respondent, vs. William Leggett, respondent. Brief for respondents. John A. Marshall, Waldemar Van Cott, attorneys for respondents.* Salt Lake [City], Star Print [1895?]

30p. 21cm.

At head of title: In the Supreme Court of Utah Territory.

Includes paper cover.

Polygamy inheritance case. Thomas Cope case.

DLC, UAr

5282c. **Marshall, Logan.** *Seeing America including the Panama Exposition. A descriptive and picturesque journey through romantic and historic cities and places, natural wonders, scenic marvels of national pride and interest.* Philadelphia, The John C. Winston Company, Publishers [c1915]

352 [i.e. 256]p. plates. 22½cm.

Mormonism briefly discussed in the chapter entitled "America's Dead Sea."

UHi, UPB

5303a. **Masonic Hall.** *Nauvoo, April 24, 1844, will be presented a grand moral entertainment, to aid the discharge of a debt, against President Joseph Smith, contracted through the odious persecution of Missouri, and vexatious law suits. His friends and the public will respond to so laudable a call, in patronizing the exertions of those who promise rational amusement with usefulness.* [Nauvoo, 1844]

Broadside. 39 x 38cm.

Brigham Young, Erastus Snow, George J. Adams, and others are included in the entertainment.

MoSHi

5303b. **Massey, Stephen L.** *James's traveler's companion. Being a complete guide through the western states to the Gulf of Mexico and the Pacific, via the Great Lakes, rivers, canals, etc. Giving full and accurate descriptions of all places on, and in the vacinity of, the western waters.* Cincinnati, Published by J. A. & U. P., 1851.

vi, 9-224p. illus., 2 fold maps. 16cm.

Has a description of Nauvoo with a note on the origins of Mormonism, p. 21-22.

DLC, KyU, MnU, NjP, NN, OOxM

5303c. **Mast, Isaac.** *The gun, rod and saddle; or, nine months in California.* Philadelphia, Methodist Episcopal Book and Publishing House, 1875.

275p. 18cm.

Returning east, he stops off in Salt Lake City and comments on the Mormons and on Brigham Young.

DLC, NjP, CU, NcD, NIC, MnU, UPB

5308a. **Matteson, John Gottlieb.** *Jesu profetier: eler von frelsers og profeternes forudsigelser fuldbyrdede af J. G. Matteson.* Battle Creek, Mich., Sundhedsvennens Forlagsexpedition, 1889.

363p. illus. 20cm.

Mormons, p. 95.

Title in English: Jesus' prophecies: or the Savior and prophets' predictions fulfilled.

UPB

5308b. **Matthews, Leonard.** *A long life in review.* [St. Louis?, 1928?]

4p.l., 178p. ports. 18cm.

Speaks of Mormons in Nauvoo and of trouble with the Mormons in Salt Lake City on July 4, 1888.

CtY, DN, InU, MnU, NcD, TxU, UPB

5308c. *He mau manao Hamama i ka Poe Hawaii a me na Lahui Polinesia o ka Moana Pakipika / kakau ia e kekahi Lunakahiko o ka Ekalesia o Iesu Kristo o ka Poe Hoano o na La Hope Nei.* Honolulu, Oahu, L.D.S. Hawaiian Mission, 1922.

12p. 18cm.

Title in English: Open thoughts to the people of Hawaii and the Polynesian nations of the Pacific Ocean written by an Elder of the Church.

Ties in Polynesian folklore with Israel and the Book of Mormon.

HLB

5311a. **Maxwell, George R.** *George R. Maxwell vs. George Q. Cannon. Papers in the case of Maxwell vs. Cannon, for a seat as delegate from Utah Territory in the Forty-third Congress. Evidence of contestant.* [Washington, 1873]

151 [2]p. 22½cm. (U.S. 43rd Cong. 1st Sess. House. Misc. Doc. No. 49)

DLC, UPB

5321a. **Mead, Elwood.** *Report of irrigation investigations in Utah, under the direction of Elwood Mead . . .* Assisted by R. P. Teele, A. P. Stover, A. F. Doremus, J. D. Stannard, Frank Adams, and F. L. Swendsen [1903]

330p. illus., plates. 30cm. (Office on Experiment Stations. Bulletin No. 124).

Early Mormon influence on irrigation.

UPB

5333a. *The members of the Iowa Conference of the Church of Jesus Christ of Latter-day Saints will hold their semi-annual conference in the G.A.R. Hall.* [Council Bluffs, April 1 and 2, 1905.]

Broadside. 30 x 23cm.

USlC

5335b. *Memorial to Congress. To the Honorable the Senate and House of Representatives in Congress Assembled:* [Salt Lake City, 1882?]

Broadside. 28 x 22cm.

The affect current legislation being passed against polygamy would have on families in Utah.

USlC

5337a. **Mensink, C.** *Het Mormonisme ontmaskerd. Eene lezing door C. Mensink. Zendeling if Marokko.* Besteladres, K. Kuipers te Sneek [ca. 1900]

32p. 16cm.

Title in English: Mormonism unmasked.

In pink printed wrapper.

Published after 1899.

UPB

5340a. **Merimee, Prosper.** *Melanges historiques et litteraires.* Quatrieme ed. Paris, Calmann Levy, 1883.

382p. 18½cm.

Title in English: Mix of history and literature.

"Les Mormons," p. 3-58.

CtY, DLC, PHi, PBM, USlC, ViU

Merriam, Florence A. See Bailey, Florence Augusta (Merriam).

5389a. **Miles, John.** *John Miles, plaintiff in error, vs. the United States. In error to the Supreme Court of Utah Territory. Filed October 13, 1879.* [Washington? 1879?]

115p. 22cm.

At head of title: Transcript of record. Supreme Court of the United States. No. 592.

Polygamy trial of John Miles with all the testimony.

DLC

5391a. **Mill, John Stuart.** *On liberty.* London, John W. Parker and Son, West Strand. M. DCCC. LIX.

207 [1]p. 20cm.

Calls Mormonism a "product of palpable imposture." Considers Mormons and especially polygamous women as slaves to their religion, p. 163-67.

CSmH, CU, DLC, MiU, NN, UPB, ViU

5398a. **Miller, Horace Elmer.** *History of the town of Savoy.* West Cummington, Mass., Published by H. E. Miller, 1879.

26p. 14½cm.

In salmon printed wrapper.

Claims that Joseph Smith founded Mormonism in Savoy, N. Y.

MWA, UPB

5404a. **Miller, O. A.** *A Journey and its ending. An address before the Rotary Club, Columbus, Ohio, September 11, 1923.* [Columbus? 1923?]

15p. 23cm.

Contains comments of his admiration of the Mormons.

UPB

Miller, Sarahanne. See *Handcart song.*

5408a. **Miller, W. H. H.** *William E. Bassett, plaintiff in error, vs. the United States, No. 110. Error to the Supreme Court of Utah. Brief for defendant in error. W. H. H. Miller, Attorney-General.* [Washington? 1890?]

12p. 22cm.

At head of title: In the Supreme Court of the United States. October, 1890.

A polygamy case, in which he is divorcing his first wife.

DLC

5413a. **Mills, W. G.** *A poem, written for the celebration of the Fourth of July, 1860, at G.S.L. City.* Great Salt Lake City, 1860.

Broadside. 29 x 22cm.

USlC

5414a.   **Mills, William Stowell.** *The story of the Western Reserve of Connecticut.* New York, Printed for the author by Brown & Wilson Press [c1900]

134, vp. 17cm.

Mormons in Kirtland, p. 105-7.

CU, DLC, OCl, OO, UPB

5433a.   **Missouri. Laws, statutes, etc.** *Laws of the State of Missouri, passed at the first session of the eleventh General Assembly, begun and held at the city of Jefferson, on Monday, the sixteenth day of November, in the year of our Lord, one thousand eight hundred and forty.* Jefferson, Printed by Calvin Gunn, 1841.

373p. 22½cm.

Order to print the Mormon documents relating to Missouri.

UPB

5433b.   _____. *Laws of the state of Missouri, passed at the first session of the twelfth general assembly, begun and held at the city of Jefferson, on Monday, the twenty-first day of November, eighteen hundred and forty-two, and ended Tuesday the twenty-eighth day of February, eighteen hundred and forty-three.* Jefferson, Printed by Allen Hammond, 1843.

494p. 23cm.

Includes material on the Mormon war.

UPB

5439a.   **Moffat, David.** *The Latter-day Saints' catechism; or, child's ladder . . . being a series of questions adapted for the use of the children of Latter-day Saints.* London, Sold by William Look at the Latter-day Saints Book and Millennial Star Office [1885]

16p. 21cm.

UHi

5439b.   **Mokler, Alfred James.** *History of Natrona County, Wyoming, 1888-1922. True portrayal of the yesterdays of a new county and a typical frontier town of the middle west. Fortunes and misfortunes, tragedies and comedies, struggles and triumphs of the pioneers. Map and illustrations.* Chicago, R. R. Donnelley & Sons Company, The Lakeside Press, 1923.

xiv, 477p. illus., plates, map. 24cm.

The Mormon trail, p. 438-46.

DLC, MjP, MtU, OrU, UHi, UPB, WHi

5441b.   **Mollhausen, Heinrich Balduin.** *Das Mormonenmadchen.* Leipzig, P. List [1911]

544p. illus. 20cm. (His Illustrierte Romane, 2 serie, lbd.)

Title in English: The Mormon Girls.

TNJ

5451a. **Monstery, Thomas Hoyer.** *California Joe's first trail. A story of the destroying angels.* New York, Beadle and Adams, 1884.

15p. illus. 29cm. (Beadle's half dime library. V. 15, No. 376)

"Fourth edition."

Story of Mormon Danites.

CtY, CU-B, NN, UPB

5453a. **Montgomery, Marcus Whitman.** *Hon._____. Dear Sir:* [Minneapolis, 1888]

Broadside. 22 x 14cm.

Form letter to accompany an article entitled "The case against Utah." Dated Feb. 4, 1888.

USlC

5458a. **Moore, Julia A.** *The death of Brigham Young. Composed and written by Mrs. Julia A. Moore, of Edgerton, Mich.* Cleveland, J. F. Ryder [1877?]

Broadside. 11 x 17cm.

Poem on the death of Brigham Young with a portrait of his eighteen wives dressed in black.

UPB

5462a. **Morcombe, Joseph E.** *Organization of Grand Lodge of Iowa, A. F. & A. M., 1844; story of beginning (now for the first time told).* [Cedar Rapids, Iowa] Cedar Rapids Gazette, 1908.

20p. ports. 22cm.

Mormons and Freemasons.

IaHi, USlC

5462b. _____. *Story of beginning (now for the first time told); Organization of Grand Lodge of Iowa, A. F. & A. M., 1844.* Cedar Rapids, Iowa, Cedar Rapids Gazette, 1930.

20p. 22cm.

Mormon lodges in Iowa.

UHi, USlC

5463a. *More trickery of Mormonism brought to light.* *Giving the full particulars of the schemes and practices of Joseph Smith, the angelite.* [n.p.] Ambler, Printer, [ca. 1838]

4p. 19½cm.

"Copied from a public journal."

Lancashire Record Office, UPB Xerox

5463b.   **Moreau, F. Frederic.** *Aux Etats-Unis. Notes de voyage.* Paris, E. Plon, Nourrit et Cie, 1888.

4p.l. 263p. 18cm.

Title in English: To the United States.

Chapter XVIII, "Les Mormons," p. 202-17.

USlC

5477a.   **Morgan, John.** *Doctrines of the Church of Jesus Christ of Latter-day Saints, its faith and teachings.* Liverpool, Printed and published at the Millennial Star Office, 1912.

26p. 18½cm.

In brown printed wrapper with "No. 1" at top.

UPB

5482a.   _____. (same, in Hawaiian) *Na kumu manaoio o ka Ekalesia o Iesu Kristo o ka hoano o na la hope nie.* Uhuhiia e J. H. Dina. [Honolulu, R. Grieve, Electric Book & Job Printer, 1899]

63p. 17cm.

HLB

5493a.   _____. *Plan of Salvation.* Chattanooga, Tenn., Published by The Southern States Mission [n.d.]

32 [1]p. 13½cm.

Includes "Church works," on page [1] following text.

UPB

5493b.   _____. (same) [Salt Lake City, Deseret News Publishing Company, n.d.]

24p. 16½cm. (Tract No. 2)

UPB

5493c.   _____. (same) [Liverpool, Millennial Star Office, n.d.]

21 [1]p. 13cm.

USlC

5495a.   _____. [Salt Lake City, Deseret News Company, 1884?]

21 [1]p. 16½cm. (Tract no. 2)

"Price list of church publications for sale by the Deseret News Company," on verso of last leaf.

UPB, USlC

5504a. _____. (same) Independence, Mo., Press of Zion's Printing & Publishing Co. [1905?]
21 [1] 17cm.
In printed wrapper.
UPB

5504b. _____. (same) [Los Angeles, California Mission] 1906.
32p. 13½cm.
In brown printed wrapper.
UPB

5507a. _____. (same) Independence, Mo., Press of Zion's Printing & Publishing Co. [1915?]
21 [1]p. 17cm.
In printed wrapper.
UPB

5508a. _____. (same) Independence, Press of Zion's Printing and Publishing Company, [1921?]
24p. 16½cm.
UPB

5508b. _____. (same) Independence, Press of Zion's Printing and Publishing Company [1923?]
24p. 17½cm.
UPB

5508c. _____. (same) Independence, Press of Zion's Printing and Publishing Company [1925?]
24p. 18cm.
UPB

5508d. _____. (same) Independence, Press of Zion's Printing and Publishing Company [1926?]
24p. 16½cm.
UPB

5508e. _____. (same) Independence, Press of Zion's Printing and Publishing Company [1926?]

24p. 17½cm.

UPB

5511c. _____. *The plan of salvation as taught by the Church of Jesus Christ of Latter-day Saints.* [Auckland] Messenger Print. [ca. 1910]

24p. 18cm.

In green printed wrapper.

At head of caption title: No. 2.

UPB

5511d. _____. (same) [Aukland] Messenger Print [ca. 1913]

24p. 18cm.

Cover title.

In green printed wrapper.

UPB

5512a. **Morgan, S. P., comp.** *Idaho facts and statistics pertaining to its early settlement and colonization with special reference to the Franklin Colony together with stories of the Indian troubles in the south eastern part of the state. Information collected and compiled for the Idaho Semi-Centennial Celebration held at Franklin, Jun 14 and 15, 1910.* Salt Lake City, Skelton Pub. Co. [1910]

36p. illus. 23½cm.

Cover title: Official program.

Numerous Mormon references.

UHi, USlC

5519a. *The Mormon centennial.* [Salt Lake City? 1930]

Broadside. illus. 53 x 36cm.

USlC

5525b. *The Mormon peril.* [New York City, n.d.]

Broadsheet. 21cm.

A similar broadsheet under same title.

MoInRC

5530a. **Mormon Tribune.** *Prospectus. The Mormon Tribune.* [Salt Lake City, 1869]

Broadside. 30 x 21cm.

Signed: W. S. Godbe, E. L. T. Harrison, publishers, Salt Lake City, Nov. 16, 1869.

USlC

5549a. *Mormonism explained;* Josiah Eardley G. A. R. *Veteran 72 years a Mormon.* [San Diego? 1922]

Broadside. 23 x 15cm.

Advertisement for church meetings in Escondido, Calif.

USlC

5550a. *Mormonism exposed.* [By a Mormon slave wife] [Chicago? n.d.]

16p. 11cm. (No. 5)

"Price 5 cents."

UPB

5550b. _____. (same) [Chicago, Ill., n.d.]

16p. 11cm. (no. 5)

Illustrated copy with drawing of a Mormon and three wives. On cover: Price 5 cents.

Half of page 14, 15-16 are advertisements.

UPB

5551a. _____. *Four Sunday evening lectures will be delivered (God willing) in the Albert Memorial Church, Queen's Road, Manchester, by the Rev. C. Fenwick Ward.* [Manchester? 1897]

Broadside. 63 x 50cm.

Four lectures Nov. 14, 24, Dec. 5, 12.

USlC

5551b. _____. *Please read, then hand to your neighbour, or mail to a friend.* [Salt Lake City? 1889?]

Broadsheet. 22 x 16cm.

In two states.

Complimentary statements concerning Mormons by various people.

UPB

5555a. *Mormonism or the Bible? A question for the times. By a Cambridge clergyman.* Cambridge, Published by T. Dixon, Sold by Wertheim & Macintosh, 1852.

31p. 22cm.

Brit. Mus.

5565a. *A Mormon's bride (the only authentic Mormon play produced).* Oldham, Bowcott & Sons, printers [188-?]

Broadside. 19 x 13cm.

Theatre Royal Wednesday.

USIC

5565b. *Mormon's catechism.* [Preston, Bateman, Printer, 184-?]

Broadside. 28 x 22cm.

Anti-Mormon polemic.

USIC

5567a. *Mormons sure of victory.* Chicago, College Free Press Bureau, 1917.

Broadside. illus. 46 x 15cm.

A free news and literary service for editors with the same address as the Church Mission Office in Chicago.

USIC

5584a. **Morrish, William John.** *Cyfeiliornadau a dichellion saint y dyddiau diweddaf a Llyfr Mormon, yn cael eu dynoethi. Gan y parch W. J. Morrish, Ledbury. Cyfieithedig, trwy ganiatad yr awdwr, Gan David Roberts.* Caernarfon, Argraffedig a Chyhoeddedig gan H. Humphreys, 1849.

24p. 16cm.

Title in English: Heresies and deceptions of the Latter-day Saints.

In printed wrapper. Title within an ornamental border.

UPB, WalN

5593a. **Morton, George F.** *In Whitingham, Vermont.* [North Adams, Mass., Byam Printing Co., 1926]

32p. graphs illus. 22½cm.

Photos of Brigham Young hill, p. 25, and birth marker, p. 32.

USIC

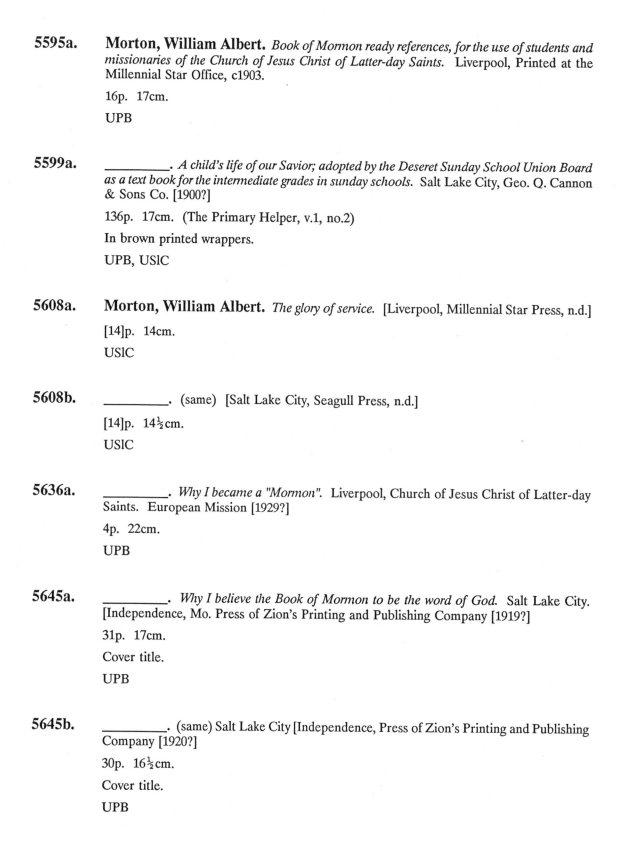

5595a.   **Morton, William Albert.** *Book of Mormon ready references, for the use of students and missionaries of the Church of Jesus Christ of Latter-day Saints.* Liverpool, Printed at the Millennial Star Office, c1903.

16p. 17cm.

UPB

5599a.   _____. *A child's life of our Savior; adopted by the Deseret Sunday School Union Board as a text book for the intermediate grades in sunday schools.* Salt Lake City, Geo. Q. Cannon & Sons Co. [1900?]

136p. 17cm. (The Primary Helper, v.1, no.2)

In brown printed wrappers.

UPB, USlC

5608a.   **Morton, William Albert.** *The glory of service.* [Liverpool, Millennial Star Press, n.d.]

[14]p. 14cm.

USlC

5608b.   _____. (same) [Salt Lake City, Seagull Press, n.d.]

[14]p. 14½cm.

USlC

5636a.   _____. *Why I became a "Mormon".* Liverpool, Church of Jesus Christ of Latter-day Saints. European Mission [1929?]

4p. 22cm.

UPB

5645a.   _____. *Why I believe the Book of Mormon to be the word of God.* Salt Lake City. [Independence, Mo. Press of Zion's Printing and Publishing Company [1919?]

31p. 17cm.

Cover title.

UPB

5645b.   _____. (same) Salt Lake City [Independence, Press of Zion's Printing and Publishing Company [1920?]

30p. 16½cm.

Cover title.

UPB

5645c. _____. (same) Salt Lake City [Independence, Press of Zion's Printing and Publishing Company 1921?]

31 [1]p. 16½cm.

Cover title.

UPB

5645d. _____. (same) Salt Lake City [1927?]

31p. 16½cm.

Cover title.

UPB

5645e. _____. (same) [Independence, Press of Zion's Printing and Publishing Company [1928?]

31 [1]p. 16½cm.

Cover title.

UPB

5651a. *Mother Goose. Mother Goose's melodies. The only pure edition, containing all that have ever come to light of her memorable writings, together with those which have been discovered among the MSS. of Herculaneum. Likewise every one recently found in the same stone box which hold the golden plates of the Book of Mormon. The whole compared, revised, and sanctioned, by one of the annotators of the Goose Family. With many new engravings.* New York and Boston: C. S. Francis and Company, c1832.

96p. 14cm.

McU, MB, MWA, PP, UPB

5651b. *Motto catechism card.* [Salt Lake City] Juvenile Instructor Print [1887?]

6 cards. 16½ x 11cm.

1. Wisdom. 2. The knowledge of God. 3. Love for one another. 4. The love of God. 5. Third commandment. 6. Prayer.

There are at least two series of these cards. The verso of card #1 at CtY varies from the USlC copy. The verso of card #2 at both CtY and UPB also vary from the USlC copy as they are blank. Card #6 at CtY has a different typeset from the USlC copy.

CtY 1,2,6., UPB #2, USlC 1-6

5652a. *The Mountaineer. The "Mountaineer" carriers' address for the new year, 1860.* [Great Salt Lake City, 1860]

Broadside. 21 x 14cm.

Text enclosed within ornamental border.

UPB, USlC

5652c. **Moxon, J. Cole.** *The Saints' Commercial Order. By Elder J. Cole Moxon.* Independence, Missouri, Ensign Publishing House, 1900.

17p. 16cm.

Established to help a better understanding of the financial law of the church.

MoInRC

5662a. **Muller, Hendrik Pieter Nicolaas.** *Door het land van Columbus een reisverhaal door Dr. Hendrik P. N. Mullet.* Haarlem, De Erven F. Bohn, 1905.

xp. [1]l., 504p. illus, ports, plates 26cm.

Title in English: Through the land of Columbus; a travelogue by Dr. Hendrik P. N. Mullet.

"Bij de Mormonen," p. 95-125.

MnHi, NN, UPB

5666a. **Munson, George A.** *Early years in Smyrna and our first old home week.* [Norwich, N. Y.] Chenango Union Presses, 1905.

208 [1]p. plates, ports. 21½cm.

Brief mention that Brigham Young was their most famous citizen, p. 118.

DLC, NN

5671a. **Murphey, Claude Charles.** *Around the United States by bicycle. Fully illustrated by Eustace Paul Ziegler.* Detroit, Press of Raynor & Taylor, 1906.

362p. plates. 18cm.

Chapter IX. "The city of the saints and the Great Salt Lake."

DLC, UPB

5673a. **Murphy, Jesse J.** *Jesse J. Murphy, appellant, vs. Alexander Ramsey, A. S. Paddock, G. L. Godfrey, A. B. Carleton, J. R. Pettigrew, E. D. Hoge and Arthur Pratt. Appeal from the Supreme Court of the Territory of Utah.* Washington, Judd & Detweiler [1884]

1p.l., 12p. 22cm.

At head of title: Transcript of record. Supreme Court of the United States. October term, 1884. No. 1027.

Cover title.

Case concerning the denial of Jesse J. Murphy to register to vote.

DLC

5676a. **Murray, Charles A.** *Newspaper career of E. D. Cowen, with biographic sketches by Charles A. Murray, Slason Thompson, R. E. M. Strickland, C. E. Arney, Hugh Hume, Frank M. Dallam, Jr.* [Seattle, Printed by Western Printing Company, c1930]

4p.l., 151 [8]p. port. 21cm.

"John D. Lee among the Indians" by E. D. Cowen, p. 47-56.

DLC, OU, TxU, UHi, UPB, WaU

5678a. **Murray, Thomas.** *Can newydd, sef, hunan fyfyrdod ar freuddwyd y Mormoniaid, y rhai sydd yn galw eu hunain yn Seintiau y Dyddiau Diweddaf, ar ei taith i Galiffornia.* [n.p., 1855]

4p. 13cm.

Title in English: A new song, namely, a meditation on the dream of the Mormons.

WalN

5684a. **Musser, Amos Milton.** *Plain facts for patriotic voters.* [Salt Lake City? 1906?]

[4]p. 23cm.

Need to vote for the Republication Party as they are defending Mormonism.

UPB, USlC

5690a. **Musser, Joseph.** *Rev. J. Musser, vs. the Saints.* East Jordan, East Jordan Press [n.d.]

4p. 31cm.

MoInRC

5695a. **Muzzey, David Saville.** *The United States of America.* Boston, Ginn and Co. [c1924]

2v. maps. 21½cm.

Mormons, v. 2, p. 152-53.

USlC

N

5705a.   **Naisbitt, Henry W.** *The veterans of our cause. Affectionately to President Woodruff on his birthday. March 1st, 1894.* [Salt Lake City? 1894]

Broadside. 24 x 18cm.

"From *Zion's Home Monthly*."

USlC

5706a.   *Names of the members of the two first Quorums of Seventies.* [Salt Lake City] Deseret News Steam Print [ca 1877]

Broadsheet. illus. 35 x 27½cm.

At head of title: Pictures of the Kirtland temple and Joseph Smith.

Printed on cardboard.

Within an ornamental border.

On the verso: "A scrap of history, from memory by Joseph Young, Sen."

UPB

5713a.   **National Reform Association.** *Mrs. Lulu Loveland Shepard. The silver-tongued orator of the Rocky Mountains.* Pittsburgh, Pa., National Reform Association [ca. 1915]

[4]p. port. 24cm.

Cover title.

Mrs. Shepard is added to the Reform Association's list of anti-Mromon speakers. Includes press clippings.

5713b.   *The National Reform Association.* *To American citizens everywhere.* [Pittsburgh, Penn., ca. 1910]

Broadside. 35 x 15cm.

USlC

5722a.   **Nauvoo Legion.** *Muster of old comrades. The Association of Veteran Artillerymen of the Nauvoo Legion.* [Salt Lake City, 1900]

Broadside. 21½cm.

USlC

5727a.   *Nauvoo Neighbor. Nauvoo Neighbor Extra, Nauvoo Hancock County, Illinois, December 9, 1843.* [Nauvoo, 1843]

Broadside. 35 x 33cm.

Concerning the State of Missouri's desire to have Joseph Smith arrested and returned to Missouri.

USlC

5731a.   _____. *Nauvoo Neighbor Extra.* July 2, 1844.

Broadside. 55 x 39cm.

"Awful assassination; the pledged."

USlC

5731b.   _____. *Nauvoo Neighbor Extra: Saturday, January 18, 1845. The voice of Nauvoo! Proceedings of the city council.* [Nauvoo, 1845]

Broadside. 41 x 28cm.

Continued thefts and other criminal acts blamed on the Mormons.

ICHi, USlC

5736a.   **Nead, Benjamin Mattias.** *The history of Mormonism with particular reference to the founding of the New Jerusalem in Franklin County.* [Chambersburg?] 1923.

411-427p. 23½cm. (Papers read before the Kittochtinny Historical Society, Chambersburg, Pa., Vol. 1, 1923)

DLC, MiU, NN, OC1WHi, PHC, PHi

5740a.   **Neal, R. B.** *Did Oliver Cowdery renounce Mormonism and join the Methodist Protestant Church at Tiffin, Ohio.* [Grayson, Ky. 1915?]

17 [1]p. illus. 21cm.

Based on the bogus "Defense in a rehearsal of my grounds for separating myself from the Latter Day Saints," by Oliver Cowdery.

UPB

5753a.   **Nebraska Territory. Supreme Court.** *Nebraska contested election. Letter from the clerk of the House of Representatives, communicating the evidence in the case of the Nebraska contested election.* [Washington? 1859]

35p. 22½cm. (U.S. 35th Cong. 2d Sess. House. Mis. Doc. No. 28)

Questions of voting by Mormon or other emigrant trains. Questions the number of Mormons in Nebraska.

UPB

5762a. **Nelson, Charles Clarence.** *Why religion? -- why the Church?* [Salt Lake City, Deseret News, 1928]

Broadside. 51 x 20cm.

At head of title: Reprint from the *Deseret News* of July 21.

Radio address given on KSL radio, July 15, 1928.

Need for spiritual food.

USlC

5764a. **Nelson, Lowry.** *Early land holding practices in Utah, and problems arising from them.* [Lancaster, Penn.?] 1927.

352-355p. 21½cm.

Reprinted from the *Journal of Farm Economics,* July, 1927.

Early Mormon land policies.

UHi

5780a. *Nephi diamond jubilee and home-coming in conjunction with Juab County Fair,* celebrating the seventy-fifth anniversary of the settlement of Nephi, 1851-1926. [Nephi, Utah, 1926]

[16]p. ports. 20½cm.

History of the founding of Nephi.

USlC

5781a. *Ein neuer zeuge fur Gott!* [Dresden, Germany, Herausgegeben von der Deutsch-Ossterreichischen Mission, ca. 1930]

[8]p. 24½cm.

Title in English: A New Witness for God.

USlC

5790a. *A new volume of scripture!* The revelations of God to the ancient Americans. [Liverpool, Millennial Star Office, n.d.]

[4]p. 22½cm.

Includes catalogue of works published by the Church of Jesus Christ of Latter-day Saints, and for sale at the Millennial Star Office.

UPB, USlC

5795a. *New West Gleaner.* Chicago, New West Education Commission, 1883?

v. bi-monthly. 30cm.

Originally organized in 1881 as a commission to promote Christianity in Utah and education against Mormonism.

Name changed to *Christian Education and New West Gleaner.*

UPB. IV; 1,2,4,5,6. V; 1,2,3,5,6. VI; 2,3,4,5,6. VII; 1,3,4,5. VIII; 1,2. USlC. IV; 1. V; 1,2,4,6. VI; 2,3,4,6. VII; 5,3. VIII; 1,2.

5795b. **New York Central Railroad Co.** *The greatest highway in the world. Historical, industrial and descriptive information of the towns, cities and country passed through between New York and Chicago via the New York Central Lines. Illustrated. Based on the Encyclopaedia Britannica.* [n.p., c1921]

130p. illus. 19cm.

Description of Joseph Smith and the "First Vision" found under the comments on Palmyra, p. 81-82.

DLC, MB, NN

5799a. **New York Woman Suffrage Society.** *Suffrage in Utah. Memorial of the New York Woman Suffrage Society, protesting against the sixth section of the bill regarding Utah.* [Washington, Govt. Print. Off.] 1873.

Broadside. 23 cm. (U. S. 42d Cong. 3d Sess. Senate. Ex. Doc. No. 44)

Letting women have the right to vote would defeat polygamy.

UPB

5805a. **Newman, Angelia French (Thurston).** *Observation No. 2.* [n.p., 1884]

Broadside. 29 x 20cm.

Reprint of Mrs. Angie F. Newman's article in *Womens Home Mission,* June, 1884. Anti polygamy article.

USlC

5805b. _____. *To the members of the Senate and House of Representatives of the 50th Congress: Sirs:* [n.p., 188-?]

Broadside. 21 x 14cm.

Against the admission of Utah as a state.

USlC

5805c. _____. *Utah. "A wonderful and horrible thing is committed in the land." Observation No. 1.* [Salt Lake City? n.d.]

Broadside. 27 x 8cm.

Reprinted from *Woman's Home Mission*? Copy torn with small amount of text missing.

USlC

5806a. **Newman, John Philip.** *Letter from Doctor J. P. Newman.* Salt Lake City, Salt Lake Tribune, 1870.

Broadside. 54 x 36cm.

Salt Lake Tribune Supplement. Aug. 1870.

Letter dated August 16, 1870.

Rebuttal after the Pratt-Newman debate.

USlC

5808a. **Newmark, Harris.** *Sixty years in southern California, 1853-1913. Containing the reminiscences of Harris Newmark. Edited by Maurice H. Newmark, Marco R. Newmark.* New York, The Knickerbocker Press, 1916.

xxviii, 688p. illus., plates, port. 23cm.

Other editions: 2nd ed., rev. New York, Knickerbocker, 1926. USlC; 3d ed rev. Boston, Houghton Mifflin Co., 1930. UPB

Contains numerous Mormon references.

CU, CU-B, DLC, MB, NN, OU, UPB

5841a. **Nielsen, Hans.** *Ex parte: In the matter of Hans Nielsen, appellant. Appeal from the First Judicial District Court of the Territory of Utah. Transcript of record.* [Washington? 1888?]

12p. 22cm.

At head of title: Supreme Court of the United States, October term, 1888. No. 1527.

Cover title.

Polygamy trial.

DLC

5850a. **Noall, Elizabeth Dette (Laker).** *He olelo ao no na hui manawalea o ko Hawaii nei paeaina.* [Honolulu, Hawaii? ca. 1894]

8p. 18cm.

Title in English: Counsel for the Relief Society in the Hawaiian Islands.

USlC

5852a. **Noall, Mathew.** *Ka hale laa o ke Akua Kiekie loa ma Loko Paakai.* [Honolulu, Hawaii, 1893]

[2]p. illus. 24½cm.

Title in English: The Holy Temple of the Most High God in Salt Lake City. Ka papa peresidena o ka Ekalesia o Iesu Kristo o ka Poe Hoano o na La Hope nei, p. [2]

USlC

5858a. *Nog een Waarschuwing tegen de Mormonen.* Haarlem, W. F. Hoogkammer [1909]

16p. 23cm.

Title in English: Yet another warning against the Mormons.

Cover title.

Title in ornamental border.

UPB

5863a. **Norlie, Olaf Morgan.** *History of the Norwegian people in America.* Minneapolis, Minn., Augsburg Publishing House, 1925.

602p. facsims., maps, music, ports. 22cm.

"Utah, 1847" p. 176-77. Includes other references throughout.

USlC copy in printed wrappers.

DLC, MH, MiU, NcU, Or, OU, UPB, USlC

5866a. **Norris, Moses.** *Speech of the Hon. M. Norris of New Hampshire, in the United States Senate, March 3, 1854 on Nebraska and Kansas.* Washington, Printed at the Sentinel Office, 1854.

16p. 23cm.

Brigham Young was appointed governor of Utah Territory while practicing polygamy.

DLC, KU, MH, OClW, Hi, UPB

5874a. *Notice : there will be a meeting held of the American citizens of Lee County, without reference to their political or religious principles, at Montrose in said county of Lee, on Saturday, the 11th inst, for the purpose of ascertaining their rights as such.* [Montrose, Iowa, 1845]

Broadside. 22 x 36cm.

Dated: Oct. 3, 1845, By order of many citizens.

Anti-Mormon meeting.

USlC

5912a. **Nutting, John Danforth.** *Mormonism proclaiming itself a fraud.* [Cleveland, Ohio, Utah Gospel Misison, 1906?]

8p. 17cm.

Reprinted from the *Union Gospel News,* March 7, 1901; revised.

Includes "Mormon morals" by Frank S. Johnson.

NN, USlC

5941a. _____. *The teachings of Mormonism and Christianity compared with the Bible and sound reason.* Cleveland, Ohio, Utah Gospel Mission, 1929.

80p. 17cm.

At head of title: Number Ten, U. G. M. Series.

"4th ed."

MH, NNUT

5948a. _____. *Utah Gospel Mission. The truth about God; being a concise statement of the main truths of reason, experience and the Bible about God, compared with the beliefs held in non-biblical lands and by Mormonism.* [Cleveland, Ohio, Utah Gospel Mission, 1909]

80p. illus. 17cm. (No. 5 of U.G.M. series)

USlC

O

5973b.   **Ochs, Milton B.** *Heart of the Rockies, illustrated, as reached by the Rio Grande Western Ry., Scenic line of the world. The new standard gauge line from Ogden and Salt Lake City to Provo, Castle Gate, Grand Junction, Glenwood Springs, Leadville, Aspen, Manitou, Colorado Springs, Pueblo, Denver and all sections of the East.* [Cincinnati, Ohio] Passenger Department of the Rio Grande Western Railway [Press of A. H. Pugh Printing Co., 1890]

199 [1]p. illus. 24cm.

Utah and the Mormons, p. 23-58.

DLC, LNHT, OClWHi, USIC

5973c.   **O'Connor, Michael Patrick.** *The life and letters of M. P. O'Connor. Written and edited by his daughter, Mary Doline O'Connor.* New York, Dempsey & Carroll, 1893.

xi, 561p. port. 23½cm.

Brief stop in Salt Lake City in 1879 and is surprised to see such genius in "this silent secluded valley."

DLC, MB, NjP, UPB, ViU

5974a.   *Oeffentlicher vortrag uber die Mormonen (Heiligen der letzten Tage) [w]ird Sonntag, den 2 Juli 1899.* [Frankfurt, F. Eichhorn, 1899]

Broadside. 34 x 64cm.

Title in English: Open discussion on the Mormons.

Public lecture with P. D. Lyman of Liverpool and A. H. Schultess of Hamburg as speakers.

USIC

5975a.   *The official publication of the Mutual Improvement Association. Maricopa Stake of Zion.* [Mesa, Ariz. 1923-   ]

v. 23cm.

UPB v. 1 #8, June, 1924.

5975b.   *Official souvenir; Independence, Missouri centennial 1827 -- 1927, October 2nd to 7th.* [Independence, Mo., Zion's Printing and Publishing Co., 1927]

[30]p. illus. 30cm.

Mormons, p. [17]

USIC

5978a. **O'higgins, Harvey.** *"Polygamy" (inside story of the play). An address by Harvey O'higgins before the Drama Society of New York.* [New York, ca. 1915]

[6]p. 16cm.

Background material on his play of the same name.

UPB

5981a. *He olelo ao no na Hui Manawalea ma ka Ekalesia o Iesu Kirsto o ka Poe Hoano o na La Hope Nei ma ko Hawaii nei Paeaina. Me kekahi mau moolelo o na luna mua o ua hui la.* Honolulu, Robert Grieve Publishing Co., Ltd., 1901.

21p. 17cm.

Title in English: Counsel for the Relief Society of The Church of Jesus Christ of Latter-day Saints for the Hawaiian Islands, and some stories of the first leaders of the organization.

HLB

O'rell, Max. See Blouet, Paul.

6020a. **Ostrander, Alson B.** *After 60 years; sequel to a story of the plains.* [Seattle, Washington, Press of Gateway Printing Co., 1925]

120p. 22½cm.

Mormons mentioned, p. 99.

CoU, DLC, IdU, NjP, USIC, UU

6022a. *Our country; its capabilities, its perils, and its hope. Being a plea for the early establishment of gospel institutions in the destitute portions of the United States, New York.* Published by the executive committee of the American Home Missionary Society, 1842.

60p. 18cm.

"Mormons and Mormon tenets," "Zeal in Proselyting," p. 47-49.

CSmH, CtY, ICN, UPB

6023a. *Our Life and Home.* Salt Lake City, Edited by C. H. Bliss, Sept. 1884.

Vol. 1 no. 1. 22cm.

Supercedes *Our Deseret Home.*

CtY, USIC

6028b. **Owen, William O.** *Life among the Mormons.* [Bristol] George Wright [1863]

Broadside. 28 x 25cm.

Lectures by Mr. Owen concerning his experiences and observations at Salt Lake City.

USIC

6030a. _____. *Seven years in the Great Salt Lake City.* London, W. J. Johnson, Printer, 1863.

Broadside. 54 x 36cm.

Lecture June 10, 1863.

CSmH, MH, USIC

P

6064a. **Page, J. D.** *J. D. Page, plaintiff and respondent, vs. J. R. Letcher, et. al., defendants and appellants. Brief and points and authorities for respondent on application for writ of mandate.* [Salt Lake City? 1894?]

20p. 22cm.

At head of title: In the Supreme Court of Utah Territory.

An election case involving the Utah Commission.

UAr

6073a. **Paine, Halbert Eleazer.** *G. Q. Cannon vs. A. G. Campbell. Contested election. Contestant's argument & reply. H. E. Paine, Counsel for contestants.* Washington, Thomas McGill & Co., Law Printers [1880]

16p. 23cm.

At head of title: House of Representatives.

Cover title.

In gray printed wrapper.

UPB

6080a. **Palmer, Eugene B.** *Impressions of Utah. Why I chose to live in Salt Lake City.* [Salt Lake City, 1925]

[10]p. 20cm.

Printed on blue paper with blue ink.

Comments on pioneer agriculture, the turmoil of earlier days.

UHi, UPB

6080b. **Palmer, Francis Leseure.** *Mahlon Norris Gilbert. Bishop Coadjutor of Minnesota, 1886-1900. With an introduction by Daniel Sylvester Tuttle.* Milwaukee, Young Churchman Company. London, A. R. Mowbray & Co., 1912.

3p.l., 303p. illus., plates, port. 20cm.

Chap. V., Life in Utah. Worked with Bishop Tuttle, Bishop of Montana, with jurisdiction in Idaho and Utah.

DLC, OClWHi, OrP, TNJ-R, UPB

6087a. **Palmer, William Rees.** *Iron County, Utah.* [Salt Lake City, Arrow Press, 1925?]

28p. illus. 22½cm.

Published by the Chamber of Commerce of Parowan, Utah. Settlements by the Mormons.

UHi

6090a. **Park, Mrs. S. E.** *The Mormons: Their religion, and identity with the Bible.* [Third edition] San Francisco, Printed by Jos. Winterrurn & Co., 1875.

2p.l. [5]-23p. 19½cm.

UPB

6095a. **Parker, James R.** *Proclamation. To all good citizens of the county of Hancock, state of Illinois, and the surrounding counties.* [Nauvoo, 1846]

Broadside. 32 x 15cm.

Dated Friday morning, August 28, 1846. States the reasons to keep the peace as the Mormons have assured him that they will leave as soon as they sell their property.

USIC

6100a. **Parkinson, Edward S.** *Wonderland; or twelve weeks in and out of the United States. Brief account of a trip across the continent -- shortrun into Mexico -- ride to the Yosemite valley-steamer voyage to Alaska, the land of glaciers -- visit to the great Shoshone Falls and a stage ride through the Yellowstone National Park.* Trenton, N.J., MacCrellish & Quigley, Book of Job Printers, 1894.

259p. illus. 19cm.

Description of their brief stay in Salt Lake City.

CtY, DLC, MtU, NNC, UPB, WaU

6113a. **Parry, Edwin Francis.** *Hur fralsning ernas.* [Stockholm, Gideon N. Hulterstrom, Broderna Olofssons Tryckeri, 1923]

4p. 22½cm.

Title in English: Saved by grace.

USIC

6120a. _____. *Een profeet der Laatste Dagen. Sterke bewijzen van de echtheid zijner zending alsmede van de waarheid van het Voek van Mormon.* Rotterdam, Netherlands, Gedrukt op last van Sylvester Q. Cannon, 1902.

31 [31]p. 21½cm.

Title in English: A prophet of Latter Days.

Includes "Het Boek van Mormon."

USIC

6121a. _____. *Simple Bible stories. No. 3. Illustrated. Adapted to the capacity of young children, and designed for use in Sabbath Schools, Primary Associations, and for home reading.* Salt Lake City, George Q. Cannon & Sons Co., Publishers, 1891.

3p. [7]-58p. illus. 22cm.

Parry given credit for the compilation in the preface of pt. l.

UPB, USIC

6138a. **Parry, Joseph Hyrum.** *Scriptural revelations of the universal apostasy.* [Liverpool? Millennial Star Office, 1908?]

4p. 21cm.

Caption-title.

Signed at end: J. H. P.

Variant of *Flake 6138.*

UPB

6146c. **Patten, Gilbert.** *Frank Merriwell among the Mormons: or, the lost tribe of Israel, by the author of "Frank Merriwell."* New York, Street & Smith, 1897.

32p. illus. 26cm. (*Tip Top Weekly.* V. 1, #62)

UHi, UPB

6149a. **Patterson, C. G.** *Cracking nuts in Utah; Little essays on tender subjects.* Salt Lake City, 1922.

[16]p. 27cm.

"The 1922 General Conference," p. [6]; comments on church business involvement, etc., p. [7]-[10].

USIC

6158a. **Paul, Hiland.** *History of Wells, Vermont, for the first century after its settlement. With biographical sketches by Robert Parks esq.* Rutland [Vermont] Tuttle & Co., Printers, 1869.

154p. 19cm.

In the section on William Cowdery, the relationship of the Cowdery family to Mormonism is discussed, p. 79-82.

MB, MH, DLC, WHi

6175a. **Pearl of Great Price. English. 1906.** *The Pearl of Great Price. A selection from the revelations, translations, and narrations of Joseph Smith, first prophet, seer, and revelator to the Church of Jesus Christ of Latter-day Saints. Divided into chapters and verses with references, in 1902, by James E. Talmage.* Salt Lake City, Published by the Deseret Sunday School Union, 1906.

iv, 103p. facsims 11½cm.

Vest pocket edition. Also published with the Doctrine and Covenants as a double combination.

UPB, USIC

6199a. _____. **German.** *Die kostliche Perle; eine auswohl aus den offenbarungen, Ubersetzungen und Erzahlungen Josph Smiths ... Funfte deutsche auflage.* Basel, Dresden, Schweizerisch-Deutschen und Deutsch-Osterreichischen Mission, 1929.

iv, 73p. facsims 17cm.

UU

6225a. **Pender, Mary Rose.** *A lady's experience in the wild west in 1883.* London, George Tucker [1888]

vii, 80p. 21cm.

Brief account of her disappointing stay in Salt Lake City.

CoD, CtY, MH, MoU, NjP, UPB

6230a. **Penrose, Charles William.** *C. W. Penrose replies to Joseph F. Smith.* [Circleville? 1892]

4p. 22cm.

Signed: Circleville, Piute County, Utah, Nov. 1, 1892.

Reasons why the people of Utah should be democrats.

USIC

6248a. _____. *Olelo ao "Moramona" moakaka a pohihihi ole He mau Lau mai ke Kumulaau mai O ke Ola. No Pres. Chas. W. Penrose.* Honolulu, L. D. S. Hawaiian Mission, 1923.

2p.l., 5-66p. 17cm.

Title in English: Mormon doctrine plain and simple.

UPB, USIC

6249a. _____. *Priesthood and presidency. Claims of the "Reorganized Church" examined and compared with reasons and revelation.* Independence, Press of Zion's Printing and Publishing Co. [n.d.]

13p. 16cm.

UPB

6256a. _____. *Rays of living light.* [Independence, Mo., Missions of the Church of Jesus Christ of Latter-day Saints, n.d.]

12 nos. 17cm.

USIC #2, 3, 5, 10

6256b. _____. *Rays of living light from the doctrines of Christ.* Liverpool, Printed and Published at the Millennial Star Office [1903?]

12 nos. 21½cm.

Cover title.

UPB

6259b. _____. (same) [n.p, ca. 1910]

12 nos. 22½cm.

USIC #1, 2, 3, 4.

6259c. _____. *Rays of living light on the one way of salvation.* Auckland, Abel, Dykes Limited, Printers [ca. 1910]

62p. 18½cm.

In pink printed wrapper.

UPB

6259d. _____. (same) [Independence, Missouri] Church of Jesus Christ of Latter-day Saints [1917]

49p. 17cm.

USIC

6259e. _____. (same) [Independence, Press of Zion's Printing and Publishing Co., 1917]

49p. [1]p. 17½cm.

In gray printed wrapper.

UPB

6259f. _____. (same) Independence, Zion's Printing and Publishing, [1918?]

48p. 17cm.

Variant cover.

USlC

6259g. _____. (same) [Independence, Press of Zion's Printing and Publishing Company, 1919?]

49[1]p. 17cm.

In tan printed wrapper.

UPB

6260a. _____. (same) [Independence? Missions of the Church of Jesus Christ of Latter-day Saints, ca. 1920]

12 nos. 18cm.

USlC #10, 11

6260b. _____. (same) [Independence, Press of Zion's Printing and Publishing Co., 1921?]

48p. 17½cm.

In gray printed wrapper.

UPB

6260c. _____. (same) [Independence, Press of Zion's Printing and Publishing Company, 1921?]

89p. 18cm.

In brown printed wrapper.

Variant printings.

UPB

6260d. _____. (same) [Independence] Church of Jesus Christ of Latter-day Saints [1921?]

89p. 18cm.

Press of Zions Printing and Publishing Company.

UHi, USIC

6260e. _____. (same) [Independence] Church of Jesus Christ of Latter-day Saints [1923?]

89p. 17½cm.

Press of Zions Printing and Publishing Company.

USIC

6260f. _____. (same) [Independence, Press of Zion's Printing and Publishing Company, 1924?]

89 [1]p. 17½cm.

In tan printed wrapper.

UPB

6260g. _____. (same) [n.p., ca. 1925]

12 nos. 22cm.

USIC

6260h. _____. (Same) [Liverpool, Mission headquarters, ca. 1925]

12 nos. 22cm.

USIC #2, 6, 7

6260i. _____. (same) [Independence] Church of Jesus Christ of Latter-day Saints [1926?]

89p. 18cm.

Press of Zions Printing and Publishing Company.

UPB, USIC

6261a. _____. (same) [Independence] Missions of the Church of Jesus Christ of Latter-day Saints, 1927?

12 nos. 17cm.

USIC

6261b. _____. (same) [Independence] Church of Jesus Christ of Latter-day Saints [1927]

89p. 18cm.

Press of Zions Printing and Publishing Company.

USIC

6261c. _____. (same) [Independence, Missions of the Church of Jesus Christ of Latter-day Saints, 1928?]

12 nos. 17cm.

USIC

6262a. _____. (same, in Danish) *Straaler af levende Lys.* [København, Udgivet og forlagt af Alma L. Peterson, n.d.]

12 nos. 25cm.

UPB #2, 9, 11, 12

6262b. _____. (same) [København, Udgivet og forlagt af Søren Rasmussen, 1908]

12 nos. 23cm.

USIC #2, 3, 6, 7, 8, 9, 10, 11, 12

6263a. _____. (same) [København, Udgivet og forlagt af Søren Rasmussen, 1908]

12 nos. 23cm.

UPB #1, 2, 4

6263b. _____. (same) [København, Udgivet og forlagt af Andrew Jenson, 1909]

12 nos. 24cm.

UPB #3, 4, 6, 7, 8, 9

6263c. _____. (same) [København, Udgivet og forlagt af Andrew Jenson, 1910]

12 nos. 25cm.

UPB #2, 3, 5-8, 10-12.

6263d. _____. (same) [København, Udgivet og forlagt af Andrew Jenson, 1911]

12 nos. 25cm.

UPB #4, 6, 8, 10

6263e. _____. (same) [København, Udgivet og forlagt af Joseph L. Petersen, 1926]

12 nos. 23cm.

USlC #1, 2, 3, 5, 7, 9, 11

6263f. _____. (same) [København, Udgivet og forlagt af Joseph L. Petersen, 1926-28]

12 nos. 23cm.

UPB #1, 3, 5, 6, 9

6264a. _____. (same, in Dutch) *Stralen van levend licht.* [Rotterdam, Utgave ban Sylvester Q. Cannon, 1908]

12 nos. 22cm.

USlC #1, 6

6265a. _____. (same) [Rotterdam, Uitgave van Chas. S. Hyde, ca. 1924]

12 nos. 22cm.

USlC #1, 2, 4, 6, 7, 8, 9, 12

6266a. _____. (same, in French) *Rayons de lumiere vivifiante.* [Rotterdam, Publie par Alex. Nibley, 1906]

12 nos. 22cm.

USlC #3, 4, 5, 6, 7

6266b. _____. (same) [Rotterdam, Publie par Alex. Nibley, 1906]

12 nos. 22cm.

UPB #7, 11

6266c. _____. (same) Bale, Suisse, Publie par Serge F. Ballif [1908?]

12 nos. 21cm.

UPB #6

6267a. _____. (same) [Leige, Belgium] Eglise de Jesus-Christ des Saints des Derniers Jours [ca. 1927]

12 nos. 22cm.

USIC #2, 4, 5, 6, 7, 8, 10

6270a. _____. (same, in German) *Strahlen lebendigen lichtes.* [Basel, Missionendder Kirche Jesu Christ der Heiligen der Letxten Tage, ca. 1930]

12 nos. 20cm.

USIC #1, 5, 6

6273a. _____. (same, in Hungarian) *Az elo vilagossag sugarai.* [Zurish, Thomas E. McKay, ca. 1910]

12 nos. 21cm.

UPB #1-4, USIC #1-4

6274a. _____. (same in Icelandic) *Geislar af lifandi lloosi.* [Gutenberg, Utgefandi ogg Kostnadarmadur, Jakob B. Josson, 1911]

12 nos. 22cm.

USIC #1, 2, 3

6285a. _____. *What "Mormons" believe. Epitome of the doctrines of the Church of Jesus Christ of Latter-day Saints.* [Salt Lake City, Bureau of Information, n.d.]

15 [1]p. 19cm.

In gray printed wrappers.

UPB

6291a. _____. (same) [Independence, Mo., Press of Zion's Printing and Publishing Company, 1928]

16p. 18cm.

UPB

6294a. _____. (same) Liverpool, Printed and published at the Millennial Star Office [1910]

27p. 17cm.

UPB

6295a. _____. (same) Liverpool, Printed and published at the Millennial Star [1911]

27p. 19cm.

In blue printed wrapper. Variant printing.

UPB

6295b. _____. (same) [Independence? Published by the missions of the Church of Jesus Christ of Latter-day Saints, ca. 1916]

8p. 17cm.

UPB

6295c. _____. (same) [Independence? Published by the Missions of the Church of Jesus Christ of Latter-day Saints, 1916?]

8p. 17cm.

Caption title.

USIC

6296a. _____. (same) [Independence, Press of Zion's Printing and Publishing Company, 1921?]

16p. 18cm.

Cover title.

UPB

6298a. _____. _Why I am a "Mormon"_ [Independence, Press of Zion's Printing and Publishing Company, ca. 1923]

15 [1]p. 18cm.

In maroon printed wrapper.

UPB

6298b. _____. (same) [Independence, Press of Zion's Printing and Publishing Company 1925?]

15 [1]p. 18cm.

Cover title.

UPB

6298c.   _____. (same) [Independence, Press of Zion's Printing and Publishing Company, 1926?]

15 [1]p.   17½cm.

Cover title.

UPB

6298d.   _____. (same) [Independence, Press of Zion's Printing and Publishing Company, 1929?]

15 [1]p.   18cm.

Cover title.

UPB

6313a.   **Perrie, George W.** *Buckskin Mose; or, life from the lakes to the Pacific, as actor, circus rider, detective, ranger, gold-digger, Indian scout, and guide. Written by himself . . . Edited, and with illustrations, by C. G. Rosenberg.* New York, H. L. Hinton, 1873.

1p.l. [5]-285p. plates. 19½cm.

Visited by Port Rockwell, Bill Hickman, Lot Smith, and other Danites, p. 210-12. Brief references to polygamy, p. 60, 285.

Another ed. New York, Worthington Co., 1890, OOxM, UPB, UU.

DLC, ICN, MH, NJP, NN, UU

6343b.   **Pfeiffer, Ida Reyer.** *Mon second voyage autour du monde par Mme. Ida Pfeiffer; traduit de l'Allemand par W. de Suckau.* Deux ed. Paris Librairie de L. Hachette et Cie., 1859.

viii, 633p. 1 col. map. 18cm.

Title in English: My second voyage around the world.

Mormon content, p. 554-55.

Another edition: Paris: Librairie de L. Hachette et Cie., 1857.

ICN, NjP, UPB

6343c.   **Phelps, A. J.** *John Taylor, President of the Church of Jesus Christ of Latter-day Saints designed and executed with a pen by Prof. A. J. Phelps.* [Salt Lake City, 1882?]

Broadside. port. 25 x 19cm.

UHi

6362a. **Phillips, Arthur Bernicie.** *The old Jerusalem gospel restored.* Lamoni [Iowa] Herald Publishing House [n.d.]

12p. 15cm. (No. 35)

UPB

Phillips, John F. See, U. S. Circuit Court.

6372b. **Phillips, S. F.** *Clawson vs. the United States. No. 1235. Brief for the United States.* [Washington? 1884?]

3p. 22cm.

At head of title: In the Supreme Court of the United States. October term, 1884.

An attempt by Clawson to obtain bail in a polygamy case.

DLC

6372c. _____. (same) [Washington? 1884?]

5p. 22cm.

At head of title: In the Supreme Court of the United States. October term, 1884.

Jury selection in polygamy case.

DLC

6372d. _____. (same) [Washington? 1884?]

13p. 22cm.

At head of title: In the Supreme Court of the United States. October term, 1884.

DLC

6372e. _____. *George Reynolds, plaintiff in error, vs. the United States. In error to the Supreme Court of the Territory of Utah. Brief for the United States.* [Washington? 1878?]

1p.l., 8p. 22cm.

At head of title: In the Supreme Court of the United States. October term, 1878. No. 180.

Cover title.

Bigamy case.

DLC

6372f.   _____. *Murphy vs. the United States, No. 1027. Pratt vs. same, No. 1028. Randall and husband vs. same, No. 1029. Clawson and husband vs. same, No. 1030. Barlow vs. same, No. 1031. Brief for the United States.* [Washington? 1884?]

33p. 22cm.

At head of title: In the Supreme Court of the United States. October term, 1884.

Voting suits as a result of the Edmunds Act.

DLC

6375a.   **Pickering, John Franklin.** *"Brain food" -- for people who love the West.* [Chicago?] Pickering's travel talks [1915?]

Broadside. 56 x 39cm.

Concerning Pickering's lectures, with endorsements from several Mormons including the First Presidency. One lecture entitled "The Mormons and their temples."

USIC

6377a.   **Pidgeon, Daniel.** *An engineer's holiday, or notes of a round trip from long. 0 [degrees] to 0 [degree].* London, Kegan Paul, Trench & Co., 1882.

2v. 20½cm.

V. 1, Chapter XX. Salt Lake City. Brief history of Mormonism and its current status. "The soul of Mormonism died with Brigham Young."

CtY, DLC, ICU, NjP, PPL, UPB

6384a.   *Pioneer celebration.* *Programme of the anniversary proceedings at the tabernacle, July 24, '76.* [Salt Lake City, 1876]

Broadside. 23 x 8cm.

UPB

6391a.   **Plank, Hiram.** *Brief sketches of the last scenes; or, A Message of warning to all people. "Cry aloud, spare not, lift up thy voice like a trumpet, and shew my people their transgression, and the house of Jacob their sins."* [Gilroy, California?] 1904.

2p.l. [5]-77p. 15cm.

In a tan printed wrapper.

Mormonism depicted as the ram spoken of in the book of Daniel.

UPB, USIC

6395a. *Political straws.* Salt Lake City [Political Straws Publishing Company] 1898.

V. 1 no. 1 [4p.] 36 x 25cm.

Dated: January 8, 1898. Only issue printed.

Newspaper to oppose the strong Mormon hold on the politics of Utah and Salt Lake City. "The gospel concerning education," by Juab, p. 4.

UPB

6410a. **Porter, James.** *Memorial of J. & R. H. Porter.* [n.p., 1859?]

37p. 20½cm.

"Brief in the case of J. C. Irwin & Co. & J. & R. H. Porter," p. [3], 10.

"Affidavits: p. [11]-37.

Utah Expedition carriers.

UPB

6413a. **Porter, Richard H.** *Hon. S. P. Chase, Secretary of the Treasury. Sir: In reflecting on your suggestion of a difficulty.* [Washington? 1861]

8p. 23cm.

Letter from Richard H. Porter of the firm of James & R. H. Porter to Mr. Chase concerning a claim for property taken by the U.S. Army during the Utah Expedition.

USIC

6421a. *Postmaster John T. Lynch of the "Mormons," a foul and frety libel!* [Salt Lake City, 1883?]

Broadside. 47 x 22cm.

Quoting from an article taken from the *St. Louis Republication*, which was quoted from the *Chicago Times* of May 27th, 1883. "Published at the request of 'Many Citizens'."

USIC

Potter, Arnold. See, Christ, Potter [pseud].

6432a. **Powell, William.** *The twenty-fourth of July.* [n.p., 187-?]

Broadside. 31 x 11cm.

Text within ornamental border.

Pioneer celebration.

USIC

Pratt, Helaman. *El bautismo a guien y como debe ser administrado por Helaman Pratt.* See Bliss, Charles H., *Flake/Draper Supplement 576a.*

6441a. **Pratt, Mary Ann M.** *Mary Ann M. Pratt, appellant, vs. Alexander Ramsey, A. S. Paddock, G. L. Godfrey, A. B. Carleton, J. R. Pettigrew, E. D. Hoge and John S. Lindsay. Appeal from the Supreme Court of the Territory of Utah.* Washington, Judd & Detweiler [1884?]

1p.l., 11p. 22cm.

At head of title: Transcript of record. Supreme Court of the United States. October term, 1884. No. 1028.

Cover title.

Case concerning the denial of Mary Ann Pratt to the right to register to vote.

DLC

6444a. **Pratt, Milson Ross.** *The House of Israel. Who and where they are.* [n.p., 191-?]

Broadside. 22 x 14cm.

The dispersion of Israel. Appears to be Mormon oriented.

USIC

6444b. _____. *The Julian calendar gives the date of our Lord's birth.* [n.p., 191-?]

Broadside. 20 x 14cm.

Dates the age of the world using the Book of Mormon.

USIC

6449a. **Pratt, Orson.** *Der Charaketer und die erforderlichen Eingenschaften, welche die Diener des Reiches Gottes besitzen mussen.* [n.p., ca. 1888]

9-13p. 24cm.

Title in English: The Character and the necessary qualities which the servant of the kingdom of God must possess.

Number 3 of 5 pamphlets from an unknown publication.

USIC

6483a. _____. *Das folgende ist eine kurze darstellung der Grundsatze, an welche die Heiligen der letzen Tage glauben.* [n.p. ca. 1888]

7-8p. 24cm.

Title in English: The next is a short description of principles, in which the Saints of the last days believe.

Number 2 of 5 pamphlets from an unknown publication.

USIC

6495a. _____. *Guds rige i de Sidste Dage, eller forberedelserne for Kristi anden tilkommelse.* Kobenhavn, Udgivet og forlagt af A. L. Skanaey. Trykt hos L. A. Nielsen, 1902.

23p. 19cm.

Title in English: God's kingdom in the last days, or the preparations for the second coming of Christ.

USIC

6523a. _____. *Maerkvaerdige syner.* 32te Tusinde. [Kjøbenhavn, Udgivet og forlagt af N. C. Flygare; Tryckt hos F. E. Bording, 1879.

16p. 22cm.

Title in English: Remarkable visions.

UPB

6539a. _____. *Sammenlikning emellan bevisen for Bibeln och Mormons bok.* [n.p.] Wilhelmsen, 1881.

23p. 23cm.

Title in English: Similarity between evidences for Bible and Book of Mormon.

Originally published in the *Journal of Discourses*, Vol. 7, p. 22-38.

USIC

6548b. _____. [Tracts] Abertawy, Cyhoeddwyd ac argraffwyd gan Daniel Daniels, 1856-1857.

224p. 17½cm.

Published in printed wrappers with title within lined borders.

Contents: 1. Y wir ffydd. 2. Gwir edifeirwch. 3. Bedydd dwfr. 4. Yr Ysbryd Glan. 5. Doniau ysbrydol. 6. Angenrheidrwydd am wyrthiau. 7. Gwrthgiliad cyffredinol. 8. Breniniaeth y dyddiau diweddaf.

Titles in English: 1. The true faith. 2. True repentance. 3. Water baptism. 4. The Holy Spirit. 5. Spiritual gifts. 6. Necessity for miracles. 7. Universal apostasy. 8. Latter-day Kingdom.

Dennis 100-107.

WalB, WalN

6561a. **Pratt, Parley Parker.** _An apostle of the Church of Jesus Christ, of Latter-day Saints, was in the island of Great Britain, for the gospel's sake; and being in the spirit on the 21st of November, A.D. 1846, addressed the following words of comfort to his dearly-beloved wife and family, dwelling in tents, in the camp of Israel, at Council Bluffs, Missouri Territory, North America; where they and twenty thousand others were banished by the civilized Christians of the United States, for the word of God, and the testimony of Jesus._ [Liverpool? 1846?]

Broadside. 40 x 31cm.

CtY, NjP, UPB, USlC

6570a. _____. _A dialogue between Joseph Smith and the Devil. From New York Herald, 1844._ Ogden, Utah, Theodore A. Smith, Book and Job Printer, 1883.

9p. 23cm.

Title within border.

In yellow printed wrapper.

UPB

6606a. _____. _Priodas a Moesau yn Utah. Annerchiad a ysgrifenwyd gan Parley P. Pratt ... Ac a ddarllenwyd yn nghyd-eisteddiad deddf-wneuthurwyr Utah, yn neuadd y cynnrychiolwyr, Fillmore, Rhag. 31, '55, gan Mr. Thomas Bullock ..._ Abertawy, argraffwyd a chyhoeddwyd gan Daniel Daniels [1856]

[14]p. 19cm.

Title in English: Marriage and morals in Utah.

Dennis 99.

USlC, WalN

6618a.   _____. *The prophet Joseph rebuking the guard at Richmond jail, Ray County, Missouri.* [Salt Lake City?] George Washington Crocheron, 1897.

Broadside. port. 40 x 51cm.

All the Mormon persons are identified in portrait.

USIC

6625a.   _____. *The true God and his worship contrasted with idolatry.* [Liverpool? Millennial Star Office? 1842?]

8p. 19cm.

Also published in v. 2, #12, April, 1842, *Millennial Star,* p. 184-89.

MH, USIC

6646a.   _____. *A voice of warning and instruction to all people; or an introduction to the faith and doctrine of the Church of Jesus Christ of Latter Day Saints. Revised. Also an analysis of Isaiah 29.* Lamoni, Iowa, Printed and published by the Reorganized Church of Jesus Christ of Latter Day Saints [c.a. 1884]

149p. 18cm.

Published after 1884.

MoInRC

6646b.   _____. (same) Seventh rev. ed. Lamoni, Iowa, Reorganized Church of Jesus Christ of Latter Day Saints, 1885.

127p. 17cm.

USIC

6649b.   _____. *A Voice of warning . . . by Parley P. Pratt.* St. John, Kansas, Indian Territory Mission [189-?]

xiii, 221p. 13cm.

USIC

6655a.   _____. (same) Electrotype edition. Chattanooga, Tenn., Published and for sale by the Southern States Mission, 1896.

xvi, 220p. 13cm.

UPB

6657a. _____. (same) Chicago, Published and for sale by the Northern States Mission, 1898.

xvi, 220p. 13cm.

In red cloth printed wrapper.

"Press of A. L. Smith & Co."

UPB

6699a. _____. (same in German) *Eine Stimme der Warnung und Belehrung fur alle Volker oder Kirche Iesu Christi der Heiligen der letzten Tage. Ubersetzt von Daniel Carn. Nachesehen und revidiert von Philipp Tadje. Herausgegeben und zu beziehen von der Schweizerisch-Deutschen Mission der Kirche Jesu Christi der Heiligen der letzten Tage.* Basel, 1914.

2p.l. [5]-138p. 19cm.

"Funfte Auglage."

USIC

6707a. _____. (same in Swedish) *En warnande rost och undervisning for alla menniskor eller inledning till fron och laran i Jesu Christi Kyrkas Uttersta Dagars Helige, af Parley P. Pratt. Ofwersatt fran engelskan.* Kopenhamn, Utgifven och forlagd af C. G. Larsen. Tryckt hos F. E. Bording, [ca. 1875]

xiii, [15]-200p. 16½cm.

"Tredje swenska upplagan."

USIC

6719a. *The Pratt family will hold a special social at recital hall. April 9, 1921.* Salt Lake City, 1921.

Broadside. 20 x 15cm.

UHi

6724a. **Presbyterian Church in the U.S.A.** *National excerpts published by the Board of National Missions, Mormon Area.* New York, 1929.

Broadside. 20 x 15cm.

UHi

6726a. **Presbyterian Church in the U.S.A. Board of Home Missions.** *The Mormons.* [New York, 1917?]

10p. 15cm. (No. 37)

OC

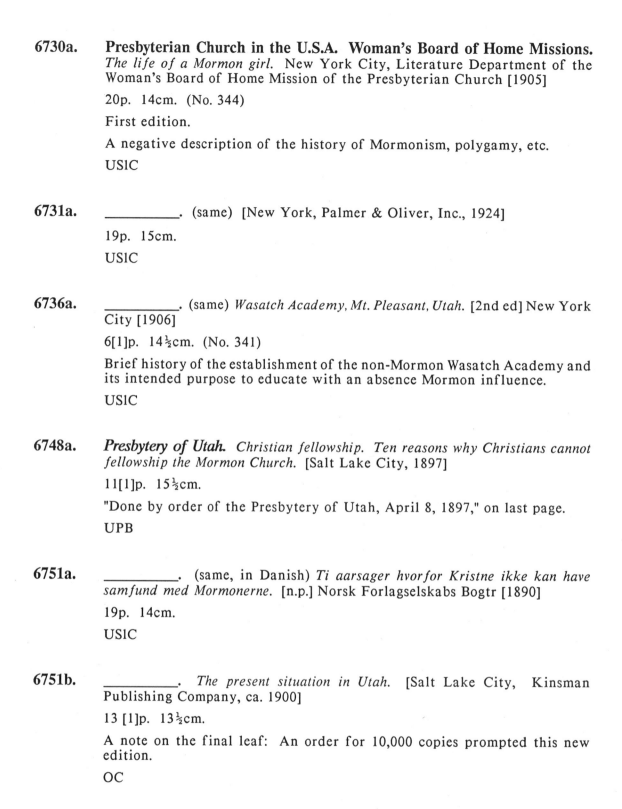

6730a.   **Presbyterian Church in the U.S.A. Woman's Board of Home Missions.**
The life of a Mormon girl. New York City, Literature Department of the
Woman's Board of Home Mission of the Presbyterian Church [1905]

20p. 14cm. (No. 344)

First edition.

A negative description of the history of Mormonism, polygamy, etc.

USIC

6731a.   _____. (same) [New York, Palmer & Oliver, Inc., 1924]

19p. 15cm.

USIC

6736a.   _____. (same) *Wasatch Academy, Mt. Pleasant, Utah.* [2nd ed] New York
City [1906]

6[1]p. 14½cm. (No. 341)

Brief history of the establishment of the non-Mormon Wasatch Academy and
its intended purpose to educate with an absence Mormon influence.

USIC

6748a.   *Presbytery of Utah. Christian fellowship. Ten reasons why Christians cannot
fellowship the Mormon Church.* [Salt Lake City, 1897]

11[1]p. 15½cm.

"Done by order of the Presbytery of Utah, April 8, 1897," on last page.

UPB

6751a.   _____. (same, in Danish) *Ti aarsager hvorfor Kristne ikke kan have
samfund med Mormonerne.* [n.p.] Norsk Forlagselskabs Bogtr [1890]

19p. 14cm.

USIC

6751b.   _____. *The present situation in Utah.* [Salt Lake City, Kinsman
Publishing Company, ca. 1900]

13 [1]p. 13½cm.

A note on the final leaf: An order for 10,000 copies prompted this new
edition.

OC

6753a. **Price, Rees E.** *To the scattered and peeled Britons.* [Mount Zion? 1845]

Broadside. 32 x 27cm.

Signed: Rees E. Price. Mount Zion, Oct. 31, 1845.

Includes a letter to Victoria, Queen Imperial of the British Empire.

Mormon poetry.

USIC

6754a. **Price, Rose Lambart.** *The two Americas; an account of sport and travel. With notes on men and manners in North and South America.* London, Sampson Low, Marston, Searle, and Rivington, 1877.

viii, 368, 24p. illus., plates. 23cm.

Includes a visit with Brigham Young; attends George A. Smith's funeral.

NIC, NjP, UPB, ViU

6757a. *Les principes fondamentaux de l'evangile de Jesus-Christ comme ils furent etablis par lui-meme. Joi, repentance, bapteme, don du St-Esprit, autorite et revelation.* Berne, Publie par la Redaction du "Stern", 1898.

16p. 18cm.

Title in English: The fundamental principles of the gospel of Jesus Christ as established by him.

UPB

6759c. *The procession of the immortals. Suggested by the death of Elder David Hoagland Cannon, while on a mission in Germany.* [Salt Lake City? 1892?]

Broadside. 26 x 17cm.

Cannon died Oct. 17, 1892.

USIC

6761b. *Program of exercises in honor of President Wilford Woodruff, (born March 1, 1807) tendered him on the eve of the ninetieth anniversary of his birth, in the Tabernacle, Salt Lake City, Utah, by the Deseret Sunday School Union, commencing at 2 o'clock p.m., Sunday, February 28, 1897.* [Salt Lake City] 1897.

[4]p. port. 19cm.

UHi, UPB

6761c. *Program of Maeser Day exercises in religion classes to officers and teachers of religion classes.* [Salt Lake City? Church of Jesus Christ of Latter-day Saints, ca. 1910]

[4]p. 20cm.

Program in honor of Karl G. Maeser.

USIC

6763a. *Programme. Grand juvenile procession.* [Great Salt Lake City, 1854]

Broadside. 32 x 21cm.

"Monday, July 24th, 1854. Being the seventh anniversary of the pioneers into the valley of the Great Salt Lake."

USIC

6769a. *Programme. 24th of July celebration.* [Great Salt Lake City, 1852?]

Broadside. 33 x 8cm.

USIC

6773a. *Protea. Talking with a Prophet. What Brigham Young himself said about his successor.* [n.p., ca. 1877]

Broadside. 83 x 13cm.

A supposed conversation at length on Mormon succession and other matters.

USIC

6779a. **Puaux, Rene.** *Decouverte des Americains.* Paris, Bibliotheque-Charpentier [c1930]

199, [1]p. 19cm.

In yellow printed wrapper.

Title in English: Discovery of the Americans.

"Chez les Mormons" p. 55-61.

CtY, DLC, IdU, NjN, NN, UPB, UU

Q

6785a. *Questions and answers on good manners.* [Salt Lake City, Juvenile Instructor Print., n.d.]

Broadside. 17½ x 11½cm.

CtY, USlC

6785b. *Questions and answers on the Godhead.* [Salt Lake City] Juvenile Instructor Print. [ca. 1887]

Broadsheet. 17½ x 10cm.

CtY, USlC

6785c. *Questions of the hour.* [Toronto? ca. 1925]

[4]p. port. 23cm.

Advertisement for "Prophetic lectures" of Daniel Macgregor with over 1,000 feet of illustrated canvas.

UPB

6785d. *Questions and answers upon the first commandment.* [Salt Lake City] Juvenile Instructor Print. [ca. 1887]

Broadsheet. 17½ x 10cm.

On the verso: Questions and answers about angels.

CtY, USlC

6785e. *Questions and answers upon the "Word of Wisdom."* [Salt Lake City] Juvenile Instructor Print. [n.d.]

Broadsheet. 18 x 12cm.

CtY, USlC

R

6805b. *Te raau a Iosepha ra.* *Te hoe vea ei na mua i te Buka a Mormona.* Papeete, Tahiti, Te Ekalesia a Iesu Mesia i te Feia Mo'a i te Mau Mahona Hopea Nei, 1906.

12p. 18cm.

Title in English: The stick of Joseph

USIC

6809a. **Rader, Perry Scott.** *School history of the state of Missouri.* Brunswick, Missouri, P. S. Rader, Publisher [c1891]

iv. 279p. ports., fold. col. map. 20cm.

Chapter V. Governor Boggs and Mormon troubles.

DLC, OCU, NIC, UPB

6809b. **Radius, J. S. C. de.** *Historical account of every sect of the Christian religion: its origin, progress rites and ceremonies, with a brief description of Judaism and Mahometanism, compiled from the latest authorities. Second ed. (rev).* London, 1864.

viii, [9]-173, 8p.

"Mormonites (or Latter-day Saints)," p. 111-20.

UPB

6814a. **Rand, Olive.** *A vacation excursion. From Massachusetts Bay to Puget Sound.* Manchester, N. H., Press of John B. Clarke, 1884.

203p. illus. 19cm.

Chapter XVII. Salt Lake City. Material on the Mormons.

CaBVaU, CSmH, OrHi, UPB, USIC, WaT

6815a. **Randall, Mildred E.** *Mildred E. Randall and Alfred Randall, appellants, vs. Alexander Ramsey, A. S. Paddock, G. L. Godfrey, A. B. Carleton, J. R. Pettigrew, E. D. Hoge and Harmel Pratt. Appeal from the Supreme Court of the Territory of Utah. Filed October 9, 1884.* [Washington? 1884?]

12p. 22cm.

At head of title: Transcript of record. Supreme Court of the United States. October term, 1884. No. 1029.

Voting rights for a non-practicing polygamist.

DLC

6821a. **Raum, George Edward.** *A tour around the world; being a brief sketch of the most interesting sights seen in Europe, Africa, Asia, and America, while on a two years' ramble.* New York, William S. Gottsberger, 1886.

2p.l., 430p. port. 21cm.

Brief stop in Salt Lake City with negative notes on the Mormons, p. 393-394.

DLC, KyU, OCl, NH, UPB, ViU

6826a. *Raymond, Alberta, Canada; a complete and comprehensive description of the agricultural, stockraising and mineral resources of Southern Alberta, Canada, near the Raymond Sugar Works.* [Raymond? ca. 1902]

36p. illus. 22cm.

Mormons, p. 4.

USlC

6828a. *Reading exercises in the English language for new beginners. Laesevesser i det engelske Sprog for Begyndere.* Kjobenhavn, Udgivit og forlagt af H. C. Haight. Trykt hos F. E. Bording, 1857.

94p. 17½cm.

Dictionary and grammar published for Danish Mormons leaving for Utah. Much of the grammar concerns information needed by the emigrant.

UPB

6830b. *Recent discussion of Mormon affairs. I. Address to the world. First Presidency of the Church. II. Review of address to the world. Ministerial Association, Salt Lake City. III. Answer to Ministerial Association review. Elder B. H. Roberts.* [Salt Lake City] The Deseret News, 1907.

17p. [1]l., 26p. [1]l., 56p. 23cm.

Each item also published separately.

UPB, USlC

6830c. *Die Rechte, Bergunstigungen und Segnungen, welcher sich Burger des Riches Gottes in Diesem Leben erfreuen.* [n.p., 188-?]

23-32p. 24cm.

Title in English: The proper encouragement and blessing, can gladden the citizen of the kingdom of God in this life.

(Number five of an unknown publication with continuous pagination).

USlC

6830d.   *Recital from Apostle Whitney's masterpiece, Elias* by Elder W. J. Kohlberg with *music and German songs.* [Salt Lake City, 1905?]

[4]p. port. 23cm.

UPB

6830e.   **Reclus, Onesime.** *A bird's-eye view of the world.* Boston, Ticknor and Company, 1887.

2p.l., v-xvi, 920p. 25cm.

Section on Utah and the Mormons in which Utah is described as an area attractive to the lower classes and the lawless due to the Mormon church.

DLC, ICRL, PPL, OCl, OO, USlC

6834a.   **Reed, Andrew.** *A narrative of the visit to the American churches, by the deputation from the Congregational Union of England and Wales. By Andrew Reed, D. D. and James Matheson, D. D.* New York, Published by Harper & Brothers, 1835.

2v. 19cm.

Brief mention of meeting "Mormonites" heading for Far West.

Another edition included in *The Christian Library.* New-York, Thomas George, 1836.

DLC, MoU, MsU, TxU, UPB, ViU

6839a.   **Rees, Cecelia.** *Dwight Peck, et. al., plaintiffs and respondents, vs. Cecelia Rees, defendant and appellant. Appellant's brief. Miller & Maginnis, attorneys for appellant.* Ogden, W. W. Browning & Co. [1891]

7p. 22cm.

At head of title: In the Supreme Court of the Territory of Utah. June term 1891.

Suit concerning money left in a will for temple work in the Logan Temple.

UAr

6839b.   **Rees, John E.** *Idaho, chronology, nomenclature, bibliography.* Chicago, W. B. Conkey Co., 1918.

125p. 21½cm.

Mormons, p. 16, 25, 28, 30, 31, 66, 78, 79, 89-90, 112.

DLC, IdU, IdTf, USlC, UU

6845a. **Reid, Agnes Just.** *Letters of long ago. Illustrated by Mabel Bennett.* Caldwell, Idaho, The Caxton Printers, Ltd. 1923.

118p. illus. 24cm.

In brown ornamental paper.

A member of the Morrisites, she relates going back to Utah in 1879 to testify at the trial of Robert T. Burton, p. 70-76. Other Mormon references.

DLC, IdU, MH, NjP, UPB, USIC

6847. **Reid, Mayne.** *The wild huntress. By Captain Mayne Reid, author of "The scalp-hunters," "The war trial," etc., etc. In three volumes.* London, Richard Bentley, New Burlington Street, 1861.

3v. 21cm.

A western novel with Mormon sections: "Squatter and saint," "An apostolic effort," a word about the "Mormon monsters."

CSmH, IU, NcU, OCU, UPB

6849a. **The Relic Library.** *Devoted to the reproduction of rare and interesting writings connected with the rise and progress of the Church of Jesus Christ of Latter-day Saints, (derisively called Mormon).* York, Neb., John K. Sheen, Publisher. April 15-May 1, 1889.

2pts. (48p.) Semi-monthly. 24½cm.

In green printed wrapper.

First series has title: "The writings of Joseph Smith, the seer." Suspended after No. 2 due to lack of support.

UPB, USIC

6854a. *Religious systems of the world; a contribution to the study of comparative religion: A collection of addresses delivered at South Place Institute, now revised and in some cases rewritten by the authors, together with some others specially written for this volume.* London, Swan Sonnenschein & Co., 1905.

viii, 824p. 22½cm.

"The Church of Jesus Christ of Latter-day Saints (commonly known as Mormons)," by James H. Anderson, p. 657-82.

MB, NBuU, OCH, USIC

6854b. **Religious Tract Society.** *Ar Mormonlaran sann, eller ej? Ester engelskan.* Malmo, Tryckt hos F. A. Hartman, 1858.

38p. 15cm.

Title in English: Is Mormonism true or not?

Translated by C. E. Venstrom.

UPB

6858a. *Remarkable delusions; or, illustrations of popular errors.* London, The Religious Tract Society [1851?]

192p. 15cm.

Chapter IX. "Delusions associated with religion." "Mormonites," p. 171-92.

"Delusions associated with religion." The final delusion discussed is "Mormonites," p. 171-88. "Some of the most extraordinary of any we have related. As its pernicious errors have extensively spread, a more detailed exposure of them may be useful."

Revised by D. P. Kidder in 1852. New York, Lane & Scott, 1852. DLC. New York, Carlton & Phillips, 1854. DLC NIC. Also published with Magic, pretended miracles, and remarkable natural phenomena. London, Religious Tract Society, 1855. DLC, INU, MH, NN, PU

DLC, UPB

6859a. _____. (same) Philadelphia, American Sunday School Union [1851?]

192p. 15cm.

DLC, NcD, UPB

6864a. *Remarks on the doctrines, practices, &c. of the Latter-day Saints: Setting forth the marvelous things connected with this new light from America.* Preston, Printed by J. Livesey [1838]

8p. 22cm.

Signed: A lover of truth.

Lancashire Record Office, UPB xerox

6864b. **Remsburg, John E.** *Bible morals. Twenty crimes and vices sanctioned by scripture.* New York, Truth Seeker Co. [c1885]

57p. 17½cm.

Mormons and polygamy, p. 46.

IdRR, KyU, NN, OCl, USIC

6903b. **Reorganized Church of Jesus Christ of Latter Day Saints.** *Concordance and reference guide to the Book of Doctrine and Covenants, published by the Reorganized Church of Jesus Christ of Latter Day Saints.* Plano, Ill., Printed at the True Latter Day Saints' Herald Steam Book and Job Office, 1870.

23p. 15½cm.

MoInRC, UPB, USIC

6910b. _____. *Epistle of the Twelve and the Bishopric. To the Church of Christ, called to be Saints, in all the World, Greeting.* [Plano, Ill., 1881]

8p. 18½cm.

Dated: April 13th, 1881.

The law of tithing in the RLDS church.

UPB

6913a. _____. *Faith and repentance.* [Plano, Ill.] Board of Publication of the Reorganized Church of Jesus Christ of Latter Day Saints [188-?]

8p. 22½cm. (No. 22)

Caption title.

Variant of *Flake 6913,* with address in Colophon.

UPB, USIC

6931a. _____. *The Kingdom of God: What is it? Whence comes it?* [Plano, Ill.] Published by the Reorganized Church of Jesus Christ of Latter Day Saints [188-?]

4p. 22cm. (No. 24)

With the place of publication in the colophon.

UPB, USIC

6943a. _____. *Laying on of hands.* [Plano, Ill.] Published by the Reorganized Church of Jesus Christ of Latter Day Saints [188-?]

4p. 22cm. (No. 25)

Caption title.

Without the place of publication in the colophon.

UPB, USIC

6953a. _____. *Ministry reports to the forty-fifth annual conference of the Reorganized Church of Jesus Christ, held at Lamoni, Iowa, commencing April 6, 1897.* Lamoni, Iowa, 1897.

50p. 22½cm. (Supplement to the *Saints' Herald,* April 7, 1897)

Cover title.

UPB

6953b. _____. *Ministry reports to the forty-fourth annual conference of the Reorganized Church of Jesus Christ, held at Kirtland, Ohio, commencing April 6, 1896.* Lamoni, Iowa, 1896.

62p. tables. 23cm. (Supplement to the *Saints' Herald.* April 1, 1896)

Cover title.

UPB

6953c. _____. *Ministry reports to the forty-third annual conference of the Reorganized Church of Jesus Christ, held at Independence, Missouri, commencing April 6, 1895.* Lamoni, Iowa, 1895.

62p. tables. 21½cm. (Supplement to the *Saints' Herald*)

Cover title.

UPB

6958a. _____. *Official facts touching the conviction of Apostle E. C. Briggs of the Reorganized Church of Jesus Christ of L.D.S. by the courts of the church upon the charge of falsehood on nine specific counts. Also for official maladministration.* [n.p., n.d.]

12p. 16cm.

MoInRC

6973a. _____. *The pure gospel of Christ.* Lamoni, Iowa [1892]

2p. 21cm. ([Tract] No. 46)

Questions and answers with scriptural notations.

MoInRC

6983a. _____. *Reports to the seventieth general conference.* [Independence] April 6, 1925

168 [1]p. 19cm.

UPB

6985a. _____. *The Sabbath question.* [Lamoni, Ia.] Published by the Reorganized Church of Jesus Christ of Latter Day Saints [n.d.]

12p. 21½cm.

UPB

7000a. _____. *Synopsis of the faith and doctrines of the Church of Jesus Christ of Latter-day Saints. Compiled from the Bible, Book of Mormon, Doctrine and Covenants, and other publications of the Church; with an appendix, containing an epitome of ecclesiastical history and a chronology of important events in the history of the Latter day work.* Plano, Ill., 1865.

448p. 12½cm.

Both this edition and the 352p. edition are complete. The 352p. edition ends with the term "glory" and the 448p. edition ends with the term "millenium-reign of Christ and the Saints on earth."

MoInRC

7003a. _____. *Trial of the witnesses of Jesus, a legal argument by Rt. Rev. Thoms Sherlock, D. D., Bishop of London, 1729 -- Revised.* Lamoni, Iowa [n.d.]

31p. 21cm. ([Tract] No. 4)

"Epitome of the faith" on verso of last leaf.

MoInRC

7026a. _____. *Youth and the Restoration; a collection of representative orations delivered during the 1929-1930 world-wide oratorical contest.* Independence, Herald House, 1930.

190p. 18cm.

MoInRC

7033b. _____. **Council of the Twelve.** *Report of the Quorum of the Twelve to the General Conference.* [n.p., n.d.]

Broadside. 31 x 21½cm.

Concerning the rights and privileges of the Council of the Twelve.

MoInRC

7033c. _____. **Daughters of Zion.** *Constitution of the General Society.* [Independence? Zion's Ensign, 1893]

7p. 14cm.

Includes "Daughters of Zion Reveille" by Mrs. M. Walter on back. First RLDS sponsored women's group.

MoInRC

7044a. _____. **General Sunday School Association.** *Constitution and by-laws adopted by the General Sunday School Association of the Reorganized Church of Jesus Christ of Latter Day Saints.* Lamoni, Iowa, 1897.

18p. 13cm.

First appeared in 1893 when the association was formed.

MoInRC

7044b. _____. (same) Lamoni, Iowa, 1900.

19p. 22cm.

MoInRC

7068b. _____. **Hymnal. English. 1920.** *Songs of redemption.* Sydney, The Standard Publishing House [1920?]

190 [5]p. music. 14cm.

UPB

7071a. _____. (same) **1924.** *Zion's praises.* Independence, Mo., Herald Publishing House, 1924 [c1903]

232 nos. music. 21cm.

Includes index.

UPB

7076b. _____. **Presiding Bishopric.** *The Church reserve and saints' home funds.* Lamoni, Iowa, 1892.

4p. 26½cm.

Dated on first page: 4th Feb., 1892, and on page 4: November 12th, 1891. Financial matters of the RLDS church.

UPB

7083b. _____. **Students Society.** *The Constitution and by-laws of the Students Society.* Lamoni, Iowa [1887]

4p. 16cm.

Society formed by Marietta Walker and a forerunner to the Zion' Religio-Literary Society.

MoInRC

7085b. **Republican Party. Utah.** *American intervention and Mexico.* [Salt Lake City, 1912]

[4]p. 22½cm.

Discusses the situation of Mormons in Mexico.

UHi

A revelation and prophecy by the prophet, seer, and revelator, Joseph Smith. See Church of Jesus Christ of Latter-day Saints. Missions. South Africa.

7090a. *Revelations.* [Great Salt Lake City, 1854?]

10p. 22cm.

Caption title.

Contains Doctrine & Covenants, Section 103, and miscellaneous teachings of Joseph Smith.

USlC

7090b. *Restoration of the Gospel.* [Salt Lake City] Juvenile Instructor Print? ca. 1887.

Broadsheet. 17½ x 10cm.

CtY, USlC

7091a. **Rewby, R.** *The fulfillment of a promise and exposure of the false teachings of the Reorganized Church of Jesus Christ of Latter Day Saints.* Coeur d'Alene, Idaho, 1921.

3p. 15cm.

MoInRC

7091b. **Reybaud, Louis (i.e. Mari Roch Louis.)** *Etudes sur les reformateurs, ou socialistes modernes. Par M. Louis Rebaud . . . Precedee d'unemouyelle preface, du Rapport de M. Jay, membre de l'Academie francaise, et de celui de M. Villemain, secretaire perpetuel.* 7 ed. Paris, Guillaumin & cie, 1864.

2 v. 18½cm.

Title in English: Studies of the reformists or modern socialists.

Mormonism not mentioned in any of the six previous editions. Very critical.

CaBVa, INS, KU, NcD, NjP, NN, PBm, PU, USlC

7098a.   **Reynolds, George.** *George Reynolds, plaintiff in error, vs. the United States, defendant in error. Brief of plaintiff in error.* [Washington? 1876?]

1p.l., 63p. 22cm.

At head of title: In the Supreme Court of the United States. October session, 1876. No. 180.

Cover title.

Polygamy case.

Attorneys for the defense: Ben Sheeks, George N. Biddle.

DLC

7098b.   _____. *George Reynolds, plaintiff in error, vs. the United States. In error to the Supreme Court of the Territory of Utah.* [Washington? 1876?]

2p.l., 30p. 22cm.

At head of title: Transcript of record. Supreme Court of the United States. No. 455. Filed October 4, 1876.

Cover title.

Bigamy case.

Same case as *Flake/Draper Supplement 7098a.*

DLC

7105a.   _____. *The "Mormon" metropolis: An illustrated guide to Salt Lake City and its environs. Containing illustrations and descriptions of principal places of interest to tourists; also interesting information and historical data with regard to Utah and its people.* Salt Lake City, J. H. Parry & Company, Publishers, 1889.

67p. illus. 20cm.

UPB

7115a.   _____. *Story of the Book of Mormon.* [Salt Lake City, Jos. Hyrum Parry, 1888]

Broadsheet. illus. 23 x 15cm.

Advertisement for a book written by Elder Reynolds. Includes information concerning the book. Verso includes a painting of the discovery of the records of the Jaredites.

USIC

7119a. _____. *The story of the Book of Mormon.* 5th ed. Chicago, Ill., Press of Hillison & Etten Co. [c1888]

xiii, [14]-386p. 20cm.

At some point the plates of this edition were acquired by Zion's Printing & Publishing Co.

UPB

7133a. **Rich, Benjamin Erastus.** A friendly discussion upon religious subjects; compiled from a work entitled, "Mr. *Durant of Salt Lake City."* [n.p., n.d.]

20p. 17½cm.

USIC

7140a. _____. (same) [n.p., n.d.]

32p. 14cm.

USIC

7142a. _____. (same) Brooklyn, T. J. Dyson & Son [ca. 1898]

31[1]p. 13cm.

Orders to be sent to Elder A. P. Kesler. A. P. Kesler was president of the Eastern States Mission from 1897 to 1899.

UPB

7142b. _____. (same) [Brooklyn, A. P. Kesler, 1898?]

31[1]p. 14cm.

USIC

7142c. _____. (same) [Brooklyn, ca. 1898]

[12]p. 21½cm.

"The baptism of water and the spirit," by A. P. K. [Alonzo Pratt Kesler], p. [11]. A description and view of the Salt Lake City, p. [12]

USIC

7161a. _____. (same, in Danish) *Den fremmede fra vesterlandet eller en venskabelig forhandling om religise Sporgsmaal.* [Kjøbenhavn, Udgivet og forlagt af Martin Christopherson, 1912]

16p. 23cm.

USIC

7164a. _____. (same, in Dutch) *Een Vriendschappelijk Onderhoud over Belangrijke Godsdienst-Waarheden.* [Rotterdam, Uitgave van de Nederlandsch-Belgische Ze ding, 1913?]

19p. 18cm.

Cover title.

In grey or green printed wrappers.

Song: We Thank Thee Oh God for a Prophet, on the recto of back cover.

UPB, USIC

7164b. _____. (same, in French) *Qu est la verite; discussion amicale sur dea sujets religieux.* Zurich, Thomas E. McKay, 1909.

21p. 17½cm.

USIC

7167a. _____. (same, in Swedish) *Framlingen fran vastern eller ett vanskapligt meningsutbyte i religiosa fragor.* Stockholm, Utgifven och forlagd af P. Sundwall, 1910.

22[2]p. 18½cm.

USIC

7168a. _____. (same) Stockholm, John H. Anderson, 1926.

24p. 18cm.

USIC

7172b. _____. *An interview in the Atlantic Constitution on the "Mormon" faith.* [Independence, Zion's Printing and Publishing Co., n.d.]

16p. 17cm.

From the *Atlanta Constitution,* March, 1899. Formerly titled: Gospel interview.

USIC

7172c. _____. (same) [Independence? Missions of the Church of Jesus Christ of Latter-day Saints? ca. 1916]

24p. 15½cm.

USIC

7183a. _____. *Mr. Durant of Salt Lake City, "that Mormon."* Chattanooga, Tenn., Published by Southern States Mission for Ben. E. Rich [1901?]

220p. [1]l. port. 13cm.

Preface of present edition dated June, 1901.

UPB

7185a. _____. (same) Independence, Mo. [Missions of the Church of Jesus Christ of Latter-day Saints, 1924?]

127p. 17½cm.

USIC

7185b. _____. (same) Independence [Missions of the Church of Jesus Christ of Latter-day Saints, 1926?]

127p. 18cm.

USIC

7231a. **Richards, Franklin S.** *Ex parte: In the matter of Hans Nielsen, appellant. Argument of Franklin S. Richards, for the appellant. Delivered April 22, 1889.* [Salt Lake City] The Deseret News Co., Printers and Publishers, 1889.

23p. 23cm.

Unlawful cohabitation case.

UPB

7232a. _____. *Rudger Clawson, appellant, vs. the United States, appellee. Appeal from the judgment on a writ of habeas corpus of the Supreme Court of the Territory of Utah. Brief of argument for appellant.* Philadelphia, Allen, Lane & Scott, [1884?]

1p.l., 14p. 22cm.

At head of title: No. 1235. October term, 1884. Supreme Court of the United States.

Cover title.

Polygamy case.

DLC

7234a.   _____. *Rudger Clawson, plaintiff in error, vs. the United States, defendant in error. Brief for plaintiff in error. From the Supreme Court of Utah.* Washington, Gibson Bros., Printers and Bookbinders, 1885.

1p.l., 26p. 22cm.

At head of title: Supreme Court of the United States. October term, 1884. No. 1263.

Cover title.

Case concerning the constitution of jury.

DLC, UPB

7237a.   _____. *United States of America, appellant, vs. the late corporation of the Church of Jesus Christ or [sic] Latter-day Saints, and others, appellees. Appeal from the Supreme Court of Utah Territory. Motion to advance cause.* [Washington, 1892]

6p. 22cm.

At head of title: Supreme Court of the United States. October term, 1892. No. 1287.

Concerning the dissolution of church property.

DLC

7237b.   _____. *The United States of America, appellant, vs. the late corporation of the Church of Jesus Christ of Latter-day Saints et al., appellees. Appeal from the Supreme Court of Utah Territory. Motion for decree. Franklin S. Richards, for appellees.* Washington, Gibson Bros., 1893.

6p. 22cm.

At head of title: Supreme Court of the United States. October term, 1893. No. 887.

Cover title.

Concerning the dissolution of church property.

DLC

7243a.   **Richards, George F.** *Salt Lake Temple. Bishop* _____ [Salt Lake City, 192-?]

[4]p. 24cm.

Instruction to bishops concerning temple garments, donations to the temple, recommends, etc.

UPB

7247a. **Richards, Louisa Lula (Greene).** *The old folks day, a jubilee song for June 25, 1925.* [Salt Lake City] Deseret News, 1925.

Broadside. 28 x 21cm.

Title within ornamental border.

Poem concerning the Old Folks Day started by Charles R. Savage, "who was no longer with us."

UHi

7247b. _____. *The thirty-sixth anniversary of . . . Evan M. Greene & Susannah K. Greene.* [Salt Lake City? 1871?]

Broadside. 18 x 11cm.

A poem honoring Evan and Susannah Greene signed by their children.

USIC

7247c. **Richards, Mary B.** *Camping out in the Yellowstone. Letters written in 1882, by Mrs. Mary B. Richards to the Salem Observer.* Salem, Mass., Published by Newcomb & Gauss, 1910.

62p. 20cm.

"Salt Lake City revisited." "A service in the Mormon temple," p. 3-7.

CtY, MH, MtBC, NjP, UHi, UPB

7249a. **Richards, Samuel Whitney.** *Creation.* [n.p., n.d.]

Broadside. 32 x 20cm.

Poetry. Signed: Samuel W. Richards, Salt Lake City.

USIC

7249b. _____. *Death of Elder Willard Snow.* [Liverpool, Millennial Star Office, 1853]

Broadside. 50 x 14cm.

An offprint from the *Millennial Star,* v. 15 (September 10, 1853), p. 598-99.

USIC

7258a. **Richardson, C. E.** *Are you brave enough to investigate?* [Independence, Mo., Press of Zion's Printing and publishing Company, c1922]

7[1]p. 18cm.

UHi, UPB, USIC

7260a. **Richardson, David M.** *To the honorable, the Senate and House of Representatives in Congress assembled.* [Detroit, Mich., 1882]

12p. 27cm.

"Polygamy," p. 5-6.

Another edition titled: Our country; its present and its future prosperity.

USIC

7261a. **Richardson, Ernest Cushing, ed.** *An alphabetical subject index and index encyclopaedia to periodical articles on religion, 1890-1899. Compiled and edited by Ernest Cushing Richardson.* New York, Published for the Hartford Seminary Press by Charles Scribner's Sons [c1907]

xlii, 1168p. 24½cm.

Mormonism, p. 748-49.

AzU, DLC, MH, MU, NjP, TU, UPB, USIC, WaS

7274a. **Riddell, Newton N.** *Child culture, according to the laws of physiological psychology and mental suggestion By N. N. Riddell . . . With a discussion of educational problems by John T. Miller.* Salt Lake City, Human Culture Publishing Co., 1902.

120[21]p. 22cm.

Discussion of Word of Wisdom, p. 101-105. Advertizement for L. D. S. garments by Cutler Brothers Co., page [9].

MH, UPB, USIC

7295a. **Rio Grande Western Railway Company.** *What may be seen crossing the Rockies enroute between Ogden, Salt Lake City and Denver on the line Rio Grande Western Railway.* Salt Lake City, 1896.

42 [2]p. illus. 15cm.

Cover-title: Crossing the Rockies.

Utah and Mormons, p. 2-14, 26-31, 41.

USIC

7295b. _____. (same) Salt Lake City, 1898.

47p. illus. 15½cm.

Utah and Mormons, p. 2-15, 20, 27.

Cover title: Crossing the Rockies.

USIC

7315a.   **Roberts, Brigham Henry.** *Cynydd a chadernid Mormoniaeth.* Gan B. H. Roberts, llynlleifiad. [n.p., 1888?]

Broadside. 42 x 23cm.

Title in English: The growth and stability of Mormonism.

USIC

7333a.   _____. *The Lord's day. Reasons for the observance by Latter-day Saints for the first day of the week as the Christian Sabbath or the "Lord's Day."* [n.p.] Published by the Missions of the Church of Jesus Christ of Latter-day Saints in the United States [ca. 1916]

13[3]p. 18cm.

USIC

7333b.   _____. (same). [Independence, Press of Zion's Printing & Publishing Co., ca. 1918]

13[3]p. 17½cm.

USIC

7343a.   _____. *Mormonism. The relation of the church to Christian sects. Origin and history of Mormonism; doctrines of church; Church organization; present status.* Independence, Press of Zion's Printing and Publishing Co., 1925.

78p. 18cm.

USIC

7356a.   _____. *Origin and faith of the Church of Jesus Christ of Latter-day Saints.* [Chicago, Press of A. L. Swift & Co., 1895]

15 [1]p. 18cm.

USIC

7368a.   _____. *The second coming of the Messiah and events to precede it.* [Liverpool] Millennial Star Office [1889?]

8p. 22½cm.

Two variants.

USIC

7368b.   _____. [Salt Lake City, The Deseret News Company, 1889?]

12p. 17cm.

UPB, USIC

7368c. _____. [Liverpool, Millennial Star Office, 189-?]
8p. 22½cm.
Variant printings
UHi, UPB, USIC, UU

7370a. _____. [Chicago? Church of Jesus Christ of Latter-day Saints, 1911?]
16p. 17cm.
UPB, USIC

7372a. _____. [Independence, Press of Zion's Printing & Publishing Co., 1915?]
12[4]p. 18cm.
Articles of faith, p. [1-2]. Price list and catalogue, p. [3].
UPB, USIC

7372b. _____. [Independence, Mo., Zion's Printing and Publishing Co., ca 1916]
12 [4]p. 17½cm.
Variants.
USIC

7372c. _____. [Independence, Missions of the Church of Jesus Christ of Latter-day Saints, 1918?]
16p. 17cm.
USIC

7372d. _____. [Independence, Missions of the Church of Jesus Christ of Latter-day Saints, 1919?]
16p. 18½cm.
UPB, USIC

7372e. _____. [Independence, Missions of the Church of Jesus Christ of Latter-day Saints, 1921?]
16p. 16½cm.
UPB, USIC

7372f. _____. [Independence, Missions of the Church of Jesus Christ of Latter-day Saints, 1923]

16p. 18½cm.

UPB, USIC

7372g. _____. [Independence, Missions of the Church of Jesus Christ of Latter-day Saints, 1925?]

16p. 18cm.

USIC

7372h. _____. [Independence, Missions of the Church of Jesus Christ of Latter-day Saints, 1927?]

16p. 17cm.

UPB, USIC

7378a. _____. *Why "Mormonism"?* [Independence, Press of Zion's Printing and Publishing Co., 1925?]

4 pts. 17cm.

UPB pt. 2, 4

7384a. **Robertson, Mrs. A. A.** *The eternity of the marriage covenant. A Mormon fallacy refuted. By Mrs. A. A. Robertson, an apostate Mormon.* [n.p., n.d.]

26p. 20cm.

Errata tipped in between p. 16 and 17.

OC

7389a. **Robinson, Fayette.** *California and its gold regions; with a geographical and topographical view of the country, its mineral and agricultural resources. Prepared from offical and other documents; with a map of the United States and California, showing the routes of the U.S. Mail steam Packets to California, also the various overland routes.* New York, Stringer & Townsend, 1849.

137p. fold. map. 21cm.

Mormons are leaving the gold fields to go to Salt Lake.

CU-B, DLC, ICN, NoU, NjP, UPB

7389b. **Robinson, Henry Cornelius.** *A few thoughts about the Pacific coast. For the Family Circle. By H. C. R.* [Hartford, 1882?]

52p. 23cm.

Travels through Salt Lake City; is not impressed with the Mormons.

CSmH, UPB

7395b. **Robottom, Arthur.** *Travels to the far West in search of borax.* [Birmingham? 1876?]

32p. illus., port. 19cm.

Travels to Salt Lake City with a Mormon. Spends a few days and describes his impressions of Mormons and Salt Lake Valley.

UPB

7395c. **Rochechouart, Julien de.** *Excursions autour du monde. Les Indes, le Birmanie, la Malaisie, le Japon et les Etats-Unis. Par le Cte Julien de Rochechouart, Ministre Plenipotentiaiare. Ouvrage onee de gravures.* Paris, E. Plon et Cie., Impremeurs-editeurs, 1879.

2p.l., iii, 282p. [1]l. plates. 18cm.

Title in English: Excursions around the world.

Visited Salt Lake City in 1876, with some comments on Mormonism.

CLU, CtY, CU, DLC, MH, PPL, USIC

7422a. **Rossiter, Ernest Crabtree.** *Te Buka a Moromona. Te mau parau i papaihia i te rima a Moromona. Te hoe mau uiraa e te pahonoraa i nia i taua buka a Moromona ra. Papaihia e Eraneta A Rositera.* Papeete, Tahiti, Te Ekalesia o Iesu Mesia o te ai Mahana Hopea Nei, 1918.

44p. 17cm.

Title in English: The Book of Mormon.

In printed cover.

Missionary tract.

USIC, UPB

7437a. **Roz, Firmin.** *L'Amerique nouvelle. Les Etats-Unis et la guerre. Les Etats-Unis et la paix.* Paris, Ernest Flammarion, 1923.

282 [1]p. 18cm.

Title in English: The new America.

Mormons, p. 63-64. Brief mention demonstrating freedom of religion in America.

UPB

7437b. *Ruin!! Ruin!! Ruin!! Influence of Mormonism!* [n.p., 184-?]

Broadside. 21 x 27cm.

Notice for parents to look after their daughters as ten girls were ruined in Claremont, N.H. by the Mormons.

USIC

7455a.   **Russell, Charles Marion.** *Trails plowed under. With illustrations in color and line by the author.* Garden City, New York, Doubleday & Company, Inc., c1929.

xx, 210p. illus. (part col). 27cm.

"Mormon Murphy's confidence," p. 69-73, "Mormon Zack, fighter," p. 117-20.

DLC, IdB, MtU, OCl, OO, UPB, USlC

7461a.   **Ryan, F. J.** *Protestant miracles. High orthodox and evangelical authority for the belief in divine interposition in human affairs. Some account of marvelous cures of illness, rescue from danger, death, poverty and suffering, through faith and prayer in recent centuries. Compiled from the Writings of Men Eminent in Protestant Churches.* Stockton, Cal., Record Publishing Co., Printers, 1899.

3p.l. [7]-198p. 17cm.

"A Mormon miracle," p. 167-68.

UPB

7462a.   **Ryland, Walter P.** *My diary during a foreign tour in Egypt, India, Ceylon, Australia, New Zealand, Tasmania, Fiji, China, Japan, and North America, in 1881-2. By W. P. R.* Brimingham, Printed by Chas. Cooper and Co., Ltd., 1886.

2p.l., iii, 263p. 19cm.

Impressions of Salt Lake City, p. 239-41.

DLC, UPB, USlC

S

7480a.   *Salt Lake City.* Salt Lake City, Published by Bureau of Information, Temple Block [ca. 1904]

[24]l. plates, 1 folded. 24 x 29cm.

Includes views of Mormon buildings.

First plate is copyrighted by the Albertype Co., Brooklyn, N.Y.

USIC

7486a.   **Salt Lake City. Chamber of Commerce.** *Annual report of Salt Lake Chamber of Commerce.* Salt Lake City, 1890-[1893]

v. 23½cm.

Includes material on Mormonism in each issue.

USIC, 1891, 1892 UPB, 1890, 1893

7492a.   _____. *Salt Lake City and Utah, "The center of scenic America."* [Salt Lake City, 1926]

[32]p. illus. 22½cm.

In colored wrapper.

Brief discussion of Temple Square and other Mormon sites.

UPB

7494a.   _____. *Utah, America's great mining and smelting center. This booklet compiled from authentic federal and state and individual sources, and issued under supervision of the Mining Committee of the Chamber of Commerce.* Salt Lake City, 1928.

32p. illus. 23cm.

Mormons, p. 3.

USIC

7495a.   _____. *Utah's importance as a mineral state. Compiled from authentic federal and state sources, 1923 statistics and issued under the supervision of the Mining Committee of the Salt Lake City Chamber of Commerce.* [Salt Lake City, 1924?]

24p. illus. 23cm.

Cover title: Utah, its mineral wealth.

Mormons, p. 4.

USIC

7495b. _____. (same) [Salt Lake City, 1925?]

24p. illus. 23cm.

Mormons, p. 22.

NjP, USlC

7495c. _____. *The western wonderland! Compliments of Salt Lake City Chamber of Commerce. Utah, her mineral and other resources. Advantages offered to the homeseeker, manufacturer and capitalist. Mineral, industrial, agricultural, commercial.* [Salt Lake City] Salt Lake Tribune Print [1888?]

31p. 22½cm.

Interestingly only brief comments on Mormonism.

DLC, NjP, UHi, UPB, USlC

7498a. *Salt Lake City directory for the year 1873,* embracing a general directory of residents, and a business directory; also general information of value to the citizens of Salt Lake City, and business men in general: Together with an appendix, full of interesting and instructive matter, regarding the condition of social, political and religious affairs in Utah Territory. Salt Lake City, Published by Hannahs & Co., 1873.

xii, 176p. 23cm.

"Boundaries of the wards," p. [89]-90. "Organization of the Mormon Church" p. 93-94.

UPB

7504a. *Salt Lake City, Utah.* Chicago, Press of Hollister Brothers, ca. 1903]

[24]p. illus. 10cm.

Advertisement for the Kenyon Hotel. Includes views of Mormons and Mormon properties.

UPB

7504b. _____. (same) [Chicago, Press of Hollister Brothers, ca. 1903]

[32]p. illus. 10cm.

Includes "Compliments of The Kenyon" on verso of the front cover. Salt Lake City, p. [2]-[3], Mormon Church history, p. [26]-[28], and Articles of Faith, p. [29]-[30].

UPB

7507a. *Salt Lake Mormons. All the people of this country have now an opportunity of seeing those men who are guilty of so many of those horrible murders which for many years have been committed in Utah.* [Chicago, 188-?]

Broadside. illus., port. 31 x 11cm.

Chicago exhibit and wax museum.

On verso: The only free gallery of anatomy in the world. "For gentlemen only."

USIC

7507b. **Salt Lake Stake Academy.** *Circular of the Salt Lake Stake Academy. Annual.* Salt Lake City, 1886-

v. 21cm.

USIC holdings include: 1886-89.

7508a. **The Salt Lake Temple.** [Salt Lake City? 1900?]

Broadside. illus. 22 x 28cm.

Brief description of the Salt Lake Temple and of Salt Lake City.

USIC

7509a. **Salt Lake Tribune.** *Death and a swift wedding; the way opened to a Tooele saint whereby his "persecutions" might cease.* [Salt Lake City] 1888.

Broadside. 28½ x 8cm.

USIC

7510a. _____. *How polygamy is dying.* Salt Lake City, 1887.

Broadside. 19 x 10cm.

Reprint of an editorial from the *Salt Lake Tribune,* Oct. 17, 1887, criticizing Ambrose Bolivar Carlton and John A. McClernand of the Utah Commission.

USIC

7519a. _____. *Tribune extra.* [Salt Lake City, 1874]

Broadside. 35 x 25cm.

Includes the people's ticket, articles against the way Mormons vote, and a poem entitled "A Mormon election" by Viva Voce and dated Feb. 8, 1874.

USIC

7519b. _____. *Tribune extra! Brigham Young versus apostates and free schools.* Salt Lake City, 1873.

Broadside. 36 x 26cm.

Includes an open letter from John Cheslett to Brigham Young.

USIC

7521a. *Salut pourles morts. Preexistence et origine de l'homme, bapteme pour les morts.* Zurich, Publie par la redaction der "Stern," Serge F. Ballif, 1906.

15p. 18cm.

Title in English: Salvation for the dead, the pre-existence and origin of man, baptism for the dead.

USIC

7521b. **Salyards, Christiana, ed.** *The Gospel Quarterly for Sunday School pupils, senior grade first year. October, November, December, 1925, Volume 33, Number 4.* Independence, Mo., Herald Publishing House, 1925.

64p. 22cm.

RLDS Sunday School manual.

USIC

7521c. *De Sande vidners: liv og laerdomme i Jesu Christi Kirke af Sidste Dages Hellige.* [Kjøbenhavn] Sidste Dages Hellige [185-]

8p. 22cm.

Title in English: The true witness.

USIC

7526a. *Sandheden sejrer. En upartisk fremstilling af et hidtil miskjendt folk. Vidnesbyrd af fremragende maend, som have besogt de Sidste-Dages Hellige i deres hjem og studeret deres liv og karakter.* [Kjøbenhavn, Udgivet og forlagt af C. N. Lund, Trykt hos F. E. Bording (V. Petersen), 1897]

8p. 22½cm.

Title in English: The truth prevails. An impartial presentation about a hitherto misunderstood people.

USIC

7526b. _____. (same) [Kjøbenhavn, Udgivet og forlagt af George Christensen, Trykt hos F. E. Bording (V. Petersen), 1898]

8p. 23½cm.

USIC

7526c.   **Sanford, Carlton Elisha.** *Early history of the town of Hopkinton, history of East Village (Nicholville) and vicinity, diaries of Elisha Risdon and Artemas Kent, soldiers of the civil war, genealogical record of sixty of the pioneer families; with two maps and a hundred and forty illustrations.* Boston, The Bartlett Press, 1903.

xiv, 604p. incl. facsims. front. plates, ports., port. groups. 25cm.

Mormon missionary work in Hopkinton, New York in 1843-44, p. 162-66.

AzU, DLC, ICU, MB, NN, PHi, WaS

7528a.   **Sauvin, Georges.** *Authour de Chicago. Notes sur les Etats-Unis.* Paris, Librairie Plon. E. Plon, Nourrit et Cie. 1893.

vii, 263p. 18cm.

Title in English: Author of Chicago. Notes on the United States.

Chapter X. "Chez les Mormons," p. 210-33.

CtY, DLC, UPB

7535a.   **Savage, Charles Roscoe.** *Pictorial reflex of Salt Lake City and vicinity.* Salt Lake City, published by C. R. Savage, c1900.

42p. 20 leaves of plates 14 x 18cm.

15th rev. edition.

The Great Temple and other places of interest.

USIC

7541a.   _____. *Views of Utah and tourists guide. Containing a description of the views and general information for the traveler, resident and public generally, from authentic sources.* Salt Lake City, Art Bazar [n.d.]

30p. [16] folded illus. 10½cm.

Description of the Mormon temple and information for tourists.

UPB

7549a.   **Scandinavian Arrangement Committee.** *A grand concert, ball and supper for the benefit of the Scandinavian Mission House, Copenhagen, Denmark, will be given at Christensen's Hall, Tuesday evening, December 31, 1901 . . . under the auspices of the Scandinavian Arrangement Committee ("Skandinavisk Farvaltnings Komite").* [Salt Lake City, 1901]

[4]p. 18½cm.

UPB

7549b. *Scandinavian conference and reunion,* Mount Pleasant, Utah, August 15th and 16th, 1925. Diamond jubilee, 1850-1925. [Mt. Pleasant, Utah, 1925]

[4]p. illus. 23cm.

Program in English and Danish.

UHi, UPB

7549c. *Scandinavian day at Saltair Beach on June 15. Souvenir program for the Scandinavian jubilee to be held in Salt Lake City, June 14, 15, 16, 17, in commemoration of the introduction of the gospel to the Scandinavian countries, June 14, 1850.* [Salt Lake City? 1900]

[12]p. illus., ports. 31cm.

The text contains words for community songs as well as for the Ogden choir.

In pink printed wrapper. Title from wrapper.

UPB, USlC

7549d. Scandinavian L.D.S. organizations of Salt Lake City. *A missionary farewell testimonial to be given by the Scandinavian L.D.S. organizations of Salt Lake City, in the Assembly Hall, Nov. 10, 1927, in honor of Elder John A. Widtsoe and wife, who leave shortly for the European Mission.* [Salt Lake City, 1927]

[3]p. ports. 23cm.

UPB

7572a. Schroeder, Theodore Albert. *Freedom of the press and "obscene" literature. Three essays by Theodore Schroeder.* New York City, Free Speech League, 1906.

71p. 23½cm.

Mormons mentioned, p. 58-59.

DLC, IEN, MnU, NN, RPB, UPB

7585a. Schroer, H. *From Piegans to the Piutes.* [n.p.] Revere Printing Co., 1926.

100p. 17cm.

Chapter V. Salt Lake City, p. 62-69. Chapter VI. Utah parks and Grand Canyon, p. 69-90. Meets Mormons on his trip through Utah.

UPB

7586a. **Schulthess, Arnold Henry.** *Friede sei in diesem hause!* [Berlin, Kunstdruckerie Georg Bannert, 1900]

[4]p. 23cm.

Title in English: May peace be in Thy house.

Missionary tract reprinted from *"Der Stern."*

"Glaubensartikel," p. [4].

USIC

7586b. _____. (same) A.H.S., Berlin, Deutschen Mission, 1901.

[4]p. 24cm.

USIC

7586c. _____. (same) Zurich, Hugh J. Cannon, [1903?]

[4]p. 23cm.

USIC

7586d. _____. (same) [Leipzig, Drud von C. G. Roder, ca. 1903]

[4]p. 23½cm.

USIC

7588a. _____. *Liebe Bruder, was soll ich thun, dass ich selig werde? Ein kurze Erklarung der fur jeden Menschen zur Seligkeit notwendigen Grundsatzen des Evangeliums Jesu Christi.* Berlin, Herausgegeben von der Redaktion des "Stern", H. Dusedann, 1901.

16p. 19cm.

Title in English: My Dear Brethren, what must I do to be saved?

UPB

7595a. **Scott, Robert, ed.** *The Church, the people and the age, ed. by Robert Scott and George William Gilmore ... analysis and summary by Clarence Augustine Beckwith.* New York, Funk & Waynalls Company, 1914.

xxi, 571p. ports. 23½cm.

"Epitome of the faith and doctrines of the Reorganized Church of Jesus Christ of Latter Day Saints," p. 526-28.

CU, LC, NjP, NNUT, OCl, OO, PPC

7601a. *The Seagull.* [Salt Lake City] Edited and published by the senior class of the Latter-day Saints' University, 1913.

[64]l. illus., ports. 20 x 28cm.

Yearbook.

UPB

7614a. *Seintiau Diweddaf.* Merthyr, Argraffwyd gan David Jones, Heol-fawr, 1846.

23p. 17cm.

Title in English: The Latter Saints.

WalN

7619a. **Seldes, Gilbert.** *The stammering century.* New York, The John Day Company [1928]

xviii, 411 [3]p. plates, ports. 24½cm.

Mormons, p. xv, xvi, 45, 101, 117, 130, 152, 182, 400. "We may discover hallucination, epilepsy, and lust in the character and person of Joseph Smith."

CtY, DLC, IdU, MB, NN, UPB

7619b. **Select Social Party.** *Mr _____. Yourself and ladies are cordially invited to attend a select social party, to be given in the music hall, Fourteenth Ward, on Wednesday eve., Oct. 29th, '75, for the benefit of Elder L. F. Branting, to enable him to go on a mission to Scandinavia.* [Salt Lake City] News Print [1875]

Broadside. 18 x 11cm.

UPB

7638a. **Shaw, George Bernard.** *The intelligent woman's guide to socialism and capitalism.* London, Constable and Company, 1928.

xxxvi, 494[1]p. 24cm.

Mormonism briefly discussed in chapter "Socialism and marriage," p. 407, 410-11, 431-32, 441, 443.

CtY, CU-B, DLC, ICU, NN, UPB, WU

7638b. **Shaw, James.** *Twelve years in America: Being observations on the country, the people, institutions and religion; with notices of slavery and the late war; and facts and incidents illustrative of ministerial life and labor in Illinois, with notes of travel through the United States and Canada. By the Rev. James Shaw, of the Illinois Conference, Methodist Episcopal Church, America. Second thousand.* London, Hamilton, Adams, and Co., 1867.

xvi, 440p. illus., fold map, plate. 19cm.

"The Mormons," p. 167-68.

CSt, DLC, ICN, MH, NjP, NN, TxU, UPB

Sheeks, Ben. See Reynolds, George. *George Reynolds, plaintiff in error, vs. the United States ... Flake/Draper Supplement 7098a-b.*

7647b. **Sheeks & Rawlins.** *H. S. Woolley, appellant, vs. C. N. Watkins and H. M. Bennett, respondents. Brief of Sheeks & Rawlins, attorneys for appellant.* [n.p. 1889?]

23p. 22cm.

At head of title: In the Supreme Court of Idaho.

Cover title.

The appellant was a member of the Mormon Church.

IAr

7677a. **Sheldon, William.** *Immaterialism.* [Buchanan, Mich., Western Advent Christian Publishing Association, 1870]

31p. 20cm.

Mormonism, p. 14-15.

UPB, WHi

7684a. **Shepherd, William.** *Prairie experiences in handling cattle and sheep.* London, Chapman & Hall, 1884.

3p.l., 266p. plates, fold. map 23cm.

Experiences among the Mormons of Utah, p. 253-64.

UPB

7684b. **Shepherd, William Nathaniel Budge.** *Biographical sketch of William Shepherd and family together with a brief narration of their early environment and migration to America.* [n.p.] 1927.

29p. illus. 25cm.

A Mormon biography.

UPB

The Sililoquy [sic] of Brigham Young. See Lambach.

7719a.   **Simonin, Louis Laurent.** *The Grand-ouest des Etats-Unis par L. Simonin. Les pionniers et les peaux-rouges. Le colons du Pacifique.* Paris, Charpentier, Libraire-Editeur, 1869.

vp. [1]l. 364p. map. 18½cm.

Title in English: The Great west of the United States.

Mormon participation in discovering gold in California.

CtY, DLC, ICN, IU, MiU, UHi, UPB, USIC

7719b.   _____. *Le monde Americain ; souveniers de mes voyages aux Etats-Unis. Par L. Simonin.* Paris, Librairie Hachette et Cie, 1876.

ii, 395p. 19cm.

Title in English: The American world.

In yellow printed wrapper.

Mormons and Utah briefly mentioned.

CtY, DLC, NN, PPL, UPB, USIC

Simple Bible stories. See Parry, Edwin Francis.

7735a.   *Sir; the religious test oaths passed by the last session of the Idaho Legislature (see copies below) place the county of Bear Lake, Idaho, in such a position that the people are compelled to get along without anything in the shape of government except paying taxes.* [n.p., 1886?]

Broadside. 25 x 22cm.

A protest from the LDS members in Bear Lake County, Idaho.

USIC

7740a.   **Sjodahl, Janne Mattson.** *Laying on of hands for the reception of the Holy Ghost.* [Salt Lake City, 1920]

4p. 18cm.

Ensign Stake of Zion. Ward teachers' leaflet. December, 1920.

USIC

7750a. **Skidmore, Charles H.** *Administration and supervision in the Box Elder School District.* Brigham City, Utah, Board of Education, 1921.

232p. illus. 20½cm.

Historic background with Mormons references, p. 9-42.

UPB

7752a. *Skriftmaessig beviis imod Mormonismens laere.* [n.p., 1854]

34p., on 17 sheets. 30cm.

Title in English: Documented evidence against the teachings of Mormonism.

USlC

7761a. **Sloan, Walter J.** *Where life is worth living. Story by Walter J. Sloan.* [Salt Lake City, Western Printing Co., 1918?]

[40]p. illus. 20cm.

Cover title: America's alpine scenic highway: the one-day wonder trip of the world.

Includes Salt Lake City with Mormon references.

UHi, UPB

7775b. **Smith, Andrew Madison.** *Luck of a wandering Dane by Hans Lykkejaeger [pseud.]* Philadelphia, Mallack & Harvey, Printers, c1885.

1p.l. [5]-130p. illus. 20cm.

Short episode in Ogden with a corrupt Mormon judge, etc.

DLC, CSmH, NN, ICN

7790a. **Smith, E. Quincy.** *Travels at home and abroad.* New York and Washington, The Neale Publishing Company, 1911.

3v. plates. 21cm.

A brief visit to Salt Lake City, v. 2, p. 58-60.

DLC, UPB

7830a. **Smith, Elbert A.** *Why a First Presidency in the Church? 2d ed.* Independence, Mo., Reorganized Church of Jesus Christ of Latter Day Saints [ca. 1929]

31p. 19½cm.

UPB

7840a. **Smith, Eliza Roxey (Snow).** *Mutual affection; a brother's and sister's love.* [Salt Lake City, C. W. Carter, 1886]

Broadside. 21½ x 17cm.

UHi

7841a. _____. *O my Father. Sacred hymn. Words by Eliza R. Snow. Arranged by Evan Stephens, sung by R. C. Easton.* Salt Lake City, Published by Coalter & Snelgrove [189-?]

[4]p. music. 26cm.

Title within ornamental border.

"Deseret News Publishing Co."

UPB

7841b. _____. *O my Father, solo and chorus as sung by Salt Lake Choir. Arranged by Evan Stephens.* Salt Lake City, Eergus Coalter Music Co. [n.d.]

[4]p. 24cm.

UPB

7842a. _____. *O my Father. Written by Eliza R. Snow. Illustrated by John Hafen.* [n.p., 191-?]

[17]p. col. illus., port., music. 28cm.

Title within ornamental border. In illustrated wrapper.

UPB

7847a. _____. *Song for the Fourth of July, 1862. By E.R.S.* [Great Salt Lake City, 1862]

Broadside. 19 x 9cm.

UPB, USlC

7906a. **Smith, Isaac M.** *The atonement of Christ and the final destiny of man. By Elder Isaac M. Smith.* [Lamoni, Iowa, Herald Publishing House, 187-?]

86p. 18½cm. (no. 1257)

Variant printing.

UPB

7931a. **Smith, Joseph, 1805-1844.** *Articles of faith of the Church of Jesus Christ of Latter-day Saints.* Liverpool, Mission headquarters [ca. 1910]

Broadsheet. 21½cm.

On verso: Utah and the Mormons. Also appeared on the verso of Volney S. Peet's "£200 reward," see *Flake 6221.*

UPB

7939a. _____. (same, in Dutch) *Aertikelen des geloofs.* [Rotterdam, Nederl. Zending, 1920?]

Broadsheet. 22cm.

UPB, USIC

7948a. _____. (same, in Spanish) *Articulos de fe, de la "Iglesia de Jesu-Christo de los Santos de los Ultimos Dias."* Salt Lake City, Deseret News [1882?]

Broadside. 10½ x 7cm.

UHi

7955a. _____. *Extraits de l'histoire du prophete Joseph Smith.* Liege, Ernest C. Rossiter [1926?]

23p. 16cm.

Cover title.

Title in English: Extracts from the history of the prophet Joseph Smith.

UPB

7957a. _____. *General Smith's views of the powers and policy of the government of the United States.* Chicago, Ill., Ellis & Fergus, Book and Job printers. 1844.

12p. 21cm.

USIC

7968a. _____. *Te hoe aratai no te mau taata i roto i te Ekalaesia a Iesu Mesia i te feia mo'a i te mau Mahana Hopea nei. Papaihia e Iosepha Heta, i Tahiti, i te Matahiti 1901, e i faarahihia e Viliamu Setemila i te Matahiti 1910. Neia i te piha neneiraa a te Ekalesia a Iesu Mesia i te Feia Mo's i te Mau Mahana Hopea Nei, i Papeete Tahiti, i te Matahiti, 1910.*

20p. 19cm.

Title in English: Another witness. To all the people of the Church of Jesus Christ of Latter-day Saints.

Translation by William Segmiller in 1910.

UPB

7968b. _____. (same) Papeete, Tahiti, Te Ekalesia, 1917.

28p. 18cm.

USlC

7968c. _____. (same) Papeete, Tahiti, Ekalesia a Iesu Mesia. 1921.

28p. 17½cm.

USlC

7976a. _____. *Joseph Smiths laerdomme; et alfabetisk ordnet udvalg af evangeliske taler og skrivelser givne af de Sidste-Dages store profet. Udvalgte fra "De Sidste-Dages Helliges Kirkeshistorie" af Edwin F. Parry. Oversatte, reviderede og omordnede af John S. Hansen.* [Salt Lake City] Bikubens Bibliotek, 1922.

4p.l. [5]-182 [6]p. 19½cm. (Bikubens Bibliotek B11. Bind)

Title in English: Joseph Smith's teachings.

Published in *The Bikuben* during 1922.

UPB, USlC

7976b. _____. (same, in Dutch) *De leeringen van Joseph Smith; een alphabetische rangschikking van de Leerstellige Predikaties en Geschriften van den Grooten Laterdaagschen Profeet door Edwin F. Parry.* [n.p.] Kerk van Jezus Christus van de Heiligen der laatste Dagen [n.d.]

xi, 132p. 19½cm.

USlC

7987. _____. *The Prophet Joseph Smith tells his own story; a brief history of the early visions of the prophet and the rise and progress of the Church of Jesus Christ of Latter-day Saints.* Chattanooga, Tenn., The Southern States Mission [ca. 1911]

32p. 14½cm.

Cover title.

UPB, USlC

7997a.   _____. *Visions of Joseph Smith, the seer; discoveries of ancient American records and relics; with the statements of Dr. Lederer (converted Jew) and others.* Plano, Ill. [1875]

43p. 17cm.

MoInRC

8027c.   **Smith, Joseph, 1832-1918.** *An answer to "What the world believes." Ways that are doubtful.* [Lamoni, Iowa, The Saint's Herald, 1888?]

Broadside. 51 x 43cm.

An answer to an article on Mormonism by Franklin D. Richards.

UPB

8036a.   **Smith, Joseph Fielding, 1838-1918.** *Garments. The following is to be regarded as an established and imperative rule.* [Salt Lake City, 190-?]

Broadside. 35 x 28cm.

How the temple garment should be worn.

USIC

8041b.   _____. *He hihio o ka hoolapanai ia ana o ka poe make.* Laie, Oahu, T.H., Ka Ekalesia o Iesu Kristo o ka Poe Hoano o na La Hope Nei [1918?]

7 [1]p. 16cm.

Title in English: Vision of the redemption of the dead.

HLB

8044a.   _____. *He Pule hoolaa no ke kie hoomanao o Iosepa Kamika, ke kaula a mea nana o ka Ekalesia o Iesu Kristo o ka poe Hoano o na La Hope nei.* Honolulu, Ka Na'i, 1906.

8p. 16cm.

Title in English: A Prayer dedicated to the memory of Joseph Smith. Dedicatory prayer for the Joseph Smith memorial.

USIC

8044b.   _____. *Onkuischheid, het heerschend kwaad van den tijd. Joseph F. Smith, uit het Engelsch door B. Tiemersma.* Rotterdam, Nederlandsche Zending [1917?]

8p. 23cm.

Title in English: Unchastity, the dominant evil of the age.

USIC

8066a.   _____. *Proceedings at the dedication of the Joseph Smith memorial monument at Sharon, Windsor County, Vermont, December 23rd, 1905. With a detailed account of the journey and visits of the centennial memorial party to Vermont and other places in the Eastern states; also a description of the Solomon Mack Farm and account of the purchase of same.* [n.p., 1905?]

88p. plates, ports. 23cm.

In tan printed wrapper.

Also bound in green cloth.

CU-B, MH, MoInRC, NN, UHi, ULA, UPB, USIC, UU

8067a.   _____. (same). [n.p., 1906?]

92p. plates, ports. 23½cm.

[89]-92 contain the poem "L'Envoi" written by Susa Young Gates December 29, 1905.

UPB, USIC

8072a.   **Smith, Joseph Fielding, 1876-1972.** *Salvation for the dead.* [Salt Lake City, 1920]

[4]p. 18cm. (Ensign Stake of Zion. Ward teachers' leaflet. September, 1920)

USIC

Smith, Sarah Bixby. See Bixby-Smith, Sarah.

8114a.   **Smith, Thomas Wood.** *Songs of Zion: For the use of the children of the kingdom, by Thomas W. Smith, an elder in the Church of Jesus Christ of Latter Day Saints.* Plano, Ill. [1875]

32p. 13cm.

MoInRC

8122a.   **Smith, Truman.** *Speech of Mr. Smith, of Conn., on the bill "to admit California into the Union -- to establish territorial governments for Utah and New Mexico, making proposals to Texas for the establishment of the western and northern boundaries." Delivered in the Senate of the United States, July 8, 1850.* Washington, Gideon & Co., Printers, 1850.

32p. 23cm.

Includes letters from John M. Bernhisel and Erastus Snow, concerned chiefly with the physical description of Deseret, and a letter from General John Wilson, concerning the people.

CU-B, NjP, UHi, UPB

8122b. **Smith, Truman.** *Speech of Truman Smith, of Connecticut, on the Nebraska question. Delivered in the Senate of the United States, February 10 and 11, 1854.* Washington, Printed by John T. and Lem. Towers, 1854.

23p. 22½cm.

What would happen if Brigham Young was elected to the Senate? Would he bring his 40 wives to Washington?

CU, DLC, MB, NN, OO, UPB, ViU

8133a. **Smith, Willard J.** *The last dispensation.* Independence, Ensign Publishing Company, 1893.

43p. 15½cm. (Ensign Circulating Library. Vest Pocket edition. No. 2, September 1893)

Reorganized Church of Jesus Christ of Latter Day Saints doctrine.

UPB

8147a. **Smith & Morton.** *1902 pocket guide to Salt Lake City and vicinity.* Salt Lake City, Smith & Morton [1902]

32p. map. 13cm.

Includes Mormon views.

UPB

8147b. **Smith & Smith.** *H. S. Woolley, plaintiff and appellant, vs. C. N. Watkins and H. M. Bennett, defendants and respondents. Sheeks & Rawlins, attorneys for appellant. R. Z. Johnson, Attorney General, and Smith & Smith, attorneys for respondents. Brief of Smith & Smith, for respondents.* [n.p., 1889?]

4p. 22cm.

At head of title: In the Supreme Court of Idaho Territory. January term, 1889.

Cover title.

An Idaho case in which the plaintiff was a member of the Mormon Church.

IAr

8148a. **Smoot, Abraham Owen.** *Circular. To the heirs of the late president Brigham Young, greeting.* [Signed A. O. Smoot, W. H. Dusenberry, H. H. Cluff, M. Tanner, Trustees of the Brigham Young Academy] [Provo, 1884]

[2]p. 21cm.

Need for funds after the January 27, 1884 fire destroyed the Brigham Young Academy buildings.

USIC

8179a. **Snow, Erastus.** *En sandheds-rost til de oprigtige af hjertet.* "106 Tusind." Kjobenhavn, Udgivet af N. C. Flygare, Trykt hos F. E. Bording, 1875.

16p. 21cm.

Title in English: A voice from the land of Zion.

UPB

8180a. _____. (same) "116 Tusind." [Kjøbenhavn, Udgivet af R. Wilhelmsen, Trykt hos F. E. Bording, 1875?]

16p. 22cm.

UPB

8198a. _____. (same, in Swedish) 10de uppl. [Kopenhamn, N. C. Flygare, 1875]

16p. 22cm.

UPB

8202a. _____. (same) Tjugotredje upplagan. Stockholm, Utgifven och forlagd af P. Sundwall, 1910.

22p. 18cm.

USIC

8242a. **Snow, Lorenzo.** *Den enda vag till salighet: En forklaring ofver begynnelselaran i" Jesu Kristi Kyrka af de Sista-Dagars Helige."* [Kopenhamn, N.C. Flygare, 1875]

8p. 22cm.

Title in English: The only way to be saved.

UPB

8248b. _____. *Ex parte: In the matter of Lorenzo Snow, petitioner, appellant, appeal from the Third Judicial District Court, Salt Lake County, Territory of Utah.* Washington, Judd & Detweiler, Printers [1886]

20p. 22cm.

At head of title: Supreme Court of the United States. October term, 1886. No. 1282.

Polygamy trial of Lorenzo Snow.

DLC

The [Soliloquy] of Brigham Young. See Lambach. *The Sililoquy of Brigham Young.*

8277a. *Songs, for the sixth of April.* [Great Salt Lake City, 1852?]

Broadside. 20 x 16cm.

The words of two songs, "In Deseret we're free," by W. W. Phelps; and "The son of God will come," by E. R. S. Eliza R. Snow's song was also published in the *Deseret News*, April 17, 1852, with a notation "For conference, April 8."

UPB

8277b. *Songs for the 24th of July, 1851.* [Great Salt Lake City, 1851]

Broadside. 41 x 28cm.

Contents: "For the pioneers," by Miss E. R. Snow; "For the 24 young men," by James Bond; "For the 24 young ladies," by Miss E. R. Snow; "A life in the desert plains," by W. W. Phelps; "Oh come, come to-day," by W. W. Phelps; "The Union," by Homer.

USIC

Songs to be Sung by The Congregation at the . . . Deseret Sunday School Union. See, Church of Jesus Christ of Latter-day Saints. Deseret Sunday School Union.

8278a. **Sorensen, Hannah.** *What women should know. By Hannah Sorensen, graduate of the Royal Hospital, Denmark.* Salt Lake City, Printed by George Q. Cannon & Sons Company [1896?]

viii, [9]-168p. illus. 18cm.

Endorsed by Joseph B. Keeler, Bishop of the Provo 4th ward. Various references to Mormon beliefs.

UPB

8279a. **Sorenson, Alfred Rasmus.** *The story of Omaha from the pioneer days to the present time. 3rd ed., rev., rearranged and enl.* Omaha, National Printing company, 1923.

5p.l., 661p. illus., ports. 22½cm.

Published in 1889 under title: *History of Omaha from the pioneer days to the present time.*

Chapter 3. "The Mormons," p. 20-29. Chapter 4. "Florence," p. 30-41.

CoU, DLC, IdRR, MoU, NcD, OKentU

8281a. **Sortrop, Marie Hansen.** *Assted.* [Kjøbenhavn, Trykt hos J. G. Salomon, n.d.]

[4]p. 21½cm.

Poem on Mormon emigration.

USIC

8293a.   *Souvenir, centennial anniversary of the birth of the prophet of Joseph Smith.* [n.p., 1905]

Broadside. illus. 10½ x 17cm.

UHi, UPB

8299a.   *Souvenir of Salt Lake, the city beautiful.* Salt Lake City, Smith & Morton [1901?]

[34]p. illus. 21cm.

Includes pictures of church buildings.

UPB

8299b.   *Souvenir of Salt Lake City, Utah.* Salt Lake City, Published by the Souvenir Novelity Co., ca. 1896.

[16]l. of plates. ports. 18 x 23cm.

Includes pictures of church buildings and church leaders.

UPB

8300a.   *Souvenir program for the Scandinavian Jubilee to be held in Salt Lake City, June 14, 15, 16, and 17, 1900, in commemoration of the introduction of the gospel to the Scandinavian countries, June 14, 1850.* [Salt Lake City] Deseret News [1900]

[12]p. illus. 30½cm.

At head of title: Scandinavian day at Saltair Beach on June 15, 1900.

UPB

8305b.   **Spalding, John A.** *From New England to the Pacific. Notes of a vacation trip across the continent in April, May, and June, 1884. J. A. S., in Hartford Evening Post.* Hartford, Conn., Press of the Case, Lockwood & Brainard Co., 1884.

4p.l. [9]-203p. 15cm.

Visits Salt Lake. The usual tourist and a detailed description of a Mormon meeting he attended.

CaBViPA, DLC, UPB

8307a.   **Sparks, Edwin Erle.** *National development 1877-1885. Commonwealth edition.* New York and London, Harper & Brothers Publishers, 1907.

xiv, 378p. maps, port. 21½cm.

Half title: The American nation, a history. [Ed. by A. B. Hart]

Mormonism and the growth of polygamy and legislation to halt it, p. 258-64.

AzU, DLC, IdU, MB, NN, OO, PU

8307b. **Sparks, Quartus S.** *Priestcraft exposed: False religion unmasked, derided, and slain; hypocrisy unveiled; Truth vindicated, sectaries mad: And Babylon falling! By Q. S. Sparks, minister of the gospel, Hartford . . .* Hartford, Printed for the publisher, 1845.

37p. 19cm.

A diatribe against the clergy by a Mormon missionary.

UPB

8313a. *Speak for themselves. Trying to upset the policy of the pioneers.* [Salt Lake City? n.d.]

Broadside. 28 x 19cm.

Recounting the actions of Brigham Young and the early Utah Legislatures in supporting home industry and criticizing the Democratic party for destroying this policy.

UPB

8318. **Spencer, George Sterling.** *De Verzoening en het Verlossingsplan van Jezus Christus, door de Ouderlingen Geo. S. Spencer en W. J. deBrij.* [Amsterdam, Netherlands? ca. 1897]

8p. 21½cm.

At head of title: Hij, de een zaak oordeel voor bij haar onderzocht heeft, is niet wijs.

Title in English: The plan of salvation and atonement of Jesus Christ.

UPB

8320a. **Spencer, Josephine.** *To Aunt Em (Emmeline B. Wells).* [Salt Lake City? n.d.]

Broadside. 23cm.

UPB

8322a. **Spencer, Orson.** *Correspondence between the Rev. W. Crowel, A. M. and O. Spencer, B. A.* [Liverpool, R. James, 1847]

4p. 20½cm.

UPB has a copy of the fourth letter which was taken from the type setting from the *Millennial Star*, June 15, 1847, v. IX, No. 12, p. 178-80. The lines have been leaded, but the type setting has been retained as in the *Star*. This is the only true first edition.

UPB

8336a. **Spencer, Samuel G.** *Joseph Smith, the prophet of the nineteenth century.* [Kansas City Mo., Edmund D. Black, Printer, ca. 1895]

36p. 15½cm.

Caption title.

UPB

8337. _____. *Joseph Smith, the prophet of XIX century.* [Kansas City, Mo., Edmund D. Black, Printer, ca. 1896]

39[1]p. 15½cm.

"The angel Moroni delivering the plates of the Book of Mormon to Joseph Smith, Jr. (September 22, 1827)." Painting by C. C. A. Christensen, copyrighted 1886.

In the caption on the last paragraph on p. 1, dying has been changed to drowning.

NN, UPB, WHi

8345a. **Spicer, Tobias.** *Autobiography of Rev. Tobias Spicer: Containing incidents and observations; also some account of the visit to England.* Boston, H. Pierce and Company, 1851.

328p. port. 20cm.

"Mormons 1833," p. 110-13.

Observes a Mormon preaching in Castleton.

DLC, OClWHi, TxU, UPB

8345b. **Spori, Jacob.** *L'evangile que Christ enseignait et son retablissement aux derniers jours. Par J. Spori, J. M. Tanner, F. F. Hintze.* Berne, Publie par Geo. C Naegle, 1894.

18p. 20½cm.

Title in English: The gospel that Christ taught and it's restoration in the latter days.

UPB

8372a. **Stebbins, Callie B.** *The silver thimbles.* Lamoni, Iowa, Printed at Herald Publishing House, 1892.

vip. [2]l. [7]-32, 4p. 16½cm. (Birth offering series No. 1)

Birth offering series. Explanation precedes the text. Final four pages are advertisements.

NjP, UPB

8378a. **Stebbins, Henry A.** *Concordance and reference guide to the Book of Doctrine and Covenants.* Lamoni, Iowa, Published by the Reorganized Church of Jesus Christ of Latter Day Saints [1883]

32p. 16cm.

Author listed on the cover title.

MoInRC, UPB

8378b. _____. (same) Lamoni, Iowa, Published by the Reorganized Church of Jesus Christ of Latter Day Saints. [n.d.]

32p. 16cm.

In tan printed wrapper. Authorship from the wrapper.

Wrapper title within ornamental border.

UPB

8383a. **Steedman, Charles John.** *Bucking the sagebrush, or The Oregon Trail in the seventies. By Charles J. Steedman. Illustrated by Charles M. Russell.* New York and London, G. P. Putman's Sons, The Knickerbocker Press, 1904.

ix, 270p. plates (one col.) fold. map. 21cm.

Chapter 2. "In Mormon land," p. 10-27.

CoU, DLC, MB, NN, PPL, UPB, UU, WaU

8383b. **Steele, John.** *Across the plains in 1850, by John Steele. Edited with introduction and notes by Joseph Schafer, Superintendent of the State Historical Society of Wisconsin. Illustrations from hitherto unpublished contemporary drawings.* Chicago, Printed for the Caxton Club, 1930.

xxxvii, 234p. [1]l. plates, fold., map. 22cm.

Various references to Mormons in Iowa in 1850.

CtY, CU, DLC, ICN, OO, UPB, UU

8409a. **Stephens, Alexander Hamilton.** *A comprehensive and popular history of the United States, embracing a full account of the discovery and settlement of the country, the history of each of the colonies until their union as states, the French and Indian wars; the War of the Revolution; the War of 1812; the long period of peace; the Mexican War; the Great War between the North and South and its results; the centennial of our independence; the assassination of President Garfield; and events down to the present time.* Philadelphia, National Publishing Co. [c1882]

1p.l., 5-6, xii-xxv, 17-1048p. front., illus. (incl. ports, maps), plates, ports., double maps. 25cm.

Briefly discusses Mormonism under chapter entitled: Administration of Buchanan, p. 547-53.

Various editions.

CSmH, CtY, DLC, TU, UPB, ViU

8433a. **Stephens, Evan.** *With song sweet and cheering serenade. (A waltz chorus or quartette). Composed by Evan Stephens and dedicated to the Deseret University Singing Society. For choirs, glee and quartette clubs.* Salt Lake City, Juvenile Instructor Office, 1884.

4p. 29cm.

UPB

8450a. **Stevens, Walter B.** *Centennial history of Missouri (The center state) One hundred years in the Union, 1820-1921. Illustrated.* St. Louis, Chicago, The S. J. Clarke Publishing Company, 1921.

5v. illus., plates, ports. 28cm.

V. 2, Chapter XXXIII. "The Mormon war and after."

DLC, GU, KyLoU, NcD, OCl, UPB, WHi

8462a. **Steward, James Zebulon.** *La Verida del Mesas.* Mexico, 1905.

8p. 14cm.

USlC

8468a. **Stillson, Henry Leonard.** *History of the ancient and honorable fraternity of Free and Accepted Masons, and concordant orders. Illustrated. Written by a Board of Editors: Henry Leonard Stillson, Editor-in-chief. William James Hughan, European Editor.* Boston and New York, U.D.S.; London, England, George Kenning, 16 Great Queen Street, European Publisher. 1896.

904p. illus., plates, ports. 25½cm.

Utah and the Mormons, p. 413-18.

Another ed. 1900 UPB, 1921 USlC

UPB

8472a. **Stoddard, Charles Augustus.** *Beyond the Rockies; a spring journey in California.* New York, Charles Scribner's Sons, 1902 [c1894]

xiii, 214p. illus. 20½cm.

Salt Lake and the Mormons, p. 134-91.

DLC, IaU, MWA, NN, OCl, TxU, UPB, WaS

8487a. **Stone, John A.** *Put's golden songster. Containing the largest and most popular collection of California songs ever published. By the author of "Put's original California songster."* San Francisco, D. E. Appleton & Co., [c1858]

64p. 14½cm.

In printed wrapper.

Without music. Tunes indicated by title.

"Sweet Betsey from Pike," p. 50-51, and "That is even so," have Mormon interest.

CtY, CU-B, DLC, MiU, TxU, UPB, ViU

8487b. _____. *Put's original California songster, giving a few words that would occupy volumes, detailing the hopes, trials and Joys of a miner's life. 4th edition, 18th Thousand.* San Francisco, Published by D. E. Appleton & Co., 1868.

vi, 7-64p. 16cm.

On cover: 5th edition, 25th thousand.

In purple printed wrapper.

Without music; tunes indicated by title.

"Seeing the elephant," p. 19-21 has Mormon interest.

CU, DLC, ICU, NcU, UPB

8490a. **Storer, Horatio Robinson.** *Is it I? A book for every man. A companion to why not? A book for every woman.* Boston, Lee and Shepard [c1867]

xix, 7-154p. 16cm.

Mormons mentioned, p. 41-42.

CtY, DLC, MH, NN, OO, UPB

8520a. **Strong, Josiah.** *Our country: Its possible future and its present crisis. By Rev. Josiah Strong ... With introduction by Prof. Austin Phelps.* New York, Baker and Taylor [c1885]

x, 229p. 19cm.

Chapter VI. "Perils -- Mormonism," p. 59-68.

UPB

8527a. *Suggestions to brethren who have been called to administer to the sick at the L.D.S. Hospital.* [Salt Lake City, 191-?]

Broadside. 28 x 22cm.

USlC

8527b. **Sullivan, John.** *Grover Cleveland, will not be elected. The Mormons won't get what they expected.* [n.p., 1884]

Broadside. 28 x 22cm.

There is a penned note: "10 Nov. 1884. Picked up in street."

USlC

Supplement to the lecture on the Mountain Meadows massacre. See, Haslam, James Holt. *Flake 3879.*

8538a. **Sutherland, J. G.** *George H. Cope, appellant, vs. Janet Cope et al. Brief for appellant.* [Washington? 1890?]

21p. 22cm.

In the Supreme Court of the United States. October term, 1890. No. 1327.

Inheritance polygamy case. It shows the inability of the state to pass laws that ignore the federal anti-polygamy laws.

DLC

8540a. **Sutherland and Judd.** *In the matter of the estate of George Handley, deceased. Sarah A. Chapman, et. al., appellants, vs. Elizabeth Handley, et. al., respondents. Brief for appellants. Sutherland & Judd, attorneys for appellants.* [Salt Lake City? 1890?]

22p. 22cm.

At head of title: In the Supreme Court of the Territory of Utah. June term, 1890.

Cover title.

A polygamy inheritance case.

UAr

8540b. _____. *In the matter of the estate of Thomas Cope, deceased. Appellant's brief. Sutherland & Judd, attorneys for petitioner.* [Salt Lake City? 1890?]

21p. 22cm.

At head of title: In the Supreme Court of the Territory of Utah. June term, 1890.

Cover title.

A polygamy inheritance trial.

UAr

8540c. _____. *Sarah A. Chapman, Ruth Newson, Benjamin T. Handley, and Harvey Handley, appellant vs. Elizabeth Handley, John Handley, William F. Handley, Charles T. Handley, and Emma N. Handley. Appeal from the Supreme Court of the Territory of Utah. Filed September 29, 1890.* [Washington? 1890?]

16p. 22cm.

At head of title: Record, case no. 14,191. Supreme Court of the United States, October term, 1891. Term No., 808.

Concerning the estate of George Handley, and whether polygamist children would inherit.

DLC

8562a. *A synoptical sketch of the life work of John Pack, the Utah pioneer of 1847.* [n.p., after 1885]

[7]p. 19cm.

Caption title. Cover title has synoptical spelled Cynoptioal.

UPB

8562b. **Sz, K. Gy.** *Tarsadalmi s allami regeneratio vagyis: a magan-s allami elet megjavitasi, a bevetel es kiadas Kozti egyensuly helyreallitasi modjai s exkozeinek nemzetgazdaszati el rendelesei. Irta: Doctor Sz. K. Gy.* [Budapest, Nyom. Markus Samunal, 1884]

259, iv p. 22cm.

Title in English: Social and state regeneration.

A discussion of Mormonism, p. 89-101, with special emphasis on religious economics.

USIC

T

8566a. **Taggart, Scott.** *West Millard County, Utah.* [Delta, Commercial Club, 1923?]

96p. illus. 22½cm.

UHi

8567a. **Takahashi, Goro.** *Morumon kyo to Morumon kyoto. Amerika dojin kigen ron.* Tokyo [the author] 1902.

12, 257p. illus., plates, ports. 20cm.

Title in English: The Book of Mormon and Mormons.

UPB, USIC

8602a. **Talmage, James Edward.** *The Book of Mormon; an account of its origin, with evidences of its genuineness and authenticity; Two lectures by Dr. James E. Talmage. Prepared by appointment, and published by the Church of Jesus Christ of Latter-day Saints.* [Independence] Church of Jesus Christ of Latter-day Saints [1915?]

47p. 17cm.

UPB

8603a. _____. (same) Independence, Press of Zion's Printing and Publishing Co. [c1924]

44p. 17½cm.

UPB

8616a. _____. *Genealogical work is essential to redemption of the dead in holy temples of the Lord.* Salt Lake City, 1918.

Broadside. 56 x 41cm.

"Address delivered in Tabernacle, Salt Lake City, Sunday, September 22, 1918, by Elder James E. Talmage."

USIC

8633a. _____. *The Great Salt Lake, present and past.* Salt Lake City, The Deseret News, 1900.

116p. 23 illus. and maps on 9 plates. 19cm.

Primarily on the lake, with a few references to the Mormons.

UPB

8660a. _____. *Mary Magdalene, Christ's friend, most maligned woman of history.* San Francisco, NEA, Pacific Bureau Service, 1917.

Broadside. illus. 54 x 36cm.

Dated: Thursday, May 10, 1917.

UPB

8662a. _____. *"Mormonism and the war."* [n.p., 1918]

Broadsheet. illus., port. 46 x 15cm.

Sunday, July 28, 1918 at Council Bluff, Iowa. Elder Talmage was giving this lecture nearly every night in a different city. Also includes "Religion, active and passive," by Elder Talmage, and "Some things for parents to ponder" by Will A. McKeever.

UPB

8662b. _____. (same) [Chicago, Winterburn Print, 1918]

Broadside. illus., port. 104 x 71 cm.

"Is Satan fighting America? Will good triumph over evil? Hear Dr. James E. Talmage. Geo. M. Cohan's Grand Opera House, Sunday, Aug. 18." Seven hundred persons attended that lecture in Chicago, the same lecture that he was making nearly every day in a different city, 1918.

UPB

8662c. _____. (same) [Chicago, Winterburn Print, 1918]

Broadside. illus., port. 103 x 71cm.

Elder Talmage was touring the Northern States Mission, and perhaps other missions, speaking on this subject, with missionaries arranging for and advertising meeting places. This broadside concerned his lecture at M. W. A. Hall, Indianapolis, Indiana, August 4, 1918.

UPB

8662d. _____. (same) *Eagles' hall, 21 North Main St., Sunday Evening, July 28th, at 8 o'clock.* [n.p., n.d.]

Broadside. 28 x 22cm.

Includes a synopsis of Dr. Talmage's statements pertinent to the topic and announces him as the speaker at the meeting.

UPB

8663a. _____. *Philosophie des "Mormonismus."* Basel, Schweiz, Serge F. Ballif [1902?]

16p. 22cm.

Title in English: Philosophy of Mormonism.

USIC

8706a. **Talmage, Thomas De Witt.** *Life and teachings of Rev. T. De Witt Talmage, D. D. Containing the noblest truths: The most delightful narratives; poetic imageries; striking similes; fearless denunciations of wrong and inspiring appeals for the right; gems of pathos and eloquessnce . . . By Rev. T. De Will Talmage . . . With an introduction by Rev. Russell H. Conwell.* [Philadelphia, National Publishing Co., 1902]

2p.l., xiv, 17-511p. illus., plates, ports. 23cm.

At head of title: Memorial volume.

"The shame of polygamy," p. 255-56.

DLC, IaU, PPLT, UPB

8710a. **Tammen, Harry Heye.** *Around the circle.* Denver, Colo., H. H. Tammen [c1888]

[12]p. illus. 15cm.

Salt Lake City, p. [12]

UPB

8753a. **Tanner, Alva Amasa.** *A message from Heaven. Given thru Alva A. Tanner.* Oakley, Idaho [1917]

[8]p. 18cm.

Variant printing.

Includes "A revelation."

UPB

8761a. _____. *Proverbs.* [Oakley, Idaho, ca. 1920]

Broadsheet. 21 x 15cm.

Mormon poetry.

USIC

8794a. **Taussig, Hugo Alois.** *Retracing the pioneers; from west to east, in an automobile.* San Francisco [The Philopolis Press] 1910.

5 p.l., 105p. illus., plans, fold. map. 18cm.

Brief mention of the Mormons.

CU, DLC, UHi

8801a. **Taylor, Alma Owen.** *Ikeru shin no kami.* 5th ed. [Tokyo] Matsu Jitsu Seito Iesu Kirisuto Kyokai Nihon Dendobu, 1911]

32p. 14½cm.

Title in English: The true and living God.

Taylor was president of the Japan Mission from 1908 to 1910.

UPB

8803a. _____, comp. *Kami wa imasu ka?* [Tokyo] Matsu Jitsu Seito Iesu Kirisuto Kyokai Nihon Dendobu [1911]

66 [2]p. 14½cm.

Compiled by Alma O. Taylor and James Anderson.

Title in English: Is there a God?

UPB

8806c. **Taylor, Benjamin Franklin.** *Between the gates. With Illustrations.* Chicago, S. C. Griggs and Company, 1883.

3p.l. [5]-292p. illus. 19cm.

Brief mention of his stop over in Utah. The profits of ZCMI belong to Brigham Young.

Other edition: 1879 UHi.

BVaU, DLC, OCl, OO, UPB, WHi

8818. **Taylor, John.** *Er de Sidste Dages-Helliges Laere Sandhed?* 8de oplag. Kjøbenhavn, F. E. Bording, 1881.

1p.l. [3]-32p. 21cm.

Title in English: Are the doctrines of the Latter-day Saints church true?

A retranslation of his: Er Mormonismen en Vranglaere?

UHi, UPB, USIC

312

8826. _____. *Er Mormonismen en Vranglaere?* 2 det oplag. Kjøbenhavn, Udgivet af Hector C. Haight. Trykt hos F. E. Bording, 1856.

31p. 23cm.

Title in English: Is Mormonism a false faith?

Translated from articles in *The Mormon.* Article I. v. 1 #43, Dec. 15, 1865. Article II. v. #44-49, Dec. 22, 1855-Jan. 26, 1856. A third part in *The Mormon* was not translated.

CSmH, NN, UPB, USIC

8826a. _____. (same) Kjøbenhavn, Udgivet af Hector C. Haight. Trykt hos F. E. Bording, 1856.

31p. 21cm.

UPB, USIC

8828b. _____. (same) 7de Oplag. Kjobenhavn, Udgivet og forlagt af N. C. *Flygare.* Trykt has F. E. Bording, 1876.

31p. 22½cm.

UPB

8834a. **Taylor, John.** *Exposition des premiers principes de la doctrine de l'Eglise de Jesus-Christ des Saints-des-Derniers-Jours, par Lorenzo Snow, elder venant de la Cite du Grand Lac Sale, Haute-Californie, Etats-Unis d'Amerique. Tranuite de l'anglais.* 2d ed. Geneve, publiee par T. B. H. Stenhouse, 1852.

16p. 19cm.

Title in English: Exposition of the first principles of the doctrine of the Church of Jesus Christ of Latter-day Saints.

UPB

8834b. _____. *[Personal duties]* [Salt Lake City, ca. 1890]

Broadside. 38 x 21cm.

Personal finances. An unidentified speech.

USIC

8843a. _____. *Propsectus. The Mormon.* [New York City, The Mormon, 1855]

Broadside. 25 x 20cm.

USIC

8844a. _____. *The seer; written for the dedication of the Seventy' Hall, and dedicated to President Brigham Young.* [Nauvoo, 1844]

Broadside. 20 x 10cm.

Printed from the same type in the *Times and Seasons*, v. 5, Jan. 1, 1844, p. 767.

UPB

8851a. _____. *Upper California.* [n.p., ca. 1850]

Broadside. 20 x 14cm.

Text surrounded by ornamental border.

Poem relating to the Mormons taking up residence on the west coast. Published as a hymn in the 1851 through 1890 editions of "Sacred hymns and spiritual songs..." Beginning in 1871 John Taylor is listed in the index as the author.

USIC

8851b. **Taylor, Joseph Henry.** *Sketches of frontier and Indian life on the upper Missouri & great plains. Embracing the author's personal recollections of frontier characters, and some observations of wild Indian life, during a continuous residence in the two Dakotas and other territories between the years 1864 and 1889.* Pottstown, Pa., Printed and published by the author, 1889.

199p. ports., plates 20cm.

Tells of the Mormons around Omaha after being expelled from Illinois and before leaving for "Deseret." Plate entitled "To the land of Deseret."

DLC, IaU, ICN, MtU, UPB, UU

8856a. **Taylor, Oliver Alden.** *Memoir of the Rev. Oliver Alden Taylor A. M., late of Manchester, Massachusetts.* Boston, Tappan and Whittemore, 1853.

xii, 396p. port. 19½cm.

Includes a visit to Nauvoo.

CoU, CtY, DLC, ICU, MB, UHi

8859a. **Teasdale, George.** *Glad tidings of great joy.* [n.p., n.d.]

4p. 17½cm.

Ascribed to Teasdale by Andrew Jenson, *Latter-day Saints Biographical Encyclopedia.*

UPB, USIC

8860a. _____. (same) [Salt Lake City, Juvenile Instructor Office, 1881?]

6[2]p. 19½cm.

Missionary tract.

The pages following text includes a Juvenile Instructor Office catalogue of church publicaitons, and an invitation to attend church meetings. Dated from the catalogue.

NjP, UHi, UPB, USIC

8867a. _____. *The restoration of the everlasting Gospel.* [Salt Lake City, Deseret News Publishing Co., ca. 1878]

8p. 22½cm.

UPB

8872a. **Teichmann, Emil.** *A journey to Alaska in the year 1868; being a diary of the late Emil Teichmann, edited with an introduction by his son Oskar.* Kensington, Priv. print. at the Cayme press, 1925.

272p. illus., 2 ports. 21cm.

Visited Salt Lake City on October 2 with a brief mention of Brigham Young.

DLC, ICN, CtY, WaU

8872b. *The Telegraph-Herald's abridged history of the state of Iowa with one hundred halftone views of interesting points on the Mississippi [and directory of Jackson County].* [Dubuque, Iowa?] 1907.

[13]p. [125]-322, 71p. illus. 23cm.

Mormons, p. 167-71.

UPB

8876a. *The temples of the Latter-day Saints.* [Salt Lake City, 1926?]

Broadside. illus. 55 x 42cm.

Purpose of temples, with a brief account of each temple.

USIC

8882a. **Tessan, Francois de.** *Promenades au Far-West.* Paris, Plon-Nourrit, 1912.

iii, 317p. 19cm.

Title in English: Travels to the Far west.

"Au pays des Mormons," p. 1-22.

UPB, USIC

8894a.   *The thirty-sixth anniversary of the wedding-day of our beloved parents.* [Smithfield? 1871]

Broadside. 18 x 11cm.

At head of title: Smithfield, August 29, 1871.

Signed by their 13 children.

Parents are Evan M. and Susannah K. Greene.

USlC

8896a.   **Thomander, Johann Henrik.** *Fem och tjugu Mormonska larosatser jemforda med den Hel. Skrifts utsagor.* Goteborg, Tryck hos Hedlund & Lindskog, 1856.

8p. 24cm.

Title in English: Twenty-five of the Mormon teachings compared with passages from the Holy Scriptures.

UPB

8911a.   **Thomas, Kate.** *The hymn of the pioneer.* Salt Lake City, c1909.

[6]p. 43 x 9cm. folded to 9 x 15cm.

On cover: G. A. R. Souvenir, Salt Lake City, Utah, 1909.

Post card on verso.

UHi

8913a.   **Thomas, Robert David.** *Hanes cymry America; a'u sefydliadau, eu heglwysi, a'u llenorion; eu belrdd, a'u llenorion; yn nghyda thiroedd rhad y llywodraeith a'r reilffyrdd* ... Utica, N. Y., T. J. Griffiths, 1872.

3v. in 1 20cm.

Brief history of the founding of Utah by the Mormons, but no mention of Welsh in Utah, v. 2, p. 164.

DLC, MH, NN, RPB, UPB, USlC

8918a.   **Thomas, Robert Moseley Bryce.** *My reasons for leaving the Church of England and joining the Church of Jesus Christ of Latter-day Saints. By a convert.* Liverpool, Millennial Star Office, 1904.

34 [1]p. 8½cm.

In salmon printed wrappers.

UPB, USlC

8926a.   _____. (same, under title) *My reasons for joining the Church of Jesus Christ of Latter-day Saints.*   Independence, Press of Zion's Printing and Publishing Co., 1918.

32p.   17½cm.

UPB, USlC

8926b.   _____. (same) Independence, Press of Zion's Printing and Publishing Co., 1921.

32p.   18cm.

UPB

8928a.   _____. (same) Independence, Press of Zion's Printing and Publishing Company, 1929.

32p.   18cm.

UHi, UPB

8933a.   **Thomassen, P. O.** *Pionererne, deras utdrifning fran Illinois, modosamma vandring ofver oknen, ankomst till Utah och svarigheter derstades. En historisk berattelse om manga tilldragelser rorande de Sista Dagarnes Helige sedan deras utdrifning fran staterne upp till senare tid.*   Salt Lake City, Svenska Boktryckeri-Aktie-Bolagets Forlag [1886]

16p.   19cm.

Title in English: The pioneers, their trek from Illinois.

UPB

8933b.   _____. *Sange til brug for de Sidste-Dages Hellige.* Kjøbenhavn, F. E. Bording [185-]

16p.   22cm.

Title in English: Songs to be used for the Latter-day Saints.

USlC

8941a.   **Thomsen, Mads.** *I Cowboyland.* Kjøbenhavn, V. Pios Boghandel, Povl Branner, 1918.

96p.   20cm.

"Med Pionererne over den store orken," p. 21-33.

Title in English: In cowboy land.

UPB

8941b. **Thomson, Edward.** *Our oriental missions.* Cincinnati, Hitchcock and Walden, New York, Carlton and Lanahan, 1870.

2v. port. 18cm.

Diatribe on Mormonism, v. 2, p. 143.

CU, DLC, MB, MH, MiU, NIC, NN, NRCR, OC, OCl

8947a. *Three generations in Council of Twelve.* [Salt Lake City, Deseret News, 1927]

Broadside. 21 x 16cm.

Concerning the three members of the Lyman family that have been apostles. Also Amasa M. Lyman's role in settling San Bernardino, California.

Reprint from *Deseret News,* August 6, 1927.

UPB, USIC

8953b. **Tillotson, M. R.** *Grand Canyon country. By M. R. Tillotson . . . and Frank J. Taylor. Foreword by Horace M. Albright . . .* Stanford, Stanford University Press, 1929.

viii, 108p. illus. 23cm.

Jacob Hamlin sent to see the Hopi Indians by Brigham Young to see if they spoke words much like Welsh.

CU, DLC, ICU, OO, PP, UHi, UPB

8955. *Times and Seasons.* Commerce, 1839.

16p. 25cm.

Volume 1 No. 1 was first printed with date: Commerce, Illinois, July, 1839. It was reprinted in Nov. 1839, with an explanation on p. 16. The text has been reset. Article by Brigham Young, p. 15-16, omitted and an explanation of the reprint added.

MoInRC

8963a. *To the Christians and gentiles, especially Christians of the United States.* [n.p., 1909?]

Broadside. 23 x 15cm.

Denouncement of Mormonism as a religion and a call for President Taft to expel Senator Smoot.

USIC

8965a. *To the non-Mormon vote of Salt Lake City.* [Salt Lake City, 1874]

Broadside. 39 x 36cm.

Withdrawal of seventeen candidates in favor of the liberal Mormon ticket headed by William Jennings.

USIC

8965b. *To the President, Senate and House of Representatives of the United States.* [n.p., 1888-?]

Broadside. 20 x 13cm.

A printed petition against polygamy with space provided for the petitioner to add his comments.

USIC

8973a. **Toncray, Dudley D.** *Dudley D. Toncray, complainant and appellant, vs. Alfred Budge, defendant and respondent. Brief of appellant. Appeal from the District Court of the Fifth Judicial District of the State of Idaho, in and for the County of Bannock.* Boise, Idaho, Syma-York Co., Printers [1908]

34p. 25cm.

At head of title: In the Supreme Court of the State of Idaho, February term, 1908]

UPB

8975a. **Topsoe, Vilhelm Kristian Siguard.** *Fra Amerika. Med afbildninger og et kort.* Kjøbenhavn, Forlagt af den Guldendalske Boghandel (F. Hegel), 1872.

498p. illus., plates, map 23cm.

Title in English: From America.

Mormon material in the chapters entitled "Saltsostaden" and "Mormonerne."

CtY, DLC, ICU, NcD, UPB, WHI

8979a. **Torry, Alvin.** *Autobiography of Rev. Alvin Torry.* Auburn, New York, 1861.

358[i.e. 360]p. illus., plates, port 19½cm.

Converted to Mormonism in 1832, but returns to Methodism, p. 246-54.

DLC

8991a. **Tracy, Joshua L.** *Guide to the great West: being a brief but carefully written, description of the country bordering upon all the principal railroads of the West, with maps and illustrations.* St. Louis, Published by Tracy & Eaton, 1870.

261[7]p. illus., 3 folded maps. 19cm.

The section on Utah, p. 81-91 includes material on the Tabernacle, the Temple, and Brigham Young's home.

AzU, CtY, DLC, ICN, MH, UPB

8991b. **Trade and Commerce Publishing Company.** *Descriptive review of the industries of Salt Lake City, 1890. Trade, commerce and manufacturer with pen sketches of her principal business houses and manufacturing establishments.* [Salt Lake City, 1890]

135p. illus. 27cm.

Cover title: Salt Lake City's trade, commerce & Industries.

Includes a brief history of Mormonism.

UPB

8991c. **Trans-Mississippi Commercial Congress.** *Official proceedings of the seventh convention of the Trans-Mississippi Commercial Congress, held at St. Louis, Mo., November 26, 27, 28 and 30, 1894. Stenographic report by Charles Freeman Johnson.* St. Louis, E. J. Schuster Printing Co., 1894.

xiv, 269[1]p. 23½cm.

Mormons and Utah, p. vi, xii, 25, 33-34, 46-47, 51-52, 56-58, 59.

DLC, MiU, OCl, Or, PU, TU, UPB

8991d. **The Trans-Mississippi West.** *Papers read at a conference held at the University of Colorado, June 18-June 21, 1929. Edited by James F. Willard and Colin B. Goodykoontz.* Boulder, University of Colorado, 1929.

xi, 366p. 20cm.

"Handcart migration across the Plains," by LeRoy R. Hafen, p. 102-121.

UPB

8991e. *Trapped by the Mormons, or The Mormon peril. In all its entirety as presented at the Piccadilly Theatre, London. Mr. W. J. Mackay, lecturer and raconteur.* [Leicester, Engl.], Willsons, 1928.

[4]p. 23cm.

At head of title: West end, Paisley. Thursday, 29th November, 1928. For three days only. Ladies only matinee, Saturday, 1st Dec. at 2 p.m.

USIC

9013a. *Tro och dop. Ar tro allena tillracklig?* 160 tusendet. [Kopenhamn, Utgifven och forlagd af Andreas Peterson, Tryckt hos F. E. Bording (V. Petersen), 1900]

8p. 23cm.

Title in English: Faith and baptism.

UPB

9015a. _____. (same) [Jonkoping, Forlagd af A. P. Anderson, A. G. Kindbergs Tryckeri & Bokbinderi, 1917]

8p. 22cm.

UPB

9015b. _____. (same) [Jonkoping, Kindbergs Tryckeri, 1926]

8p. 22cm.

UPB

9019a. **Trowbridge, Richard B.** *The cart before the horse. The weak link in the activities of the restoration movement is the failure to heed God's command "build my temple" (in Jackson County, Missouri). By a student of it for fifty years.* Independence, Mo. [ca. 1925]

[8]p. 22½cm.

Signed: R. B. Trowbridge.

UPB

9019b. _____. *Do you want to know the truth? This is a time of crisis. To meet this crisis we must have the facts. Facts have been and are still being suppressed.* [Independence, Mo.? 192-]

[3]p. port. 25cm.

At head of title: "Ye shall know the truth -- the truth shall make you free." RLDS church finances.

USIC

9021a. *The true Church of Jesus Christ contrasted with the systems of men.* [Manchester] Jacques, Printer, Oldham Road [1845]

Broadside. 22 x 14½cm.

USIC

9021b. *The true lamplighter, and Aunt Mary's cabin.* Sketches of Franklin Gray, Queen Victoria, Joe Smith and the Mormons, P. T. Barnum, Ward trial in Kentucky, wooden nutmegs, John Burrill, Jona. Whilson. Boston, Published by Cushing, Perkins & Fay, 1854.

40p. 20cm.

A fictional account of Mormonism.

MH, UPB

9021c. *True versus modern Christianity.* [n.p., 1888]

[3]p. 19½cm.

"The public are respectfully invited to attend a discourse to be delivered at by Elder _____."

UPB

9027a. *Truth revealed "to the law and to the testimony."* The inhabitants of _____ and its vicinity are respectfully informed that a course of lectures will be delivered (D.V.) [sic] in the _____. [Bedford? 1849]

Broadside. 39 x 25cm.

Spaces provided for locations and times to be filled in. A list of twelve topics to be discussed.

Elder T. Smith . . . and Elder J. H. Flanigan are the lecturers.

USlC

9031a. **TSimmerman, Edward Romanovich.** *Puteshestvie po Amerike V 1869-1870 Eduarda TSimmermanna. Izdanie tret'e, ispravlennos, K. T. Soldatenkova.* Moskva, Tipografiia gracheve i k., u prechistenskikh v., d. chilovoi, 1872.

448p. 21cm.

Title in English: Journey through America in 1869-1870.

Description of the author's travels in America 1869-72. Chapter 15 is devoted to Salt Lake City and the Mormons.

DLC, UPB

9037b. **Tullidge, Edward Wheelock.** *Biographical sketch of Franklin S. Richards as published in Tullidge's History of Salt Lake City.* Salt Lake City, 1886.

10p. 22cm.

UPB

9049a. **Turenne d'Aynac, Gariel Louis Comte de.** *Quatorze mois dans l'Amerique du nord (1875-1876) par le Cte Louis de Turenne avec Carte d'une partie du Nort-Quest* . . . Paris, A. Quantin, Imprimeur-editeur, 1879.

2v. fold. map 19cm.

Title in English: Fourteen months in North America.

V. 1, Chapter VI. "Une excursion dans l'Utah."

UPB, USlC

9051a. **Turner, D. B.** *That "veiled gospel." Mr. Penrose denies that the Mormon missionaries carry a "veiled gospel."* [Salt Lake City, Kinsman Publishing Co., ca. 1910]

6p. 13½cm.

At head of title: Kinsman supplement.

Letter written to "Florida Philosopher."

UPB

9066a. **Typographical Association of Deseret.** *Original songs, composed for the first annual festival of the Typographical Association of Deseret, February 2, 1855.* [Great Salt Lake City, 1855]

Broadside. 26 x 16cm.

Songs by John Davis and E. R. Snow.

USlC

U

9068a.   *Udfald fra Christi Kirke mod Mormonerne og falsklaerere, af Ustrom.*
Kjøbenhavn, Faaes hos boghandler J. R. Møller, Trykt hos S. L. Møller, 1857.

61 [2]p. 20cm.

Title in English: An attack from Christ's Church against Mormonism and false teachers of the West.

UPB

9071a.   **Undertaker.** *A few facts. About the modern monogamic parson.* [Salt Lake City, 1885]

Broadside. 42 x 27cm.

Written to the editor of the *Herald* concerning polygamy and those who persecute polygamists.

USlC

9074a.   **Union Pacific Railroad Company.** *Along the Union Pacific system.* [Chicago, Ill., ca. 1925]

86p. illus. 23cm.

Mormons and Utah, p. 6, 24-31, 40-41.

Variant printings.

UPB

9079a.   _____. *A description of the western resorts for health and pleasure reached via Union Pacific Railway, "The overland route."* [Omaha?] Rand McNally & Co., 1889.

120p. illus., fold. map. 23cm.

Points in Utah, p. 85-101. Includes some material on the Mormons.

Other editions: 4th, Chicago, Knight & Leonard Co., 1891. UC-B, USlC; 5th, Chicago, 1892. USlC; 5th, Chicago, 1892. USlC; 6th, Chicago, 1893. USlC.

UHi, UPB

324

9079b. _____. *En route to California. Souvenir and views of the Union Pacific, "The overland route." World's pictorial route.* Omaha, 1901.

[72]p. [1]l. col. illus. 13 x 20cm.

"Fourth ed."

Describes Granger, Wyoming as a Mormon trading post. Description of temple square in Salt Lake City.

UPB

9083b. _____. *History of the Union Pacific Railroad. Issued by the Union Pacific Railroad on the occasion of the celebration at Ogden, Utah, May 10th, 1919, in commemoration of the 50th anniversary of the driving of the golden spike.* [Omaha, Nebraska? 1919]

42p. 23cm.

Mormons mentioned, p. 5, 11, 16.

UPB

9083c. _____. *Irrigation, its history, methods, statistics and results. Lands irrigated along the Union Pacific System.* St. Louis, Woodward & Tiernan Printing Co., 1894.

124[4]p. 20cm.

Mormons, p. 7-8. Irrigation in Utah, by C. W. Aldrach, p. 63-67.

DLC, DNAL, OCl, UPB

9088b. _____. *Union Pacific sketch book: A brief description of prominent places of interest along the line of the Union Pacific Railway and connections. With numerous illustrations.* Omaha, Neb., Gibson, Miller & Richardson, Art printers, 1887.

78 [2]p. illus., maps. 27cm.

"Compliments of the Passenger Department," Union Pacific Railway, Omaha, Neb.

Ogden, p. 47-50. Brief mention of Mormons, Salt Lake, p. 51-53. Mention of Brigham Young's grave; his residence with a picture of it.

UPB

9089a. _____. *Utah: its people, resources, attractions, and institutions. 1903. Compiled from authentic information and the latest reports. Compliments of the Passenger Department.* [Omaha, Neb., 1904]

118p. 21cm.

Cover title: Utah, a complete and comprehensive description.

11th ed.

Brief discussion of the settlement of Utah by the Mormons.

UPB

9089b. _____. *Utah; its resources and attractions, 1899. Compliments of the Passenger Department. 9th ed.* Chicago, Rand, McNally & Co., 1899.

128p. 20½cm.

Tourist information with Mormon references

ICN, NN, UPB

9104a. **U.S. Circuit Court. Illinois.** *Circuit Court of the United States of America District of Illinois vs.; The United States of America, to the marshall of the District of Illinois; greeting.* [Nauvoo?] Icarian Community Printing Establishment, 1850.

Broadside. 21 x 16cm.

Concerning the estate of Joseph Smith. The writ names his family and numerous other people.

USIC

9113c. **U.S. Congress. House. Committee on Claims.** *Emma Bidamon. [To accompany bill H. R. No. 290] April 22, 1856. Mr. Giddings, from the Committee of Claims, to whom was referred the petition of Emma Bidamon, report.* [Washington, 1856]

4p. 22cm. (U. S. 34th Cong. 1st Sess. House Report. No. 66)

Concerning land sold to pay off debts of Joseph Smith and others.

UPB

9113d. _____. *Richard H. Porter and James Porter.* [Washington, Govt. Print. Off. 1886]

3p. 23cm. (U.S. 49th Cong. 1st Sess. House. Report. No. 2696)

Compensation for cattle lost during the Utah Expedition.

UPB

9113e. _____. *Richard J. Porter and James Porter ... Report: [To accompany bill H. R. 4540.]* [Washington, Govt. Print. Off.] 1882.

3p. 23cm. (U.S. 47th Cong. 1st Sess. House. Report. No. 1181)

Claims for property impressed by the Utah Expedition and lost.

UPB

9113f. _____. *Utah Expedition.* [Washington, Govt. Print. Off.] 1885.

2p. 22cm. (U.S. 48th Cong. 2d Sess. House. Report. No. 2650)

Payment for property seized from Richard H. and James Porter during the Utah expedition.

UPB

9113g. **U.S. Congress. House. Committee on Election of President, Vice-President, and Representatives in Congress.** *Amendments to the Constitution prohibiting polygamy, etc.* [Washington, Govt. Print. Off.] 1899.

16p. 23cm. (U.S. 55th Cong. 3rd Sess. Report No. 2307).

The selection of Brigham H. Roberts in 1899 started new efforts to have a constitutional amendment against polygamy. A summary of polygamy and legislation against it.

UPB

9113h. _____. *Amendments to the Constitution prohibiting polygamy, etc.* Washington, Govt. Print. Off., 1899.

16p. 26cm.

UPB

9115a. **U.S. Congress. House. Committee on Elections.** *Cannon vs. Campbell, contested election case from the Territory of Utah.* [Washington, Govt. Print. Off.] 1882.

66p. 23½cm. (U.S. 47th Cong. 1st Sess. House. Report No. 559)

Polygamy and other reasons for denying George Q. Cannon a congressional seat by the Committee on Elections.

UPB, USIC

9115b. _____. *Delegate from the Territory of Utah ... Report: The Committee on Elections, to whom was referred the application and accompanying papers of John T. Caine, asking to be admitted to a seat in the Forty-seventh Congress as a delegate from the Territory of Utah, having had the same under consideration, beg leave to report as follows:* [Washington, Govt. Print. Off.] 1883.

4p. 23cm. (U.S. 47th Cong. 2d Sess. House. Report. No. 1865)

Special election after the disputed Cannon vs. Campbell election.

UPB

9116a. _____. *George Q. Cannon, delegate from Utah.* [Washington, 1875]

10p. 23cm.

The Committee recommends that Cannon not be seated because he had four wives.

UPB, USIC, UU

9116b. _____. *George Q. Cannon, delegate from Utah. Views of the minority.* [Washington, 1875]

8p. 23cm.

The case of George Q. Cannon's right to a seat in congress be dismissed.

UPB, USIC, UU

9119a. **U.S. Congress. House. Committee on Naval Affairs.** *House of Representatives, The Committee on Naval Affairs, Tuesday, May 16, 1911 ... with reference to the silver service that is proposed to be presented to the battleship Utah.* [Washington? Govt. Print Off.? 1911?]

15p. 23½cm.

Brief history of Utah with Mormon references.

UPB

9126a. **U.S. Congress. House. Committee on the Judiciary.** *J. and R. H. Porter ... Report: [To accompany bill S.905.] The committee on the Judiciary, to whom was referred the bill [S.905] for the relief of J. and R. H. Porter, having had the same under consideration, would respectfully report.* [Washington, Govt. Print. Off.] 1882.

22p. 23cm. (U.S. 47th Cong. 1st Sess. House. Report. No. 1637)

Information on the Utah expedition. Redress for destroyed wagons.

UPB

9126b. _____. *Polygamy . . . Report: [To accompany H. Res. 176.] The Committee on the Judiciary to whom have been referred House resolutions 16, 50, 140, and 143, for the amendment of the constitution of the United States, beg leave to report.* [Washington, Govt. Print. Off., 1886]

12p. 22cm. (U. S. 49th Cong. House. 1st Sess. Report. No. 2568)

Discussion on polygamy, but recommends caution in altering the constitution.

NjP, ULA, UPB

9148a. _____. **Committee on the Territories.** *Carson Valley, Utah -- annexation to State of California -- and eastern boundary of California.* [Washington, Cornelius Wendell, Printer] 1857.

2p. 23cm. (U.S. 34th Cong. 3d Sess. House. Report. No. 116)

Desire of Carson Valley residents to be divided from Utah due to Mormon discrimination, etc.

UPB

9160a. _____. *Territory of Nevada. [To accompany Bill H. R. No. 567] May 12, 1858. Mr. William Smith, from the Committee on the Territories, made the following report.* [Washington, James B. Steedman, Printer?] 1858.

5p. 23cm. (U.S. 35th Cong. 1st Sess. House. Report. No. 375)

Necessity of dividing the state to get the loyal citizens of Nevada out from the control of the Mormons.

UPB

9166d. _____. **Senate. Committee on Claims.** *In the Senate of the United States . . . Report: [To accompany S. 1198]* [Washington, Govt. Print. Off.] 1892.

23p. 23cm. (U.S. 52d Cong. 1st Sess. Senate. Report. No. 625)

Heirs of James Bridger, attempting to receive reparation for Fort Bridger, which was burned by the Mormons during the Utah Expedition.

UPB

9166e. _____. *Report: To accompany bill S. 905.* [Washington, Govt. Print. Off., 1882]

4p. 22cm. (U.S. 47th Cong. 1st Sess. Senate. Report. No. 154)

Compensation to Richard H. and James Porter for property taken during the Utah Expedition.

UPB

9166f. _____. (same) *Report: [To accompany bill S. 1368]. The Committee on Claims, to whom was referred the bill (S. 1368P) for the relief of Richard H. Porter and James Porter, having had the same under consideration, beg respectfully to submit the following report.* [Washington, Govt. Print. Off.] 1886.

3p. 22cm. (U. S. 49th Cong. 1st Sess. Report No. 209.)

Reimbursement for property lost during the Utah Expedition.

UPB

9184a. **U.S. Congress. Senate. Committee on Territories.** *Resolutions.* [Washington, Govt. Print. Off.] 1888.

[1]p. 22cm. (U.S. 50th Cong. 1st Sess. Senate. Mis. Doc. No. 89)

The second resolution proposes that Utah not be granted statehood until polygamy is no longer practiced and the territory is not controlled by the Mormon Church.

DLC, UPB

9189a. **U.S. Department of the Interior.** *Compensation of commissioners under the act for the suppression of bigamy, etc. Message from the President of the United States, transmitting a communication from the Secretary of the Interior, recommending amendments to the act in reference to bigamy, approved March 22, 1882.* [Washington, Govt. Print. Off.] 1882.

2p. 23cm. (U.S. 47th Cong. 1st Sess. House. Ex. Doc. No. 152)

Compensation for members of the Utah Commission.

UPB

9189b. _____. *Enforcement of the anti-polygamy act. Letter from the Secretary of the Interior, transmitting certain petitions for enforcing the anti-polygamy act of 1862.* [Washington, Govt. Print. Off., 1879]

6p. 22½cm. (U. S. 45th Cong. 3d Sess. House. Ex. Doc. No. 58)

List of petitions to congress to enforce the polygamy law of 1862.

UPB

9189c. _____. *Indians of Skull Valley and Deep Creek, Utah. Letter from the Secretary of the Interior, transmitting report of the special agent appointed July 3, 1911, to visit the Indians of Skull Valley and Deep Creek and other detached Indians of Utah.* [Washington, Govt. Print. Off.] 1912.

9p. 23cm. (U.S. 62 Cong 2d Sess. House. Doc. No. 389.)

Includes the Mormon treatment of the Indians.

UPB

9194b. _____. **Census Office.** *Report on cattle, sheep, and swine, supplementary to enumeration of live stock on farms in 1880. Clarence Gordon, special agent in charge.* Washington, Govt. Print. Off., 1884.

162p. tables. 29½cm.

Utah Territory, p. 117-24. Other Mormon references, p. 93, 98-99, 102.

UPB

9199a. **U.S. General Land Office.** *Letter from the Secretary of the Interior, transmitting, in response to Senate resolution of 23d March, the report of the Commissioner of the General Land Office upon the subjects embraced therein . . . May 19, 1880.* [Washington, Govt. Print. Off.] 1880.

136p. 1 fold. map. 24cm. (46th Cong., 2d Sess. Senate. Ex. Doc. No. 181).

Includes material on Mormon land claims, individual Mormons, etc.

UPB, USlC

9199b. _____. *Letter from the Secretary of the Interior, transmitting, in response to Senate resolution of 23d March, the report of the Commissioner of the General Land Office upon the subjects embraced therein.* [Washington, Govt. Print. Off.] 1880.

138p. 2 fold. maps. 23cm. (U.S. 46th Cong. 2d Sess. Senate, Ex. Doc. No. 181)

Discrimination of land use by the Mormons.

UPB

9209a. **U.S. National Park Service.** *Circular of general information regarding Grand Canyon National Park, Arizona.* [Washington] Govt. Print. Off., 1929.

72p. illus. 23½cm.

Mormons, p. 22, 24, 62.

UPB

9209b. _____. *Glimpses of our national monuments.* [Washington] Govt. Print. Off., 1930.

vi, 74p. illus. 22cm.

Mormons mentioned at Pipe Springs National Monument, p. 52-53 and Scotts Bluff National Monument, p. 57.

UPB

9225a. **U. S. President, 1885-1889 (Cleveland).** *Message of the President of the United States communicated to the two houses of Congress at the beginning of the Second Session of the Fiftieth Congress.* Washington, Govt. Print. Off., 1888.

32p. 23½cm.

Mormons, p. 25.

USlC

9236a. **U.S. Utah Commission.** *Minority report.* [Springfield, Ill., Springfield Printing Co., 1887?]

24p. 22½cm.

No more legislation on polygamy or the Mormon Church needed.

NjP, UPB, UU

9236b. _____. *Minority report of the Utah Commission. Presented by Gen. John A. McClernand.* [Salt Lake City? 1891?]

18p. 22½cm.

Dated: Salt Lake City, September 25th, 1891.

Concerning polygamy legislation.

UHi, UPB

9237a. _____. *Polygamy in Utah. Message from the President of the United States, transmitting a communication from the Secretary of the Interior relative to polygamy in Utah.* [Washington, Govt. Print. Off.] 1884.

15p. 23cm. (U.S. 48th Cong. 1st Sess. House. Ex. Doc. No. 153)

Cover title: Special report of the Utah Commission made to the Secretary of the Interior, 1884.

Political situation and status of polygamy as a result of the Edmunds Act.

UPB

9239a. _____. *Report of the Utah Commission as to the management of the Industrial Christian Home of Utah Territory.* [Washington, Govt. Print. Off., 1889]

10p. 22cm. (U.S. 51st Cong. 1st Sess. Senate. Misc. Doc. No. 34)

Industrial Christian Home was for polygamist wives.

UHi, UPB

9254a. **U.S. War Department.** *Military posts. Letter from the Secretary of War, in answer to a resolution of the House of the 5th December, transmitting a report of inspection of military posts.* [Washington, Govt. Print. Off.] 1867.

15p. 23cm. (U.S. 39th Cong. 2d SEss. House. Ex. Doc. No. 20).

"Mormons," p. 7-11.

UPB, USlC

9254b. _____. *Protection across the continent. Letter from the Secretary of War, in answer to a resolution of the House of December 6, 1866, transmitting information respecting the protection of the routes across the continent to the Pacific from molestation by hostile Indians.* [Washington, Govt. Print. Off., 1867]

55p. 22cm.

Food grown in Colorado would solve the Indian and Mormon problem.

UPB

9254c. _____. *Report of the Secretary of War, in answer to a resolution of the Senate calling for a copy of the contract made with Russell, Majors & Waddell for beef cattle; and also a statement of contracts made by the department, or under its authority, during the present session of Congress in connection with the Utah Expedition, without public notice.* [Washington, Govt. Print. Off., 1858]

9p. 22½cm. (U.S. Congress. 35th Cong. 1st Sess. Senate. Ex. Doc. No. 46.)

UPB, USlC

9257a. **Unity Club, Nauvoo.** *Nauvoo, the beautiful.* [Nauvoo, 1926?]

[8]p. folder, illus., port. 16cm.

Includes the history of the Mormons in Nauvoo.

UHi, UPB

9257b. **University of Chicago Press.** *A study of Mormonism as a laboratory of ethics and psychology.* [Chicago, 1922]

[4]p. 15½cm.

A brochure for Ephrain E. Ericksen's dissertation "The psychological and ethical aspects of Mormon group life."

UPB

9264a. *Das ursprungliche evangelium.* *Ein kurze abhandlung uber kie lehre der Kirche Jesu Christi der heiligen der letzten Tage. Funste auflage.* Bern, Herausgegeben von Geo. C. Naegle, 1895.

26p. 22½cm.

Title in English: The original gospel.

UPB

9273a. **Utah. Constitution.** *Constitution of the State of Utah as framed by the Constitutional Convention in Salt Lake City, Utah, from March 4th, to May 8th, 1895. Published by authority of the convention under the supervision of Hon. Richard G. Lambert, chairman of committee on printing.* Salt Lake City, Tribune Job Printing Company, 1895.

iii, [1]48p. 22½cm.

Bans the practice of polygamy, p. 3.

UPB, UU

9294a. **Utah. Manufacturers Association.** *Utah, your state; pertinent facts for speakers.* [Salt Lake City, ca. 1925]

[16]p. 22cm.

Includes 1918 conference address of Heber J. Grant.

UPB

9297a. **Utah. Mormon Battalion Monument Commission.** *Mormon Battalion Monument now being erected on the southeast corner of the state capitol grounds, Salt Lake City, Utah, to be completed May 1st, 1927.* [Salt Lake City, 1927?]

[6]p. illus. 23cm.

UPB

9311a. **Utah Semi-Centennial Commission.** *From the Press Bureau of the Utah Semi-Centennial Commission, having in charge the Utah Pioneer Jubilee, in commemoration of the arrival of "the pioneers of 1847." Special correspondence, Salt Lake City, May 18, 1897.* [Salt Lake City, 1897]

Broadside. 24 x 15½cm.

UPB

9312a. _____. *To the people of Colorado. Greetings.* [Salt Lake City, 1897?]

[4]p. 20½cm.

The arrival of the pioneers to Utah.

UPB

9313a. _____. *Utah Pioneer Jubilee, Salt Lake City, July 20 to 25, 1897.* [Salt Lake City, 1897]

[2]p. 16cm. (Bulletin No. 2)

UPB

9314a. **Utah. State Board of Health.** *Circular issued by the State Board of Health, Utah.* [Salt Lake City, 1900]

14p. illus. 22½cm.

"Recommendation to the Latter-day Saints by the First Presidency, published in the *Deseret Evening News*, November 17th, 1900," p. 14.

UPB

9314b. **Utah. State Conservation Commission.** *Report of the Utah Conservation Commission.* Salt Lake City, Arrow Press, Tribune-Reporter Printing Co., 1913.

206p. illus. 23½cm.

Mormons, p. 42-43, 202.

UPB

9327a. **Utah (Territory) Citizens.** *Territory of Nevada ... The Committee on Territories, to whom was referred the petition of numerous citizens of the United States residing in the Territory of Utah, asking for the creation of a new territory, to be formed from the western portion thereof.* Washington, James B. Steedman, 1858.

5p. 24cm. (U.S. 35th Cong. 1st Sess. House. Report No. 375.)

Petition to be separated from the Mormons in Utah Territory.

UPB

9329a. **Utah (Territory). Commission for the Appointment and Government of Registrars.** *Registration rules. Adopted by the Commission for the Appointment and Government of Registrars, etc., for the delegate election in November.* [Salt Lake City, 1882]

4p. 23cm.

Includes restrictions on polygamists.

UPB

9329b. **Utah (Territory). Commissioner of Schools.** *Biennial report of the Territorial Superintendent of Common Schools, for the years 1874-5, with historical sketch of education in Utah, and the new school law.* Salt Lake City, David O. Calder, Public Printer at the Deseret News Steam Printing Establishment, 1876.

70p. 23cm.

Brigham Young Academy, p. 18-19, Mormons p. 43.

UPB

9341a. **Utah (Territory) Constitutional Convention.** *Memorial to the honorable, the Senate and House of Representatives of the United States, in Congress assembled* . . . [Salt Lake City? 1882?]

Request for statehood for Utah Territory.

4p. 23cm.

UPB

9361a. **Utah (Territory) Governor, 1871-1875 (Woods).** *Governor's message to the Legislative Assembly of the Territory of Utah.* [Salt Lake City, 1874]

16p. tables. 22cm.

Speaks of the Perpetual Emigration Fund Company, and its ability to assume the property of a deceased person.

UPB

9369a. **_____, 1881 (Thomas).** *Governor's message, with accompanying documents. Message of his excellency A. L. Thomas.* [Salt Lake City, 1881]

27p. tables. 21cm.

Political power weilded the by the church authorities, assessments for political purposes; polygamy mentioned.

UPB

9382a. **_____, 1893-1896 (West).** *Report of the Governor of the Territory of Utah to the Secretary of the Interior.* Washington. Govt. Print. Off., 1895.

47p. 23cm.

"We have inhibited for all time polygamous or plural marriages."

UHi, UPB

9382b. _____, **1893-1896 (West).** *Report of the Governor of the Territory of Utah to the Secretary of the Interior.* Washington, Govt. Print. Off., 1896.

5p. 23cm.

Includes material on the polygamy question.

UPB

9391a. _____. *Legislative Assembly. Protest of Legislative Assembly of Utah. Memorial of the Legislative Assembly of the Territory of Utah, protesting against the passage of the bills now pending in Congress, or any other measures iminical to the people of said Territory, until after a full investigation by a Congressional committee.* [Washington, Govt. Print. Off.] 1884.

13p. 23cm. (U.S. 48th Cong. 1st Sess. House. Mis. Doc. No. 45)

A review of anti-Mormon legislation.

UPB

9391b. _____. *Resolution in relation to a constitutional convention.* [Salt Lake City, 1882]

Broadsheet. 24½cm.

Dated: March 4, 1882. Signed: F. M. Lyman, Speaker House of Representatives, Jos. F. Smith, President of Council.

UPB

9391c. _____. *Utah. Memorial of the members and officers of the Legislative Assembly of the Territory of Utah, setting forth their grievances, and praying Congress to give them a voice in the selection of their rulers.* [Washington, James B. Steedman, 1858]

5p. 22cm. (U.S. 35th Cong. 1st Sess. House. Mis. Doc. No. 100)

Objections to the territorial appointees as well as redress of Missouri lands.

UPB

9393a. _____. **Committee of the Judiciary.** *Report on the Governor's message by the Committees on the Judiciary and Education.* [Salt Lake City, 1882]

15p. 21½cm.

Cover title: Council. Thirty-third day. Signed: Daniel H. Wells . . . Moses Thatcher.

UPB

9401a. **Utah Territory. Superintendent of Common Schools.** *Annual report of the Territorial Superintendent of Common Schools. For the year 1867.* Salt Lake City, Geo. Q. Cannon, Public Printer, "Deseret Evening News" office, [1868]

19p. 18½cm.

Need for the introduction of the Deseret alphabet in the schools. This need for a phonetic alphabet is also the main theme of the 1868 report.

UPB, USlC

9401b. _____. *Annual report of the Territorial Superintendent of Common Schools for the year 1869.* Salt Lake City, Joseph Bull, Public Printer, "Deseret News" office [1870]

17p. 20cm.

Need for the adoption of the Deseret Alphabet.

UPB, USlC

9403a. **Utah Tract and Bible Society.** *Pre-existence.* Salt Lake City [ca. 1910]

8p. 18cm.

UPB

V

9409a.   **Vahl, Jens.** *Joseph Smith's Levnet. 3 dte oplag.* Kjøbenhavn, Udgivet af Foreningen til gudelige Smaaskrifters Udbredelse, 1888.

80p. 17cm. (No. 78)

Cover title.

Signed: J. Vahl and D. Rothe on verso of cover.

Title in English: The life of Joseph Smith:

USlC

9411a.   _____. *Mormonernes laerdomme ifolge deres egne skrifter og betragtede i Christendommens Lys. udgivet ved J. Vahl.* 2det Oplag, ny Udgave. Kjøbenhavn, Udgiver af Foreningen til gudelige Smaaskrifters Udbredelse, 1883.

24p. 16cm.

"No. 249."

USlC

9413a.   *Valgberettigede i Utah, giv agt!* [Salt Lake City? Republican Party? 1894?]

[2]p. 22cm.

Title in English: Voters of Utah, beware!

USlC

9414a.   **Valk, M. H. A. Van Der.** *De Mormoonsche leer, door M. H. A. Van Der Valk.* Rotterdam, Handelmaatschappij Goudswaard [ca. 1920]

33[3]p. 19cm.

Title in English: Of the Mormon teaching.

In grey printed wrapper.

Advertisement for other Valk anti-Mormon pamphlet found on page [3] following text.

UPB

9448a. **Varley, Thomas.** *Utah's mineral wealth, represented by statistics and graphic charts compiled from official government and state reports. By Thos. Varley, C. C. Stevenson, W. Spencer Reid* ... Salt Lake City, Commercial Club, Chamber of Commerce, 1921.

31 [1]p. illus., map. 23cm.

Early Mormon church's discouragement of prospecting; its participation in establishing iron mines.

CoD, CU-B, NjP, UPB, USlC

9460a. *Et venligt ord.* [København, Udgivet og forlagt af J. M. Christensen, Trykt hos P. S. Christiansen, Aarhus, 1905]

4p. 23½cm.

Title in English: A friendly word.

USlC

9460b. *Die Verbannung des Mormonenvolkes.* [Bern, Buchdruckerei Steiger & Cie., 1895?]

[4]p. 23½cm.

Title in English: Banishment of the Mormon people.

Reprinted from the *Millennial Star.*

USlC

9464a. **Vermont Party.** *Annual reunion of the Vermont party, 1905-1907.* [Salt Lake City, Deseret News, 1907]

[8]p. illus. 19cm.

Reunion of those persons attending the dedication of the Joseph Smith monument in Vermont.

UHi

9466a. *Verstaat gij ook hetgeen gij leest?* [Rotterdam? Netherlands-Belgian Mission? n.d.]

4p. 23½cm.

Title in English: Do you understand what you read?

Includes: Articles of Faith.

USlC

9466b. **Vest, George Graham.** *Ellen C. Clawson and Hiram B. Clawson, appellants, vs. Alexander Ramsey, A. S. Paddock, G. L. Godfrey, A. B. Carleton, J. R. Pettigrew, E. D. Hoge, and James T. Little, appellees. Appeal from judgment of the Supreme Court of Utah. Brief and argument for appellants.* Washington, Gibson Bros., 1885.

1p.l., 12p. 22cm.

At head of title: Supreme Court of the United States. October term, 1884. No. 1030.

Cover title.

Polygamy case.

DLC

9466c. _____. *James M. Barlow, appellant, vs. Alexander Ramsey, A. S. Paddock, G. L.. Godfrey, A. B. Carleton, J. R. Pettigrew, E. D. Hoge, and Harmel Pratt, appellees. Appeal from judgment of the Supreme Court of Utah. Brief and argument for appellant.* Washington, Gibson Bros., 1885.

[1]p. 22cm.

At head of title: Supreme Court of the United States. October term, 1884. No. 1031.

Cover title.

A bigamy case.

DLC

9466d. _____. *Jesse J. Murphey, appellant, vs. Alexander Ramsey, A. S. Paddock, G. L. Godfrey, A. B. Carleton, J. R. Pettigrew, E. D. Hoge, and Arthur Pratt, appellees. Appeal from judgment of the Supreme Court of Utah. Brief and argument for appellant. George G. Vest, Wayne MacVeagh, Franklin S. Richard, Charles W. Bennett, for appellant.* Washington, Gibson Bros., Printers and bookbinders, 1885.

3p. 22cm.

A bigamy case.

DLC

9467a. _____. _Mary Ann M. Pratt, Appellant vs. Alexander Ramsey, A. S. Paddock, G. L. Godfrey, A. B. Carleton, J. R. Pettigrew, E. D. Hoge, and John S. Lindsay, Appellees. Appeal from judgment of the Supreme Court of Utah. Brief and argument for appellant. George G. Vest, Wayne MacVeagh, Franklin S. Richards, Charles W. Bennett, for appellant._ Washington. Gibson Bros., Printers and Bookbinders, 1885.

42p. 23cm.

At head of title: Supreme Court of the United States. October term, 1884. Cover title.

Polygamy trial.

UPB, USlC

9467b. _____. _Mildred E. Randall and Alfred Randall, appellants, vs. Alexander Ramsey, A. S. Paddock, G. L. Godfrey, A. B. Carlson, J. R. Pettigrew, E. D. Hoge, and Harmel Pratt, appellees. Appeal from judgment of the Supreme Court of Utah. Brief and argument for appellants._ Washington, Gibson Bros., 1885.

1p.l., 3p. 22cm.

At head of title: Supreme Court of the United States. October term, 1884. No. 1029.

Cover title.

Case concerning a Mormon attempting to register to vote.

DLC

9479a. **Violette, Eugene Morrow.** _A history of Missouri._ New York, D. C. Heath & Co. [c1918]

xxxiii, [1]l. 500p. illus., maps, col. plate. 20½cm.

Chapter IV. "Mormon troubles in Missouri."

CoU, CU, DLC, MiU, OCl

9484a. **Vogel, Hermann Wilhelm.** _Vom indischen Ocean bis zum Goldlande. Reisebeobachtungen und Erlebnisse in pier Velttheilen._ Berlin, Verlag von Theobald Grieben, 1877.

vi, 452[2]p. 21½cm.

Title in English: From the Indian Ocean to the gold fields.

Includes his trip through Salt Lake City.

DLC, USlC

9490a. **Vollenweider, J.** *Der Glaube und die Lehre der Kirche Jesu Christi der Heiliggen der letzten Tage, oder Der wahre Weg selif zu werdwn Ein Wort an das Schweizervolk zur Warnung und Delchrung von J. Wollen-wider.* Zurich, Herausgageben von G. Hafen, 1861.

34p. 23cm.

Title in English: The beliefs and teachings of the Church of Jesus Christ of Latter-day Saints.

USIC

9490b. *Eine vollkommene Religion.* Basel, Fred Tadje [19--?]

4p. 20cm.

Title in English: A complete religion.

Missionary tract used in the Swiss-German Mission.

USIC

9491a. **Von Klenner, Katherin (Evans). Baroness.** *The greater revelation. Messages from unseen world received through automatic writing in various languages, including Chinese and Japanese, in the chirography and with verified signatures of those sending the messages.* New York, Siebel Publishing Corporation, 1925.

ix, 259p. illus. 21cm.

A paragraph from Brigham Young, p. 121.

UPB

9492a. **Voorhees, Luke.** *Personal recollections of pioneer life on the mountains and plains of the great West.* [Cheyenne, 1920]

76p. 21½cm.

"Early experiences in Salt Lake City," p. 38-29.

CtY, ICN, NN, RPB, UPB, UU

W

9502a. *Wahrer und falscher Gottesdienst.* [Bern, Herausgegeben von F. W. Schonfeld, ca. 1885]

[4]p. 23½cm.

Title in English: True and false worship of God.

Missionary tract.

USIC

9516a. **Walker, Charles L.** *In commeration of the 25th anniversary of the giving of endowment for the dead, as well as for the living, in the St. George Temple, by desire of press. David H. Cannon.* [St. George, Utah? 1902]

Broadside. 38½ x 24½cm.

USIC

9516b. _____. *Lines kindly solicited by President David H. Cannon for the occasion of the 23rd anniversary of giving endowments for the dead in the St. George Temple on the 11th January, 1877, the date being the first of such sacred work in this dispensation.* [n.p.] 1900.

Broadside. 35 x 18cm.

USIC

9516d. _____. *Lines written for the St. George Female Relief Society.* [St. George, Utah?] 1892.

Broadside. 21 x 28cm.

Consists of two poems, each on the same subject.

USIC

9525a. **Walker, Marietta (Hodges).** *Gospel story and footsteps of Jesus.* Lamoni, Herald House, 1904.

108p. 19½cm. (Birth offering series)

USIC

9536a. **Walker, Samuel Frye.** *The ruins revisited, and the world-story retold. By an Americanist.* [Lamoni, Iowa? 1887]

240p. 20½cm.

American antiquities. Walker was the husband of Marietta Walker.

CU, DLC, MH, MoInRC, NjP

9536b. _____. *The spoilers of Jerusalem; a historical poem.* [Lamoni, Iowa? Herald House? 1889]

8p. 18cm.

MoInRC

9537a. *Valkomsthelning vid ankomsten till Sion.* [Rock Island, Ill., Augustana Tract Society, 188-?]

4p. 23cm.

Title in English: A word of welcome upon arrival in Zion.

Excerpts from the Swedish hymnal, *Journal of Discourses,* etc., concerning Mormon beliefs.

USIC

9537b. **Wallace, Charles, d. 1850.** *A confession of the awful and bloody transactions in the life of Charles Wallace, the fiend-like murderer of Miss Mary Rogers, the beautiful cigar-girl of Broadway, New York, whose fate has for several years past been wrapt in the most profound mystery: Together with an authentic statement of the many burglaries and murders of Wallace and the notorious and daring thief, Snelling: And an account of the murder and robbery of Mr. Parks, of Newport, Kentucky, also perpetrated by Wallace.* New Orleans, Published by E. E. Barclay & Co., 1851.

vi, [7]21[1]p. ill., plates 22cm.

Includes a visit to Nauvoo with a derogatory view of Joseph Smith.

DLC, MH, NcD, NIC, UPB, ViU

9600a. *Warning to parents & employers. Mormons or Latter Day Saints.* [England, 190-?]

Broadside. 22 x 14cm.

"Abominable doctrines of Mormonism and when a young woman convert is finally secured, she is persuaded to leave this country for Salt Lake City where polygamy is believed in as part of their religion."

USIC Incomplete copy.

9604a. **Warsaw Committee of Safety.** *To his excellency Thomas Ford, Governor of the State of Illinois.* [Warsaw? 1844]

Broadside. 45 x 22cm.

Request for protection against the Mormons.

USIC 2 variants

9605a. **Warsaw Message.** *Extra. V. 1. Warsaw, Ill., July 12, We are again compelled to allow another publication day to pass without issuing a paper* . . . [Warsaw, 1843]

Broadside. 57 x 31cm.

Includes two articles concerning the arrest of Joseph Smith.

NN

9610a. **Warsaw Signal.** *Warsaw Signal extra. Warsaw, January 8, 1846. Important from Carthage.* [Warsaw, 1846]

Broadside. 32 x 16cm.

Money furnish to Backenstos' posse passed by the two Mormon commissioners.

USIC

9616a. _____. *Supplement to the Warsaw Signal. This supplement to the warsaw Signal contains a complete documentary history of the late difficulties with the Mormons, and an account of the late expedition of Gov. Fort to Nauvoo* . . . [Warsaw, 1846]

[4]p. 58cm.

Correspondence and documents on the Mormon war.

NN

9673a. **Weiffenbach, Eugen.** *Der Mormonismus.* Cincinnati, Chicago, Kansas City, San Francisco, Jennings & Graham, c1907.

72p. 19½cm.

Title in English: The Mormons.

NNUT

9678a. **Welling, Milton Holmes.** *Relief Society -- wheat. 1918 June 7.* [Washington, Govt. Print. Off., 1918]

Broadsheet. 23 x 15cm.

Speech given in the United States House of Representatives by Milton Holmes Welling, congressmen from Utah, concerning the wheat collected by the Relief Society and given to the government.

USIC

9679a. **Wells, Daniel Hanmer.** *General orders No. 1.* Great Salt Lake City, 1852.

Broadside. 25 x 20cm.

At head of title: Head Quarters, Nauvoo Legion, G.S.L. City, Utah Territory, April 12, 1852.

Organization of the Nauvoo Legion.

USIC

9679b. _____. *Military circular. Head Quarters, Nauvoo Legion ... General orders No. 5.* [Great Salt Lake City, 1857]

Broadside. 36 x 22cm.

Dated July 31, 1857.

Additional men called into the legion due to the approach of the Utah Expedition.

USIC

9686a. **Wells, Emmeline Blanche (Woodward).** *The wife to her husband. [By] Emile.* Salt Lake City, 1874.

Broadside. 18 x 11cm.

Dated at end: Salt Lake City, Nov. 17, 1874.

Mormon poetry.

UPB

9690a. **Wells, Samuel Roberts.** *Wedlock; or, the right relations of the sexes: Disclosing the laws of conjugal selection, and showing who may, and who may not marry.* New York, Samuel R. Wells, Publisher. 1870.

vi, [7] 238p. 20cm.

"The Mormon system," etc., p. [138]-140.

Another ed. 1872. KU, WM

CU, DLC, OU, RPB, UPB, ViU

9693a. **Werff, B. Van Der.** *Het Mormonisme, door B. Van Der Werff, Geref. predikant te Helder.* Zutphen, J. B. Van Den Brink & Co. [ca. 1920].

24p. 19½cm. (Ons arsenaal. 3e serie Onder leiding van Dr. H. Kaajan, Rotterdam en Ds. J. Waterink, Zutphen).

Title in English: The Mormons.

At head of title: Christelijke Brochurenreeks.

Cover title.

In mauve printed wrapper.

UPB

9704a. **Westermarck, Edward Alexander.** *The history of human marriage.* 2d ed. London, Macmillan and Co., 1894.

xx, [1]-644, [1]-4p. 22cm.

Includes brief comments about Mormon polygamy, p. 434, 448, and 470.

Other editions in 1889, 1891, 1901, 1903, 1921, 1922, 1925.

USIC

9704b. _____. *A short history of marriage.* New York, Macmillan Company, 1926.

xiii, 327p. 21½cm.

Another edition: New York, 1930 CoU, CU, OLI, PP, UPB.

Based on his History of human marriage. Mormons regard polygamy as a divine institution.

CU, DLC, MBOU, PU

9713a. *He Whakamsharatanga aroha ki a Hirini Whaanga.* Salt Lake City, Deseret News, 1905.

15p. ports. 15cm.

Title in English: Memories of love for Hirini Whaanga.

Message from the First Presidency on p. 14-15.

USIC

9714a. *What shall we do to be saved?* [n.p., Church of Jesus Christ of Latter-day Saints, 18--]

Broadside. 19 x 13cm.

Has some general comments on religion and announces services every Sabbath at 2:30 and 6:30 p.m. at Swansea and Cardiff.

Mormonism in Wales.

USIC

9727a. **White, Bartholomew.** *Brief sketch of the life of Bartholomew White, a compendium of travel, adventure and pioneer life west of the Rocky Mountains.* Oakland [the author] 1878.

52p. 22 x 14cm.

Cover title.

Spent a month among the Mormons at Ogden and Salt Lake City.

Or

9729a. **White, Eugene E.** *Service on the Indian reservations. Being the experiences of a special Indian agent while inspecting agencies and serving as agent for various tribes; including explanations of how the government service is conducted on the reservations; descriptions of agencies; anecdotes illustrating the habits, customs, and peculiarities of the Indians; and humorous anecdotes and stories of travel.* [Little Rock, Arkansas Democrat Company, 1893]

336p. illus. 20cm.

Visits Salt Lake City and comments on the Mormons.

AAP, DLC, MH, NNC, UPB

9768a. **Whitney, Orson Ferguson.** *Hail to the Prophet who pointed the way.* [Salt Lake City? n.d.]

Broadside. 17 x 11½cm.

Sung to music by H. E. Giles. Words to a song concerning restoration of the gospel.

USIC

9782a. _____. *The soul's captain. (A reply to William Ernest Henley's poem "Invictus," ending with the line, "I am the captain of my soul.")* [Salt Lake City? n.d.]

Broadside. 23 x 13½cm.

Mormon poetry.

USIC

9783. _____. *Speeches of Hon. O. F. Whitney in support of woman suffrage; delivered in the Constitutional Convention of Utah, March 30th, April 2nd, and April 5th, 1895.* [Salt Lake City] Utah Woman Suffrage Association [1895]

23p. 24cm.

"Mormon women and church government."

CU-B, UPB, USIC

9786a. _____. *The strength of the "Mormon" position.* Independence, Press of Zion's Printing & Publishng Co. [1918?]

40p. 18cm.

In gray printed wrapper.

Copies with and without copyright information on the verso of the title page.

UPB

9787a. _____. (same) Independence, Zion's Printing and publishing Co. [ca. 1924]

48p. 17cm.

In blue printed wrapper.

UPB

9788a. _____. *Two poems. Invictus by William Ernest Henley. The Soul's captain by Orson F. Whitney.* [n.p., n.d.]

[2]l. 21½cm.

Whitney's answer to Invictus.

UPB

9798a. Whittemore, C. O. *C. O. Whittemore, appellant, vs. Thomas H. Cope, et al., respondents, and George H. Cope, appellant. Brief for appellants. C. O. Whittemore and George H. Cope. Appeal from Third District Court . . . C. O. Whittmore, attorney for appellant Whittemore. S. P. Armstron, attorney for appellant George H. Cope.* [Salt Lake City? 1895?]

17p. 22cm.

At head of title: No. 530. In the Supreme Court of Utah Territory. January term, 1895.

Cover title.

Polygamy inheritance case.

DLC

9832a. Widtsoe, Leah Eudora (Dunford). *A mothers' letter . . . to the Elders of the European Missions.* Liverpool, 1929.

[4]p. 18½cm.

Signed by Leah D. Widtsoe and nine other mission mothers.

USlC

9853a. Wight, John W. *Home training of children. Pt. I-II.* Lamoni, Iowa, 1895.

i, 8p. 15½cm. (Daughters of Zion leaflets, No. 10, 11)

MoInRC

9865a. Willers, Diedrich. *Centennial historical sketch of the town of Fayette, Seneca County, New York.* Geneva, N. Y., Press of W. F. Humphrey, 1900.

157p. 23cm.

Mormons, p. 47-51, 152.

AU, DLC, NIC, NNC, PHi

9868a. *William Smith, patriarch & prophet of the Most High God.* [n.p., 185-?]

Broadside. 51 x 30cm.

Includes a revelation to William Smith dated Aug. 28, 1847, also other writings by William Smith and Aaron Hook.

USlC

9870a. **Williams, David.** *Twyll y seintiau diweddaf yn cael ei ddynoethi mewn nodiadau byr ar draethawd a ysgrifenwyd yn ddiweddar gan Capt. D. Jones, dan yr enw, "Traethawd ar Anghyfnewidioldeb Teyrnas Dduw," &c. Gan David Williams, Silo, Abercannaid. Yr ail argraffiad.* Merthyr, Argraffwyd gan D. Jones, Heol-fawr, 1846.

32p. 16½cm.

Title in English: The deceit of the Latter Saints exposed in brief notes on a treatise written recently by Capt. D. Jones.

WalCS

9881a. **Williams, Rufus K.** *James N. Kimball, respondent, vs. Franklin D. Richards, appellant. Mandamus. Brief and argument of R. K. Williams and F. S. Richards, attorneys for appellant.* [Salt Lake City, 1882?]

14p. 23cm.

At head of title: In the Supreme Court of Utah Territory.

In purple printed wrapper.

UPB, USlC

9881b. **Williams, Samuel.** *Mormonism exposed. By S. Williams.* [Pittsburg? 1842?]

16p. 24cm.

An anti-Mormon work aimed particularly against Sydney Rigdom. Quotes from E. D. Howe, W. Swartzell, W. Harris, and others.

USlC

9902a. **Williams, Warner W.** *The great secret of freemasonry; a study in the relation between economics, psychology and religion; a generalization.* Salt Lake City, Warner, W. Williams, c1923.

28p. 19½cm.

Mormon references throughout.

NN, USlC

9902b. _____. (same) Rev. ed. Boston, The Christopher Publishing House [c1926]

50p. 21cm.

LU, NN, USlC

9902c. **Williams, Wilbur Herschel.** *Uncle Bob and Aunt Becky's strange adventures at the world's great exposition.* Chicago, Laird & Lee [1904]

1p.l., 358p. 19½cm.

Visit to Salt Lake City, p. 332-37, with observations about the Mormons.

DLC, Uhi

9903a. **Willis, Alfred.** *Mormonism: Whence is it? The true history of Joseph Smith and of the Book of Mormon.* [London, Society for Promoting Christian Knowledge, ca. 1890]

8p. 17cm. (No. 2809)

A polemic against Mormonism and particularly against Joseph Smith.

UPB

9933a. **Wilson, Robert A.** *Mexico and its religion; with incidents of travel in that country during parts of the years 1851-52-53-54, and historical notices of events connected with places visited.* New York, Harper & Brothers, 1855.

406p. illus. 20cm.

Mormons, p. 290-91.

Other edition: New York, Harper & Brothers, London, Sampson Low, 1856.

CU, NCU, OCl, UPB, USlC, WHi

Wilton, Mark. See Manning, William Henry.

9954a. **Wipper, Frank F.** *Church of Christ. Temple Lot.* [Independence, 1926]

[10]leaves. 33cm.

Mimeographed.

Dated in ink: August 11, 1926.

Chronology of the Churches history and doctrines.

UPB

9967a. **Wistar, Isaac Jones.** *Autobiography of Isaac Jones Wistar, 1827-1905.* Philadelphia, Printed by the Wistar Institute of Anatomy and Biology, 1914.

2v. ports. 30cm.

Crosses the plains in 1849. On July 5, two men come east from Salt Lake. On July 22, five go south to the Great Salt Lake, "a rather uninviting place." Comments on the Mormons.

DLC, PHi, PPD, TxU

9968a. **Withers, Ethel Massie, comp.** *Clay County, Missouri, centennial souvenir, 1822-1922.* Liberty, Alexander Doniphan Chapter, Daughters of the American Revolution, Liberty Tribune, 1922.

196p. illus., ports. 30cm.

Mention of the Mormon war. Reference to the Mormons coming to Clay County from Jackson County, and meetings to get rid of them. Notes that they were all gone by 1838.

UHi

Woman in all ages and in all countries. See Larus, John Rouse. *Woman of America.*

9976a. **Woman's Christian Temperance Union of Utah.** *Minutes of the fifteenth annual convention of the Woman's Christian Temperance Union of Utah. Held at Salt Lake City, Utah, October 20-21, 1905. With directory, superintendents, etc.* [Salt Lake City, 1905]

16p. 21½cm.

Mormons mentioned, p. 6.

USlC

9978a. **Woman's Hygiene-Physiological Reform Class.** *Closing exercises of the Woman's Hygiene-Physiological Reform Class held in Springville. Term commencing May 25, ending September 8, 1891. Motto: "Woman, know thyself."* [Springville, Utah? Dispatch Steam Print, 1891]

16p. 21½cm.

Classes taught by Sister Hannah Sorensen. W. Woodruff's signature on the cover.

USlC

9982a. **Wood, Edward James.** *E i ai i lenei tusi nai tusi itiiti e igoa. "O le taitai," "O le ala," O le faitotoa," "o le malo o le atua," atoa ma "O le pogai." Ia fai ia tusi ma tulaga o le Apefai o le Evagelia Moni, Ina ia Maua ai le tonu i e Savavali i ai. Na tusia e Ed. J. Laau.* Salt Lake City, The Deseret News [1900-02]

2p.l., 26, 31, 47, 22, 36, 4, 4, 6, 3, [37]-40p. 15cm.

Each part has a separate title page, dated 1900, 1901, 1902 and n.d.

In gray printed wrapper.

Title in English: This book contains the following titles: "Leader," "Path," "Door," "Kingdom of God," and "Foundation."

Mormon doctrine.

UPB

9982c. _____. (same) Salt Lake City, The Deseret News [1910]

186p. 17cm.

In gray printed wrapper.

UPB, USIC

9985a. **Wood, Samuel.** *A fatal mistake as I saw it.* [Fresno, Ca.? ca. 1924]

[4]p. 20cm.

Published after 1924. Printed in Mayfield, Ca. by Harris & Ely.

The question of supreme directional control in the RLDS church.

UPB

9999a. **Woodruff, Wilford.** *To the Presidents, Bishop's agents and Bishops of the several stakes and wards of Zion: Dear brethren:* _____, Salt Lake City, 1887.

4p. 21½cm.

Signed: Wilford Woodruff, Wm. B. Preston.

Dated: December 13, 1887.

Instructions for annual settlement of tithes and offerings.

USIC

10,007a. **Woodward, George.** *Auto-biography of George Woodward. Feb., 1903.* [St. George] Dixie Advocate Print [1903?]

14p. port. 16cm.

In pink printed wrapper.

A pioneer of Southern Utah.

UPB, USIC

10,014a. **World's Christian Citizenship Conference.** *Official program of the Third World's Christian Citizenship Conference.* Pittsburgh, National Reform Association, 1919.

[12]p. 22½cm.

November 9th to 16th, 1919.

"Conference on Mormonism," p. [6]

UPB

10,017a. **World's Congress of Representative Women.** *The World's Congress of Representative Women. A historical resume for popular circulation of the World's Congress of Representative Women, convened in Chicago on May 15, and adjourned on May 22, 1893, under the auspices of the Woman's Branch of the World's Congress Auxiliary. Edited by May Wright Sewall.* Chicago and New York, Rand, McNally & Company, 1894.

2v. illus., ports. 23½cm.

The legal and political status of women in Utah -- Address by Emily S. Richards of Utah.

UPB

10,025a. **Wright, John Livingston, 1869- .** *Mr. Eagle's U. S. A. As seen in a buggy ride of 1400 miles from Illinois to Boston. [By] John Livingston Wright and Mrs. Abbie Scates Ames.* Hartford, Conn., Truman Joseph Spencer, 1898.

224p. plates. 19cm.

"Original shrine of Mormonism," p. 110-116. Kirtland Temple.

DLC, ICN, MB, NN, PP, UPB

10,033a. **Wunderlich, Jean, tr.** *Ein Leitfaden zum studium des Buches Mormon. Bearb. von Jean Wunderlich.* Basel, Kirche Jesu Christi der Heiligen der Letzten Tage, Schweizerrisch-Deutschen Mission [1928]

128p. illus., front. 20½cm.

Title in English: A Manual for the study of the Book of Mormon.

UPB

Y

10,056a. **Young, Brigham.** *Circular. G.S.L. City _____ 1862. To the Bishop of _____ U. T.* [Great Salt Lake City, 1862]

3p. 20½cm.

Form letter concerning contract with Ben Holladay to deliver grain for the overland stations.

UPB, USlC

10,058a. _____. *Discourse by President Brigham Young, at Logan, Cache County: Monday morning, May 25, 1877, at the priesthood meeting, held for the purpose of organizing a stake of Zion.* [Salt Lake City?, 1877?]

8p. 24cm.

Reported by G. F. Gibbs.

UPB

10,062a. _____. *Instructions to the bishops.* [Salt Lake City, 186-?]

Broadside. 31 x 21cm.

Notice for members to begin liquidating the indebtedness especially the "Fund." [Perpetual Emigrating Fund]

USlC

10,063a. _____. *Pic-nic party at the head waters of Big Cottonwood. Pres. Brigham Young respectfully invites _____ and family to attend a pic-nic party at the lake in Big Cottonwood Kanyon on Friday, 24th of July.* Great Salt Lake City, 1857.

Broadside. 26 x 21cm.

Dated July 18, 1857.

It was at this party that news of Johnston's Army was announced.

USlC

10,063b. _____. *Proclamation.* [Great Salt Lake City, 1851]

Broadside. 17 x 19cm.

Manuscript corrections upon this copy indicates an election was planned for Nov. 16, 1853.

USlC

10,096a. **Young, Joseph Watson.** *Om Israels insamling och Zions forlossing.* [Kobenhamn, Utgiven och R. C. Flygare, Tryckt hos F. E. Bording, 1875]

16p. 21cm.

Title in English: The gathering of Israel and the redemption of Zion.

"Tjunde upplagan."

UPB

10,096b. **Young, Junius.** *Views on the scenic line of the world.* [Salt Lake City, Denver & Rio Grande Western Railway, 1887?]

10p. [12] col. photographs. 10½ x 15cm.

Includes views on the Salt Lake Temple, Tabernacle, etc. with descriptions of them.

DLC, UPB

10,105a. **Young, LeGrande.** *Edwin B. Ayres and Edward A. Kessler appellants, vs. Mary Ann Jack, respondent, vs. William Leggett, respondent. Additional abstract. LeGrande Young and Zane and Putnam, attorneys for appellants. Waldemar Van Cott and John A. Marshall, attorneys for respondents.* [Salt Lake City? 1890?]

37p. 22cm.

At head of title: In the Supreme Court of Utah Territory.

Cover title.

Inheritance case of a polygamist marriage.

UAr

10,105b. _____. *In the matter of the estate of Oscar A. Amy, deceased; Jennie Amy, appellant, vs. Royal D. Amy, et al., appellants, vs. Adelia Young, et al., respondents. Brief of respondents Adelia Young, et al. Appeal from Third District Court, Hon. S. A. Merritt, presiding.* [Salt Lake City?] 1895.

36p. 22cm.

At head of title: In the Supreme Court of Utah Territory. June term, 1895.

Includes paper cover.

The problems of Probate Courts in Utah after the Poland Act.

UAr

10,105c. _____. *In the matter of the estate of Thomas Cope, deceased. Respondents brief. LeGrande Young and John M. Zane, attorneys for respondents. C. O. Whittemore, S. P. Armstrong and Sutherland & Judd, attorneys for appellant.* [Salt Lake City, 1890?]

10p. 22cm.

At head of title: In the Supreme Court of the Territory of Utah.

Cover title.

A polygamy inheritance trial.

UAr

Z

10,120a. **Zane & Zane.** *J. D. Page, plaintiff and appellant, vs. J. R. Letcher, George W. Thatcher, A. G. Norrell, Hoyt Sherman, Jr., and E. W. Tatlock, defendants. Proceedings in prohibition. Brief of respondent.* Salt Lake [City] Star Print [1895?]

8p. 22cm.

At head of title: In the Supreme Court of Utah Territory.

Cover title.

Election dispute due to action of the Utah Commission.

UAr

10,120b. **Zardetti, Otto.** *Westlich! Oder Durch den fernen Westen Nord-Amerikas.* Mainz, Verlag von Franz Kirchheim, 1897.

vii, [1]220p. illus. 28cm.

Title in English: Westward! Or through the district Western North America.

Chapter 17. "Die Mormonen und der Salzsee," p. [180]-89.

CtY, CU, DS, MiU, MnHi, TxU, USIC

10,122a. **Zimmer von Ulbersdorf, Gustav Adolf.** *Im Schatten von Mormons Tempel. Erzuhlungen aus der Deutschen evangelischen Mission in Utah. Ein neuer Beitrag zur Kenntnis der Mormonen, von G. A. Zimmer von Ulbersdorf, Derfosser von Unter den Mormonen in Utah"* etc. Neukirchen, Erziehungsvereins [1911?]

3p.l. [7]-112p. illus., plates. 18½cm.

Title in English: In the shadow of the Mormon Temple.

UPB, USIC

10,129a. **Zion's Co-operative Mercantile Institution.** *Agreement, order, certificate of incorporation & by-laws. Incorporated December 1st, 1870.* Salt Lake City, Printed at the Deseret News Book and Job Office, 1870.

22p. 21cm.

In a gray printed wrapper.

At head of title: Holiness to the Lord.

MH, UPB

10,130a.   . *Constitution and by-laws.* [Salt Lake City] Deseret News Print [1869?]

8p. illus. 20cm.

UPB, USIC

10,138a.   **Zion's Home Monthly.** *Prospectus of Zion's Home Monthly.* [Salt Lake City, 1888]

Broadside. 28 x 22cm.

Prospectus for a new magazine, signed by Joseph Bull, Jr., Publisher, April 15th, 1888.

UPB, USIC

10,139a.   **Zion's Messenger.** [Council Bluffs, Iowa? 1855?]

76p. 17½cm.

Sub-title on p. 4, "The messenger to the nations."

In the only known copy, the first leaf is missing, which is probably the title page. This publication identifies the name of the Gladden church as The Church of Jesus Christ of the New Jerusalem.

ULA

10,145a.   *Zur geschichte des Sabbats.* [Basel, Schweiz, Herausgegeben von der Schweizerisch Deutschen Mission, ca. 1915]

4p. 22½cm.

Title in English: On the history of the Sabbath.

USIC

Title Index

A

A. M. Crary memoirs and memoranda. 2575a.

Aandelige sange til brug i mission og Sondagsskole. 1849a.

Abfall vom ursprunglichen evangelium und dessen wiederherstellung. 10a.

Abraham, yourself and Jacob; a changeable God. 4881a.

Across America with the kings of the Belgians. 3608a.

Across the continent by the Lincoln Highway. 3588b.

Across the plains. 8383b.

Action of the Utah Methodist Episcopal Church Mission. 13a.

Added upon. 131a.

Address of the Hon. William Bross. 889a.

Address. The Church of Jesus Christ of Latter-day Saints to the world. 1310a, 1649a.

Address to Franklin D. and Samuel W. Richards. 5066b.

Address to my children. 4613a.

Address to the officers and members of the Church of Jesus Christ of Latter-day Saints. 1652a.

Address to the visitor to conference . . . 3869a.

Administration and supervision in the Box Elder School District. 7750a.

Admission of Utah as a state in the union. 25a.

Adobe days. 538a.

Adventures of a forty-niner. 4668a.

Adventures of James Capen Adams. 4053a.

Aertikelen des geloofs. 7939a.

Afskrift. Til Bergens politimester! 3956a.

After 60 years. 6020a.

Afterglow. 27a.

Agreement, order, certificate of incorporation & by-laws. 10,129a.

Ai diw duw ddanfonodd Joseph Smith? 4457a.

Ai dwyfol oedd cenadwri Joseph Smith? 4457b.

Alberta, Canada. 40a.

Alberta Temple. 40b.

Album of State and other public officers of Utah. 4587a.

All round the world. 35a.

All the western states and territories. 298a.

All together again. 49a.

Along the Union Pacific system. 9074a.

Arizona under our flag. 2972a.

Around the circle. 8710a.

Around the United States by bicycle. 5671a.

Arrest of Ammon by the guards of King Limhi. 1532a.

Artemus Ward among the Mormons. 918a.

Artemus Ward, "Among the Mormons" and "His book". 918b.

Artemus Ward, his book. 923a.

Artemus Ward, his programme. 924a.

Artemus Ward, (his travels) among the Mormons. 924b-c.

Artemus Ward's travels. 934.

Articles of faith of the Church of Jesus Christ of Latter-day Saints. 207a, 7931a.

Articulos de fe. 7948a.

As I remember them. 3618a.

Assted. 8281a.

At a meeting held at Independence Hall. 3618b.

Atebydd y gwrthddadleuon a ddygir yr fwyaf . . . 4463a.

Atonement of Christ and the final destiny of man. 7906a.

Au pays des gratte-ciel (Etats-Unis). 3611b.

Augusta's story. 228a, 2671b.

Authour de Chicago. 7528a.

Auto-biography of George Woodward. 10,007a.

Autobiography of a Shaker. 3210b.

Autobiography of Isaac Jones Wistar. 9967a.

Autobiography of James Crooks. 2597a.

Autobiography of John Brown the cordwainer. 901a.

Autobiography of Rev. Alvin Torry. 8979a.

Autobiography of Rev. Tobias Spicer. 8345a.

Autorite divine. 235a.

Aux Etats-Unis. 5463b.

B

Baptism for the dead. 294a.

Baptism, how and by whom administered. 295a-b, 296a.

Baptism of the Holy Ghost. 1101a.

Baptism of the spirit. 3841a.

Battle of Mormon. 335a.

Begin van het evangelie van Jezus Christus. 378a.

Bekesseg legyen e hazban! 380a.

Beitrage zur Charakteristik der Vereinigten Staaten von Nord-Amerika. 3733b.

Beksrivning ofver Nord. 581b.

Benson Stake ward teachers' message. 2161a.

Beproeft alle dingen; behoudt het goede. 439b.

Beth ydyw yr efengyl? 4463b.

Between the gates. 8806c.

Beyond the Rockies. 8472a.

Bible morals. 6864b.

Biblische Hinweisungen. 495a.

Bibliska anvisningar. 501a.

Bibliu tilvisanir. 540a.

Biennial message of Edward A. Stevenson. 1886. 4180b.

Biennial message of Edward A. Stevenson. 1888. 4180c.

Biennial message of John B. Neil. 4179a.

Biennial message of William M. Bunn. 4180a.

Biennial report of the Territorial Superintendent of Common Schools. 9329b.

Biglow papers. 5001a.

Bijbelsche Aanhalingen. 479a.

Biographical and historical record of Ringgold and Decatur Counties. 522a.

Biographical and historical record of Wayne and Appanoose Counties. 522b.

Biographical sketch of Franklin S. Richards. 9037b.

Biographical sketch of the life of Elder Thomas Dobson. 2851b.

Biographical sketch of the life of William B. Ide. 4183a.

Biographical sketch of William Shepherd. 7684b.

Biographical sketches of the life Major Ward Bradford. 790a.

Bird's-eye view of the world. 6830e.

Birth control. 5195a.

Birthday of the Lion House. 529a.

Bishop _____ Dear Brother. 1652b, 2096a.

Bishop _____ Dear Sir: 2404b.

Bishopric of Canada. 3233a.

Bishop's message for April 1928. 2216a.

Blijde boodschap. 563a.

Boadicea: the Mormon wife. 385a.

Boek der Leer en Verbonden. 2853b.

Book of Doctrine and Covenants. 2944a, 2945a-c, 2960a, 2962a, 2968a.

Book of Mormon. 1900. 632a.

Book of Mormon: an account of its origin. 8602a, 8603a.

Book of Mormon ready references. 5595a.

Book of Mormon weighed in the balances of the scriptures. 4304a.

Book of startling revelations! 748a.

Book of the words. 4148a.

Born in the living law. 4874a.

Boulevards all the way-maybe. 3373a.

Bp._____ We today forward to you blank forms . . . 1321a.

"Brain food" for people who love the West. 6375a.

Brief historical sketch of the life of Josiah Rhead. 813a.

Brief history and financial summary of the Gallands Grove. 4135a.

Brief history of the Church of Jesus Christ of Latter-day Saints. 87a.

Brief sketch of the life of Bartholomew White. 9727a.

Brief sketches of the last scenes. 6391a.

Brigham Young. 3543a, 5213.

Brigham Young and the Mormons of the Salt Lake. 829a.

Brigham Young College bulletin series. 830.

Brigham Young College catalog. 831.

Brigham Young's birthday celebration. 845a.

Brigham Young's funeral march. 2734b.

Buch der Lehre und Bundnisse. 2933a-b.

Bucking the sagebrush. 8383a.

Buckskin Mose. 6313a.

Buffalo Bill and the Danite kidnappers. 1001b.

Buffalo-Bill; le Complot des Mormons. 1001c.

Buffalo Bill's own story of his life and deeds. 2445a.

Buka a Moromona. 7422a.

Bulletin for Primary Associations . . . 2117a.

By land and sea. 3420a.

By-laws of the Church Association of _____ Stake of Zion. 1324a.

By-laws of the church association . . . 2233a.

By the Golden Gate or San Francisco. 1187a.

C

C. O. Whittmore, appellant, vs. Thomas H. Cope. 2514a, 9798a.

C. W. Penrose replies to Joseph Smith. 6230a.

California and its gold regions. 7389a.

California Joe's first trail. 5451a

Californians and Mormons. 2779a.

Calimis. 1089a.

Camping out in the Yellowstone. 7247c.

Can newydd, sef, hunan fyfyrdod ar freuddwyd y Mormoniaid. 5678a.

Cannibals all: or, slavers without masters. 3372a.

Cannon vs. Campbell. 9115a.

Cannoneer. Recollection of service in the Army of the Potomac. 9001a.

Carson Valley, Utah. 9148a.

Cart before the horse. 9019a.

Carthage Jail. 1222a.

Case against delegate Cannon, of Utah. 1224a.

Case of Brigham H. Roberts. 3733e.

Catalog and price list. 2780c.

Catalogue of books and rules and regulations of the Masonic library . . . 3447a.

Catalogue of price-list of church publications. 1174a, 1176a.

Catalogue of publications of the Church of Jesus Christ of Latter-day Saints. 1329, 2811a.

Catalogue of works published by the Church of Jesus Christ of Latter-day Saints. 1884b-c.

Catechism for children. 4325a.

Catechism on the first principles of the gospel. 1238a.

Celestial marriage. 3991a, 4958a.

Celestial marriage? 864a.

Centennial historical sketch of the town of Fayette. 9865a.

Centennial history of Missouri. 8450a.

Central railroad route to the Pacific. 3450a.

Chapter on prayer. 1256a.

Character of the Latter-day Saints. 1887a.

Charaketer und die erforderlichen Eingenschaften. 6449a.

Child culture. 7274a.

Child's life of our Savior. 5599a.

Children on the plains. 258a-b.

"Children's Friends" as a missionary. 1265a.

Children's jubilee of the Primary Association. 2117b.

Christensen's grand historical exhibition. 1275b.

Christian fellowship. 6748a.

Christian messenger to all people. 1276a.

Christmas testimonial to our missionaries in the field. 2258b.

Christ's brode. 1283a.

Church. 1283c.

Church and its divine mission. 4010a.

Church of Christ. Temple Lot. 9954a.

Church of Jesus Christ. 4496a, 4897a.

Church of Jesus Christ of Latter-day Saints. 108a.

Church of Jesus Christ of Latter-day Saints, Mormons. 2007a.

Church reserve and Saint's home funds. 7076b.

Church, the people and the age. 7595a.

Cigarette evil. 2155a.

Circuit Court of the U. States of America. 9104a.

Circular. 5050a.

Circular. G. S. L. City. 10,056a.

Circular issued by the State Board of Health. 9314a.

Circular of general information regarding Grand Canyon National Park, Arizona. 9209a.

Circular of instructions. 1337c-d.

Circular of instructions; 1655b.

Circular. To Bishop . . . 2098a.

Circular. To the citizens of Utah. 2374a-b.

Circular. To the heirs of the late Brigham Young. 838a.

Circular. To the heirs of the late President Brigham Young. 8148a.

Circular. To the members of the Hooper Irrigation Company: 2240b.

Class work for 1917. 1539a.

Clawson vs. the United States. 6373b-d.

Clay County, Missouri. 9968a.

Closing exercises of the woman's hygiene-physiological reform class . . . 9978a.

Collect 1930 dime fund in one day. 1539b.

Collection of sacred hymns. 1762a, 1766.

Collection of sacred hymns for the use of all the saints. 2367a.

College Record. 2457a.

Compensation of commissioners under the act for the suppression of bigamy, etc. 9189a.

Compilation of statements on plural marriage. 2466a.

Complete works of Charles F. Browne. 940a.

Comprehensive and popular history of the United States. 8409a.

Concordance and reference guide to the book of Doctrine and Covenants. 2471a, 6903b, 8378a-b.

Conference meetings. 1895. 1942c.

Conference minutes of the Church of Jesus Christ of Latter-day Saints. 1945b.

Conference of the Cheltenham Branch. 1911a.

Conference of the Church of Jesus Christ of Latter-day Saints. 2473b.

Conference. The Church of Jesus Christ of Latter-day Saints. 1904a.

Confession of the awful and bloody transactions. 9537b.

Congregational hymns for general conference. 1344a.

Constitution and by-laws. 10,130a.

Constitution and by-laws adopted by the General Sunday School Association. 7044a-b.

Constitution and by-laws. Daughters of Utah Pioneers. 2672a.

Constitution and by-laws of the Student Society. 7083b.

Constitution of the general society. 7033c.

Constitution of the State of Deseret. 2787a.

Constitution of the State of Utah. 9273a.

Convention of the Elder of the British Mission. 1888a.

Correct account of the murders of Generals Joseph and Hyrum Smith . . . 2659a.

Correspondence between the Rev. W. Crowel . . . 8322a.

Course humoristique autour bu Monde. 3498a.

Course of study for the quorums of the priesthood. 1349a.

Course of study for the Y.M.M.I.Association . . . 2165a.

Courses of study; Adult Women's Department . . . 2335a.

Courtship, marriage in the home. 4755a.

Cracking nuts in Utah. 6149a.

Creation. 7249a.

Crime and treason of the Mormon Church exposed. 1264c.

Crofutt's trans-continental tourist guide's. 2596a.

Crossing the plains with ox teams in 1862. 752a.

Cruise of a schooner. 3863a.

Cwyn yr ymfudwr, a'i ddau anerchiad. 4493a.

Cyclopaedia of religious denominations. 2637a.

Cyfeiliornadau a dichellion saint y dyddiau diweddaf a Llyfr Mormon. 5584a.

Cynydd a chadernid Mormoniaeth. 7315a.

D

Daab, hvorledes og af hvem udfores den. 2640a.

Dadl rhwng Bedyddiwr ac anffyddiwr. 4467a.

Dairy [sic] of a voyage from Liverpool to New Orleans. 5066c.

Dammeg y pren a ddwg naw math o ffrwythaw! 4467b.

Danger to your wives and daughters. 3975a.

Daniel Hanmer Wells Association. 2657b.

Danite chief. 5264a.

Dansk Amerikansk historie. 1275a.

Darlithiau ar dwyll Mormoniaeth. 4128a-b.

Darlun o'r byd crefyddol. 4467c.

Daughters of Zion. 1139c.

Day school in Utah. 2734a.

De l'Atlantique au Pacifique . . . 4131a.

Dear Brethren: 1658a.

Dear Brother . . . 1873a.

Dear Brother: 1658c, 1658e, 2099a.

Dear sir: At a mass meeting held in this city on the 23rd ultimo. 1264a.

Dear sir: We are today faced with polygamous Mormonism. 1264b.

Dear Sister. The dedication of the great Temple. 1658f.

Death and a swift wedding. 7509a.

Death of Brigham Young. 5458a.

Death of Elder Willard Snow. 7249b.

Decouverte des Americains. 6779a.

Dedication, 22nd Ward Chapel and Amusement Hall. 2262a.

Dedicatory services, Ensign Ward Chapel. 2249a.

Defense of Mr. Bright and rationalism. 3869b.

Del Plata al Niagara. 3733d.

Delegate from the Territory of Utah. 9115b.

Descendants of John Walker . . . 3128b.

Description of the Joseph Smith Monument. 2779c-d.

Description of the western resorts for health and pleasure . . . 9079a.

Descriptive catalogue of Dr. Williams & Co. 2853a.

Descriptive review of the industries of Salt Lake City. 8991b.

"Deseret". Program of closing meeting. 1942a.

Deseret alphabet. 2780b.

Deseret anthems. 1495a.

Deseret News white book. 2811c.

Deseret Sonntagschulliederbuch . . . 1636a.

[Deseret Sunday School Hymnal] 1605a-b.

Deseret Sunday School songbook. 1622a.

Deseret Sunday School songs. 1623a-c.

Deseret Sunday School union leaflets. 1551a-b, 1552a.

Dialogue between Joseph Smith and the Devil. 6570a.

Diary of a trip through Mexico and California. 1283b.

[Diary] of a voyage from Liverpool to New Orleans. 5066c.

Dick's Ethiopian scenes. 2829a.

Dictionary of doctrinal and historical theology. 577c.

Did Oliver Cowdery renounce Mormonism . . . 5740a.

Dimmed vision [a genealogical story]. 141a-b.

Directory of Ogden City. 2841b.

Dirgelion Saint v Dyddiau Diweddaf, yn cael cu dinoethi. 4485b.

Disciplism. 5152a.

Discourse by President Brigham Young. 10,058a.

Discourse for home missions. 1047a.

Distinguishing characteristics. 4595b.

Divine authority. 1350a.

Do you want to know the truth. 9019b.

Do you wish the world to go Mormon. 2851a.

Doctrine and Covenants of the Church of Jesus Christ of Latter-day Saints. 2881a, 2888a, 2895a, 2900a.

Doctrine of Christ. 3726a.

Doctrine of the first resurrection. 2969a.

Doctrines of the Church of Jesus Christ of Latter-day Saints. 5477a.

Door het land van Columbus. 5662a.

Drumms manual of Utah. 3013a.

Dudley D. Toncray, appellant, vs. Alfred Budge, defendant. 965a.

Dudley D. Toncray, complainant and appellant. 8973a.

Dvacet tisic mil po sousi a po mori. 2973a.

Dwight Peck, et. al., plaintiffs and respondents. 6839a.

Dynoethiad Mormoniaeth: 3083a.

E

E i ai i lenei tusi nai tusi itiiti e igoa. 9982a-c.

Early history of the town of Hopkinton. 7526c.

Early land holding practices in Utah. 5764a.

Early years in Smyrna and our first old home week. 5666a.

Egwyddorion Saint y Dyddiau Diweddaf . . . 4498d.

Eighteenth Message. 3332a-b.

Eighty-ninth anniversary of the birth of Joseph F. Smith. 3123a.

Ein jahr auf den Sandwich-Inseln. 366a.

Einzig wahre evangelium. 991a.

Elder _____ Dear Brother: 1640b.

Ellen C. Clawson and Hiram B. Clawson. 9466b.

Ellen C. Clawson and Hiram B. Clawson, appellants. 2404a.

Elo vilagossag sugarai. 6273a.

Emma Bidamon. 9113c.

En route to California. 9079b.

Enda vag till salighet. 8242a.

Enest sande Evangelium eller de forste Kristnes Tro. 989a.

Enforcement of the anti-polygamy act. 9189b.

Engineer's holiday. 6377a.

England to Holland, Belgium and France. 2635a.

Enkele getuigenissen aangaande . . . 1995a.

Epistle of Demetrius, Jr. 2761a-b.

Epistle of Elder J. Haven. 3891a.

Epistle of the Council of the Twelve Apostles . . . 1502.

Epistle of the First Presidency. 1662-a.

Epistle of the Twelve and the Bishopric. 6910b.

Epistle to the Church of Jesus Christ of Latter-day Saints in France. 1978a.

Er daab en betingelse for frelse? 575b-c.

Er de Sidste-Dages Hellige Kristne? 3178a.

Er de Sidste Dages-Helliges Laere Sandhed? 8818.

Er Mormonismen en Vranglaere. 8826, 8826a-b.

Erde und ihre Volker. 3946a.

Erlosung fur die Toten. 2021a, 2022a.

Errors and inconsistencies concerning the presidency . . . 5005a.

Ervaringen van een Hollandsche vrouw in het land der Mormonen. 848a, 2744a.

Es el bautismo esencial a la salvacion? 576a-c.

Etats-Unis d'Amerique. 2846a.

Etats-Unis d'Amerique. 3183a.

Etats-Unis en 1900. 5045a.

Eternity of the marriage covenant. 7384a.

Ett gladt bundskap; inbjudning till Guds rike. 3589a-c.

Etudes sur les reformateurs. 7091b.

Evangile. 4112a.

Evangile que Christ enseignait et son retablissement aux derniers jours. 8345b.

Event of the 19th century. 4871b.

Everybody should read the Book of Mormon. 3278a.

Ewige wahrheit. 2018a, 3278b.

Ex parte: In the matter of Hans Nielsen. 5841a, 7231a.

Ex parte: In the matter of Lorenzo Snow. 2614a, 8248b.

Excentricites Americaines. 3284b.

Excursions autour du monde. 7395c.

Expedition of Captain Fisk to the Rocky Mountains. 3368a.

Exposition des premiers principes de la doctrine . . . 1970a, 8834a.

Exposure of clerical slander. 3283a.

Exposure of Mormonism. 4963a.

Extermination of the Latter Day Saints . . . 3284a.

Extract from "Solid facts from a loyal man". 2833a.

Extraits de l'histoire du prophete Joseph Smith. 7955a.

F

Fac-simile from the Book of Abraham. 3289a.

Facts about the Bible and what it teaches. 4975a.

Facts for thinkers. 2365a-b, 3291a.

Facts in the case. 5170a-b.

Faith. 2648a.

Faith and repentance. 6913a.

Families in Heaven. 992c.

Farewell entertainment and dance in honor of Elder Louis Iverson. 3301a.

Farewell Hymn. 4937a.

Farragut Post. 3662d.

Fatal mistake as I saw it. 9985a.

Faulty creeds. 3241a.

Fellow country women. 3319a.

Fem och tjugu Mormonska larosatser. 8896a.

Few thoughts about the Pacific coast. 7389b.

Fight with distances. 221a.

Financial review no. 561. 2635b.

Financing and distributing Sunday School lessons. 1555a.

First impressions of America. 3770a.

First Presidency, Council of the Twelve. 3359a.

Flower of the Mormon city. 3380a.

Folgende ist eine kurze darstellung Grundsatze. 6483a.

Folly and falsehood of the golden Book of Mormon. 2727a.

For all kinds of Mormon publications . . . 2811b.

Forces morales aux etats-unis. 1261b.

Forste store drama. 3956b.

Fort Sutter papers. 3405a.

Forty-third national encampment. 3662a.

Fourth annual session of the Baptist Congress. 297a.

Fox and Hoyt's quadrennial register of the Methodist Episcopal Church. 3415a.

Fra Amerika. 8975a.

Fra Amerika, af Henrik Cavling. 1242.

Fralsningens vag. 4692a.

Framlingen fran vastern eller. . . . 7167a, 7168a.

Framstaende mans vittnesbord om de sista dagars heliga. 3419a.

France mystique. 3179a.

Frank Merriwell among the Mormons. 6146c.

Fraternal greeting issued by Old Folks' Central Committee. 2087a.

Free lecture on character education. 3434b.

Free love and its votaries. 3155a.

Free outing for Old Folks. 2087b.

Freedom of the press and "obscene" literature. 7572a.

Freemasonry in Utah. 3622a, 3624a.

Fremmede fra vesterlandet eller. . . . 7161a.

Friede sei in diesem hause! 7586a-c.

Friendly discussion upon religious subjects. 7121a, 7140a, 7142a-c.

From Geneva to Mexico. 3270a.

From New England to the Pacific. 8305b.

From ocean to ocean. 3476a.

From Piegans to the Piutes. 7585a.

From the Clyde to California with jottings by the way. 35b.

From the press bureau of the Utah-semicentenial commission. 9311a.

Fruit in the season thereof. 2734d.

Fruits of the gospel of Jesus Christ. 1229a.

Fulfillment, a panorama of Christian cycle. 1013a.

Fulfillment of a promise and exposure of the false teachings. . . . 7091a.

Full and reliable guide by railway . . . 192a.

Funeral sermon of President Joseph Smith. 5018a.

Funeral services for Mrs. Phileus Tempest. 3492a.

Funeral services for Mrs. Rebecca N. Nibley. 3492b.

Funeral services, Patriarch John Smith. 3494a.

G

G. Q. Cannon vs. A. G. Campbell. 6073a.

Garments. 8036a.

Garretty's guide. 3509a.

Gazetteer and business directory of Ontario County, N. Y., for 1867-8. 1264f.

Gazetteer and business directory of Wayne County, N. Y., for 1867-8. 1264g.

Geislar af lifandi loosi. 6274a.

Genealogical record of the Keeler family. 4536a.

Genealogical Society of Utah. 1709a.

Genealogical work is essential to redemption of the dead . . . 8616a.

General orders No. 1. 9679a.

General Smith's views of the powers and policy of the Government of the United States. 7957a.

George H. Cope, appellant, vs. Janet Cope et. al. 8538a.

George H. Cope, appellant, vs. Thomas H. Cope and Janet Cope, respondents. 328a.

George Q. Cannon, delegate from Utah. 9116a-b.

George R. Maxwell vs. George Q. Cannon. 5311a.

George Reynolds, plaintiff in error. 7098a-b.

George Reynolds, plaintiff in error vs. the United States. 6372e.

Geschichte der Mormonen. 1155a.

Gidex (registered) for Utah. 4837b.

Gita intorno alla terra dal gennaio al Settembre dell' anno 1876. 3323a.

Glad Tidings. 3588a.

Glad tidings of great joy. 8859a, 8860a.

Glaube und die Lehre der Kirche Jesu Christi . . . 9490a.

Glimpses of Mexico and California. 4865a.

Glimpses of our national monuments. 9209b.

Glory of service. 5608a-b.

Gold region, and scenes by the way. 891a.

Golden state. 5117a.

Goldkoerner von wahrheit und auszueg aus den reden . . . 3610a.

Gone to rest. 3611a.

Good news for the aged. 2087c.

Gospel Banner. 3638a.

Gospel message. 968a.

Gospel pioneer. 4376a.

Gospel Quarterly for Sunday School pupils. 7521b.

Gospel story and footsteps of Jesus. 9525a.

Gottliche offenbarung und Belehrung uber den Ehestand. 1354a.

Governor's message to the First Legislature of the State of Idaho. 4181a.

Governor's message to the Legislative assemble. 9361a.

Governor's message with accompanying documents. 9369a.

Grand Canyon country. 8953b.

Grand concert. 3662e, 7549a.

Grand-ouest des Etats-Unis par L. Simmonin. 7719a.

Grand Scandinavian jubilee concert. 3662f.

Great deserts and forests of North America. 3412a.

Great highway. 3489a.

Great Mormon fraud. 4442.

Great Mormon remedy! 3698b.

Great Salt Lake country. 3698d.

Great Salt Lake present and past. 8633a.

Great secret of freemasonry. 9902a-b.

Great West; a vast empire. 2657a.

Greater revelation. 9491a.

Greatest highway in the world. 5795b.

Greeting: Beloved Brethren. 1668a.

Greetings from the First Presidency. 1669a.

Griffith's parliamentary chart and key to parliamentary practice. 3727a.

Grover Cleveland will not be elected. 8527b.

Growth of a century. 3768a.

Grundprinzipien des Evangeliums Jesu Christi . . . 3734a-b.

Grundung und lehren der Kirche Jesu Christi der Heiligen der letzten Tage. 801a.

Guds rige i de Sidste Dage. 6495a.

Guide to the first year's courses of study . . . 2338a.

Guide to the great West. 8991a.

Gun, rod and saddle. 5303c.

H

Haapiiraa evaneria. 2632a.

Haapiiraa I-[XXI] 2632.

Hail to the prophet. 9768a.

Hale laa o ke Akua Kiekie loa ma Loko Paakai. 5852a.

Half yearly report of the London Conference. 1940b.

Half-yearly report of the Southhampton Conferences. 1953a.

Handbook for the officers and teachers in the religion classes . . . 1518a.

Handbuch fur die bienenkorbaadchen . . . 2350a.

Handcart song. 3829a.

Hanes chwech o benboethiaid crefyddol sef, Joseph Smith. 4891a.

Hanes cymry America. 8913a.

Hans Freece, popular lectures. 3436a.

Happiest Christ. 3508b.

He that readeth, let him understand. 1366a, 3930a-b.

Hear, O ye people. 3935a, 4059a.

Hear the testimony -- then judge ye. 3935b.

Heart of the continent: 2976a.

Heart of the Rockies. 5973b.

Helldorado, bringing the law to the Mesquite. 803a.

Help! Twelve men met in solemn conclave. 3948a.

Henry S. Tanner. 3957a.

Herald Publishing House and book bindery. 3961a-b.

Heroes of the plains. 997a.

Hihio o ka hoolapanai ia ana o ka poe make. 8041b.

Hints for Sunday School Superintendent. 1557a.

His final admonition. 4485a.

Historic and literary miscellany. 577a.

Historical account of every sect of the Christian Religion. 6809b.

Historical and descriptive sketches of Salt Lake City. 1267a.

Historical biography of the United States. 4020c.

Historical collections of the great West. 4110.

History Company. 4022a.

History of Adams County, Illinois. 4023.

History of America B.C. 200 - 420 A.D. 1366b-d.

History of Hawaii. 4690a.

History of Howard and Chariton Counties. 4031a-b.

History of Fort Leavenworth. 4141a.

History of human marriage. 9704a.

History of Middletown. 3469a.

History of Missouri. 9479a.

History of Mormonism . . . 5736a.

History of Natrona County, Wyoming. 5439b.

History of the American people. 3584a.

History of the ancient and honorable fraternity of Free and Accepted Masons. 8468a.

History of the Norwegian people in America. 5863a.

History of the town of Savoy. 5398a.

History of the Union Pacific Railroad. 9083b.

History of the United States. 759a.

History of the United States for schools. 3402a.

History of the United States in Rhyme. 23a.

History of Washington County. 2581a, 3403a.

History of Wells, Vermont. 6158a.

Hith almenna truarfrafall. 539a.

Hoe aratai no te mau taata i roto . . . 2632b.

Home library of knowledge. 4076a.

Home training of children. 9853a.

Hon. . . . . Dear Sir: 5453a.

Hon. S. P. Chase, Secretary of the Treasury. 6413a.

House of Israel. 6444a.

House of Representatives, the Committee on Naval Affairs. 9119a.

How polygamy is dying. 7510a.

How to prevent sickness. 5090a.

Hull to Holland. 2635c.

Hur fralsning ernas. 6113a.

Hymn of the pioneer. 8911a.

[Hymnau, wedi eu Cyfansiddi a'u Casglu] 1870b.

Hymns and spiritual song, original and selected . . . 1298a.

Hymns for semi-annual conference Latter-day Saints. 1369a.

Hymns to be sung at the dedication of the Masonic Temple. 4177a.

Hymns used by the Latter-day Saints. 1822a.

Hyrum Ricks & Company. 4177b.

I

I cowboyland. 8941a.

Idaho, chronology . . . 6839b.

Idaho facts and statistics . . . 5512a.

Ikeru shin no kami. 8801a.

Im Schatten von Mormons Tempel. 10,122a.

Immaterialism. 7677a.

Important from Carthage. 9610a.

Important from the Great Salt Lake. 4210a.

Important to all. 4210b.

Important. To whom this may concern. 4210c.

Impressions of the prophet Joseph Smith. 394a.

Impressions of Utah. 6080a.

In cabins and sod-houses. 5100b.

In commemoration of the 25th anniversary of the giving of endowment of the dead. 9516a.

In consequence of the sickness of President Brigham Young. 4213a.

In memoriam. George A. Blakeslee. 4217a.

In memoriam; President Anthon H. Lund. 4219a.

In opposition to the resolution. 4669a.

In the cult kingdom. 905a.

In the matter of the estate of George Handley, deceased. 8540a.

In the matter of the estate of Orson Pratt, deceased. 404a.

In the matter of the estate of Oscar A. Amy. 2834a, 10,105b.

In the Senate of the United States. 9166d.

In to the Yukon. 3118a.

In Whitingham, Vermont. 5593a.

Incidents in American history. 299a.

Indbydelse til Guds Rige. 4232a.

Independence, Missouri. 4237a.

Indians of Skull Valley and Deep Creek, Utah. 9189c.

Information for tourist. 1461a.

Inspired translation of the Holy Scriptures. 554a.

Installation, Nauvoo Lodge. 4255a.

Instruction to the Bishops. 10,062a.

Instructions and suggested program. 2103a.

Instructions to officers of the Primary Association. 2119a.

Instructor. 3728a-b.

Intelligent woman's guide to socialism and capitalism. 7638a.

Interesting address on "The three witnesses . . ." 4586a.

International Association of Municipal Electricians. 1671a.

Interview with the Atlantic Constitution. 7172b-c.

Into the unknown. 3377a.

Invitation . . . 1883a.

Invitation! A great and marvelous work has come forth . . . 1891a.

Invitation. All persons are respectfully invited to attend the Latter-day Saints' meetings. 1891b-c.

Invitation to attend the dedication of the Granite Stake Tabernacle. 2176a.

Iowa contested election case. 4272a.

Ire ar; Forenta Staterna. 2465b.

Iron County, Utah. 6087a.

Iron heel. 4972a.

Irrigation; its history, methods, statistics and results. 9083c.

Is baptism essential. 572a. 573a.

Is it I? A book for every man. 8490a.

Is your heart in the work. 4516a.

Isms, fads & fakes. 3348a.

J

J. and R. H. Porter. 9126a.

J. D. Page, plaintiff and appellant. 10,120a.

J. D. Page, plaintiff and respondent; vs. J. R. Letcher. 6064a.

James M. Barlow, appellant, vs. Alexander Ramsey. 303a, 9466c.

James N. Kimball, respondent, vs. Franklin D. Richards. 9881a.

James' railroad and route book . . . 3733c.

James' river guide . . . 4316a.

James's traveler's companion. 5303b.

Jefferson County centennial. 2542a.

Jesse C. Murphey, appellant, vs. Alexander Ramsey. 9466d.

Jesse J. Murphy, appellant, vs. Alexander Ramsey. 5673a.

Jesu profetier. 5308a.

Jimin no tokucho. 4382a.

John Bull & Co. 577b.

John Miles, plaintiff in error vs. the Unites States. 5389a.

John Miles vs. United States. 2823a.

John Taylor. 6343c.

John the Baptist has come. 3333a-b.

John the Baptist (Resurrected) has come. 3333c.

Jordan Stake of the Church of Jesus Christ of Latter-day Saints. 2185a.

Joseph P. Ledwidge as county clerk . . . 3976a.

Joseph Smith, the martyr. 4502a-b.

Joseph Smith, the prophet of the nineteenth century. 8336a.

Joseph Smith, the prophet of the XIX century. 8337.

Joseph Smith, was he a prophet of God? 3251a.

Joseph Smith's laerdomme . . . 7976a.

Joseph Smith's Levnet. 9409a-b.

Josiah Rhead Family. 4503a.

Journal of army life. 3599a.

Journey and its ending. 5404a.

Journey to Alaska. 8872a.

Jubilee songs. 4510.

Jubilee songs as sung by one thousand children . . . 331a.

Judas of Salt Lake. 2530a.

Judge A. B. Carlton's views on the qualification if voters . . . 1192a.

Julian Calendar gives the date of our Lord's birth. 6444b.

Junction extra! 4511a-b.

Just published, the Mormon Bible. 4318a.

K

Kami wa imasu ka? 8803a.

Kansas, Utah, and the Dred Scott decision. 2983b.

Keep apichinin. 4543a.

Kerk van Jezus Christus van de Heiligen der Laatste Dagen aan de wereld. 1383a.

Key to the floral record of the Savior. 102a

Ki nga Hunga Tapu o te Mihana . . . 5195b.

Kingdom of God. 6931a.

Ko nga korerohari mo te haringa nui. 877a.

Kostliche Perle; eine auswohl aus den Offenbarungen. 6199a.

Ko te inoi. 4675a.

Ko te whakahokinga mai o te rongo pai. 4675b.

Ko te Whanautanga o thu karati. 4675c.

Kumu manaoio o ka Ekalesia o Iesu Kristo . . . 5482a.

L

L.D.S. Hymns for the Scandinavian Conference in the Assembly Hall. 1387a.

Lady's experience in the wild west in 1883. 6225a.

Lamoni illustrated. 4013a.

Land der unbegrenzten Moglichkeiten. 3609a.

Last dispensation. 8133a.

Late corporation of the Church of Jesus Christ of Latter-day Saints et al., appellants, vs. the United States. 867a.

Latter day pilgrim. 4764a.

Latter-day Saint literature. 4765a.

Latter-day Saint seminaries. 4765b.

Latter-day Saints. 4765c.

Latter-day Saints anthems book. 2734c.

Latter Day Saints' belief. 4766a.

Latter-day Saints' catechism. 5439a.

Latter-day Saints church office building. 1386a.

Latter-day Saints' faith. 4774a.

Latter Day Saints' hymns. 1767a.

Latter-day Saints: The dupes of a foolish and wicked imposture. 4768a.

Law of tithing. 259a, 2258a.

Laws of the State of Missouri. 5433a-b.

Laying on of hands. 6943a.

Laying on of Hands . . . 7740a.

Leavitts of America. 4822a.

Lecture! Rattling roaring rhymes. 4837a.

Leer en leven der Mormonen. 848b.

Leeringen van Joseph Smith. 7976b.

Lehi City Rustler Supplement. 4870a.

Leitfaden zum studium des Buches Mormon. 10,033a.

Leo kahes. 2738a.

Lessons for mothers work. 2229a.

Letter from Doctor J. P. Newman. 5806a.

Letter from Mr. James Hole. 4056g.

Letter from the editor. 326a.

Letter from the Secretary of the Interior . . . 9199a-b.

Letter of the delegate of the Territory of Utah. 2787b.

Letters. 1644a.

Letters and journal by the Hon. Francis Charteris. 1257a.

Letters. Dear Brethren of the Seventies: 1391a.

Letters of long ago. 6845a.

Levensvragen. 4683a.

Liebe Bruder, was soll ich thun. 1179a-c, 1180a, 1182a, 7588a.

Life among the Mormons. 6028b.

Life and letters of M. P. O'Conner. 5973c.

Life and teaching of Rev. T. De Witt Talmage. 8706a.

Life history of brother Lars R. Jensen. 4923a.

Life of a Mormon girl. 6730a, 6731a.

Life of Amos A. Lawrence. 4812a.

Life sketch of Lydia Mamreoff von Finkelstein (Madame Mountford). 4925a.

Life, travels and adventures of an American wanderer. 3368b.

Light for Utah. 5078a.

Light interviews with shades. 4496a.

Lincoln's earliest home. 2635d.

Lines kindly solicited by President David H. Cannon . . . 9516b.

Lines written for the St. George Female Relief Soceity. 9516d.

List of Mormon emigrants of 1852. 2804a.

List of persons shipped at Liverpool. 2804b.

List of tithing prices, weights and measures. 1397a.

Little giant cyclipedia and treasury of ready reference. 201a.

Little talk. 4956a.

Llanymddy, Argraffwyd gan E. Morris. 4483b.

Llyfr cronicl prophwydi Mormonaidd. 4969a.

Llyfr Mormon, ei darddiad. 4477a-b.

Llyfrau Saint y Dyddiau Diweddaf . . . 2702a.

Long life in review. 5308b.

Lord's day. 7333a-b.

Lord's Supper from a revelation given to Joseph the Prophet in April, 1830. 1565a.

Lover of truth. 4995a.

Lovers of truth are most respectfully invited to attend a course of lectures. 1884a.

Loyal celebration of Utah County. 5001b.

Luck of a wandering Dane by Hans Lykkejaeger. 7775b.

M

M.I.A. banquet. 2053a.

M.I.A. outlines for summer work. 2165c.

M. Official publication. 5075a.

Mackinac and lake stories. 1239b.

Madras "Christian Instructor" versus Mormonism. 5238a.

Maerkvaerdige syner. 6523a.

Magic, pretended miracles. 5242a.

Mahlon Norris Gilbert. 6080b.

Manchester semi-annual conference. 1942b.

Manual, 1897-8. 2279.

Manual of the churches of Seneca County . . . 2542b.

Marriage suit. 2832b.

Mary Ann M. Pratt, appellant, vs. Alexander Ramsey. 6411a, 9467a.

Mary Magdalene, Christ's friend. 8660a.

Masonic Hall. 5303a.

Matzsu Jitsu Seito sanbika. 1845a.

Mau haawina no ke kula ana i ka Oihana Kahuna a me na lala o na Hui Manawalea . . . 1399a.

Mau manao Hamama i ka Poe Hawaii a me na Lahui Polinesia. 5308c.

Meine dritte Amerika-fahrt. 4020a.

Melanges historiques et litteraires. 5340a.

Members of the Iowa Conference. 5333a.

Members of the Iowa Conference of the Church of Jesus Christ of Latter-day Saints . . . 1498a.

Memoir of the Rev. Oliver Alden Taylor. 8856a.

Memorial events in the life of Captain Jason W. James. 4315a.

Memorial of J. & R. H. Porter. 6410a.

Memorial of the celebration at Palmyra. 3104a.

Memorial to Congress. 5335b.

Memorial to the Honorable, the Senate and House of Representatives . . . 9341a.

Men and manners in America. 3807a.

Message from heaven. 8753a.

Message of the President of the United States communicated to the two houses of Congress . . . 9225a.

Methods of Mormon missionaries. 1126a.

Mexico and its religion. 9933a.

Mg'rdouthiun eagan eprgoutean. 576d.

Mildred E. Randall and Alfred Randall. 6815a, 9467b.

Military circular. 9679b.

Military memoirs of a Confederate. 46a.

Military posts. 9254a.

Milk of the gospel. 53a.

Ministry reports to the forty-fifth conference . . . 6953a.

Ministry reports to the forty-forth conference . . . 6953b.

Ministry reports to the forty-third conference . . . 6953c.

Minnen fran mina resor genom Norra Amerikas . . . 3580a.

Minority report. 9236a-b.

Minutes of a meeting of the stock holders of the Kirtland Safety Society Bank. 4656b, 4657a.

Minutes of annual conference meeting of the Sunday School Union. 1566a.

Minutes of the fifteenth annual convention of the Woman's Christian Temperance Union of Utah. 9976a.

Missionaer-sang. 3956c.

Mississippi River and its wonderful valley. 1250a.

Mistakes of Latter Day Saints. 4742a.

Mistakes of Moses. 4248a.

Mkrdouthuune eakan e phyyuthean. 575a.

Moeurs et voyages ou recits du monde nouveau. 1261a.

Mon second voyage autour du monde. 6343b.

Monde Americain. 7719b.

Monoraa mau i te toroa peretiteniraa . . . 2634a.

More misrepresentative men. 3656a.

More trickery of Mormonism brought to light. 5463a.

Mormon centennial. 5519a.

Mormon defiance to the nation. 2455a.

Mormon Elder and how to meet him. 3443a.

Mormon horrors exposed or why I left the Mormon Church. 4761.

"Mormon" metropolis. 7105a.

Mormon peril. 3444a, 5525b.

Mormon problem. 5048a.

Mormon prophet. 2983a.

Mormon Tabernacle Choir. 2241a.

Mormon Tribune. 5530a.

Mormonaren spelstykke i ei vending. 303b.

Mormonenmadchen. 5441b.

Mormonernes Laerdomme . . . 9411a.

Mormonism. 7343a.

Mormonism and exhibition of Mormon life. 4360a.

Mormonism and its author. 1235a, 1236a.

"Mormonism and the war." 8662a-d.

Mormonism, by an ex-Mormon Elder. 160a.

Mormonism explained. 5549a.

Mormonism exposed. 763a, 5550a-b, 5551a-b, 9881b.

Mormonism or the Bible. 5555a.

Mormonism proclaiming itself a fraud. 5912a.

Mormonism: Whence is it? 9903a.

Mormonisme. 9693a.

Mormonisme ontmaskerd. 5337a.

Mormonismus. 9673a.

Mormonlaeth: neu draethawd . . . 209a.

Mormons. 6090a, 6726a.

Mormon's bride. 5565a.

Mormon's catechism. 5565b.

Mormon's mistake; or, what is the gospel? 4275a.

Mormons, or, Latter-day Saints. 3755a.

Mormons sure of victory. 5567a.

Mormoonsche leer . . . 9414a.

Morumon kyo to Morumon kyoto. 8567a.

Mother Goose. 5651a.

Mothers' letter. 9832a.

Motto catechism card. 5651b.

Mountain Meadow massacre. 4362a.

Mountaineer. 5652a.

Mr. Buchanan's administration on the eve of the rebellion. 952a.

Mr. Dooley's philosophy. 3047a.

Mr. Durant of Salt Lake City. 7183a, 7185a-b.

Mr. Eagle's U. S. A. 10,025a.

Mrs. Lulu Loveland Shepard. 5713a.

Murphy vs. the Unites States. 6372f.

Muster of old comrades. 5722a.

N

O

O my Father. 7841a-b, 7842a.

Observation No. 2. 5805a.

Octogenarian's. 594.

Oeffentlicher vortrag uber die Mormonen. 5974a.

"Of all that Thou shall give me . . ." 2192a.

Offenbarungen der Neuzeit. 2303a-b.

Official announcement . . . 1674b.

Official declaration. To whom it may concern. 1411.

Official facts touching the conviction of Apostle E. C. Briggs. . . . 6958a.

Official proceedings of the seventh convention of the Trans-Mississippi Commercial Congress. 8991c.

Official program of the Third World's Christian Citizenship Conference. 10,014a.

Official program, pioneer day celebration. 2233b.

Official publication of the Mutual Improvement Association. 5975a.

Official souvenir. 5975b.

Ogden Stake Relief Society work . . . 2202b.

Old Folks day. 7247a.

Old Folks day a big jubilee. 2087d.

Old Folks excursion. 2086c.

Old Folks will go to Brigham City. 2087e.

Old Jerusalem gospel restored. 6362a.

Olelo ao "Moramona" . . . 6248a.

Olelo ao no na Hui Manawalea ma ka Ekalesia o Iesu Kirsto. 5981a.

Olelo ao no na hui manawalea o ko Hawaii nei paeaina. 5850a.

Om Israels insamling och Zions forlossing. 10,096a.

On Liberty. 5391a.

On the departure from earth of Beatrice Lillian Driggs. 3373b.

On the first principles of the gospel. 3891b.

Onkuischheid, het heerschend kwaad van den tijd. 8044b.

Only true gospel. 978a.

Onze buurman, de heer S. 2001a.

Open letter from Nathan Baldwin Jr. 258c.

Order of Enoch. 1201a.

Ordinations and ceremonies. 2250d.

Organists manual. 2042c.

P

Pioneer west. 3461a.

Pionerene, deras utdrifning fran Illinois. 8933a.

Plain facts for patriotic voters. 5684a.

Plan and program for the study of child culture . . . 2136a, 2137, 2233c-d.

Plan of campaign for the Anti-polygamy Constitutional Amendment. 4258a.

Plan of salvation. 5495a, 5504a-b, 5507a, 5508a-e.

Plan of salvation as taught by the Church of Jesus Christ of Latter-day Saints. 5511c-d.

Plea for religious liberty . . . 2618a.

Poem, written for the celebration of the Fourth of July, 1860. 5413a.

Political aspects of Mormonism. 1127a.

Political straws. 6395a.

Polygamie aux Etats-Unis. 3027b.

Polygamy. Report. 9126b.

Polygamy. [signed] Truth conquers. 817a.

Polygamy! World wide after the war. 3522a.

"Polygamy" (inside story of the play). 5978a.

Polygamy in Utah. 9237a.

Polygamy, or the mysteries and crimes of Mormonism. 355a, 356a-e.

Polynesiens orientauz au contact le la civilisation. 1066a.

Popular songs of the Church of Jesus Christ of Latter-day Saints. 1419a.

Postmaster John T. Lynch. 6421a.

Practicability of railroads through South Pass. 4735a.

Prairie experiences in handling cattle and sheep. 7684a.

Praktische hinweisung auf Bibelstellen . . . 4576a.

Pratt family will hold a special social. 6719a.

Pre-existence of spirits. 994a.

Pregeth gwrth-Formonaidd. 2702b.

Present situation in Utah. 6751b.

Present truth. 5152b.

Presentation of a flag to Governor Ford and his troops by the ladies of Hancock County. 3397a.

Presidency and priesthood. 4562a.

Presidential reception to the Old Folks of Utah . . . 2087i.

Presidents of _____ Quorum of Seventy: 1644b.

Press comments on Mr. Charles Ellis' lectures. 3150a.

Price list: Publishing Department of the European Mission. 1973a.

Priestcraft exposed. 8307b.

Priesthood and presidency. 6249a.

Priesthood conferences. 1928. 1510a.

Priesthood convention of Weber Stake. 2238a.

Primary song book. 2121a.

Principes fondamentaux de l'evangile de Jesus-Christ. 6757a.

Principles of the junior church. 548a.

Priodas a Moesau yn Utah. 6606a.

Prize ode to irrigation. 5116a-b.

Proceeding of the Democratic State Convention . . . 2762a.

Proceedings at the dedication of the Joseph Smith memorial monument . . . 8066a, 8067a.

Procession of the immortals. 6759c.

Proclamation. 6095a, 10,063b.

Proclamation by the Governor. 4199a.

Proclamation from the Lord to his people scattered throughout the earth. 533b.

Proclamation from the Rocky Mountains. 1050a.

Profeet der Laatste Dagen. 6120a.

Profion o eirwiredd Llyfr Mormon. 4478b.

Program dedicatory services, Brooklyn Chapel. 1968b.

Program, District Sunday School convention. 1571a.

Program, 1918 Apr. 7, Salt Lake City, Utah. 1571d.

Program for Sunday School annual stake conferences to be held during the year 1900. 1571c.

Program for ward teaching and home evening. 2177a.

Program of dedicatory and opening services. 2260a.

Program of exercises in honor of President Wilford Woodruff. 6761b.

Program of Maeser Day exercises. 6761c.

Program: the Elders' missionary benefit. 2254a.

Programme. Grand juvenile procession. 6763a.

Programme. 24th of July celebration. 6769a.

Programme of exercises of the joint conference . . . 2210c.

Programme of the Daughters of the Utah Pioneers. 2674a.

Prohibition: not state controlled. 5063a.

Promenades au Far West. 8882a.

Promenades dans les deux Ameriques. 2536a.

Prophecy and revelation concerning the present war . . . 2916a.

Prophet Joseph rebuking the guard at Richmond jail. 6618a.

Prophet Joseph Smith tells his own story. 7987.

Prospectus of eleven lectures and recital on sociology . . . 2074a.

Prospectus of the 15th volume of the Deseret News Weekly . . . 1210a.

Prospectus. The Mormon. 8843a.

Prospectus to the Liahona. 4911a.

Protea. 6773a.

Protection across the continent. 9254b.

Protest of Legislative Assembly of Utah. 9391a.

Protestant miracles. 7461a.

Proverbs. 8761a.

Psychological and ethical aspects of Mormon group life. 3180a.

Pule hoolaa no ke kie hoomanao o Iosepa Kamika. 8044a.

Pure gospel of Christ. 6973a.

Puteshestvie po Amerike. 9031a.

Put's golden songster. 8487a.

Put's original California songster. 8487b.

Q

Qu est la verite. 7164b.

Quatorze mois dans l'Amerique du nord. 9049a.

Questions and answers on good manners. 6785a.

Questions and answers on the Godhead. 6785b.

Questions of the hour. 6785c.

Questions and answers upon the first commandment. 6785d.

Questions and answers upon the "Word of Wisdom." 6785e.

R

Raau a Iosepha ra. 2042a-b.

Rainbow Bridge. 439h.

Raymond, Alberta, Canada. 6826a.

Rayons de lumiere vivifiante. 6266a-c, 6267a.

Rays of living light. 6256a-b, 6259b-g, 6260a-i, 6261a-c.

Reading course books adopted by the Mutual Improvement Association. 2780d.

Reading exercises in the English language for new beginners. 6828a.

Ready references. 489a, 490a.

Reasons why B. H. Roberts should be expelled . . . 1129a.

Recent discussion of Mormon affairs. 6830b.

Rechte, Bergunstigungen and Segnungen, welcher sich Burger des Riches Gottes. 6830c.

Recital from Apostle Whitney's masterpiece. 6830d.

Recollections and reflections. 3871a.

Red men on the war path. 772a.

Regarding law enforcement. 2210b.

Registration rules. 9329a.

Regulations for the guidance of Sunday School. 1576a.

Reina: Los Angles in three centuries. 3998a.

Reise durch den Stillen Ozean. 961a.

Rejected manuscript. 3280a.

Relief Society -- wheat. 9678a.

Religion in America. 250a.

Religious forces of the United States enumerated. 1214a.

Reminiscences of the happy life of a teacher. 4056e.

Reorganization of the Church of Jesus Christ of Latter-Day Saints. 5006a, 5008a.

Report of cattle, sheep, and swine . . . 9194b.

Report of irrigation investigations in Utah. 5321a.

Report of Mr. Flint, of the select committee. 1087a.

Report of the Every-community survey . . . 4181b.

Report of the Governor of Idaho to the Secretary of the Interior. 4180d-f.

Report of the Governor of the Territory of Utah. 9382a-b.

Report of the Nottingham Conference. 1945c.

Report of the Nottinghamshire Conference. 1947a.

Report of the Quorum of the Twelve. 7033b.

Report of the Scheffield Conference. 1952a.

Report of the Secretary of War. 9254c.

*Report of the Utah Commission as to the management of the Industrial Christian Home of Utah Territory.
9239a.*

Report of the Utah Conservation Commission. 9314b.

Report on barracks and hospitals. 518b.

Report on the Governor's message . . . 9393a.

Report on the subject of the massacre at the Mountain Meadows. 1189, 1190, 1190b.

Report: to accompany bill S. 905. 9166e.

Report: to accompnay bill S. 1368. 9166f.

Reports to the seventieth general conference. 6983a.

Resolution in relation to a constitutional convention. 9391b.

Resolution of the legislature of the State of California. 1085a.

Resolutions. 9184a.

Resolutions of respect to the memory of Miss Evelyn Billings. 2233e.

Restoration of the everlasting gospel. 8867a.

Results of the anti-polygamy crusade. 4259a.

Relic Library. 6849a.

Religious systems of the world. 6854a.

Remarkable delusions; or, illustrations of popular errors. 6858a.

Remarks on the doctrines, practices, &c. of the Latter-day Saints. 6864a.

Restoration of the Gospel. 7090b.

Retracing the pioneers. 8794a.

Rev. J. Musser, vs. the Saints. 5690a.

Rev. Wm. R. Campbell. 1129b.

Revelation and prophecy. 2916b-c.

Revelation and prophecy . . . 2015a.

Revelations. 7090a.

Reverence. 1579a.

Revised Odd-Fellowship illustrated. 562a.

Richard H. Porter and James Porter. 9113d-e.

Robert N. Baskin, contestant, v. George Q. Cannon. 3127a.

Rogers -- Cornish debate. 2520a.

Roihani ilahiler. 1870a.

Roll of honor. Church of Jesus Christ of Latter-day Saints. 1945a.

Roll of honor of the Fifteenth Ward Sunday School. 2250a.

"Round the world". 3382a.

Rudger Clawson, appellant vs. the United States. 2411a, 7232a.

Rudger Clawson, plaintiff in error, vs. the United States. 2411b, 7234a.

Ruin!! Ruin!! Ruin!! 7437b.

Ruins revisited and the world-story retold. 9536a.

Rules and regulations for conduct of Elders in Northern States Mission. 2011a.

Rules for the guidance of members . . . 2239a.

Rules for the guidance of Sunday School in the stakes of Zion. 1579b.

Run through the states. 35c.

Rural comedy drama, the Mormon wife. 755a.

S

Sabbath question. 6985a.

Sacred spot is definitely located. 1291a.

Saint y dyddiau diweddaf a doniau gwyrthiol. 3210a.

Saints' Commercial Order. 5652c.

Saints of a latter-day. 5282a.

Salt Lake City and Utah. 7492a.

Salt Lake City and Utah by pen and pictures. 3383a.

Salt Lake City busy man's pocket directory. 3434a.

Salt Lake City directory for the year 1873. 7498a.

Salt Lake City, Utah. 3662c, 7504a-b.

Salt Lake Mormons. 7507a.

Salt Lake Stake Academy. 7507b.

Salt Lake Stake Sunday Schools. 1640a.

Salt Lake Temple. 7243a, 7508a.

Salt Lake's fall carnival . . . 2080b.

Salut pourles morts. 7521a.

Salvation for the dead. 8072a.

Sammenlikning emellan bevisen for Bibeln och Mormons bok. 6539a.

San Diego Mission. 3166a.

Sande vidners: 7521c.

Sandheden sejrer. 7526a.

Sandheds-rost til de oprigtige af hjertet. 8179a, 8180a, 8198a, 8202a.

Sange til brug for de Sidste-Dages Hellige. 8933b.

Sanna evangeliet eller de forsta kristans tro. 992a-b.

Sarah A. Chapman. 8540c.

Sarah A. Chapman et al. 4056c.

Scandinavian conference and reunion. 7549b.

Scandinavian day at Saltair Beach. 7549c.

Scandinavian L.D.S. organizations of Salt Lake City. 7549d.

Scenes from every land. 4671a.

School history of the state of Missouri. 6809a.

Scriptural revelations of the universal apostasy. 6138a.

Seagull. 7601a.

Seagull girls. 2126a.

Second biennial message of John B. Neil. 4179b.

Second coming of the Messiah. 7368a-c, 7370a, 7372a-h.

Second elders' conference of the Liberty Stake . . . 2192b.

Second quarterly report of the Church of Jesus Christ of Latter-day Saints. 1948a.

Second visit to the United States . . . 5046a.

Seeing America including the Panama Exposition. 5282c.

Seeing the West. 3028a.

Seer; written for the dedication of the Seventy' Hall. 8844a.

Seintiau Diweddaf. 7614a.

Selected works of Artemus Ward. 942a.

Selection from the songs of Zion. 1815a.

Service on the Indian reservations. 9729a.

Seven presidents of the Mormon Church. 2780e.

Seven years in the Great Salt Lake City. 6030a.

Seventy. 4498c.

Seventy's calling, and local service in the Church. 1645a.

Seventy-fifth anniversary celebration. 2011b.

Shepherd Saint of Lanai. 3560a-c.

Short history of marriage. 9704b.

Signs of the day. 2505a.

Sililoquy [i.e. soliloquy] of Brigham. 4711a.

Silver thimbles. 8372a.

Simple Bible stories. 6121a.

Sir; the religious test oaths passed by the last session of the Idaho Legislature. 7735a.

Sixty years in Southern California. 5808a.

Sketch of the travels and ministry of Elder Orson Hyde. 4169a.

Sketches of frontier and Indian life. 8851b.

Skriftmaessig beviis imod Mormonismens laere. 7752a.

Societe americaine. 3027a.

[Soliloquy] of Brigham. 4711a.

Some account of the rulers of the world. 1260a.

Some distinctive features of Mormonism. 4010b.

Song for the Forth of July, 1862. 7847a.

Songs, for the sixth of April. 8277a.

Songs for the 24th of July, 1851. 8277b.

Songs of praise. 2734e.

Songs of redemption. 7068b.

Songs of Zion. 1798a, 8114a.

Songs to be sung by the congregation at the semi-annual Sunday School conference. 1580a.

Soul's captain . . . 9782a.

South be west; or, winter in the Rocky Mountains. 4633b.

Souvenir. 187a.

Souvenir, centennial anniversary of the birth of the prophet Joseph Smith. 8293a.

Souvenir of Mesa City and environments. 5220a.

Souvenir, of Salt Lake, the city beautiful. 8299a.

Souvenir of Salt Lake City Utah. 8299b.

Souvenir program for the Scandinavian Jubilee. 8300a.

Souvenir program. Formal opening of Wells Ward Chapel. 2264a.

Souvenir program, Hull District. 1929a.

Speak for themselves. 8313a.

Speaking of the Era. 3676a.

Special organ recital in honor of H. R. H. Gustavus Adolphus. 1677a.

Special organ recital in the Tabernacle, Salt Lake City, Utah. 1677b.

Speech of John M. Clayton of Delaware. 2423a.

Speech of Mr. Smith, of Conn. 8122a.

Speech of the Hon. M. Norris of New Hampshire. 5866a.

Speech of Truman Smith. 8122b.

Speeches of Hon. O. F. Whitney in support of woman suffrage. 9783.

Speeches of Sam Houston of Texas. 4099a.

Spiritual gifts and Seer of Palmyra. 585b.

Spiritual gifts and spirit manifestations. 585a.

Spoilers of Jerusalem. 9536b.

Stammering century. 7619a.

Statement from Josiah Quincy. 1968a.

States and Territories of the great West. 3331a.

Stimme der Warnung und Belehrung . . . 6699a.

"Stone" in the "hat." 4643a-b.

Stories from the Old Testament for the primary department of the Sunday School. 1583a.

Story of beginning (now for the first time told). 5462b.

Story of Detroit. 1239c.

Story of Omaha. 8279a.

Story of the Book of Mormon. 7115a, 7119a.

Story of the Western Reserve. 5414a.

Straaler af levende Lys. 6262a-b, 6263a-f.

Strahlen lebendigen lichtes. 6270a.

Stralen van levend licht. 6264a, 6265a.

Stray lights on different principles. 2370a.

Strength of the "Mormon" position. 9786a, 9787a.

Striking and remarkable vision. 2914b.

Struggle to attain righteousness. 1184a.

Study of Mormonism as a laboratory of ethics and psychology. 9257b.

Suffrage in Utah. 5799a.

Suggestions for Melchizedek Quorum Committees. 1512a.

Suggestions to brethren . . . 8527a.

Summer scamper along the old Santa Fe Trail. 2629a.

Sunday morning in the kindergarten. 1585a.

Sunday School conferences, 1917. 1588a.

Sunday School manual. 2167a.

Sunday School officers and teachers handbook. 1595a.

Sunday School outlines of the parents' department. 1599a.

Sunday School plan for the First Intermediate Department . . . 2165b.

Superintendents will report on the following questions . . . 1599b.

Supplement revelations on the building of the Temple. 3338d-f.

Supplement to History of Indian depredation. 3649a.

Supplement to the manual of coins and bullion. 3107a.

Supplement to the Warsaw Signal. 9616a.

Synopsis of the faith and doctrine of Church of Jesus Christ of Latter-day Saints. 7000a.

Synoptical sketch of the life of John Pack. 8562a.

T

Tahiti, by Tihoti. 1081a.

Tarsadalmi s allami regeneratio vagysis. 8562b.

Te hoe aratai no te mau taata i roto i te Ekalaesia. 7968a-c.

Te raau a Iosepha ra. 6805b.

Teachings of Mormonism and Christianity . . . 5941a.

Telegraphic-Herald's abridged history. 8872b.

Temple records adjusted and genealogical information obtained. 5044a.

Temple report for June 14, 1900. 4622a.

Temples of the Church of Jesus Christ of Latter-day Saints. 5099b.

Temples of the Latter-day Saints. 8876a.

Ten years in Oregon. 50a.

Ten years of my mission. 3099a.

Territory of Nevada. 9160a, 9327a.

Territory of Utah, County of Box Elder. 1259a.

Testimonial presented to Elder Henry Clegg. 1930a.

Texas ranch life: 4354a.

That "veiled gospel". 9051a.

Theological dictionary. 961b.

Theology. D. & C., sec. 88: 77. 2196a.

Thirty-one years on the plains and mountains. 3001a.

Thirty-sixth anniversary of . . . 7247b.

Thirty-sixth anniversary of the wedding-day of our beloved parents. 8894a.

Thoughts on tithing. 2114a.

Three degrees of glory. 272a.

Three district meetings of the Church of Jesus Christ of Latter-day Saints. 1900a.

Three generations in Council of Twelve. 8947a.

Thrilling adventures, travels and exploration of Dr. Elijah White among the Rocky Mountains and in the far West. 50b.

Through storyhood to the sunset seas. 4659a.

Ti aasagerr hvorfor Kristne . . . 6751a.

Tim. 5078b.

Times and Seasons. 8955.

Tithing. 851a.

To all presidents and members of the Seventies' Quorums. 1645b.

To American citizens everywhere. 5713b.

To Aunt Em (Emmeline B. Wells). 8320a.

To California and back. 3994a.

To conductor Evan Stephens, and members of the Tabernacle Choir. 1680b.

To Cyrus H. Wheelock. 5068a.

To his excellency Thomas Ford. 9604a.

To my friends. 2587a.

To presidents of stakes and bishops of wards: 1681a.

To stake and ward officers Y.M.M.I.A. 2318a.

To the bishops and members of the Church of Jesus Christ of Latter-day Saints. 1682a.

To the Christians and gentiles. 8963a.

To the citizens of Hancock. 3459a.

To the honorable, the Senate and House of Representatives in Congress assembled. 7260a.

To the member of the Senate and the House of Representatives . . . 5805b.

To the non-Mormon vote of Salt Lake City. 8965a.

To the people of Colorado. 9312a.

To the presidency and bishopric of _____ Stake. 1685a.

To the President. 8965b.

To the presidents and clerks of the Quorum of Seventies. 1645c.

To the presidents, bishop's agents and bishop . . . 1685b, 9999a.

To the presidents of stakes and bishops of wards. 1685c-1685e.

To the presidents of stakes and their counselors. 1687c.

To the presidents of stakes, bishops and parents in Zion. 1691a.

To the presidents of stakes, bishops of wards and Stake tithing clerks in Zion. 1691b.

To the presidents of the _____ Quorum of Seventies. 1644c-d, 1646a-b, 1648a.

To the priesthood quorum generally. 5199a.

To the scattered and peeled Britons. 6753a.

To the stake officers, Y.M.M.I.A. 2318b.

To the superintendents and Sunday School worker. 2169a.

To those interested in the Mexican Mission. 4484a.

Toilers of land and sea. 3498b.

Tour around the world. 6821a.

Tourists' guide book to Salt Lake City. 2608a.

Tracks of a rolling stone. 2449a.

Tradition and the Book of Mormon. 5127a.

Traethodau ar ail-ddyfodiad Crist. 4498a.

Traethodau ar y doniau gwyrthiol. 4498b.

Trails plowed under. 7455a.

Trans-Mississippi West. 8991d.

Trapped by the Mormons. 8991e.

Travelers handbook across the continent. 3137a.

Travels at home and abroad . . . 7790a.

Travels to the Far West in search of borax. 7395b.

Tre digte. 3956d.

Treason in Washington. 581a.

Trente-quatre etoiles de l'union Americaine. 3284c.

Trial of the witness of Jesus. 7003a.

Tribune extra. 7519a-b.

Trip around the world. 2504a.

Trip to the United States in 1887. 342a.

Trips and travel. 2841a.

Tro och dop. 9013a.

True church. 3849b.

True Church of Jesus Christ. 9021a.

True God and his worship contrasted with idolatry. 6625a.

True lamplighter. 9021b.

True story of the lost shackle. 2641a-b.

True versus modern Christianity. 9021c.

Truth about the "Mormons". 1449a.

Truth made manifest. 3133a-b.

Truth revealed "to the law and to the testimony". 9027a.

Twelfth visitation of the messenger to Elder Otto Fetting. 3338g.

Twelve Apostles . . . The Seven Presidents of the Seventy . . . 1450a.

Twelve years in America. 7638b.

Twentieth general annual conference of the Y.M. and Y.L.M.I.A. 1450b.

Twenty-five letters to a young lady. 3693a.

Twenty-forth of July. 6432a.

Twenty-second Message. 3338h.

Twenty-third Message. 3338i.

Twin monsters. 3040a-c.

Two Americas. 6754a.

Two hundred men with teams wanted . . . 1186b.

Two poems. 9788a.

Two prayers. 3809a.

Twyll y seintiau diweddaf yn cael ei ddynoethi mewn nodiadau . . . 9870a.

U

U. S. A. Uncle Sam's abscess. 4363a.

Uber charakterbilding und lebensfuhrung. 2319a.

Udfald fra Christi Kirke mod Mormonerne. 9068a.

Uintah Stake Relief Society outlines. 2232a.

Uncle Bob and aunt Becky's strange adventure at the worlds great exposition. 9902c.

Uncle Sam says the Mormons still practice polygamy. 3445a.

Undertaker. 9071a.

Union Pacific sketch book. 9088b.

United States, appellant, vs. the late corporation of the Church of Jesus Christ of Latter-day Saints et al. 1450c.

United States of America. 5695a.

United States of America, appellant, vs. the late corporation of the Church of Jesus Christ or [sic] Latter-day Saints. 7237a-b.

United States of America, plaintiff, vs. Horace S. Eldredge. 3128a.

United States of America, plaintiff, vs. the Late corporation of the Church of Jesus Christ of Latter-day Saints. 546a.

United States vs. the corporation of the Church of Jesus Christ of Latter-day Saints. 870a, 5142a.

United States, vs. the late corporation of the Church of Jesus Christ of Latter-day Saints. 4510a.

United States with an excursion into Mexico. 243a.

Unsre Sonntagsschule. 1988a.

Up from the hills. 3837a.

Upper California. 8851a.

Ursprungliche evangelium. 9264a.

Utah. 5805c.

Utah, Americas great mining and smelting center. 7494a.

Utah Battalion Monument . . . 9297a.

Utah: being a concise description of the vast resources. 2976b.

Utah contest. 2762b.

Utah directory and gazetteer for 1879-1880. 2608b.

Utah Expedition. 9113f.

Utah Gospel Mission. 5948a.

Utah: its people, resources, attractions, and institutions. 1485a, 9089a.

Utah; its resources and attractions. 9089b.

Utah. Memorial of the members and officers of the Legislative Assembly of the Territory Utah. 9391c.

Utah pioneer jubilee. 9313a.

Utah revealed. 2450a.

Utah. The prize poem. 2430a.

Utah women in politics. 3525a.

Utah, your state. 9294a.

Utah's importance as a mineral state. 7495a-b.

Utah's mineral wealth. 9448a.

V

Vacation excursion. 6814a.

Valgberettigede i Utah, giv agt! 9413a.

Valkomsthelsning vid ankomsten till Sion. 9537a.

Venligt ord. 9460a.

Verbannung des Mormonenvolkes. 9460b.

Verheerlijkt een verhaal. 135a.

Verida del Mesas. 8462a.

Vermont Party. 9464a.

Vermoorden van ongeboren kinderen. 2999a.

Verstaat gij ook hetgeen gij leest? 9466a.

Verzoening en het verlossingsplan van Jezus Christus. 8318.

Veterans of our cause. 5705a.

Viaje al pais de los Mormones. 1029b.

Vie, la confession et l'execution de l'eveque John D. Lee. 4848a.

Views of Utah and tourist guide. *7541a.*

Views on the scenic line of the world. *10096b.*

Visions of Joseph Smith. *7997a.*

Voice of the good shepherd. *2777a.*

Voice of warning. *6649b.*

Voice of warning an instruction to all people. *6646a-b, 6656a.*

Vollkommene Religion. *9490b.*

Vom indischen Ocean bis zum Goldlande. *9484a.*

Von New York nach San Francisco. *4020b.*

Voyage au pays du petrole. *2434a.*

Voyages du Capitaine Burton a la Mecque. *1029b.*

Vriendschappelijk Onderhoud over Belangrijke Godsdienst-Waarheden. *7164a.*

W

Wahrend der Konferenz der Kirche Jesu Christi der letzten Tage. *1986a.*

Wahrer und falscher Gottesdienst. *9502a.*

Wanderings in the West. *1049a.*

Wanted! One hundred thousand men and women . . . 2011c.

Ward Teachers Department. *2240a.*

Ward teachers manual. *2202a.*

Ward teachers' subjects. *2214a.*

Ward teaching, explanation and revelation. *2235a.*

Warnande rost och undervisning . . . 6707a.

Warning to all. *3892a.*

Warning to all people of the second coming of Christ. *3338j, 3339a.*

Warning to parents & employers. *9600a.*

Was ist aus der Mission Jesu Christi geworden? *302a.*

Wasatch Academy, Mt. Pleasant, Utah. *6736a.*

Way called heresy. *5035a.*

Ways that are doubtful. *8027c.*

We are again compelled to allow another publication day to pass without issuing a paper. *9605a.*

We carry a full line of curios and souvenirs. *2460a.*

Wedlock: or, the right relations of the sexes. *9690a.*

Welsh District Conferences. *1956a.*

West Millard County, Utah. *8566a.*

Word of wisdom. 1977a, 2086a.

World as it is and has been. 3617a.

World's Fair ecclesiastical history of Utah. 1264e.

Y

Y casgl; neu grynhoad o draethodau . . . 2697a.

Y drych cywir. 4483a.

Y seintiau diweddaf. 2682b.

Yankee trader in the gold rush. 961c.

Yoniau gwyrthiol fel eu darlunir yn yr ysgrythyrau sanctaidd . . . 2681a.

Youth in the Restoration. 7026a.

Z

Zetetic sermon. 3033a.

Zion's Home Monthly. 10,138a.

Zion's Messenger. 10,139a.

Zion's praises. 7071a.

Zions sanger en samling af utvalda sanger . . . 1866.

Zion's trumpet. 3571a.

Zondagsschool-bladeren. 1600a.

Zondagsschool-schetsen. 1600b-f.

Zur geschichte des Sabbats. 10,145a.

Chronological Index

1855:   385a, 945b, 1087a, 1087b, 1298a, 1930a, 2404b, 3617b, 3891a, 4099a, 4457a-b, 4467b-c, 4477a, 4477b, 5050a, 5242a, 5678a, 8843a, 9066a, 9536c, 9933a, 10,139a

1856:   3331a, 3733c, 5238a, 6606a, 8826, 8826a, 8896a, 9113c

1857:   192a, 1236a, 2983b, 3372a, 6828a, 9068a, 9148a, 9254a, 9679b, 10,063a

1858:   1085a, 2787b, 3179a, 4318a, 4735a, 6854b, 8487a, 9160a, 9254c, 9327a, 9391c

1859:   50b, 5391a, 5753a, 6343b, 6410a

186-:   10,062a

1860:   1189, 1190, 2465b, 3284b, 4053a, 5413a, 5652a

1861:   6413a, 6847, 8979a, 9490a

1862:   335a, 3284c, 7847a, 10,056a

1863:   2015a, 4316a, 6028b, 6030a

1864:   258a, 817a, 2374a, 2374b, 2916a, 2916b, 3283a, 3368a, 6809b, 7091b

1865:   518a, 918a, 924a, 924b, 1210a, 1658c, 7000a

1866:   889a, 952a

1867:   258b, 1264f, 1264g, 3469a, 5246b, 7638b, 8490a, 9254a, 9254b

1868:   35a, 298a, 901a, 1257a, 2096a, 2098a, 8487b, 9401a

1869:   366a, 2780b, 3210b, 4088a, 4169a, 5530a, 6158a, 7719a, 10,130a

187-:   934, 4248a, 6432a, 7906a

1870:   518b, 2471a, 3137a, 3155a, 3543a, 3869a, 4325a, 5213, 5806a, 6903b, 7677a, 8941b, 8991a, 9401b, 9690a, 10,129a

1871:   191a, 829a, 1049a, 2581a, 3325a, 3476a, 4543a, 4659a-b, 4741a, 7247b, 8894a

1872:   577c, 1029a, 2787a, 2943a, 3382a, 3498a, 3618b, 8913a, 8975a, 9031a

1873:   1029b, 2596a, 2829a, 5311a, 5799a, 6313a, 7498a, 7519b

1874:   2240b, 3373b, 3599a, 4633b, 5117a, 7519a, 8965a, 9361a, 9686a

1875:   577a, 5303c, 6090a, 6707a, 7619b, 7997a, 8114a, 8179a, 8180a, 8180b, 8198a, 8242a, 9116a, 9116b, 10,096a

1876:   329a, 578a, 826a, 1682a, 1884a, 3104a, 3127a, 4232a, 4667a, 6384a, 7098a, 7098b, 7395b, 7719b, 8828b, 9329b

1877:   1276a, 1605a, 2473b, 2734b, 3323a, 3793a, 4511a, 4511b, 4848a, 5458a, 5706a, 6754a, 6773a, 9409c, 9410a, 9484a, 10,058a

1878:   961a, 2841b, 2851b, 2853a, 2969a, 3571a, 6372e, 8867a, 9727a

1879: 968a, 978a, 1605b, 1884c, 2608a, 2608b, 2846a, 4023, 5389a, 5398a, 6523a, 7395c, 9049a, 9189b

188-: 1640b, 1646b, 4711a, 5565a, 5805b, 6830c, 6913a, 6931a, 6943a, 7507a, 9537a

1880: 180a, 394a, 2823a, 3447a, 4179a, 4183a, 6073a, 9199a, 9199b

1881: 13a, 748a, 1224a, 2777a, 2779a, 2845a, 4360a, 6539a, 6910b, 8818, 8860a, 9369a

1882: 25a, 35b, 355a, 918b, 924c, 997a, 1264a, 1264b, 1275b, 2434a, 2455a, 2504a, 2944a, 2976a, 3472a, 3560a, 3560b, 3560c, 4179b, 4765a, 5335b, 6343c, 6377a, 7260a, 7389b, 7948a, 8409a, 9113e, 9115a, 9126a, 9166e, 9189a, 9329a, 9341a, 9391b, 9393a, 9881

1883: 160b, 877a, 991a, 1397a, 1646a, 2505a, 2629a, 2630a, 2811a, 3368b, 3498c, 3584a, 3869b, 4031a, 4031b, 5340a, 5795a, 6421a, 6570a, 8378a, 8806c, 9115b, 9409c, 9411a

1884: 23a, 303a, 838a, 1391a, 1644a, 2404a, 2779b, 3693a, 4180a, 4363a, 4514c, 5451a, 5495a, 5673a, 5805a, 6023a, 6372b, 6372c, 6372d, 6372f, 6441a, 6646a, 6814a, 6815a, 7232a, 7684a, 8148a, 8305b, 8433a, 8527b, 8562b, 9194b, 9391a

1885: 160a, 297a, 1050a, 1139a, 1139b, 2370a, 2411a, 2411b, 3040a, 3040b, 3319a, 4020c, 4056e, 4442, 4711b, 4812a, 5090a, 5439a, 6646b, 6864b, 7234a, 7775b, 8520a, 8562a, 9071a, 9113f, 9466b, 9466c, 9466d, 9467a, 9467b, 9502a

1886: 522b, 1259a, 1645b, 1645c, 1662, 1662a, 2086c, 2536a, 2614a, 2618a, 3040c, 3991a, 4056g, 4180b, 4180d, 4484a, 4958a, 5048a, 6821a, 7462a, 7507b, 7735a, 7840a, 8248b, 8933a, 9037b, 9113d, 9126b, 9166f

1887: 102a, 342a, 522a, 870a, 1192a, 1260a, 1283b, 1283c, 1321a, 1329, 1502, 1685b, 2945a, 3128a, 4213a, 4515, 4865a, 5001b, 5142a, 5264a, 5651b, 6785b, 6785d, 6830e, 7090b, 7083b, 7510a, 9088b, 9236a, 9536a, 9999a, 10,096b

1888: 221a, 554a, 867a, 1691b, 2250a, 2587a, 2738a, 4020b, 4131a, 4180c, 4180f, 4812a, 5453a, 5463b, 5841a, 6225a, 6449a, 6483a, 7115a, 7119a, 7315a, 7495c, 7509a, 7510a, 8027c, 8710a, 8965b, 9021c, 9184a, 9225a, 9409a, 10,138a

1889: 360a, 801a, 1190b, 1687c, 2099a, 2210c, 2657a, 3278a, 3698b, 4022a, 5308a, 5551b, 6849a, 7105a, 7231a, 7368a, 7368b, 7647b, 8147b, 8851b, 9079a, 9239a, 9536b

189-: 1186b, 3975a, 4498c, 4516a, 4675a, 4675b, 4675c, 5035a, 6649b, 7368c, 7841a

1890: 175f, 201a, 328a, 331b, 585a, 1001a, 1214a, 1238a, 1411, 1551a, 1565a, 1655b, 2087h, 3509a, 4056bb, 4181a, 4376a, 4562a, 4586a, 5408a, 5973b, 6751a, 8538a, 8540a, 8540b, 8540c, 8834b, 8991b, 9903a, 10,105a, 10,105c

1891: 404a, 404b, 585b, 790a, 1267a, 1644c, 1652b, 1685a, 1685c, 2318b, 2945b, 3023a, 3023b, 3150a, 4536a, 4737a, 6121a, 6809a, 6839a, 9236b, 9978a

1892: 27a, 69a, 546a, 1155a, 1644d, 2233d, 2461a, 2520a, 2762b, 3377a, 3588a, 4013a, 4510a, 4514b, 4671a, 6230a, 6759c, 6973a, 7076b, 7237a, 8372a, 9166d, 9516d

1893: 940a, 1264e, 1405a, 1450c, 1648a, 1652a, 1658f, 2457a, 3171a, 3270a, 3508b, 3757a, 3976a, 3994a, 4056c, 5852a, 5973c, 7033c, 7237b, 7528a, 8133a, 9729a

1894:   35c, 540a, 577b, 1210b, 1406a, 1566a, 1674b, 1685d, 2165a, 2233a, 2564a, 2945c, 3768a, 4354a, 4668a, 5220a, 5705a, 5850a, 6064a, 6100a, 8345b, 8472a, 8991c, 9083c, 9413a, 9704a, 10,017a

1895:   108a, 772a, 1350a, 1551b, 1579b, 1680b, 1681a, 1685e, 1942c, 2338a, 2514a, 2811b, 2833a, 2834a, 3610a, 3655a, 3957a, 3961a, 4515a, 4659a, 5076a, 5282b, 6953c, 7356a, 8336a, 9225a, 9264a, 9273a, 9382a, 9460b, 9704a, 9783, 9798a, 9853a, 10,105b, 10,120a

1896:   175a, 994a, 1337c, 1658e, 2241a, 2430a, 2450a, 2542b, 3013a, 3027a, 3935a, 4059a, 6655a, 6953b, 7295a, 8278a, 8299b, 8337, 8468a, 9382b

1897:   331a, 452a, 479a, 1176a, 1242, 1337d, 1532a, 1873a, 1942b, 2021a, 2053a, 2641a, 2641b, 2827a, 3301a, 3580a, 4870a, 5551a, 6146c, 6618a, 6748a, 6761b, 6953a, 7044a, 7510a, 7526a, 8318, 9311a, 9312a, 9313a, 10,120b

1898:   1324a, 1599b, 1640a, 2258a, 2279, 3278b, 3734a, 4595a, 4595b, 4692a, 6395a, 6657a, 6757a, 7142a, 7142b, 7142c, 7295b, 7526b, 10,025a

1899:   243a, 845a, 1129b, 1239b, 1870a, 2983a, 3001a, 3611a, 3734b, 4643b, 5482a, 5974a, 7172b, 7461a, 9089b, 9113g, 9113h

19--:   2224a, 9490b

190-:   8036a, 9600a

1900:   64a, 207a, 295a, 295b, 632a, 969a, 992c, 1090a, 1127a, 1129a, 1174a, 1179a, 1183a, 1256a, 1571c, 1576a, 1600a, 1900a, 2018a, 2087f, 2087g, 2169a, 2489a, 2597a, 2657b, 2881a, 3047a, 3662c, 3662f, 3728a, 3733e, 3841a, 3961b, 4258a, 4259a, 4622a, 4633a, 4643a, 4871b, 4923a, 5337a, 5414a, 5599a, 5652c, 5722a, 6751b, 7044b, 7508a, 7535a, 7549c, 7586a, 8300a, 8633a, 9013a, 9314a, 9516b, 9865a, 9982a

1901:   489a, 755a, 1179b, 1179c, 1986a, 2224a, 3181, 3412a, 4587a, 5005a, 5981a, 7183a, 7549a, 7586b, 7588a, 8299a, 9079b

1902:   307a, 562a, 594, 1001b, 1179c, 1187a, 1552a, 1644b, 2136a, 2165b, 2233c, 2976b, 2968a, 3251a, 3280a, 4237a, 6120a, 6495a, 6826a, 7274a, 8147a, 8567a, 8663a, 8706a, 9516a

1903:   439b, 461a, 1849a, 2137, 2176a, 2233d, 2235b, 3609a, 5078b, 5116b, 5321a, 5595a, 6256b, 7504a, 7504b, 7526c, 7586c-d, 10,007a

1904:   356a, 356b, 356c, 356d, 356e, 439c, 1419a, 1970a, 1995a, 2011a, 2011d, 2022a, 2074a, 2087b, 2229a, 2888a, 3118a, 3348a, 3728b, 3755a, 3956a, 4787a, 6391a, 7480a, 8383a, 8918a, 9089a, 9525a, 9902c

1905:   49a, 378a, 439d, 539a, 540a, 1369a, 1498a, 1571a, 1845a, 1891a, 2007a, 2087e, 2121a, 2449a, 2460a, 2542a, 2779c, 3807b, 3948a, 3956b, 3956c, 3956d, 4020a, 4276a, 4295a, 4683a, 5333a, 5504a, 5662a, 5666a, 6730a, 6830d, 6854a, 8066a, 8293a, 8462a, 9460a, 9713a, 9976a

1906:   439e, 1580a, 1599a, 2042a, 2042b, 2087d, 2185a, 2318a, 2481a, 3359a, 3434b, 3698d, 3946a, 5078a, 5504b, 5671a, 5684a, 5912a, 6175a, 6266a, 6266b, 6736a, 6805b, 7521a, 7572a, 8044a, 8067a

1907:   10a, 46a, 175c, 439f, 1180a, 1310a, 1383a, 1600b, 1600c, 1600d, 1600e, 1600f, 1649a, 2192b, 4150a, 4669a, 4683b, 4911a, 5116a, 6830b, 7261a, 8307a, 8872b, 9464a, 9673a

1908:   457a, 581a, 965a, 1139c, 1622a, 1798a, 2011c, 2080b, 2087a, 2165c, 2239a, 2632, 3443a, 3589a, 4502a, 4502b, 4758a, 4925a, 4972a, 5462a, 6138a, 6262b, 6263a, 6264a, 6266c, 8973a

1909:   235a, 571a, 851a, 1066a, 1623a, 1623b, 1623c, 2634a, 2744a, 2895a, 3233a, 3436a, 3589b, 3662a, 3662b, 5858a, 5948a, 6263b, 7164b, 8911a, 8963a

191-:   5044a, 6444a, 6444b, 7842a, 8527a

1910:   187a, 302a, 380a, 562a, 1126a, 1250a, 1848b, 1866, 2799a, 3402a, 4177b, 5511c, 5512a, 5713b, 6259b, 6259c, 6263c, 6273a, 6294a, 6761c, 7167a, 7247c, 7931a, 7968a, 8202a, 8794a, 9051a, 9403a, 9982c

1911:   294a, 925b, 1911a, 2087i, 3494a, 3863a, 4315a, 5199a, 5441b, 6263d, 6274a, 6295a, 7370a, 7790a, 7987, 8801a, 8803a, 9119a, 10,122a

1912:   131a, 458a, 573a, 576a, 1264c, 1366b, 1366c, 1645a, 1887a, 2087c, 2233b, 3380a, 3680a, 4135a, 4896a, 5477a, 6080b, 7085b, 7161a, 8882a, 9189c

1913:   175g, 759a, 989a, 1229a, 1888a, 2202b, 2232a, 3183a, 3383a, 3419a, 3445a, 5511d, 7164a, 7601a, 9314b

1914:   2119a, 2210b, 2960a, 3099a, 3525a, 3727a, 6699a, 7595a, 9967a

1915:   1450b, 1968a, 2365a, 2575a, 2635b, 2900a, 3291a, 3588b, 4148a, 4514a, 4761a, 5282c, 5507a, 5713a, 5740a, 5978a, 6375a, 7372a, 8602a, 10,145a

1916:   87a, 1366d, 1539a, 2530a, 2734c, 2762a, 3665a, 5195a, 5808a, 6295b, 6295c, 7172c, 7333a, 7372b

1917:   175b, 490a, 1585a, 1588a, 1677b, 2011b, 2240a, 2445a, 2632a, 2659a, 3522a, 3871a, 5567a, 6259d, 6259e, 6726a, 7968b, 8044b, 8660a, 8753a, 9015a

1918:   303b, 573b, 905a, 1571d, 2208a, 3849b, 3953a, 3953a, 4485a, 5018a, 6259f, 6839b, 7333b, 7372c, 7422a, 7761a, 8041b, 8616a, 8662a, 8662b, 8662c, 8926a, 8941a, 9479a, 9678a, 9786a

1919:   1945a, 1968b, 2155a, 2262a, 2780e, 2962a, 3589c, 4432a, 5645a, 6259g, 7372d, 9083b, 10,014a

192-:   1822a, 7243a, 9019b

1920:   114a, 439g, 1261b, 1386a, 1399a, 1658a, 1956b, 1973a, 2238a, 2303a, 2635a, 2635c, 2635d, 2648a, 2933a, 2933b, 3033a, 3128b, 3166a, 3535a, 3649a, 4382a, 5064a, 5645b, 6260a, 7068b, 7740a, 7939a, 8072a, 8761a, 9414a, 9492a, 9693a

1921:   228a, 259a, 1583a, 1709a, 2254a, 2671b, 3027b, 3319b, 3405a, 3608a, 3770a, 3837a, 5150a, 5508a, 5645c, 5795b, 6260b, 6260c, 6260d, 6296a, 6719a, 7091a, 7372e, 7750a, 7968c, 8450a, 8926b, 9448a

1922:   272a, 1081a, 1089a, 1182a, 1691a, 2811c, 3180a, 3434a, 4496a, 5195b, 5308c, 5549a, 6149a, 7258a, 7976a, 9257b, 9968a

1923:   40b, 79a, 575a, 576c, 992a, 1019a, 1239c, 1344a, 2042c, 2249a, 2250b, 2734e, 3461a, 3809a, 4181b, 5404a, 5439b, 5508b, 5736a, 5975a, 6113a, 6248a, 6260e, 6298a, 6845a, 7372f, 7437a, 8279a, 8566a, 9902a

1924:   439h, 495a, 942a, 1518a, 1815a, 2018b, 2161a, 2177a, 2258b, 2319a, 2672a, 3622a, 3624a, 4076a, 4219a, 4822a, 5075a, 5695a, 6260f, 6265a, 6731a, 7071a, 7185a, 7495a, 8603a, 9787a, 9985a

1925:   58a, 141b, 258c, 573c, 576b, 1349a, 1449a, 1822a, 1837a, 2126a, 2214a, 2235a, 2250d, 2303b, 3373a, 3611b, 3676a, 3733d, 5231a, 5508c, 5863a, 6020a, 6080a, 6087a, 6260g, 6260h, 6298b, 6785c, 6983a, 7247a, 7343a, 7372g, 7378a, 7495b, 7521b, 7549b, 8872a, 9019a, 9074a, 9294a, 9491a

1926:   175d, 529a, 538a, 575b, 813a, 1579a, 1677a, 2264a, 2640a, 3178a, 3403a, 3420b, 3498b, 3528a, 4141a, 4503a, 4690a, 5508d, 5508e, 5593a, 5780a, 6260i, 6263e, 6263f, 6298c, 7168a, 7185b, 7492a, 7585a, 7955a, 8876a, 9015b, 9257a, 9704b, 9902b, 9954a

1927:   175e, 175h, 1275a, 1495a, 1671a, 1942a, 1956a, 2117a, 2365b, 2780c, 2851a, 3123a, 4210c, 4755a, 5645d, 5764a, 5975b, 6261a, 6261b, 6267a, 7372h, 7549d, 7684b, 8947a, 9297a

1928:   576c, 803a, 1184a, 1485a, 1510a, 1524a, 1555a, 2086a, 2117b, 2192a, 2216a, 2350a, 2674a, 2972a, 3492a, 3492b, 4010a, 4765b, 4837a-b, 5100b, 5127a, 5308b, 5645e, 5762a, 6261c, 6291a, 7494a, 7619a, 7638a, 8991e, 10,033

1929:   417a, 864a, 1291a, 1512a, 1595a, 1636a, 1669a, 2103a, 2196a, 2841a, 2929, 2973a, 3338g, 3338e, 3873a, 3998a, 5636a, 5941a, 6199a, 6298d, 6724a, 7455a, 7830a, 8928a, 8953b, 8991d, 9209a, 9832a

1930:   548a, 575c, 752a, 961c, 992b, 1013a, 1539b, 1929a, 1988a, 2202a, 2335a, 2552a, 2780d, 3028a, 3332a, 3332b, 3333a, 3338c, 3338d, 3338f, 3338h, 3338i, 3338j, 3339a, 3526a, 4742a, 5063a, 5099b, 5462b, 5519a, 5676a, 5781a, 5808b, 6270a, 6779a, 7026a, 8383b, 9209b

410

Foreign Language Index

Armenian:	575a
Czech:	2973a
Danish:	575b-c, 989a, 1275a, 1242, 2640a, 3178a, 3778a, 5308a, 6262a-b, 6263a-f, 6682, 6751a, 6495a, 6523a, 6828a, 7161a, 7521c, 7526a-b, 7752a, 7976a, 8179a, 8180b, 8281a, 8818, 8826, 8826a-b, 8828b, 8933b, 8941a, 8975a, 9068a, 9409a, 9411a, 9413a, 9460a
Dutch:	135a, 378a, 439b-g, 479a, 563a, 848a-b, 1383a, 1600a-f, 1995a, 2001a, 2744a, 2853b, 2999a, 4683a-b, 5337a, 5662a, 5858a, 6120a, 6364a, 6265a, 7164a, 7939a, 7976b, 8044b, 8318, 9414a, 9466a, 9693a
French:	235a, 1001c, 1029b, 1066a, 1261a-b, 1970a, 2434a, 2536a, 2846a, 3027a-b, 3179a, 3183a, 3284b-c, 3498a, 3498c, 3611b, 4131a, 4711b, 4848a, 5045a, 5340a, 5463b, 6266a-c, 6267a, 6343b, 6757a, 6779a, 7091b, 7164b, 7395c, 7437a, 7521a, 7528a, 7719a-b, 7955a, 8345b, 8834a, 8882a, 9049a
German:	10a, 175a, 175f-g, 302a, 366a, 380a, 495a, 801a, 961a, 991a, 1155a, 1179a-c, 1180a, 1182a, 1354a, 1636a, 1986a, 1988a, 2018a-b, 2021a, 2022a, 2303a-b, 2319a, 2350a, 2933a-b, 3278b, 3609a, 3610a, 3733b, 3734a-b, 3946a, 4020a-b, 4576a, 4667a, 5441b, 5781a, 5974a, 6199a, 6270a, 6449a, 6483a, 6699a, 6830c, 7586a-d, 7588a, 8663a, 9264a, 9460b, 9484a, 9490a-b, 9502a, 9673a, 10,033a, 10,120b, 10,122a, 10,145a
Hawaiian:	1399a, 2738a, 5308c, 5482a, 5850a, 5852a, 5981a, 6248a, 8041b, 8044a
Hungarian:	6273a, 8562b
Icelandic:	539a, 540a, 4232a, 6274a
Italian:	3323a
Japanese:	1845a, 4382a, 8567a, 8801a, 8803a
Maori:	877a, 1848b, 4675a-c, 5195b, 9713a
Norwegian:	303b, 1849a, 3956a-d
Russian:	9031a
Samoan:	9982a
Spanish:	576a-c, 1029a, 3733d, 7948a

Swedish: 65a, 501a, 581b, 992a-b, 1866, 2465b, 3419a, 3580a, 3589a-d, 4692a, 6113a, 6539a, 6854b, 7167a, 7168a, 8198a, 8202a, 8242a, 8896a, 8933a, 9013a, 9015a-b, 9829a, 10,096a

Tahitian: 2042a-b, 2632, 2632a-b, 2634a, 6805b, 7422a, 7968a-c, 9537a

Turkish: 1870a

Welsh: 209a, 576d, 1870b, 2681a, 2682b, 2697a,, 2702a-b, 3083a, 3210a, 4112a, 4128a-b, 4457a-c, 4463a-b, 4467a-c, 4477a-b, 4478a-b, 4483a-b, 4484b, 4485b, 4493a, 4498a-b, 4498d, 4891a, 4969a, 5584a, 5678a, 6548b, 6606a, 7315a, 7614a, 9870a

References

Cowan

Cowan, Robert Ernest, and Robert Granniss Cowan. *A Bibliography of the history of California, 1510-1930.* IV volumes in one. Los Angeles: 1964

Dennis

Dennis, Ronald D. *Welsh Mormon writing from 1844 to 1862. A Historical bibliography.* Provo, Utah: Brigham Young University Religious Studies Center, 1988.

Fales/Flake

Fales, Susan L., and Chad J. Flake, comps. *Mormons and Mormonism in U. S. Government Documents. A Bibliography.* Salt Lake City: University of Utah Press, 1989.

Flake

Flake, Chad J., ed. *A Mormon bibliography, 1830-1930. Books, pamphlets, periodicals, and broadsides relating to the first century of Mormonism.* Salt Lake City: University of Utah Press, 1978.

Flake/Draper

Flake, Chad J., and Larry W. Draper, comps. *A Mormon bibliography, 1830-1930. Ten year supplement.* Salt Lake City: University of Utah Press, 1989.

Howes

Howes, Wright, comp. *U. S.iana (1650-1930).* 2d ed., rev. & enl. New York: R. R. Bowker Company, 1962.

Wagner/Camp

Wagner, Henry R., and Charles L. Camp. *The Plains and the Rockies: A Bibliography of original narratives of travel and adventure, 1800-1865.* Fourth edition rev, enlarged and edited by Robert H. Becker. San Francisco: John Howell -- Books, 1982.